Victorian Writers and the Environment

Applying ecocritical theory to the work of Victorian writers, this collection explores what a diversity of ecocritical approaches can offer students and scholars of Victorian literature, at the same time that it critiques the general effectiveness of ecocritical theory. Interdisciplinary in their approach, the chapters take up questions related to the nonhuman, botany, landscape, evolutionary science, and religion. The contributors cast a wide net in terms of genre, analyzing novels, poetry, periodical works, botanical literature, life-writing, and essays. Focusing on a wide range of canonical and noncanonical writers, including Charles Dickens, the Brontës, John Ruskin, Christina Rossetti, Jane Webb Loudon, Anna Sewell, and Richard Jefferies, *Victorian Writers and the Environment* demonstrates the ways in which nineteenth-century authors engaged not only with humans' interaction with the environment during the Victorian period, but also how some authors anticipated more recent attitudes toward the environment.

Laurence W. Mazzeno is President Emeritus at Alvernia University, USA.

Ronald D. Morrison is Professor of English at Morehead State University, USA.

Among the Victorians and Modernists
Edited by Dennis Denisoff

This series publishes monographs and essay collections on literature, art, and culture in the context of the diverse aesthetic, political, social, technological, and scientific innovations that arose among the Victorians and Modernists. Viable topics include, but are not limited to, artistic and cultural debates and movements; influential figures and communities; and agitations and developments regarding subjects such as animals, commodification, decadence, degeneracy, democracy, desire, ecology, gender, nationalism, the paranormal, performance, public art, sex, socialism, spiritualities, transnationalism, and the urban. Studies that address continuities between the Victorians and Modernists are welcome. Work on recent responses to the periods such as Neo-Victorian novels, graphic novels, and film will also be considered.

1. Arthur O'Shaughnessy, A Pre-Raphaelite Poet in the British Museum
   By Jordan Kistler

2. Dialectics of Secrecy and Disclosure in Victorian Fiction
   By Leila May

3. Louise Jopling
   By Patricia de Montfort

Victorian Writers and the Environment
Ecocritical Perspectives

Edited by Laurence W. Mazzeno and
Ronald D. Morrison

LONDON AND NEW YORK

First published 2017
by Routledge
2 Park Square, Milton Park, Abingdon, Oxon OX14 4RN

and by Routledge
711 Third Avenue, New York, NY 10017

Routledge is an imprint of the Taylor & Francis Group, an informa business

© 2017 selection and editorial matter, Laurence W. Mazzeno and Ronald D. Morrison; individual chapters, the contributors.

The right of Laurence W. Mazzeno and Ronald D. Morrison to be identified as the author of the editorial material, and of the authors for their individual chapters, has been asserted in accordance with sections 77 and 78 of the Copyright, Designs and Patents Act 1988.

All rights reserved. No part of this book may be reprinted or reproduced or utilised in any form or by any electronic, mechanical, or other means, now known or hereafter invented, including photocopying and recording, or in any information storage or retrieval system, without permission in writing from the publishers.

Trademark notice: Product or corporate names may be trademarks or registered trademarks, and are used only for identification and explanation without intent to infringe.

British Library Cataloguing in Publication Data
A catalogue record for this book is available from the British Library

Library of Congress Cataloging in Publication Data
Names: Mazzeno, Laurence W., editor. | Morrison, Ronald D., editor.
Title: Victorian writers and the environment : ecocritical perspectives / edited by Laurence W. Mazzeno and Ronald D. Morrison.
Description: New York : Routledge, 2017. | Series: Among the Victorians and modernists | Includes bibliographical references and index.
Identifiers: LCCN 2016030169 | ISBN 9781472454706 (alk. paper)
Subjects: LCSH: English literature--19th century--History and criticism. | Ecocriticism--Great Britain. | Nature in literature. | Environmental protection in literature.
Classification: LCC PR143 .V53 2017 | DDC 820.9/36--dc23
LC record available at https://lccn.loc.gov/2016030169

ISBN: 978-1-4724-5470-6 (hbk)
ISBN: 978-1-315-54823-4 (ebk)

Typeset in Sabon
by Saxon Graphics Ltd, Derby

Contents

Acknowledgments		vii
Introduction: Practical ecocriticism and the Victorian text LAURENCE W. MAZZENO AND RONALD D. MORRISON		1
1	Reading nature: John Ruskin, environment, and the ecological impulse MARK FROST	13
2	Between "bounded field" and "brooding star": a study of Tennyson's topography VALERIE PURTON	29
3	Celebration and longing: Robert Browning and the nonhuman world ASHTON NICHOLS	47
4	"Truth to nature": the pleasures and dangers of the environment in Christina Rossetti's poetry SERENA TROWBRIDGE	63
5	The zoocentric ecology of Hardy's poetic consciousness CHRISTINE ROTH	79
6	Early Dickens and ecocriticism: the social novelist and the nonhuman TROY BOONE	97
7	Bleak intra-actions: Dickens, turbulence, material ecology JOHN PARHAM	114

8 Dark nature: a critical return to Brontë country 130
DEIRDRE D'ALBERTIS

9 Anna Sewell's *Black Beauty*: reframing the pastoral tradition 142
ERIN BISTLINE

10 The environmental politics and aesthetics of Rider Haggard's *King Solomon's Mines*: capital, mourning, and desire 157
JOHN MILLER

11 Jane Loudon's wildflowers, popular science, and the Victorian culture of knowledge 174
MARY ELLEN BELLANCA

12 Falling in love with seaweeds: the seaside environments of George Eliot and G. H. Lewes 188
ANNA FEUERSTEIN

13 Agriculture and ecology in Richard Jefferies's *Hodge and His Masters* 205
RONALD D. MORRISON

14 Edward Carpenter, Henry Salt, and the animal limits of Victorian environments 220
JED MAYER

Sources for further study 236
Editors and Contributors 246
Index 250

Acknowledgments

First and foremost, the editors of *Victorian Writers and the Environment* want to thank the volume's contributors for their hard work, patience, and enthusiastic support for this project. It has been a great pleasure to work with each of them.

We also acknowledge the support provided by Ann Donahue of Ashgate. In addition, we also wish to thank the team at Routledge for their assistance in getting this volume into print.

Laurence W. Mazzeno extends a note of thanks to the staff of the Frank A. Franco Library at Alvernia University, particularly Sharon Neal, Roberta Rohrbach, and Derek Smith, and to the staff of the Earl Gregg Swem Library at the College of William & Mary for their cheerful (and invaluable) assistance.

Ronald D. Morrison extends his gratitude to Tom Williams, Chair of the Department of English at Morehead State University, and Scott McBride, Dean of the Caudill College of Arts, Humanities, and Social Sciences at Morehead State University, for negotiating a reduced teaching load during the final stages of this project.

Introduction
Practical ecocriticism and the Victorian text

Laurence W. Mazzeno and Ronald D. Morrison

Victorian Writers and the Environment: Ecocritical Perspectives is a collection of fourteen essays on Victorian writers whose work touches directly or indirectly on matters of the environment. Twenty years ago this volume would have been revolutionary. Today it can best be described as evolutionary, building on the fine work done by ecocritics (some of whom have contributed to this collection) on Victorian writers and their work. However, the notion of applying principles of ecocriticism to Victorian literature has been relatively late in developing; the field is still being shaped. We hope this volume helps to clarify some principles by which ecocritics may interrogate Victorian texts and suggests productive directions for further study.

In conceiving this volume, we have relied first on the broad definitions of ecocriticism provided by Cheryl Glotfelty and Richard Kerridge in the Introductions to their seminal anthologies, *The Ecocriticism Reader* (coedited with Fromm 1996) and *Writing the Environment* (coedited with Sammells 1998). Glotfelty defines ecocriticism as "the study of the relationship between literature and the physical environment" (viii). Kerridge claims that the ecocritic "wants to track environmental ideas and representations wherever they appear, to see more clearly a debate which seems to be taking place, often part-concealed, in a great many cultural spaces" (Kerridge and Sammells 5). Under this broad umbrella, a rapidly expanding branch of literary analysis has developed that has consciously moved away from the postmodernist trend of considering a text as a web of words with no substantive connection to a world outside it. Ecocriticism is one of the new approaches to literature that have "presented themselves as correctives or enhancements to literary theory's preexisting toolkit" (Buell, *Future* 11). Contemporary ecocriticism is both deliberate in its focus on the materiality of the environment and interdisciplinary in its approach. On the one hand, "ecological" critics—ecocritics—have drawn freely from various theoretical or disciplinary models such as animal studies, feminist theory, the history of science, Marxist theory, New Historicism, and post-colonial theory, often employing these methodologies in unique combinations. On the other hand, examining the material reality of the environment has caused others to embrace a more activist, "environmentalist" stance. While Heidi C. M. Scott helpfully distinguishes between "ecological" and "environmentalist" positions (6), the boundaries between these stances are seldom tidy. Most of the essays in this volume can be labeled as "ecological," although there are powerful "environmentalist" implications in many of them as well.

Although several scholars have traced the roots of ecocriticism to ancient Greece, the idea that literary texts can have something to contribute to the larger debates about the future of the ecological systems (of which humankind is a part) remains a relatively new phenomenon. The possibility that literature might contribute to an understanding of ecological issues has its origins in works such as Joseph Meeker's 1972 study *The Comedy of Survival: Studies in Literary Ecology* and William Reuckert's 1978 essay "Literature and Ecology: An Experiment in Ecocriticism." Curiously, however, anyone scanning bibliographies or indexes for ecocritical works on Victorian writers and texts will quickly notice that they have been underrepresented. Early anthologies such as Glotfelty and Fromm's *The Ecocriticism Reader* and even Kerridge and Sammells's *Writing the Environment*, where one might expect some mention of the contributions Victorian writers might make to an understanding of ecological issues, contain limited material. Karla Armbruster and Kathleen Wallace's *Beyond Nature Writing* includes only Kerridge's essay "Ecological Hardy," while other literary periods are more generously represented. Despite the growing number of ecocritical studies of Victorian texts after 2000, surveys of environmental literature such as Bryan Moore's *Ecology and Literature: Ecocentric Personification from Antiquity to the Twenty-First Century* (2008) or Timothy Clark's *The Cambridge Introduction to Literature and the Environment* (2011) give little more than a passing nod to the Victorians. Clearly, some explanation for this phenomenon seems called for, in part for those using this volume as an introduction to their study of the Victorians from an ecocritical perspective, and in part to explain why this volume makes sense at this time.

Two decades ago Cheryll Glotfelty suggested that ecocriticism, like other new approaches to texts, would likely undergo three phases of development similar to those through which feminist literary criticism evolved during the decades between the 1960s and the time the *Ecocriticism Reader* appeared. During the first phase, she expected that ecocritics would interrogate texts to identify stereotypes and misconceptions of the natural world as a kind of conscious-raising exercise. In the second phase, critics would identify an ecological "literary tradition"—by which Glotfelty means writings about nature.[1] In the third phase, ecocritics would develop appropriate theory to "examin[e] the symbolic construction of species" and "attempt[] to develop an ecological poetics" (xiii–xxiv).

That progression might have been followed if the genesis of environmental criticism had taken place three decades earlier. As it happened, however, the rise of ecocriticism coincided with the growing trend to privilege theory in literary studies. Consequently, one finds in the work of early ecocritics considerably more attention paid to developing theories of ecocriticism than to the application of those theories to texts. A second factor contributing to the inattention paid to the Victorians was the initial interest of ecocritics in American writers. For example, despite its title, Lawrence Buell's *The Environmental Imagination*, perhaps the most influential early book employing techniques of ecocriticism, is almost exclusively devoted to an examination of Henry David Thoreau's work. Indeed, looking farther back into the tradition of environmentalist writings, one discovers that Leo Marx, author of the influential 1964 study *The Machine in the Garden*, stresses the challenges to the American ideal of pastoral posed by the ascendency of technology in the nineteenth century. Following Marx's lead, the first wave of ecocritics writing in the 1990s celebrated American nature writing and pointed out threats to the natural world posed by human intervention during the past two centuries.

Given this initial impetus to equate ecocriticism with analysis of nature writing, it is probably not surprising that ecocritics investigating British texts would find the Romantics obvious candidates for ecocritical critiques. Celebrators of natural landscapes and the rural countryside, and critics of the city and industrial "progress" (or so conventional mythology goes), Romantic writers were particularly adept at recreating in their work the kinds of environments being challenged by industrial capitalism, technological nightmares, and environmental disasters.[2] As a result, they were the subjects of the first influential works of British ecocriticism: Jonathan Bate's *Romantic Ecology: Wordsworth and the Environmental Tradition* (1990) and Karl Kroeber's *Ecological Literary Criticism: Romantic Imagining and the Biology of Mind* (1994). As critics of American literature found it useful to trace the origins of their work to Leo Marx, ecocritics of British literature found a critical forerunner in Raymond Williams, whose 1973 study *The Country and the City* became for many a point of departure for the kind of ecological study most adaptable to British texts. Williams's dual focus—on rural landscapes where agriculture is practiced in harmony with the ecological systems of as-yet-undisturbed forests and fens, and on the city, the created environment in which humans must learn to establish sustainable ecological systems one or more steps removed from "natural" habitats—offered convenient entrée for discussing some of the ecological issues that critics, and the population at large, find pressing as humankind moves into the twenty-first century.[3]

While relatively little attention was paid to the Victorians' views on the environment before 2000, there were some notable exceptions. Michael Wheeler's *Ruskin and Environment*, a collection of essays demonstrating Ruskin's environmental awareness, appeared in 1995. Beginning in the 1990s, some ecocritics began writing regularly about Thomas Hardy, whom Richard Kerridge calls "one obvious candidate for the ecocritical canon" ("Ecological

Hardy" 126), and Gerard Manley Hopkins. That work has continued, even as interest in other Victorian writers has resulted in the publication of ecocritical scholarship during the first decade of the twenty-first century.

In his essay "Was There a Victorian Ecology?" and again in the Introduction to a special issue of *Green Letters* on Victorian ecology (2011), John Parham has offered a systematic defense for the study of the Victorians from an ecocritical perspective. First, he argues, "the proximity to the scientific developments" that "converge[d] to form ecology" allowed the Victorians to develop "an understanding, although incomplete," that humans are part of an interrelated network of species. Second, from the new scientific knowledge emerged "a broadly materialistic awareness" that the concept of "human being" resides in "the nature and quality of humanity's relationship with other species and the surrounding physical environment." Third, the awareness of humankind's interdependence on other species and the physical environment led to the emergence of "an early environmental activism and 'green politics.'" The final, and "most interesting" reason, in his view, is that, reacting to these new discoveries, Victorian writers, "often ambivalent about new scientific ideas" and sometimes "alarmed by the implications of their own social-environmental critiques, constantly 'shuttled' between a bewildering array of influences" as they tried to make sense of "the scientific, social and epistemological complexities with which they were confronted." Hence, the "utility" of considering the Victorians from an ecocritical perspective lies in considering the "multiplicity of ways" that Victorian writers dealt with the complexities "intrinsic to ecological thought" (Parham, "Introduction," 5–6).[4]

The appropriateness of studying the Victorians from an ecocritical perspective is reinforced by Ashton Nichols in the Prologue to his *Beyond Romantic Ecocriticism: Toward Urbanatural Roosting*, in which he employs the term "urbanature" to describe his belief that "nature and urban life are not as distinct as human beings have long supposed." Nichols insists that "human beings are not *out of* nature when they stand in the streets of Manhattan"—or, we might substitute, London—"any more than they are *in* nature when they stand above tree-line in Montana"—or amid the hills of England's Lake District. That "human beings are never cut off from wild nature by human culture," is, Nichols says, "the central truth of all ecology" (xiii, xv). Hence, if ecology is the study of humankind in city as well as country, then where better to start than with analysis of the literature that first described (and often decried) the modern urban environment?

Since 2000, the growth of ecocritical studies of the Victorians has been steady, if somewhat overshadowed by ecological criticism of figures from the Renaissance, the Romantics, and American writers. Scholars have produced insightful essays on canonical figures such as Dickens, the Brontës, Ruskin, Morris, Carlyle, and Tennyson, as well as critiques of lesser-known writers such as Richard Jefferies and Jane Webb Loudon. Books like Parham's and Nichols's now sit on shelves beside more than a dozen others that have expanded our knowledge of the Victorians' understanding of their environment and the challenges facing its preservation—even its survival—in a growing industrial age. Not only have articles on Victorian texts appeared in journals such as *ISLE* and *Green Letters*; ecocriticism of the Victorians has made it into *PMLA* (Gold, "Consolation") and even into rather unusual places such as the *Contemporary Justice Review* (Delveaux). Scholarly conferences have been organized on Victorian writers' interest in and use of the environment, and panels have been sponsored at major scholarly gatherings. Clearly, ecocriticism of Victorian literature is now an established and accepted practice.

But where will such study lead? If ecocriticism of Victorian texts is not simply to be another theoretical exercise, there must be some practical reason for using this methodology. Hence, in our estimation, the key question for ecocritics interested in Victorian literature and culture is: How best can we interrogate Victorian writers and works by using the tools of ecocriticism to enhance understanding of their work, develop a broader definition of "Victorian ecology," and find correspondences that might help us approach contemporary issues related to the environment with a deeper understanding of questions that have been on the minds of writers at least since the nineteenth century?

Although advances in ecocritical theory may occur as a result of close analysis of individual writers and texts, our chief interest in *Victorian Writers and the Environment* is in practical criticism, applying current theories of ecocriticism to individual texts and writers. However, we are not using the term "practical criticism" in the same way I. A. Richards and his colleagues employed it when they encouraged close readings of texts independent of what might be called the context in which a work was produced. Unlike New Critics, for whom Richards's technique of analysis was central, ecocritics actively engage both texts and contexts. The contributors to *Victorian Writers and the Environment* are "practical" critics in the sense that they are primarily concerned with reading specific writers and texts for what they reveal about human interactions with the environment, although it is also evident that each of them is informed by recent theory.

As their most significant contribution, the essays in *Victorian Writers and the Environment* assess a variety of writing across a wide range of genres: imaginative literature, descriptive writing, and argument. The essays in this volume fall into three broad categories:

- Five broad overviews of canonical writers from an ecocritical perspective;
- Five more narrowly focused readings of fiction that has traditionally been considered canonical or which has received increasing attention in recent years; and
- Four examinations of nonfiction by several writers who deal with matters of environment and the nonhuman world.

The contributions are unified, however, by their interest in what these writers reveal about the Victorians' interest in the world around them.

In the first group is Mark Frost's overview of John Ruskin, who might be considered the most "ecological" writer among the Victorians. Frost explains how Ruskin developed a powerful method of "reading" natural phenomena that foregrounded their dynamism and embeddedness within larger systems and anticipated the ambitious and multi-faceted nature of ecological thought. Focusing closely on Ruskin's concept of "Vital Beauty" and his chapter "The Law of Help" from *Modern Painters*, Frost demonstrates that Ruskin's environmental consciousness was formed equally of religiously informed hermeneutical methods and insights drawn from his engagements with modern materialist science. Although Ruskin ultimately rejected evolutionary theory and many of the implications of materialist science, his proto-ecological positions as well as his environmental interventions in the 1870s remain an important part of his legacy.

By contrast, Valerie Purton introduces her essay on Tennyson by noting how he initially appears to be an "unpromising subject for an environmental or ecocritical reading"—especially since Tennyson's poetry seldom directly addresses threats to the environment. But, through her analysis of a range of Tennyson's poetry from both early and late in his career, Purton asserts that a re-examination of the concepts of "place" and "space" from an ecocritical perspective reveals helpful insights into Tennyson's liminal position between a Romantic idealization of nature and a coldly scientific view of nature from a post-Darwinian perspective. Purton's far-ranging, nuanced reading of familiar materials explores the foundational question of what it means to be a "nature poet." Writing of Robert Browning, another poet not often described as ecocritical, Ashton Nichols argues that, as much as any other writer of the period, Browning regarded plants and animals as central focal points of his work. Nichols argues that, for Browning, "nature" was not so much a category distinguished by its "otherness" as it was a part of a continuum of living creatures (as well as nonliving natural entities) that helped humans to understand their own role in ecological systems. Linking Browning to other figures studied in this volume, Nichols concludes that Browning's engagement with the environment was a function of his early understanding of Darwin combined with an almost Hardyesque, or Tennysonian appreciation of the brevity of life and the value of living in the moment, especially in terms of our awareness of the nonhuman world around us.

In a revisionist reading of the ecological dimensions of Christina Rossetti's poetry, Serena Trowbridge challenges earlier critical readings that figure Rossetti as a poet of nature who offered an uncomplicated and "womanly" depiction of the natural world. Echoing the conclusions Mark Frost draws about Ruskin, Trowbridge examines how, for Rossetti, the experience of the natural world is filtered through the medium of her faith, situating humankind in a landscape of both delight and fear, a position which must be constantly and conscientiously negotiated. The co-existence of the sublime and the wicked in the natural world, and the duty of the artist to render it truthfully, complement and reflect Rossetti's Tractarian beliefs, as Trowbridge demonstrates through insightful readings of selected poems from *Sing-Song* and from Rossetti's devotional writings. Trowbridge concludes that Rossetti's work might be regarded as an early version of ecotheology.

Thomas Hardy is the subject of Christine Roth's essay, one of several that draw attention to the Victorians' growing interest in the complex nature of nonhuman (animal) life. Rather than concentrate on Hardy's oft-discussed novels, Roth instead interrogates a wide range of his poetry, much of which she believes is driven by an increasingly zoocentric, ethical, and activist attention to the nonhuman animal. She claims that Hardy's poetic treatment of the intrinsic value of nonhuman animal life as an active and guiding motif uses animals less as metaphors or commodities than as ethical touchstones. Much like Nichols's assessment of Browning, Roth finds that the trajectory of Hardy's career as a poet attests to his growing interest in the relationship of humans to other animals as a continuum rather than a sharp division, spurred in part by his reading of Darwin. Increasingly, he associated traits and feelings previously associated only with humans, such as compassion and embarrassment and pride, to animals, resulting in an ecological vision in which readers are called to transcend the human into the collective biosphere—taking with them an unsettling new aesthetic.

The first two essays in the second section of *Victorian Writers and the Environment* consider novels by Dickens, another figure not often associated with "nature writing." Troy Boone's examination of nonhuman nature in the early novels argues that, while many critics continue to regard Dickens primarily as a social novelist, when read ecocritically, Dickens's fiction reveals a broader understanding of the human's place in the world. Focusing on the writings Dickens produced before he became identified as an urban novelist, Boone recovers a Dickens more aligned with posthumanist ecocriticism and works in the emerging field of animal studies. As he demonstrates, the early Dickens is committed to a critique of the centrality of the human in the social theories that are still profoundly with us. Hence, Boone brings to the surface a potentially more radical view of nature than most critics of Dickens's fiction have recognized. Concentrating on Dickens's later novels, John Parham provides a complex and multi-faceted analysis of "material ecology" that seems to connect the material, linguistic, and social realms in Victorian literature. Parham argues that Dickens's interest in material ecology is particularly evident through his treatment of miasma theory, a subject that appears in both his periodical writings from the 1850s and, most notably, in *Bleak House*. Dickens's attention to this and related topics reflect what Parham describes as "the materiality of the social," or ways in which the material effects of things—particularly waste products—have a broader social impact, exemplified by how various forms of pollution and putrefaction disproportionately affect the lives of the poor and laboring classes.

Offering a strategy for reading a canonical text from an ecological perspective, Deirdre d'Albertis argues for a revision of the long-standing dualistic critical approach to Emily Brontë's *Wuthering Heights* that sets up a fundamental conflict between nature and culture symbolically connected to the novel's two houses. Anchoring her analysis in the work of two recent ecocritical studies—Tim Morton's analysis of dark ecology in *Ecology Without Nature: Rethinking Environmental Aesthetics* and the writings of Paul Kingsnorth in connection with the Dark Mountain Project—d'Albertis concludes that the concept of dark nature can be an effective tool to approach this novel, since it offers a view of humans locked in cycles of violence and irrationality, and a context in which humans and animals become indistinguishable from one another. D'Albertis also employs the concept of "ferality," as articulated by Greg Garrard and George Monbiot, to problematize earlier readings that promote a simplistic approach to nature.

Similarly, Erin Bistline argues that a more nuanced reading of another classic text, Anna Sewell's *Black Beauty*, reveals problems with the simplistic notion of the form of the pastoral in the nineteenth century. Bistline asserts that, far from accepting conventional ideas about the divide between country and city, Sewell consistently questions the belief that country life offers an idyllic environment for humans and animals alike. Instead, Sewell leads her readers to re-interpret Black Beauty's experiences, juxtaposing them with those of city laborers to highlight startling similarities. Drawing on Raymond Williams's *The Country and the City* and William Cronon's work on American literature, Bistline explores the relationship between the pastoral tradition and Sewell's novel and the social changes reflected in the text, concluding that Sewell's novel is far more culturally significant than its current status as a "children's classic" would perhaps indicate.

In another essay employing contemporary critical theory to bolster an ecological reading, John Miller argues that Rider Haggard's *King Solomon's Mines* can be read in light of recent developments in postcolonial ecocriticism to reassess the uneasy relationship between environmental politics and aesthetics in Haggard's writing. Miller argues that, not only might the novel be read as *either* a justification of imperial exploitation of African resources *or* a denunciation of the same in favor of an idealization of the natural, the unspoiled and the primitive; it might also legitimately be understood to be *both* of these at the same time. Miller significantly re-contextualizes Haggard's work by examining his voluminous writings on agriculture as a means of fully comprehending his environmental aesthetics. Moreover, Miller analyzes the ways in which Haggard uses a sexualized portrayal of the African landscape to promote a broader agrarian political position.

With the exception of Frost's critique of Ruskin, the chapters in the first two sections of this volume offer assessments of imaginative literature (poetry and fiction). To fully appreciate the significance of the impact of environmentalist concerns on poets and writers of imaginative prose, however, we believe their work must be placed in a larger context of environmentally oriented writing that includes articles, personal essays, tracts, descriptive monographs, and notebooks. The four essays in the third section of this volume deal with such work. The Victorians' interest in botany yields insight into their attitudes toward the environment, as Mary Ellen Bellanca's essay on Jane Webb Loudon's *British Wild Flowers* (1844) reveals. Bellanca argues that Loudon's book can be read as an index to competing discourses in Victorian botanical study as a cultural pursuit. Although principally interested in conveying botanical information in this volume, Loudon also incorporates other discourses, juxtaposing factual knowledge with folk practices, literary quotations, and her own pointed opinions. Her personal narratives of discovery and comments on flowers' beauty leaven the book's technical material with pleasure, grounding the desire for knowledge in readers' lived encounters with flowers growing wild. Amid many contested issues in botanical publishing, often strongly inflected by gender, *British Wild Flowers* demonstrates Loudon's confidence in her publishing niche, her canny identification of and with her audience, and her acumen in seizing or creating opportunities in the popular science market.

Anna Feuerstein's essay on George Eliot and G. H. Lewes focuses upon their time spent at the seashores of Ilfracombe and Tenby and the influence these visits had upon their subsequent writings. Claiming that both writers formulated a secular ecological awareness quite different from that of other Victorian writers, who typically accepted the theologically influenced model of natural history of the day, Feuerstein uncovers a striking engagement with the environment and an appreciation of nonhuman life forms, both plant and animal, that de-centers the human and moves out of a hierarchical view of nature toward a more inclusive ecological understanding.

Ronald D. Morrison's essay investigates the journalism of an important figure generally characterized as a Victorian "nature writer": Richard Jefferies. Morrison argues that literary scholars have often oversimplified and distorted Jefferies's views of the environment, largely because they have typically focused only on selected parts of Jefferies's large body of work, routinely ignoring the agricultural writings. Morrison examines Jefferies's *Hodge and His Masters*, an interconnected and cohesive series of articles that initially appeared in the Tory periodical *The Standard*. In these essays Jefferies analyzes the economic, social, political, and natural environments of agricultural communities in the southern county of Wiltshire in the late 1870s during a time of prolonged economic depression. Morrison concludes that this collection should be read as an early example of what we today consider ecocriticism and a precursor to the modern georgic, as exemplified by the writings of Wendell Berry and others. Moreover, he argues that Jefferies's conservative positions exemplify what Katey Castellano has termed "Romantic conservatism," which can be reconciled with a developing ecological awareness in the nineteenth century.

Finally, the Victorians' interest in the nonhuman world is addressed directly by Jed Mayer in his essay on animal rights champion Henry S. Salt and social activist Edward Carpenter. Mayer contends that both writers extended principles of communitarianism and equality to the nonhuman world through their work with the Humanitarian League and its publications. Both developed philosophical creeds based on their belief in the interrelatedness of living things and the moral responsibility such kinship entails. Both writers associated cruelty and insensitivity not only with capitalism, but also with aspects of masculine behavior that flourished in acquisitive and unequal societies. Mayer's reading of these early advocates of environmentalism and animal rights links their work with contemporary eco-feminism and queer ecology. Moreover, he argues that both writers offer insightful possibilities that might address points of conflict between ecocriticism and the developing field of animal studies in our own century.

While we have not set out with the express purpose of creating a new canon composed solely of works that offer insights into ecology, it is certainly possible that exploring the connections between Victorian writers and the environment may lead to a reconsideration of the value of some works included in the traditional canon and expand our interests beyond the novels, poems, and essays that were the staple of Victorian literature courses for nearly a century. Ecocriticism has already done much to blur traditional genre distinctions, and (as more than one essay in this volume demonstrates) it is likely that future work will continue that trend. Ecocritics may do for Victorian literature what critics of sensation fiction have done in the recent past: Open up the canon to include new works that contribute to an overall understanding of the period.[5]

Ecocritics of Victorian literature may also end up providing new ways to read canonical works, not to challenge their merit but to point out nuances of meaning and unrecognized ideological assumptions that further enhance their value as objects of cultural interest. However, the critic examining Victorian literature from an ecological perspective would do well to heed Glen Love's admonition in *Practical Ecocriticism*. In applying the tools of this new approach to works of the past, Love says he wishes to "avoid the 'gotcha' manner of an eco-policeman, dragging past writers to the dock for violations of today's sense of environmental incorrectness. For the most part the thinking, or nonthinking, of past writers on nature-related matters was simply part of the cultural givens of their times. This particular given, or the writer's unique diversion from it, however, may well be worth examining" (11). We believe that, when viewed through the lens of ecocriticism, Victorian writers can be seen to have anticipated more recent attitudes regarding a range of topics associated with the environment. Our hope is that the essays in *Victorian Writers and the Environment* will suggest ways in which Victorian writers and works may be studied to illuminate their insights into questions of environment and prove useful for the study of literature and its application to contemporary questions of ecology.

Notes

1 It is inevitable that ecocritics must use such imprecise terms as "nature writing" or "writings about nature," even as they problematize these terms. In one way or another, all of the essays in this volume critique the various meanings of "nature writing."
2 The Romantics' responses to challenges to the natural environment are the subject of the essays in Ben P. Robertson's newly published essay collection, *Romantic Sustainability: Endurance and the Natural World, 1780–1830*.
3 It is worth noting, however, that in his early chapters, Williams points out that the elements of what we now call capitalism were present in many earlier agrarian societies. One might argue that Williams offers a proto-deconstruction of the concepts of "country" and "city" that anticipates much current criticism.
4 Recommendations for how one might read the Victorians ecologically began to appear at about the same time as Parham's 2002 book. Among these are Nicholas Frankel's "The Ecology of Victorian Poetry" (2003) and Joseph Carroll's "The Ecology of Victorian Fiction" (2001). Carroll must be considered a reluctant participant in the ecocritical movement, as he has insisted that "ecology cannot by itself generate a theory of literature or serve as the basis for a theory of literature"; instead, he says, "responsiveness to the sense of place is an elemental component of the evolved human psyche and that it thus can and should be integrated into a Darwinian literary theory" ("Ecology of Victorian Fiction," 296). In "Energy, Ecology, and Victorian Fiction," Barri Gold provides a useful summary of recent scholarship on Victorian writers and ecology. See also Ursula Heise, "The Hitchhiker's Guide to Ecocriticism."
5 See, for example, Barri Gold, "Embracing the Corpse: Discursive Recycling in Rider Haggard's *She*" and John Miller's *Empire and the Animal Body: Violence, Identity and Ecology in Victorian Adventure Fiction*.

Works cited

Armbruster, Karla and Kathleen Wallace, eds. *Beyond Nature Writing: Expanding the Boundaries of Ecocriticism*. Charlottesville: U of Virginia P, 2001.
Bate, Jonathan. *Romantic Ecology: Wordsworth and the Environmental Tradition*. London: Routledge, 1990.
Buell, Lawrence. *The Environmental Imagination: Thoreau, Nature Writing, and the Formation of American Culture*. Cambridge, MA: Belknap, 1995.
——. *The Future of Environmental Criticism*. Malden, MA: Blackwell, 2005.
Carroll, Joseph. "The Ecology of Victorian Fiction." *Philosophy and Literature* 25.2 (2001): 295–313.
Clark, Timothy. *The Cambridge Introduction to Literature and the Environment*. Cambridge: Cambridge UP, 2011.
Delveaux, Martin. "'O Me! O Me! How I Love the Earth': William Morris's *News From Nowhere* and the Birth of Sustainable Society." *Contemporary Justice Review* 8.2 (2005): 131–46.
Frankel, Nicholas. "The Ecology of Victorian Poetry." *Victorian Poetry* 41 (2003): 629–35.
Glotfelty, Cheryll and Harold Fromm, eds. *The Ecocriticism Reader*. Athens: U of Georgia P, 1996.
Gold, Barri. "The Consolation of Physics: Tennyson's Thermodynamic Solution." *PMLA* 117.3 (2002): 449–64.

——. "Embracing the Corpse: Discursive Recycling in Rider Haggard's *She*." *English Literature in Transition* 38.3 (1995): 304–27.
——. "Energy, Ecology, and Victorian Fiction." *Literature Compass* 9.2 (2012): 213–24.
Heise, Ursula. "The Hitchhiker's Guide to Ecocriticism." *PMLA* 121.2 (2006): 503–16.
Kerridge, Richard. "Ecological Hardy." In Armbruster and Wallace, eds., *Beyond Nature Writing*, 126–42.
Kerridge, Richard and Neil Sammells, eds. *Writing the Environment: Ecocriticism and Literature*. London: Zed Publications, 1998.
Kroeber, Karl. *Ecological Literary Criticism: Romantic Imagining and the Biology of Mind*. New York: Columbia UP, 1994.
Love, Glen. *Practical Ecocriticism: Literature, Biology, and the Environment*. Charlottesville: U of Virginia P, 2003.
Marx, Leo. *The Machine in the Garden: Technology and the Pastoral Ideal in America*. New York: Oxford UP, 1964.
Meeker, Joseph. *The Comedy of Survival: Studies in Literary Ecology*. New York: Scribner's, 1972.
Miller, John. *Empire and the Animal Body: Violence, Identity and Ecology in Victorian Adventure Fiction*. London: Anthem, 2012.
Moore, Bryan. *Ecology and Literature: Ecocentric Personification from Antiquity to the Twenty-First Century*. New York: Palgrave Macmillan, 2008.
Nichols, Ashton. *Beyond Romantic Ecocriticism: Toward Urbanatural Roosting*. New York: Palgrave Macmillan, 2011.
Parham, John, ed. *The Environmental Tradition in English Literature*. Burlington, VT: Ashgate, 2002.
——. Introduction. *Green Letters* 14 (2011). Special Issue on Victorian Ecology.
——. "Was There a Victorian Ecology?" In Parham, *Environmental*, 156–71.
Reuckert, William. "Literature and Ecology: An Experiment in Ecocriticism" *Iowa Review* 9.1 (1978): 71–86.
Robertson, Ben, ed. *Romantic Sustainability: Endurance and the Natural World, 1780–1830*. Lanham, MD: Rowman & Littlefield, 2016.
Scott, Heidi C. M. *Chaos and Cosmos: Literary Roots of Modern Ecology in the British Nineteenth Century*. University Park: Pennsylvania State UP, 2014.
Wheeler, Michael, ed. *Ruskin and Environment: The Storm-Cloud of the Nineteenth Century*. Manchester: Manchester UP, 1995.
Williams, Raymond. *The Country and the City*. New York: Oxford UP, 1973.

1 Reading nature
John Ruskin, environment, and the ecological impulse

Mark Frost

Since its beginnings ecology has been strongly characterized by its multiple nature. Its scientific insights produce critiques of environmental policy, resource management, and social organization, and for many ecological actors engagement with nature involves a combination of scientific, social, aesthetic, and spiritual approaches. Ecological science invites political action, as well as questions about lifestyle choices and social organization. Ecology destabilizes customary disciplinary and cultural boundaries, and inclines towards advocating a holistic attitude to every subject. All of the modern features of ecology reflect the conditions of its genesis in the mid-nineteenth century, as well, of course, of all that followed. Rather than being merely an offshoot of evolutionary science, early ecology represented the coming together of Darwinism and many other strands of thought, including anatomical science, Romanticism, transcendentalism, human geography, religion, and politics. Ecology is marked by a wider nineteenth-century tendency to draw together often disparate and sometimes conflicting ideas. I will be exploring a particular instance of the nineteenth-century roots of ecology in the work of John Ruskin. Although he ultimately rejected evolutionary theory and the implications of materialist science, his nature writings participated in nascent ecological thinking, and his approach represented many of the contradictions and opportunities that define ecology.

Like many others of his generation, Ruskin was caught between two conceptualizations of environment—one based on eighteenth-century and evangelical notions of a hierarchical nature, the other informed by both Romantic and scientific claims about the interdependence of environment. Ruskin's ambivalent perspective generated a powerful method of reading natural phenomena that foregrounded their dynamism and their embeddedness within larger systems, and anticipated the ambitious multivalence of ecological thought. Beginning with examples from the 1840s and 1850s of Ruskin's extraordinarily acute nature-reading, I will underline his insistence that observers pay close attention to nature; that the environment represents a precious resource; and that environmental engagement offers opportunities for self-improvement and collapses the distance between observer and observed by revealing what they share. While his nature-reading techniques were profoundly indebted to scriptural hermeneutics, his insistence on close scrutiny led him to discern the systematic connections of nature and to reach for explanations of environment that bore distinctive ecological markers. Acknowledging, scrutinizing, and embracing an environment made up of endless connections and characterized by infinite variety led him to query the place of humanity within this newly conceived realm. By turn, it led him at times to challenge (but ultimately never to reject or overturn) those hierarchical and anthropocentric readings of nature that he inherited from Evangelicalism. Like ecology, Ruskin's approach to nature was complex, multiple, and in a state of productive tension.

Having explored Ruskin's nature-reading methods and the ways this led him to think of nature as a helpful system, I will turn to the manner in which he directed this towards nature conservancy. Ruskin's activities in the 1870s are significant not merely as indicators of his environmentalist credentials but also for the manner in which they deployed the nature-reading processes established early in his career. Uniquely gifted in reading the signs of a healthy environment, Ruskin was also unusually sensitive in discerning environmental breakdown, partly because of his attentiveness to nature and partly because, as a religious thinker, the stakes could not have been higher. Focusing closely on his observations of moments in which the various "bodies" of nature begin to lose their ecological order, I will demonstrate that Ruskin's environmental consciousness was informed both by evangelical hermeneutics and materialist science. Committed to the preservation of divine nature, and to the salvational possibilities of environmental stewardship, Ruskin's vision of nature-as-system also carried unmistakable ecological markers.

An ecological model of nature emerged distinctively around mid-century in the work of Ernst Haeckel, George Perkins Marsh, and others who drew upon Darwin's notion of the "economy of nature," a vision of nature as a complex whole made up of dynamic, interactive parts in various states of competition, co-operation, and co-dependence.[1] Ecology was influenced by nineteenth-century biology, anatomy, natural history, geology, and organic chemistry, but its multiple roots can also be traced to Romanticism, transcendentalism, human geography, and to emerging disquiet about intensive exploitation of resources. Its genesis belongs in a process of scientific and cultural change taking place throughout the century. Conceptualizing nature as a complex continuum made up of dynamic, interactive elements, ecologists immediately promoted environmental and social programs, arguing that lessons about natural systems provide powerful arguments for better management of the planet. Ecology represents a holistic way of seeing that pays close attention to microcosmic and macrocosmic elements of natural systems, and valorizes the dynamic connectedness of heterogeneous phenomena—that which Ruskin perceived as early as 1843 when he notes that "there is indeed in nature variety in all things" (3: 368) and that "the truths of nature are one eternal change—one infinite variety" (3: 145).[2] Ecologists attempt to reject anthropocentric assumptions, rooted in western philosophy, that subordinate environment to humanity, insisting instead that priority be placed upon environmental systems. Intensely programmatic, ecology engages in wider debates about resource management that go beyond normally constituted boundaries of scientific discourse. Ecologists simultaneously operate at scientific, social, and cultural levels; and elaborate a holistic view of human activity that includes political economy, creative practices, and epistemology. Philosophies predicated on linearity, hierarchy, and division are often rejected in favor of inclusive, organic modes of inquiry. As I hope to demonstrate, Ruskin's characteristic approach to nature-reading placed him close to many of the emerging features of ecological thought that I have so far described.

Ruskin's nature-reading began in youthful scientific articles and *The Poetry of Architecture* (1837–1838), but emerged most powerfully in *Modern Painters* (5 vols., 1843–1860), a work whose fame was in no small part due to its author's reputation as a "word-painter" whose descriptions of nature were uniquely vivid. His ability to transcribe visual experience into textual form, enabling readers to feel that they saw *with* Ruskin, relied on being both a gifted reader and writer of nature. *Modern Painters* was at once a defense of J. M. W. Turner and a call for landscape artists to engage intensively with environment in order to observe and describe its various "truths."[3] For Ruskin, this meant science and the arts working in harmony. In "The Moral of Landscape," a chapter from *Modern Painters III* (1856), he spoke impatiently of Wordsworth's anxieties about scientific investigation of nature. "The chief narrowness of Wordsworth's mind," he complained, was that "he could not understand that to break a rock with a hammer in search of crystal may sometimes be an act not disgraceful to human nature" or that "to dissect a flower may sometimes be as proper as to dream over it" (5: 359). Deeply indebted to Wordsworth, and Romanticism, Ruskin nonetheless believed that poetic engagement was insufficient, and that "a curiously balanced condition of the powers of mind is necessary to induce full admiration of any natural scene" (5: 357). While many were incapable of achieving this rare balance, a true observer combined the reading techniques of the artist, poet, botanist, engineer, and divine. Each of these specialists, he argued, could perceive in a natural object only a single, distorting aspect—its aesthetic qualities, poetic connotations, taxonomic status, structural function, or role in God's creation. Only in individuals like Turner were "these perceptions and trains of ideas" presented in "a mingled and perfect harmony" (5: 358) that embraced the multiple aspects of natural phenomena. Building this proto-ecological model of engagement, Ruskin called on readers to particularly observe what he termed the "Vital Beauty" and "leading lines" of nature: by noting the ways in which the functional life history of an organism or inorganic matter were inscribed in their forms, Ruskin invited readers to engage sympathetically with them, and to recognize their locatedness within environmental networks.

In *Modern Painters II* (1846), he attempted to divide natural beauty into two aesthetic categories:

> By the term Beauty, then, properly are signified two things. First, that external quality of bodies already so often spoken of, and which, whether it occur in a stone, flower, beast, or in man, is absolutely identical, which, as I have already asserted, may be shown to be in some sort typical of the Divine attributes, and which therefore I shall, for distinction's sake, call Typical Beauty: and, secondarily, the appearance of felicitous fulfilment of function in living things, more especially of the joyful and right exertion of perfect life in man; and this kind of beauty I shall call Vital Beauty.
>
> (4: 64)

Vital Beauty was among the most significant tools in Ruskin's nature-reading methodology. It cannot be understood in isolation from its conceptual twin, Typical Beauty, which he located in environmental features that revealed divine order and intention. Typical Beauty echoed the evangelical Bible study methods with which Ruskin was so familiar. Just as scriptural hermeneutics suggested that Old Testament figures and events were divine types because they prefigured Christ, so Ruskin's six natural types symbolized aspects of divine purpose as revealed through environment. While Ruskin's principal aim in *Modern Painters* was indeed to declare "the perfectness and eternal beauty of the work of God," narrowly contextualized religious readings of his work often deflect attention from the manner in which Ruskin's preoccupation with the intricate material workings of environment distanced him from evangelical concerns about the snares of postlapsarian creation. Engagement with Vital Beauty, defined as "the appearance of felicitous fulfilment of function in living things" and of their "joyful and right exertion of perfect life," was not merely a matter of producing a "homiletic register" in which "each species has its own assigned function to perform, and its own particular sermon or message from God to convey" (Finley 205). While Ruskin argued that "there is not any organic creature, but in its history and habits it shall exemplify or illustrate to us some moral excellence or deficiency" (4: 156), he found it difficult to share the certainty of fellow Christians about the unique and separate role of *Homo sapiens* in creation. Understanding natural sermons made it necessary to "not only love all creatures well, but esteem them" (4: 100). Doing so involved deep sympathy with the lived experience and physical being of the natural form under observation, an engagement that tended in practice to draw human subject and natural object together by acknowledgement of their shared experience of life. Pursuing the various communions of sympathy that Vital Beauty opened up led Ruskin to re-evaluate what it meant to be creative, and to see humans, animals, rocks, paintings, buildings, and societies as sacred participants in cooperative "building," each seeking a helpful place in nature's wider "circles of vitality" (16: 378).

Vital Beauty moved Ruskin beyond familiar sermons in stones, inviting readers to sympathetically identify with environment: our place in creation is re-imagined when we recognize or believe that everything in nature feels with us the pleasures of "felicitous fulfilment of function" (4: 64) in joyful exertions. In a study of Ruskin, design, and much else besides, Lars Spuybroek suggests that sympathy indicates "deep-rooted engagement between us and things," a "relationship with caring," and "an immediate seeing-feeling-thinking relationship" (146, 171) which extends beyond organic life. Building on Ruskin's Vital Beauty, Spuybroek argues that this "reciprocity between us and things" is "not something extra, added on top of our relations with things and with each other," but "*at the core of those relations*" (146, 173–4). Sympathy must not be confused with empathy: we sympathize when we are able to enter into another's mode of existence, even when that existence is repulsive to us. Spuybroek draws on Henri Bergson's example of solitary wasps that paralyze caterpillars, arguing that they experience sympathy because their success "requires a form of knowledge between intelligence and instinct" (163). Describing Vital Beauty in individuals of a species, Ruskin counseled readers that we are not "called to pronounce upon worthiness of occupation or dignity of disposition" because "the animal's position and duty" is fixed by its divine design. The task instead is "to determine how far it worthily executes its office; whether, if scorpion, it hath poison enough, or if tiger, strength enough, or if dove, innocence enough, to sustain rightly its place in creation" (4: 101). To do this, we must sympathetically enter their lived experience, and in order to do so, we must be mindful of organic functionality.

The concept of sympathy was familiar in an age of Romantic poetry and nature tourism, but it was also through contact with nineteenth-century materialist anatomy, natural science, and geology that Ruskin predicated his version on proto-ecological concepts of interpenetration, cooperation, and the function-form relationship. As an exemplar of Vital Beauty, Ruskin drew attention to "a slender, pensive, fragile flower" poking out of "lines and gradations of unsullied snow" in an Alpine spring. The bloom of *Soldanella alpina* "shudders over the icy cleft ... partly dying of very fatigue after its hard won victory" (4: 146) in piercing the snow. While "the dead ice and the idle clouds" evoke "very pure and high typical beauty," the *Soldanella* offered "a totally different impression of loveliness" in which "there is now uttered to us a call for sympathy" for its heroic efforts, and "an image of moral purpose and achievement, which, however unconscious or senseless the creature may indeed be that so seems to call, cannot be heard without affection, nor contemplated without worship" (4: 147). Vital Beauty occurs when we recognize effort and energy as something familiar: founding this concept on what we share with other parts of nature, and inviting identification with humble organisms routinely regarded as "unconscious or senseless" (4: 89), Ruskin complicated anthropocentric divisions underlying Evangelicalism, just as the sentence above fails to quite clarify whether the object of worship is God or flower. We "look upon those as most lovely which are most happy" because "the pleasure afforded by every organic form is in proportion to its appearance of healthy vital energy" (4: 90, 92). Subject and object draw closer in a moment of recognition of one another's common experience of pleasure and energy. Ruskin hoped that by receiving "the utmost of pleasure from the happiness of all things" (4: 90), the observer would begin to conceive the wider environmental systems within which humanity was embedded.

Vital Beauty led Ruskin to ever-closer studies of environment and to insights that were reliant on the intensity of his gaze. His reading process involved tracing stories that stressed interconnectedness and dynamic process. In *The Elements of Drawing* (1857), a volume of art instruction, Ruskin told students "I have directed your attention early to foliage" because "its modes of growth present simple examples of the importance of leading or governing lines." In these leading lines, the artist accesses "a kind of vital truth to the rendering of every natural form … because these chief lines are always expressive of the past history and present action of the thing." In a mountain, leading lines reveal, "how it was built or heaped up; and secondly, how it is now being worn away, and from what quarter the wildest storms strike it." In a tree, "they show what kind of fortune it has had to endure from its childhood: how troublesome trees have come in its way, and pushed it aside, and tried to strangle or starve it; where and when kind trees have sheltered it, and grown up lovingly together with it, bending as it bent; what winds torment it most; what boughs of it behave best, and bear most fruit" (15: 91). Acute readers could access these dynamic histories and myriad interactions through an approach that was not purely scientific, religious, or aesthetic, but instead combined insights drawn from the materiality of organic and inorganic forms, their cultural significance, and their connections to the observer, a process that again encouraged a close and sympathetic gaze.

Ruskin's nature-reading methodology could even be applied to mythical nature. "Of the True Ideal" (*Modern Painters III*), offers an astonishing reading of two images of griffins (Fig. 1), "a piece of true grotesque, from the Lombard-Gothic, and of false grotesque from classical (Roman) architecture" (5: 140). Illustrating the reasons for Ruskin's preference for organic gothic design over the synthetic orderliness of classicism, the two griffins were also a lesson in the nature-reading possibilities opened up by Vital Beauty and leading lines. Acknowledging the griffin's mythical status, Ruskin nonetheless insisted that because we know that it "is a beast composed of lion and eagle," we can use knowledge of their material function and lived experiences to judge whether or not the representations revealed "the united power of both" (5: 141, 142). The classical griffin repeatedly failed this test because the design had "no other intent than that of covering a level surface with entertaining form." The other griffin was "a profound expression of the most passionate symbolism" (5: 147) arising out of instinctive love of natural form. The classical griffin, Ruskin complained, unnaturally raises its left foot in an absurd manner, and "sets it on the tendril of a flower so lightly as not even to bend it down" and that "in order to reach it, his left leg is made half as long again as his right." Inattentive to nature, the Roman carver achieves compositional balance by distorting anatomical and behavioral functions: "we may be pretty sure, if the carver had ever seen a griffin, he would have reported of him as doing something else than that with his feet" (5: 142). The Lombard griffin, by contrast, reproduces leonine nature because it "has the carnivorous teeth bare to the root, and the peculiar hanging of the jaw at the back, which marks the flexible and gaping mouth of the devouring tribes." It is also quintessentially aquiline:

> Among things essential to the might of an eagle ... are his claws. It is no use his being able to tear anything with his beak, if he cannot first hold it in his claws; he has comparatively no leonine power of striking with his feet, but a magnificent power of grip with them. Accordingly, we see that the real griffin, while his feet are heavy enough to strike like a lion's, has them also extended far enough to give them the eagle's grip with the back claw; and has, moreover, some of the bird-like wrinkled skin over the whole foot, marking this binding power the more: and that he has besides verily got something to hold with his feet, other than a flower.
>
> (5: 143)

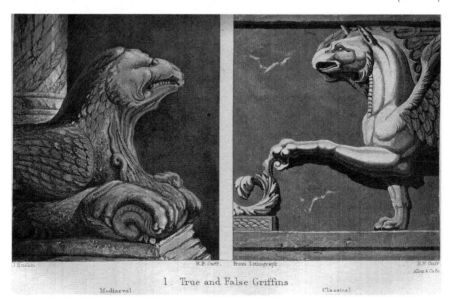

Figure 1.1 John Ruskin and R. P. Cuff, "True and False Griffins."
Source: Cook and Wedderburn Vol. 5, page facing 140.

Ruskin valued representations in which exterior physiology revealed a creature's functionality—even when this function can only be logically inferred. In this respect he was attuned to an important thread of early nineteenth-century science that would ultimately do much to prompt the emergence of Darwinism. In *Discourse On The Revolutionary Upheavals On The Surface Of The Globe And On The Changes Which They Have Produced In The Animal Kingdom* (1825), Baron Cuvier helped revolutionize anatomy by revealing that internal connections between organs were crucial to understanding animal organization:

> The form of a tooth leads to the form of the condyle, that of the scapula to that of the nails ... Similarly, the nails, the scapula, the condyle, the femur, each separately reveal the tooth or each other; and by beginning from each of them the thoughtful professor of the law of organic economy can reconstruct the entire animal.
>
> (98–9)

Cuvier argued that every anatomical feature of an animal contributed to an animal's functional purpose and helped fulfill its organic requirements. Anatomy revealed organisms as systems. In early correspondence to a clerical friend, Ruskin rubbished the prevailing evangelical notion that prelapsarian lions had laid down peaceably with lambs, arguing that leonine physiology meant carnivorous functionality: insisting in Cuvierian terms that "the gift of an instrument supposes the appointment to a function," he argued that "the claw is to catch with, the teeth are to tear with, and there is a particular juice in the stomach to digest meat with." To imagine "that these were given without intention of being used" is akin to supposing "that your tongue was given to you without your being intended to talk or taste with it" (1: 476).

In recognizing the functional mutuality of a lion's claws, teeth, and stomach, Ruskin applied Cuvierian methods to his dissection of Genesis.[4] They are also evident in the discussion of griffins. The false griffin would simply be incapable of rapid aquiline flight: "it would be difficult to impede him more thoroughly than by giving him two cocked ears to catch the wind [because] as he flew, there would be a continual humming of the wind on each side of his head, and he would have an infallible ear-ache when he got home," while "the real griffin has his ears flat to his head, and all the hair of them blown back, even to a point, by his fast flying." While its ear apertures face downwards, so that "he may hear anything going on upon the earth, where his prey is," the false griffin's apertures face upwards (5: 143–4). The true griffin's jowly neck facilitates the devouring of large prey, while the ornamental bosses on the false griffin's "must be infinitely in his way when he is swallowing." The true griffin combined leonine indolence and aquiline watchfulness, and because it had "such a little matter" as having "a poisonous winged dragon to hold," he does so "lying down and at his ease, looking out at the same time for any other piece of work in his way." The false griffin "is quite sleepy and dead in the eye," an unreal creature "putting himself to a great deal of unnecessary trouble with his paws, holding one in a most painful position merely to touch a flower" (5: 144, 145). Preferring elegance and compositional symmetry to organic verisimilitude, the Roman carver lacked interest in anatomy, natural processes, or the interaction of species with environment, while the medieval carver grasped these things intuitively and sympathetically.

Ruskin's preference for the materialist truth of the Lombard griffin exemplified his desire to understand environmental phenomena as networks of internal (anatomical) and external (environmental) co-dependencies. His nascent ecological vision was most fully theorized in "The Law of Help" (*Modern Painters V*, 1860), a work that also helped foster his growing concern that environment was not being properly read or properly valued. "The Law of Help" defined aesthetic composition as "the help of everything in the picture by everything else." If even one element of a well-composed artwork were removed, the rest became "helpless and valueless" (7: 205), but environment, rather than painting, provided the principal examples through which he illustrated this statement of co-determinant relationality. Ostensibly a chapter on art, "The Law of Help" was preoccupied with fundamental principles of order and collapsed distinctions between aesthetic and other forms of organization. Surveying helpfulness in environment, Ruskin noted differing degrees of natural composition. Atoms of clouds and stones "cohere to each other, or consist with each other, but they do not help each other," so that "removal of one part … does not injure the rest," whereas in plants removal might sometimes be injurious, and in animals decidedly so: "we may take away the branch of a tree without much harm to it; but not the animal's limb" (7: 205). Emphasizing the dynamic mutuality of natural forms, and the dangers inherent in meddling with organic systems, Ruskin insisted that "intensity of life is also intensity of helpfulness," and began to think about what happens when inherent helpful impulses are hindered. Because "the ceasing of this help is what we call corruption," Ruskin concluded that "the more intense the life has been, the more terrible is its corruption," and established a scale of decay:

> The decomposition of a crystal is not necessarily impure at all. The fermentation of a wholesome liquid begins to admit the idea slightly; the decay of leaves yet more; of flowers, more; of animals, with greater painfulness and terribleness in exact proportion to their original vitality; and the foulest of all corruption is that of the body of man.
>
> (7: 205–6)

These corresponding scales of decay and creative composition saw Ruskin simultaneously pursuing two opposing visions of nature: on the one hand a hierarchical model descending from *Homo sapiens*, through other animals, flowers, and leaves, down to crystals and clouds; on the other, a mutualistic principle that saw every part of an organic system as vital to its harmonious functionality, and anticipated a biodynamic understanding of systematic interdependence.

At the heart of all creative endeavor, "Help" represented a universal co-operative principle, so that aesthetic composition, as he argued in *The Elements of Drawing*, was merely "the type, in the arts of mankind, of the Providential government of the world" (15: 161–2). For Ruskin, "composition means, literally and simply, putting several things together so as to make *one* thing out of them; the nature and goodness of which they all have a share in producing." In composition—aesthetic, social, or environmental—every element "should be in a determined place, perform an intended part, and act, in that part advantageously for everything that is connected with it" (15: 161). "The Law of Help" had powerful social applications for Ruskin, but also led him towards environmental campaigns as he came to represent composition and competition as an eternally warring binary:

> therefore, is that in which all its parts are helpful or consistent ... The highest or organic purities are composed of many elements in an entirely helpful state. The highest and first law of the universe—and the other name of life is, therefore, "help." The other name of death is "separation." Government and co-operation are in all things and eternally the laws of life. Anarchy and competition, eternally, and in all things, the laws of death.
>
> (7: 207)[5]

The most striking early evidence of Ruskin's growing environmental anxieties emerged in his 1858 lecture, "The Work of Iron." In that lecture, Ruskin chastised his audience for thinking that iron was best in polished form, and that "rusty iron [was] spoiled iron." Counter-intuitively, he insisted, "it is not a fault in the iron, but a virtue, to be so fond of getting rusted, for in that condition it fulfils its most important functions in the universe." Anticipating the binary opposition between cooperation and competition in "The Law of Help," he argued that "in a certain sense, and almost a literal one, we may say that iron rusted is Living; but when pure or polished, Dead" (16: 376–7). In his analysis of oxidization, iron actively inhales air, revealing itself and oxygen as dynamic substances that participate in physical transformations: only by rusting can iron be creative. By respiring as we do, iron is revealed as part of a communion of the living and nearly living that interacts at a formative environmental level. Iron and other metals only reach their "most perfect and useful state" when they have "breath put into them," a breath of life that is both physical and spiritual (16: 376, 377). The dynamic changes which the consummation of oxygen and iron enact are endless, but its commercial products are relatively insignificant: "the main service of this metal is not in making knives, and scissors, and pokers, and pans," but instead "in making the ground we feed from, and nearly all the substances first needful to our existence." All soils are "metals which have undergone this ... vital change ... by permanent unity with the purest air" (16: 377), and these products of metallic re-composition produce the varied hues of landscapes, the coloration of rocks and gemstones, and the iron-rich shades of tiles, bricks, and slates. The interpenetration of iron oxide with all aspects of organic life revealed a realm of mutual dependence that subtly challenged scriptural differentiation between *Homo sapiens* and the rest of creation. In what can be seen as a case study of "The Law of Help," Ruskin embraced the co-dependence of humanity within the biocentric "circles of vitality" by invoking the religious symbolism of blood: "is it not strange," he asks, "to find this stern and strong metal mingled so delicately in our human life that we cannot even blush without its help?" (16: 384). In this intimate, sensual internalization of the work of iron, Ruskin reached his most advanced ecological position in tracing the "delicate mingling [and] binding" of a vitally helpful environmental system, and by declaring ourselves to be part of it.

The lecture was keen to do much more, however, for to recognize the delicate connections of environment was to seek their preservation. Ruskin therefore warned his audience that human interference with such systems risked substituting corruption for help. Predominately elegiac, the lecture also reflected an anxiety to be found in much nineteenth-century ecology. Pushing again at their preference for unrusted iron, Ruskin challenged his audience to imagine a world in which "all your meadows, instead of grass, grew nothing but iron wire." Articulating disquiet at a technological desire to arrest, harness, or nullify natural forces in pursuit of artificial commodities, he provoked them by asking if they would be content "if the whole earth, instead of its green and glowing sphere, rich with forest and flower, showed nothing but the image of the vast furnace of a ghastly engine." By failing to read nature correctly, a desire to command environment and achieve synthetic perfection would transform a vitalistic world of intricately helpful connections into "a globe of black, lifeless, excoriated metal" (16: 378). In a rhetorical sleight of hand, Ruskin withdrew from the audience the world, as it still exists, in which iron *does* rust, in which change *is* perpetual, and offers in its place a static monochromatic dystopia that might follow the cessation of iron ecology. Restoring the real world to the audience, he urged them, in biblical cadences, to sympathetically embrace ordinary, but miraculous experience:

> [The earth *would* be 'lifeless'] were it not that all the substance of which it is made sucks and breathes the brilliancy of the atmosphere; and, as it breathes, softening from its merciless hardness, it falls into fruitful and beneficent dust; gathering itself again into the earths from which we feed, and the stones with which we build;—into the rocks that frame the mountains, and the sands that bind the sea.
>
> (16: 378)[6]

Ruskin's direct environmental interventions began in the 1870s. One of the most prominent of these, his preface to Robert Somervell's 1877 pamphlet objecting to the creation of Thirlmere reservoir in Cumberland, attacked the scheme for its materialist value-system and insensitivity to the lake ecosystem.[7] Anticipating current debates about how (and whether) to ascribe monetary value to environments and environmental resources, Ruskin argued that "even if it be conceded that no considerations are valid the worth of which cannot be estimated in £.s.d., it can easily be shown that tried by this test, the charms, for the effacement of which this scheme is a bold initiatory step, are of no trifling value, we have no price-current for the beauties with which God has clothed our world." Moreover, "the immense sums which people of all degrees and classes spend every year, to procure for themselves, in one way or another, the enjoyment which these beauties … can afford, would be sufficient, one would think, in itself, to prove to the most unsentimental mind, that the best and rarest materials for such enjoyments are very far from worthless" (11).[8] Ruskin also argued that loss of landscape value registered at visual and environmental levels:

> There can be no object in raising the level of the Lake, or in extending its area, but that of creating a reserve during the wet season to be drawn upon in summer. At that season then, when the District is visited by Tourists, the Lake will be reduced to its old dimensions and for every acre of water remaining there will be an equal extent of mud and rotting water-weeds, or of desolate stony ground, like the bed of an Italian river, which will form a margin to the lake round its whole circumference, and this to replace the present shore, which nature has been beautifying for centuries, and harmonizing by means of moss and lichen, and varied herbage with the watery surface within, and the rocks and hills without.
> (10)

That Thirlmere's shoreline remains unsightly and scarred is evident to today's summer visitors, but Ruskin's argument showed that his habitual methods of nature-reading, his sense of environment as composition, and his preoccupation with natural functionality made him keenly aware of the effects of thoughtless intervention. By enormously increasing its potable water, Manchester Corporation had degraded a functioning natural environment.

More catastrophic still was the situation Ruskin discovered at Carshalton in 1870. In the introduction to *The Crown of Wild Olive* written that year (and published in 1873), he recollected a childhood idyll that he immersed in biblical rhythms and allusions:

> Twenty years ago, there was no lovelier piece of lowland scenery in South England, nor any more pathetic, in the world, by its expression of sweet human character and life, than that immediately bordering on the

sources of the Wandel ... No clearer or diviner waters ever sang with constant lips of the hand which "giveth rain from heaven."

(18: 384)

Surveying the same site in 1870, Ruskin had "never seen anything so ghastly in its inner tragic meaning ... as the slow stealing of aspects of reckless, indolent, animal neglect, over the delicate sweetness of that English scene." This "insolent defiling of those springs by the human herds that drink of them" symbolized an underlying "blasphemy or impiety" (18: 385) that had produced a grotesque inversion of the Law of Help. In one of the finest readings of a single Ruskin work, David Carroll argues that Ruskin found in scenes of natural beauty figures of a broader divine power of elemental arrangement, so that "each act of ordering implies vividly for him both the chaos before creation and the cosmos called into being by the imagination brooding, like the Holy Spirit, over the waters on the first day of creation" (6). Ruskin experienced strong emotion when encountering beauty or its loss, because "the moment in which form becomes formlessness, or vice versa, is charged with great intensity." Pollution was a synecdoche of a broader disordering brought about by deliberate human interference with vital helpfulness. Describing what he saw as the breaking of a sacred covenant, Ruskin's method in the Introduction was to place "the original sacred scene and the polluted view ... side by side, processes of growth in the former and decay in the latter described together" (Carroll 12). This, I would suggest, also involved provocative shifts between the modes of pastoral idyll (recalling the former Wandel) and pastoral elegy (describing its current state). Within the passage, the light, movement, and energy of pure water was starkly contrasted with the poisoned immobility of impure matter:

> Just where the welling of stainless water, trembling and pure, like a body of light, enters the pool of Carshalton, cutting itself a radiant channel down to the gravel, through warp of feathery weeds, all waving, which it traverses with its deep threads of clearness ... just in the very rush and murmur of the first spreading currents, the human wretches of the place cast their street and house foulness; heaps of dust and slime, and broken shreds of old metal, and rags of putrid clothes; which, having neither energy to cart away, nor decency enough to dig into the ground, they thus shed into the stream, to diffuse what venom of it will float and melt, far away, in all places where God meant those waters to bring joy and health.

(18: 386)

Serpentine rubbish that refused to decompose, that was immune to the cleansing power of divine water, was sacrilegious. Thus, the "ragged bank of mortar, and scoria, and bricklayer's refuse," "dead earth," and "black slime" (18: 386) represented "the *topos* of sacred contagion," rendering the

Wandel "a powerful focus for the forces of good and evil arrayed against each other in the latter half of the nineteenth century" (Carroll 72). The scene's wider significance saw Ruskin revisit the binary thinking so powerfully articulated in "The Law of Help":

> For Ruskin the opposing powers are those validating his natural theology and those of devilish Mammon ... They are held in balance as his childhood self wanders in memory through the sacred sites in which he now stands knee-deep in rubbish. The two coexist under enormous pressure in his (and the reader's) mind, as the endless metonymies of modern civilization are superimposed upon the precise metaphors of Eden, and the precious pastoral composition is decomposed before our eyes.
>
> (Carroll 75)

Modern society needed to decide whether "to worship God in Creation or the Divinity of Decomposition" (Carroll 74), where decomposition meant failure to helpfully compose, rather than the welcome biological process. This choice would be at the heart of Ruskin's attempts, via his utopian organization, the Guild of St George, to remedy environmental blasphemy. Enraged and despairing, he suggested that "half-a-dozen men, with one day's work could cleanse those pools, and trim the flowers about their banks, and make every breath of summer air above them rich with cool balm; and every glittering wave medicinal," but despondently added that the "day's work is never given, nor, I suppose, will be; nor will any joy be possible to heart of man, for evermore, about those wells of English waters" (18: 387). By 1872 he was no longer willing to wait for others, and took the lead himself in a remarkable project that kept the Wandel's spring so clear that trout returned to these waters for at least a decade.[9]

Projects like the Wandel underline Ruskin's environmentalist credentials, but his approach to such matters arose naturally—*help*fully—out of the nature-reading methods that this chapter has sought to describe. For Ruskin, environment represented a resource of multiple value and wider cultural significance. His insistence on the personal, cultural, social, spiritual, and material importance of landscape gained much strength from his simultaneous immersion in a range of influences, including Romanticism, Evangelicalism, Natural Theology, art, architecture, and science, but the positions he reached as a result make him one of the key nineteenth-century forbears and parents of ecology. He anticipated, and to some extent participated in, ecological thought not simply in his tendency to make connections (between natural phenomena and elements of an ecosystem, between observer and observed, between subjects and discourses), but also in his desire to dissolve boundaries between these things, to combine rather than divide. In his understanding of nature narratives, of organismic functionality, and of the role of process and interaction (in organisms and natural systems) Ruskin helped shape ecological approaches, while also finding a method of seeing and feeling the world that went beyond environment and that continues to be relevant today. For Ruskin, the ability to read nature created opportunities to alter and shape consciousness in ways that reflected everything that he saw and valued in the environment, as his advice to readers of *Modern Painters V* suggests:

> Let him [sic] be assured of this, that unless important changes are occurring in his opinions continually, all his life long, not one of those opinions can be on any questionable subject true. All true opinions are living, and show their life by being capable of nourishment; therefore of change. But their change is that of a tree—not of a cloud.
>
> (7: 9)

For modern readers, facing the existential threat of global warming and environmental degradation, the ability to read nature in order to transform our thought processes and to find helpful relationships with the world is more sorely needed than ever.

Notes

1. Ernst Haeckel defined his newly coined science of ecology as emerging from "the body of knowledge concerning the economy of nature" or "the study of all those complex interrelationships referred to by Darwin as the condition of the struggle for existence" (trans. and qtd. in Stauffer 141). See also Marsh.
2. All subsequent quotations from Ruskin will be from Cook and Wedderburn, given parenthetically in the text in the form of volume number and page number(s).
3. For Ruskin's early articles and *The Poetry of Architecture*, see Cook and Wedderburn, vol. 1.
4. For a fuller analysis of Ruskin's materialist critique of evangelical readings of Eden, see Frost, "A Vital Truth." See also Conner (15) and Spear (45).
5. On the social and political implications of "The Law of Help," see Atwood; Eagles; and Frost, "Of Trees and Men."
6. For a comparison of "The Work of Iron" and Ruskin's studies of Moss, see Frost, "Everyday Marvels." On "The Work of Iron," see also Shrimpton.
7. On Thirlmere's role in the emergence of modern environmentalism, see Ritvo.
8. It is instructive to compare Ruskin's thoughts on landscape value and those of the modern landscape historian Oliver Rackham in his 1990 Reflection Riding Memorial Lecture.
9. For a detailed account of this restoration project (previously thought to have been an abject failure) see Frost, *Lost Companions* 73–80.

Works cited

Atwood, Sara. *Ruskin's Educational Ideals*. Aldershot: Ashgate, 2011.
Carroll, David. "Pollution, Defilement and the Art of Decomposition." *Ruskin and Environment*. Ed. Michael Wheeler. Manchester: Manchester UP, 1995. 58–75.
Conner, Patrick. *Savage Ruskin*. London: Macmillan, 1979.

Cook, E. T., and Alexander Wedderburn, eds. *The Library Edition of John Ruskin's Works*. 39 vols. London: George Allen, 1903–12.

Cuvier, Baron Georges. *Discourse On The Revolutionary Upheavals On The Surface Of The Globe And On The Changes Which They Have Produced In The Animal Kingdom*. Paris: Defour and D'Ocagne, 1825.

Eagles, Stuart. *After Ruskin: The Social and Political Legacies of a Victorian Prophet*. Oxford: Oxford UP, 2010.

Finley, C. Stephen. *Nature's Covenant: Figures of Landscape in Ruskin*. University Park: Pennsylvania State UP, 1992.

Frost, Mark. "The Everyday Marvels of Rust and Moss: John Ruskin and the Ecology of the Mundane." *Green Letters: Studies in Ecocriticism* 13 (2011): 10–22.

———. *The Lost Companions and John Ruskin's Guild of St George: a Revisionary History*. London: Anthem, 2014.

———. "Of Trees and Men: The Law of Help and the Formation of Societies in *Modern Painters V*." *Nineteenth Century Prose* 38.2 (2011): 85–108.

———. "'A Vital Truth': Ruskin, Science and Dynamic Materiality." *Journal of Victorian Literature and Culture* 39.2 (2011): 367–83.

Haeckel, Ernst. *Generelle Morphologie der Organismen*. 2 vols. Berlin: Verlag von Georg Reimer, 1866.

———. *The Riddle of the Universe at the Close of the Nineteenth Century*. Trans. Joseph McCabe. London: Watts, 1900.

———. *God-Nature*. London: n.p., 1914.

Marsh, George Perkins. *Man and Nature*. 1864. Ed. David Lowenthal. Cambridge: Harvard UP, 1965.

Rackham, Oliver. "Landscape and the Conservation of Meaning." Reflection Riding Memorial Lecture to the Society of Arts. *RSA Journal* (1991): 903–15.

Ritvo, Harriet. *The Dawn of Green: Manchester, Thirlmere, and Modern Environmentalism*. Chicago: U of Chicago P, 2009.

Ruskin, John. Preface. Robert Somervell. *Water for Manchester from Thirlmere: the Manchester and Thirlmere Scheme: an Appeal to the Public on the Facts of the Case*. Manchester: Heywood, 1877.

Shrimpton, Nick. "'Rust and Dust': Ruskin's Pivotal Work." *New Approaches to Ruskin: Thirteen Essays*. Ed. Robert Hewison. London: Routledge, 1981. 51–67.

Spear, Jeffrey L. *Dreams of an English Eden: Ruskin and His Tradition in Social Criticism*. New York: Columbia UP, 1984.

Spuybroek, Lars. *The Sympathy of Things: Ruskin and the Ecology of Design*. Rotterdam: v2/NAI, 2011.

Stauffer, Robert. "Haeckel, Darwin, and Ecology." *Quarterly Review of Biology* 32 (1957): 138–44.

2 Between "bounded field" and "brooding star"
A study of Tennyson's topography

Valerie Purton

> We ranging down this lower track,
>   The path we came by, thorn and flower,
>   Is shadowed by the growing hour,
> Lest life should fail by looking back.
>
> So be it: there no shade can last
>   In that deep dawn behind the tomb,
>   But clear from marge to marge shall bloom
> The eternal landscape of the past.
>
> A lifelong tract of time revealed;
>   The fruitful hours of still increase;
>   Days ordered in a wealthy peace,
> And those five years its richest field.
>
> O Love, thy province is not large,
>   A bounded field, nor stretching far;
>   Look also, Love, a brooding star,
> A rosy warmth from marge to marge.
>
> (*In Memoriam* XLVI 1–16)[1]

Tennyson seems initially an unpromising subject for an environmental or ecocritical reading. Yes, he was noted from his earliest poetic successes as a "poet of nature" but, coming from rural Lincolnshire, he never seems to have seen "nature" as vulnerable, as worthy of protection. His most famous line paints "her" in very different colors—as "red in tooth and claw" (*In Memoriam* LVI 15)—as an indifferent, indeed, Monstrous Mother. Where Matthew Arnold can praise Wordsworth as one who "laid us where we lay at birth, / In the cool, flowery lap of Earth" ("Memorial Verses" 48–9), Tennyson seems rather the ruthless Victorian poet of science, for whom "nature" is at best indifferent to, at worst the enemy of human aspirations.

And yet there are other ways in which he lends himself to just such a reading—indeed, I am going to argue in this chapter that his use of two key concepts in ecocriticism, "place" and "space," takes us to the heart of his poetic vision while also inevitably forcing us to engage with the complex and vexed issue of what it is to be a "nature poet."

Tennyson as "nature poet"

Cheryll Glotfelty's seminal list of questions for the potential ecocritic includes two which are particularly germane to this study of Tennyson: "How can we characterize nature writing as a genre?" and "In addition to race, class, and gender, should *place* become a new critical category?" (xix). Tennyson's "nature writing" at first glance seems to lack one element essential to its inclusion in the ecocritical tradition. Timothy Clark in mapping that tradition links Jonathan Bate with William Wordsworth, arguing that both tend "to idealise what was *under threat* in the Lake District" (19, my italics). Tennyson, living first in the village of Somersby and then in Cambridge, seems relatively untroubled by the "threat" of industrialization and it is perhaps this single omission that has led to his relative neglect by ecocritics. A recent critic exploring "the literary roots of modern ecology in the British nineteenth century" goes so far as to borrow her title, *Chaos and Cosmos*, from Tennyson's "Locksley Hall Sixty Years After"—without mentioning him at all (Scott 2014). There are in fact key moments in which a sense of threat does emerge in Tennyson's poetry. Consider, for example in *Maud*, when the narrator describes his father's death as directly the result of capitalist speculation and industrial exploitation: "that old man, now lord of the broad estate and the Hall, / Dropt off gorged from a scheme that left us flaccid and drained" (19–20). In the same poem, Maud's

> old grandfather has lately died,
> Gone to a blacker pit, for whom
> Grimy nakedness dragging his trucks
> And laying his trams in a poisoned gloom
> Wrought, till he crept from a gutted mine
> Master of half a servile shire,
> And left his coal all turned to gold,
> To a grandson, first of his noble line …
>
> (334–41)

There are many such attacks on capitalist greed, sometimes only sideswipes, as in "Edwin Morris": "new-comers in an ancient hold / New-comers from the Mersey, millionaires" (9–10), or in "The Golden Year," when the speaker envisages a time "when wealth no more shall rest in mounded heaps / … / And light shall spread, and man be liker man" (32, 35). That poem ends with a sound which, for the young Tennyson in the Lincolnshire Wolds, would have been all that he knew of early nineteenth-century industry: "He spoke; and, high above, I heard them blast / The steep slate-quarry, and the great echo flap / And buffet round the hills, from bluff to bluff" (74–6) .

Tennyson, then, *is* aware of the dangers of industrial capitalism, but it is an awareness that he expresses, I would argue, not so much in grand statements about *protecting* the natural world, as in clear-sighted *looking* at that world. Timothy Clark, attempting to identify "the natural" as it developed through and beyond the Romantic tradition, declares that "What Bate and Wordsworth idealise as 'natural' is more accurately described as a mode of relatively non-exploitative and stable *settledness*, a locally focussed pre-capitalist lifestyle" (19). The key phrase here for Tennyson is "locally-focussed." His best poetry has "a local habitation and a name"—and it is a local habitation minutely described.

The appreciation of Tennyson as an observer of the natural world began to re-emerge, after the eclipse of his reputation during the ascendancy of Modernism, as early as 1951, in Marshall McLuhan's sharply perceptive "Tennyson and Picturesque Poetry," which examines the poet's depiction of landscape. McLuhan's central claim is that "if anybody ever had and consciously cultivated a movie-camera eye it was Tennyson" (83). He made what was at the time a bold prediction: For future readers "it will be the Tennyson of the precise ear and eye who will provide the most unexpected and persistent enjoyment" (81). That notion was followed up by Carol Christ and John Jordan who identified Tennyson's "legendary fidelity to visual detail." They recall the character in Elizabeth Gaskell's *Cranford* who declared that it was Tennyson's poetry which had taught him that "ash buds are black at the beginning of March," and record the poet "falling to his knees in the grass to observe a rose through a dragonfly's wings" (xx). Laurence Mazzeno summarizes the point: Tennyson "was always intensely interested in minute details; he had a habit of reversing the adage expressed by Dr. Samuel Johnson in *Rasselas* that the business of the poet is not with tracing the streaks of the tulip, but in describing general properties" (134).

Arthur Hallam was one of the first critics to identify Tennyson's peculiar poetic relationship to "nature." One of the young poet's "distinctive excellencies," he declared, was his "vivid, picturesque delineation of objects" (qtd. in Jump 42). W. J. Fox declared that Tennyson could "personate anything he pleases, from an angel to a grasshopper" (qtd. in Jump 26). Christopher North, on the other hand, attacked the young poet for not investing "nature" with meaning: poets such as Wordsworth, he declares, "shun not the sights of common earth … But beneath the magic of their eyes the celandine grows a star or a sun. What beauty is breathed over the daisy by lovingly blessing it because it is so common! 'Sweet flower! Whose home is everywhere!'" (qtd. in Jump 52). In the mid-twentieth century, at the nadir of Tennyson's reputation, John F. Danby condemned him on precisely these grounds, presenting him as simply a recorder of (in Danby's scathing phrase) "nature-notes." Danby posited a "rough scale of 'nature-poetry'" of which "the first level is that of 'nature-notes,' the counting of the streaks of the tulip, observations like 'black as ash-buds in the front of March' or like 'willows whiten, aspens quiver.' Tennyson is a notorious repository of such *detachable and detailed accuracies*" (46, my italics). What the insights of ecocriticism now allow us to see is that it may be this very unintrusive reporting of the natural world which is Tennyson's great and peculiarly modern achievement. The specificity of "nature poetry" for him is a specificity which denies the symbolizing tendency of the Romantics, and instead produces a natural description in which a stone is just a stone—and nonetheless mysterious for that. When Wordsworth speaks pityingly of Peter Bell, for whom "a primrose by the river's brim / A yellow primrose was for him / And it was nothing more" ("Peter Bell" 248–50) his pity reveals a key difference in attitude between the Romantics and their successors, whether Victorians, modernists, postmodernists, or ecocritics.

Arthur Hallam identified Tennyson's ability simply to "see" an object in his essay in *The Englishman's Magazine* (1831), in which he had placed his friend as a poet of the Keatsian rather than the Shelleyan mode: "Shelley and Keats were indeed of opposite genius; the one was vast, impetuous and sublime, the other … does not generalise or allegorise nature; his imagination works with few symbols, and reposes willingly on what is freely given" (qtd. in Jump 36). John Ruskin followed that line of argument when, in 1851, he introduced the Pre-Raphaelites to the world and identified "[t]he sudden and universal Naturalism, or inclination to copy ordinary natural objects" (qtd. in McLuhan 73). Tennyson's greatest contribution to the cause of nature poetry, then, may be precisely his energetic engagement in what Christ and Jordan see as the debate "between objective and subjective paradigms of perception'"(xx). Arguably, it is precisely in his "nature-notes," about which Danby was so scathing, that Tennyson liberates the natural world from the domination of human meaning-making and simply looks steadily at all its manifestations. A key characteristic of this "looking," and of Tennyson's peculiar observational gift as a nature poet, is his juxtaposition of the vast and the minute—as in his dizzying swoop, in *In Memoriam* CXXIV, from "world and sun" in one line to "eagle's wing, or insect's eye" in the next. This is the move I identified at the beginning of the chapter, between "space" and "place" and it returns us to Glotfelty's second question quoted above: "should *place* become a new critical category?"

"Place" and "space"

As the *In Memoriam* stanzas quoted at the beginning of this chapter suggest, Tennyson was a poet with a strong topographical bent. He was also notoriously shortsighted and never able completely to compensate for this with monocle or spectacles (See Martin 93). The result was a double vision which many fellow myopics will recognize: he had a preternaturally vivid and detailed awareness of objects close to hand, but a different, undifferentiated vagueness about the distant, the seas, the heavens, "vastness." It is easy to illustrate this from the poems:

"a million emeralds break from the ruby-budded lime"
(*Maud* 102)

"rosy plumelets tuft the larch"
(*In Memoriam* XCI 1)

the sunflower "shining fair/Ray[s] round with flames her disk of seed"
(*In Memoriam* CI 5–6)

the dragonfly emerges from its chrysalis displaying "plates of sapphire mail"
("The Two Voices" 12)

At the other extreme are "the starry heavens of space" (*In Memoriam* LXXVI 3) and "star and system rolling past" ("Epilogue," *In Memoriam* 122). Or consider this striking evolutionary vision of *The Princess*:

This world was once a fluid haze of light
Till toward the centre set the starry tides,
And eddied into suns, that wheeling cast
The planets ...

(101–4)

I want in this chapter to suggest that ecocritical approaches to "place" and "space" can take us to the heart of Tennyson's unique achievement as a liminal poet working between subjectivity and objectivity, between the Romantics' idealization of nature and the scientific predations of the post-Darwinian world.

Ecological criticism has made much of definitions of place and space. Cultural geographer Yi-Fu Tuan laid the groundwork in *Space and Place: The Perspective of Experience* (1977): space and place, he says, "require each other for definition. From the security and stability of place, we are aware of the openness, freedom and threat of space, and vice versa ... Human lives are a dialectical movement between shelter and venture, attachment and freedom. In open space one can become intensely aware of place; and in the solitude of a sheltered place the vastness of space beyond acquires a haunting presence" (6, 54). Other critics went on to make the crucial link between place and identity: "Knowledge of place is ... closely linked to knowledge of the self, to grasping one's own position in the larger scheme of things, including one's own community, and to securing a confident sense of who one is as a person" (Basso 34).

Yi-Fu Tuan's comment that "Human lives are a dialectical movement between shelter and venture, attachment and freedom" neatly suggests the Tennysonian dialectic. One might begin by examining his use of the word "space" in a poem in which "shelter and venture" are indeed central. In "The Lady of Shalott," the nameless Lady herself is defined by an absence: "Four gray walls, and four gray towers / Overlook a space of flowers" (15–16). That space, surrounded by the limitations imposed by (male) castle-builders, suggests the amorphousness of the Lady's identity, that is, before she enters the world of language and inscribes her name upon the boat that carries her to her death. Basso's link between place and identity is relevant here. In the case of the Lady, the place in which she lives is described as a "space" precisely because she has not been able to impose her identity upon it: she has no knowledge of self.

At the end of the poem the word "space" recurs, but this time with a temporal rather than a topographical meaning: "But Lancelot mused a little space" (168). "Space," then, can be used more abstractly than "place," as a link, in fact, between place and time—an idea running through the *In Memoriam* stanzas quoted at the beginning of this chapter, and one which I will develop later. "Space" is a shifting, subjective concept. It can be linked to individual experience, to a sense of identity, rather than simply to objective geography. As applied to the heavens and to the ambition of human beings to imagine beyond the comfort of terrestrial "place," for Tennyson "space" can also suggest danger and imaginative boldness, as evidenced in the Conclusion to *The Princess* ("Through all the silent spaces of the worlds" [114]) and *In Memoriam* ("And rolled the floods in grander space" [CIII, 26]).

The "space" side of Tennyson's poetry has always commanded respect and indeed awe. Readers and critics have recognized the grandeur of his imaginative struggle, beyond that of any other Victorian poet, with the new and terrifying insights of nineteenth-century science. As T. H. Huxley remarked, Tennyson "is the only poet since Lucretius who truly understood scientific thought" (2: 338). When Lawrence Buell identified the present environmental crisis as "a crisis of imagination" (2), he would have done well to enlist the help of Tennyson, who, in his imaginative swoops from the vast to the microscopic, seems to presage the insights of twentieth-century nuclear science. In *In Memoriam*, looking ahead into a "secular abyss," he imagines a moment "Where all the starry heavens of space / Are sharpened to a needle's end" (LXXVI 3–4). Admiration for Tennyson's cosmic vision, then, is well deserved, but it has developed largely at the expense of his local "nature poetry."

"Place," until ecocriticism reassessed it, has often been regarded as *limitingly* small and local, linked to the "nature notes" which were the object of Danby's blistering condescension. It is certainly true that there is a side to Tennyson's poetry which is full of enclosed, circumscribed spaces; even the major poems are usually safely anchored in time and place. His, it could be argued, is a world of gardens, parks, "landscapes," a world (according to his detractors) of safety, both emotional and political. Sir

Walter Vivian may open his gardens to the *hoi polloi* but he has no intention of permanently sharing them. The narrator of *The Princess*, returning from his chivalric world of myth and romance, implicitly approves of the reinstatement at the end of the poem of both the poetic and the political status quo. There are many such circumscribed places in Tennyson's poetry, beginning with the intimacy of the much-loved domestic place—the *home*:

> What shall sever me
> From the love of home?
> Shall the weary sea,
> Leagues of sounding foam?
>
> Shall extreme distress,
> Shall unknown disgrace,
> Make my love the less
> For my sweet birth-place?
>
> Though my brains grow dry,
> Fancy mew her wings,
> And my memory
> Forget all other things—
>
> Though I could not tell
> My left hand from my right,—
> I should know thee well,
> Home of my delight!
>
> ("Home" 1–16)

This poem was written only five years earlier than "Ulysses," in 1828, presumably when Alfred first left Somersby for Cambridge. "Home" attempts to *enact* the desired stasis and security with end-stopped lines and safe, enclosed *abab* quatrains. The movement of the imagery is from the vastness of "perilous seas" to the safety of one's own territory, indeed, one's own body. The neatness is almost parodic, but the emotion obviously heartfelt.

The next space Tennyson's poetry offers us is that of the *Garden*, initially his father's garden memorably captured in an early poem, "Amphion" (written 1837–1838, published 1842). This poem makes it clear that the literal garden at Somersby was also for the poet a metaphorical garden, the poetic inheritance left to him by his father but also sometime tutor, George Clayton Tennyson (see Sturman and Purton 1993):

> My father left a park to me,
>   But it is wild and barren,
> A garden too with scarce a tree,
>   And waster then a warren:

> Yet say the neighbours when they call,
>   It is not bad but good land,
> And in it is the germ of all
>   That grows within the woodland.
>
>   (1–8)

Here "park" and "garden" are closely allied and offer the opportunity to reach out into the "woodland." The poem goes on to explore the ancient cultivators of that garden (which has by now metamorphosed into the garden of English poetic tradition) and contrasts them with the greatly inferior "modern Muses" who read "botanic treatises" but have no natural affinity with the land. Despite this, the speaker has no choice but to work in the limited place in which he finds himself:

> And I must work through months of toil,
>   And years of cultivation,
> Upon my proper patch of soil
>   To grow my own plantation.
> I'll take the showers as they fall,
>   I will not vex my bosom:
> Enough if at the end of all
>   A little garden blossom.
>
>   (97–104)

The sense of "belatedness" of the young, early Victorian poet is wistfully apparent in the verbal and rhythmic limitations of this poem which bear witness to the sense of inferiority he experiences when measuring himself against the grandeur of the achievements of his Romantic forebearers. What is significant, though, is that Tennyson feels the need to define his task topographically. He had already done so even more specifically in "Ode to Memory," in mapping out "the seven elms, the poplars four / That stand beside my father's door" (56–7). The trope of the garden haunted him to the end of his life. In the last *Notebook* (*Tennyson Notebook* 34 [1892]) he reacted angrily to an American editor who had, as so often happened, ignored his wishes and printed poems he had decided to suppress, with the squib:

> I weeded my garden for hours and hours,
> To make it a pleasure for women and men;
> But a Yankee planted the weeds again,
> Little he cared for the flowers.
>
>   ("I weeded my garden" Ricks 1449)

The garden for Tennyson, then, was a place of beauty, but also a place of productivity, of livelihood. Gardens in earlier times were, after all, smallholdings producing a peasant's means of subsistence. Bourgeois they may appear to twenty-first-century eyes, but to Tennyson they also meant an inheritance that might provide the means to be independent from authority. In his work they appear in many forms. There are garden-bowers, garden gates, garden-herbs, garden-isles, garden lawns, garden roses, garden squares, garden tools, garden trees, garden walks and garden walls. Passion does of course also occur in the garden, notably in *Maud*, but even here there is a tendency towards domestication: "I have led her *home*, my love, my only friend" (659, my italics).

Beyond the garden may be the *park*, private property that democratically minded owners such as Lilia's father in *The Princess* may, with other like-minded landowners, open at certain times of year to the public:

> Sir Walter Vivian all a summer's day
> Gave his broad lawns until the set of sun
> Up to the people: thither flocked at noon
> His tenants, wife and child, and thither half
> The neighbouring borough with their Institute
> Of which he was patron.
>
> ("Prologue" 1–6)

Tennyson's poetic world, selectively read, is full of such cultivated places: the "suburb grange" ("To Fitz"); the "well-beloved place" (*In Memoriam*, CII); alleys and cultivated flowers, and "old familiar fields" ("Enoch Arden"); and even a quintessentially English "privet hedge" ("The Gardener's Daughter" 110). It is mapped, familiar, circumscribed. Tennyson seems to "know his place" in every sense—both his familiar native land and the poetic tradition within which he writes.

On the other hand, the language itself works to collapse the distinction between place and space, for example, across the liminal space of "The Gardener's Daughter":

> Not wholly in the busy world, nor quite
> Beyond it, blooms the garden that I love.
> News from the humming city comes to it
> In sound of funeral or of marriage bells;
> And, sitting muffled in dark leaves, you hear
> The windy clanging of the minster clock;
> Although between it and the garden lies
> A league of grass, washed by a slow broad stream,
> That, stirred with languid pulses of the oar,
> Waves all its lazy lilies, and creeps on,
> Barge-laden, to the three arches of a bridge
> Crowned with the minster-towers.
>
> (33–44)

In these *English idylls* are imbricated the larger *idylls* of Arthurian legend and the Laureate poems of public space. In the confinement of the English garden can already be heard the sounds of funerals and weddings, as in "The Lady of Shalott," the "windy clanging," as on the "ringing plains of windy Troy" in "Ulysses"; the "league of grass" could so easily become the Light Brigade's "half a league onwards," the "[b]arge-laden" "slow broad stream" could be that which was to bear away King Arthur. Language knows no geographical limits, cannot easily be policed, least of all by a poet. Tennyson's gardens, his parks, his enclosed places, I hope to suggest, always give unwitting access to his wildernesses, the large dark "interstellar spaces" of his unconfined imagination.

Limits

It is certainly true, however, that one of Tennyson's favorite words is "limit": the "limit of the hills" in "Audley Court" (83), "the quiet limit of the world" in "Tithonus" (7), the "laughter at the limit of the wood" in "Pelleas and Ettarre"(49), "the glimmering limit far withdrawn" in "The Vision of Sin" (223). Tennyson was in every sense aware of his limitations. In his choice of the *abba* stanza form in *In Memoriam*, in particular, he sets up rigid poetic limits which perhaps provide their own sense of security, even while the ideas with which the poem struggles reach beyond the limits of the human imagination. Poetic form itself is, like a garden, a place of cultivation and confinement—and within that form Tennyson sets up self-imposed limits while openly expressing a desire for greater freedom. Christopher Decker in his wittily titled "Tennyson's Limitations" reminds us that "Tennyson confessed that he liked the confinements of the sonnet form somewhat less than Wordsworth: 'I hate the perfect sonnet with a perfect hatred,' was one of his splenetic outbursts against its straitjacketing constraints" (66). Decker goes on to point out the other side of Tennyson's adherence to "place":

> "Mariana," "The Lady of Shalott," "Ulysses" and "Tithonus" embody the wish to exceed the bounds of what they know ... The figures central to these poems wish to move abroad, beyond the confinement of their spatial limitations ... [S]pace in Tennyson is a recurrent central metaphor for experience—whether a pane of glass, a verge, or a fading margin, an arch, a glimmering threshold, or the space demarcated by or contained within these limits—... [while] the poems themselves are ... clearly bounded by their own limits, their margins.
>
> (65)

In an early sonnet addressed almost certainly to Arthur Hallam, the topography illustrates Decker's point, mapping what is to become a typically Tennysonian emotional journey:

Me my own Fate to lasting sorrow doometh:
   Thy woes are birds of passage, transitory:
   Thy spirit circled with a living glory,
In summer still to summer joy resumeth.
Alone my hopeless melancholy gloometh,
   Like a lone cypress, through the twilight hoary,
From an old garden where no flower bloometh,
   One cypress on an island promontory.
But yet my lonely spirit follows thine,
   As *round the rolling earth night follows day:*
But yet thy lights on my horizon shine
   Into my night, when thou art far away.
I am so dark, alas! And thou so bright,
When we two meet there's never perfect light.
                        ("Me My Own Fate," my italics)

The sonnet was published in the album *Friendship's Offering* in 1832 but never reprinted—obviously having been "weeded out" by the poet later in his career. The octave is set firmly in a "place"—a withered garden with a "lone cypress"—but the *volta* imposed by the sonnet form allows the poet to move effortlessly out in the sestet into "space"—the rolling earth, the horizon—before he attempts an awkward reconciliation of the much-travelled Hallam and his own provincial Lincolnshire self in the bathetic but immensely touching last line. Here the very limits and constrictions of the sonnet form structure the thought in a way impossible in any other poetic form, and allow the young poet to track what was to become his favorite poetic movement—from the local to the global.

The exotic

Beginning often with his "Love of Home," then, Tennyson's poetry compulsively moves out beyond such limits. The young poet writing of home and of gardens was at the same time, after all, writing of Babylon, the Peruvians and Timbuctoo (Timbuktu). Tennyson the poet of "Home" is also, and equally, a poet of exploration, of transgression, of the lure of the exotic (literally, "an outside place"). His poetic environment from the beginning extended "Far, far away": "Before I could read, I was in the habit on a stormy day of spreading my arms to the wind, and crying out 'I hear a voice that's speaking in the wind,' and the words 'far, far away' had always a strange charm for me" (qtd. in Hallam Tennyson *Memoir* 1: 11).

Tennyson's poetry is thus characterized by the tension between "place" and "space," between the domestic and the exotic. This makes more explicable the fact that one of his earliest responses to Arthur Hallam's death was "Ulysses," a poem, he said, about "the need to go on," to journey "far, far away"—"beyond the sunset and the baths / Of all the western stars until I die" (60–1). Ulysses is an old man with no specific goal except covering distance. He perceives a threat coming, significantly, from staying in one place, from domesticity, from being "matched with an agèd wife" (3). The harsh consonants do not suggest tenderness: they snap with frustration. This is no domestic idyll but a life-in-death sentence. The interlocking vowels, the use of "ee" and "a," trap both the verse and Ulysses himself in linguistic confinement. There is a noticeable sense of escape, of expansion, as he moves out into the world: the end-stopped lines change as he finds his natural rhythm, the natural shape of his thoughts: they expand and flow through enjambments from line 6 to line 11, where they do find resolution. The whole first movement of the poem is from "know not me" (5) to "I am become a name" (11), where the soft "m" sounds at last bring some comfort. For the purposes of my argument, the key lines are 6 and 7: "I cannot rest from travel: I will drink / Life to the lees." Tennyson, or rather Ulysses, sees travel itself (simply the journey, not the prospect of a destination) as a form of fulfillment. The colon in the middle of that line equates one side with the other: travelling itself, irrespective of aim, equals "drinking life to the lees." This may sound like a rather dubious impulse towards escapism, but it is followed by the perhaps more admirable desire to lose oneself in other cultures:

> For always roaming with a hungry heart
> Much have I seen and known; cities of men
> And manners, climates, councils, governments,
> Myself not least, but honoured of them all.
>
> (12–15)

The use of "For" is estranging: I have always taken it to mean "As a result of," but the preposition simultaneously suggests reward—that such travel, motivated though it is by a sense of inner emptiness, is rewarded by the acquisition of knowledge of other lands and cultures. R. B. Martin picks up a similar phrase from *In Memoriam* for the title of his biography: *Tennyson: The Unquiet Heart*. In the stanza from *In Memoriam* to which the title refers, it is the actual writing of poetry that calms the heart; in "Ulysses," equally a poem of bereavement, the poet uses the distance of the dramatic monologue precisely to address one of the symptoms of grief: the desire to distance oneself from the source of the pain, to travel "far, far away," to lose oneself in alien spaces.

Arthur Hallam, in his entry for the Chancellor's Medal competition of 1828 whose subject was "Timbuctoo," envisaged Timbuctoo much more positively than did Tennyson in his winning poem. To Hallam, it was a place full of "Love, and Truth, and all that cannot die" (qtd. in Reynolds 220). Hallam's youthful love of the exotic might well have encouraged Tennyson's own early "exotic" poems, notably the second "Mariana" poem, "Mariana in the South," in which Tennyson transports his lonely heroine from a "moated grange" in Lincolnshire to the Pyrenees where the two young men had been walking in the summer of 1830. Hallam wrote enthusiastically in 1831 to W. B. Donne: "You will, I think, agree ... that ... The *Southern Mariana*" requires "a greater lingering on the outward circumstances" than the former poem (qtd. in Ricks 362). Certainly, both Hallam and Tennyson were inspired by the subject of "Timbuctoo." Tennyson sent his imagination soaring from the Pillars of Hercules, over the sunken city of Atlantis, over Eldorado (which he places on the wrong continent, possibly confusing New Guinea with Guinea), on to the Acropolis in Greece and thence to the Pyramids. He positions his speaker on a peak overlooking the known and unknown world:

> I stood upon the Mountain which o'erlooks
> The narrow seas, whose rapid interval
> Parts Afric from green Europe, when the Sun
> Had fallen below the Atlantick
>
> ("Timbuctoo" 1–4)

This is the sort of commanding view which prompts Alan Sinfield's argument that Tennyson's exoticism is part of an imperialist project, involving a *threat* to what is remote and unknown from Western colonialism—that, as postcolonialist readings of "Ulysses" also suggest, the attraction of the distant space is that it is there to be colonized, controlled, overwhelmed. It is Tennyson himself, and the imperial culture he represents, says Sinfield, which form "the ultimate threat" to the remote spaces he describes (50). In his defense, it might be argued that Tennyson's exoticism is always essentially literary rather than political. He found his inspiration for "Timbuctoo" close to home, in the travel books in his father's library. In fact, everything begins for Tennyson in what is local, in the Lincolnshire landscape of his childhood.

From place to space: the exotic in the local

Like Charles Dickens, Tennyson was adept at showing "the romantic side of familiar things" (Dickens, Preface to *Bleak House* 42). Unlike Dickens, though, Tennyson stayed during his own lifetime in relatively familiar surroundings, refusing all invitations to explore the New World. His Timbuctoo is very firmly located in the realms of his imagination. Similarly, when he read the classics in childhood he had envisaged the towers of Troy as rising on the beach at Mablethorpe in Lincolnshire:

> Here often, when a child, I lay reclined,
>   I took delight in this locality.
> Here stood the infant Ilion of the mind,
>   And here the Grecian ships did seem to be,

> And here again I come, and only find
> The drain-cut levels of the marshy lea—
> Grey sandbanks, and pale sunsets,—dreary wind,
> Dim shores, dense rains, and heavy-clouded sea!
>
> ("Lines" 1–8 [Ricks 500])

This is a wonderful, easily ignored, little poem which charts the typically Tennysonian movement I have been outlining, from specific local place to boundless imaginative space and back again. In the first lines, the adult's coldly disparaging vocabulary anticipates, distances itself from, and diminishes that of the child, translating and reducing childhood experience into its own controlled register: "I took delight in this locality." The child's enraptured, myth-entranced vision then bursts into the landscape, enlarging it: "Here stood the infant Ilion of the mind / And here the Grecian ships did seem to be." An estranging Tennysonian alliteration, the "infant Ilion," is buttressed in the line by strong monosyllables. All the years between childhood and adulthood are neatly encompassed in five simple words: "And here again I come." Then occurs, officially, the moment of adult recognition, the *anagnorisis*, where the poem is meant to turn from glory to bleakness: "... and *only* find / The drain-cut levels of the marshy lea" (my italics). There is obviously, in the poem's official reading, a "falling-off" intended here—a falling-off associated with climate, if you like the "Mariana climate" in which Lincolnshire weather presages, indeed enforces, hopelessness. It is surely intended as a Wordsworthian fragment, conveying the loss of vision with adulthood: "Whither is fled the visionary gleam? / Where is it now, the glory and the dream?" (Wordsworth, "Ode: Intimations" 56–7). That, I am sure, is the "official" reading—but the poetry itself undercuts it, picking up speed, rhythm, and intensity again as the speaker actually *looks* intently at what is before him: "Grey sandbanks, and pale sunsets—dreary wind, / Dim shores, dense rains, and heavy-clouded sea!" Ilion this very obviously isn't; but nor is it merely a wet Saturday afternoon in Skegness: Tennyson's genius for clear *looking* fuses the objective and the subjective, irradiating even Lincolnshire. "Pale sunsets," "dim shores" belong with Keats's "magic casements, opening on the foam / Of perilous seas in fairy lands forlorn" (Keats, "Nightingale" 69–70). The plurals make this into a magic landscape, suggesting excess; they are overwhelming, all-absorbing. "Dreary," "dense," "heavy-clouded" produce an accumulated weight which anticipates the heavy mythical landscape of "The Lady of Shalott": "By the margin, willow-veiled / Slide the heavy barges trailed / By slow horses" (19–21). Enchantment steals back through concentration on the actual. The final exclamation mark, paralleling that at the end of "Timbuctoo," is meant to drive home the painful contrast between the exotic and the local, to indicate disillusionment. Its effect on the reader, however, is to produce a new access of wonder at the immediately accessible natural world. This is a prime example of Tennyson's innate ability to see "the romantic side of familiar things," to find the exotic within the local, to reconcile "place" and "space."

The motif of travel and return is a recurrent one throughout Tennyson's poetry, from the errant Ulysses to the tragically exiled Enoch Arden. It wasn't until old age, however, that Tennyson made clear, in another little-read but key poem, the way his imagination needed to move constantly between home and abroad, between bounded garden and limitless wilderness. In 1888 he wrote a short poem, "To Ulysses," to William Gifford Palgrave, the missionary brother of his friend F. T. Palgrave. W. G. Palgrave had recently published a book of his travels that he had called *Ulysses*, avowedly as much in recognition of Tennyson's hero as of Homer's. He died in Montevideo, before he could read Tennyson's poetic tribute, and Tennyson read the poem instead to his brother Francis, in November 1888. This is not a dramatic monologue like the brilliant 1833 "Ulysses": it is a conversation poem, written in the intimate *In Memoriam* stanza form. In this late poem, Tennyson makes explicit the working of his topographical imagination:

> Ulysses, much-experienced man,
>   Whose eyes have known this globe of ours,
> Her tribes of men, and trees, and flowers,
>   From Corrientes to Japan,
>
> To you that bask below the Line,
>   I soaking here in winter wet—
> The century's three strong eights have met
>   To drag me down to seventy-nine
>
> In summer, if I reach my day—
>   To you, yet young, who breathe the balm
> Of summer-winters by the palm
>   And orange grove of Paraguay,
>
> I tolerant of the colder time,
>   Who love the winter woods, to trace
> On paler heavens the branching grace
>   Of leafless elm, or naked lime,
>
> And see my cedar green, and there
>   My giant ilex keeping leaf
> When frost is keen and days are brief—
>   Or marvel how in English air
>
> My yucca, which no winter quells,
>   Although the months have scarce begun,

> Has pushed toward our faintest sun
>   A spike of half-accomplished bells—
>
> Or watch the waving line which ere
>   The warrior of Caprera set,
> A name that earth will not forget
>   Till earth has rolled her latest year—
>
> I, once half-crazed for larger light
>   On broader zones beyond the foam,
> But chaining fancy now at home
>   Among the quarried downs of Wight …
>
> (1–32)

There is a fascinating poetic dialogue going on between traveler and poet here: in his own book, *Ulysses*, Palgrave refers to the Philippines as "isles of Eden, lotus-lands." Tennyson's "The Lotos-Eaters" has given Palgrave a new way of seeing the Philippines; in return, Tennyson quotes Palgrave's "Your Orient Eden-isles" (38) in his own poetry. The "warrior of Caprera" is Garibaldi, who came to Farringford in 1864 and commemorated the visit by planting a Wellingtonia (which was later stripped bare by souvenir hunters). Here at last is the *explicit* integration of local nature poetry and the poetry of distance and exoticism. Tennyson has quite literally "domesticated" the exotic both by writing the poem and by planting a yucca in his English garden.

Tennyson's interest in other cultures, especially in religions and belief systems, deepened as he grew older, but a more general passion for the exotic seems always to have informed his writing, from the earliest days. As he reveals in "To Ulysses," his imagination is essentially dialogic: he needs constantly to move back and forth between the immediate and local and the distant and mysterious, to liberate his imagination, both geographically and emotionally, from the limits of the Lincolnshire "Englishness" where he began, but always recognizing that the latter, the "local habitation," remains essential to his work.

Space and time

As the *In Memoriam* stanzas quoted at the start of this chapter suggest, Tennyson was prone to map his poetry both geographically and chronologically, often simultaneously: "clear from marge to marge shall bloom / The eternal landscape of the past" (*In Memoriam* XLVI 8). Space and time were to him deeply interfused and his "Passion of the Past" was most often conceived in terms of landscape. "The Past" for him is at a geographical as well as a temporal distance. The French critic Yves Bonnefoy conceives a similar idea as "*l'arriere-pays*."[2] The place itself may be "real"—identifiable on a map—but it also contains the past, crucially the early years of the writer. The opening scene of *Great Expectations* would be a prime illustration of the concept. It is observable in Tennyson in several places, in "the high Hall-garden" perhaps, in *Maud*, or in "By night we linger'd on the lawn" (XCV) from *In Memoriam*. It may not be very far from what Bakhtin calls a "chronotope." Crucially, for ecocritical purposes, it focuses the debate between objective or subjective approaches to the natural world by collapsing the distinction between place and time while maintaining that between "geography" and landscape. Jane Avner explains:

> The distinction between geography and landscape is ... a fundamental one: unlike the objective spatial configuration of the map ... a landscape is an aspect of the land perceived or constructed from a specific point of view ... landscape is not an object but a relationship, an encounter, one shaped by the horizon [which] both defines the landscape ... yet at the same time denotes an "elsewhere"—one which moves as we move.
> (95)

Avner neatly suggests here the point at which the subjective and the objective approaches to the natural world merge. She may not be consciously thinking of Tennyson, but in that final phrase she seems unmistakably to be alluding to "Ulysses."

In concluding this preliminary "mapping" of Tennyson's poetry of place and space, "Ulysses" is the obvious *locus*, in every sense, on which to end. The "horizon" suggests the limits of poetic form. Tennyson needs limits, geographical, political, and poetic. He may find the sonnet form confining, but he creates for *In Memoriam* his own form of confinement in the *abba* tetrameter stanza. The swooping movements in his poetry between the "bounded field" and the "brooding star," between place and space, the domestic and the exotic, past and present, the objective and the subjective, fuse and dissolve in that image of the horizon, both a geographical truth *and* the limit of human consciousness, "whose margin fades / Forever and forever as we move" ("Ulysses" 20–1).

Notes

1   All quotations from Tennyson's poetry are taken from Ricks, ed. *The Poems of Tennyson* and are identified by line number in the text except where additional clarifying information is required.
2   Jane Avner discusses this concept in "A Medway Childhood."

Works cited

Arnold, Matthew. *The Poetical Works of Matthew Arnold*. Ed. C. B. Tinker and H. F. Lowry. Oxford: Oxford UP, 1961.

Avner, Jane. "A Medway Childhood: The Dickensian *'arrière pays'*?" *Dickens and the Imagined Child*. Ed. Peter Merchant and Catherine Waters. Farnham, Surrey: Ashgate, 2015. 93–110.

Bakhtin, Mikhail. *The Dialogic Imagination: Four Essays*. Ed. Michael Holquist. Trans. Caryl Emerson and Michael Holquist. Austin: U of Texas P, 1981.

Basso, Keith. *Wisdom Sits in Places: Landscape and Language Among the Western Apache*. Albuquerque: U of New Mexico P, 1996.

Bate, Jonathan. *Romantic Ecology: Wordsworth and the Environmental Tradition*. London: Routledge, 1991.

Buell, Lawrence. *The Environmental Imagination: Thoreau, Nature Writing, and the Formation of American Culture*. Cambridge: Harvard UP, 1995.

Christ, Carol and John O. Jordan. *Victorian Literature and the Victorian Visual Imagination*. Berkeley: U of California P, 1995.

Clark, Timothy. *The Cambridge Introduction to Literature and the Environment*. Cambridge: Cambridge UP, 2011.

Danby, John F. "William Wordsworth: Poetry, Chemistry, Nature." *The Green Studies Reader: From Romanticism to Ecocriticism*. Ed. Laurence Coupe. London: Routledge, 2000. 44–9.

Decker, Christopher. "Tennyson's Limitations." *Tennyson among the Poets*. Ed. Robert Douglas-Fairhurst and Seamus Perry. Oxford: Oxford UP, 2009. 57–65.

Dickens, Charles. *Bleak House*. London: Penguin, 1971.

Glotfelty, Cheryll. *The Ecocriticism Reader: Landmarks in Literature*. Athens: U of Georgia P, 1996.

Huxley, T. H. *Life and Letters of Thomas Henry Huxley*. 2 vols. Ed. Leonard Huxley. London: Macmillan, 1900.

Jump, John D., ed. *Tennyson: The Critical Heritage*. London: Routledge & Kegan Paul, 1967.

Keats, John. *The Poems of Keats*. Ed. Miriam Allott. London: Longman, 1970.

Martin, R. B. *Tennyson: The Unquiet Heart*. Oxford: Clarendon P, 1980.

Mazzeno, Laurence W. *Alfred Tennyson: The Critical Legacy*. Rochester, NY: Camden House, 2004.

McLuhan, H. Marshall. "Tennyson and Picturesque Poetry." *Essays in Criticism* 1.3 (1951): 262–82. Rpt. in *Critical Essays on the Poetry of Tennyson*. Ed. John Killham. London: Routledge and Kegan Paul, 1960. 67–85.

Reynolds, Matthew. *The Realms of Verse: English Poetry in a Time of Nation-Building*. Oxford: Oxford UP, 2001.

Ricks, Christopher, ed. *The Poems of Tennyson*. London: Longman, 1969.

Scott, Heidi C. M. *Chaos and Cosmos: Literary Roots of Modern Ecology in the British Nineteenth Century*. University Park: Pennsylvania State UP, 2014.

Sinfield, Alan. *Alfred Tennyson*. Rereading Literature. Oxford: Basil Blackwell, 1986.

Sturman, Christopher and Valerie Purton. *Poems by Two Brothers: The Lives, Work and Influence of George Clayton Tennyson and Charles Tennyson d'Eyncourt*. Stamford, Lincs: Paul Watkins, 1993.

Tennyson, Hallam. *Alfred Lord Tennyson: A Memoir by his Son*. Two vols. London: Macmillan, 1899.

Tuan, Yi-Fu. *Space and Place: The Perspective of Experience*. Minneapolis: U of Minnesota P, 1977.

Wordsworth, William. *Wordsworth: Poetical Works*. Ed. Ernest DeSelincourt. Oxford: Oxford UP, 1990.

3 Celebration and longing
Robert Browning and the nonhuman world

Ashton Nichols

Robert Browning—although not yet the subject of a great deal of scholarship that could be described as "ecocritical"—was the Victorian poet who, as much as any other, saw the plant and the animal kingdoms as central aspects of his work as a lyricist. From his earliest Shelleyan verses in the 1820s, up through the masterpiece lyrics, dramatic monologues, and other poems of the 1830s–1860s, all the way to the now-obscure narrative, dramatic, and translated verses of the 1870s and 1880s, Browning saw the natural world as a crucial index for understanding our human world and the nonhuman reality that surrounds us. For him, "nature" was not so much a category distinguished by its "otherness" as it was a part of a continuum of living creatures and even nonliving entities. These natural elements help us to understand and appreciate our place, as *Homo sapiens*, the most fully self-aware beings on earth.

As early as 1902, Stopford Brooke noted that there was "no poet whose love of animals is greater than Browning's, and none who has so frequently, so carefully, so vividly described them … from the river-horse to the lizard, from the eagle to the wren, from the loud singing bee to the filmy insect in the sunshine" (83). In addition, Browning is masterful in his ability to fuse the activities of human life and contents of the human mind with the active, organic universe around us. While some earlier critics have focused on Browning's use of nature in relation to his view of the divine, this essay will focus, not on the theological implications of Browning's engagement with the environment (as we might now say) but on his understanding of Charles Darwin. This awareness of Darwin is then combined with a Hardyesque—or at least a Tennysonian—appreciation of the beauty and the shortness of life, as well as the value of living *in* the moment, especially in terms of our connectedness to the natural world around us.

In addition, this essay will emphasize an evolutionary organicism that could sometimes produce a less positive view of the nonhuman world in Browning's generally optimistic writing. In terms of the rapidly expanding field of ecocritical (animal and plant) studies, Browning is an important transitional figure between the Romantic natural history of the early nineteenth century and the modernist naturalism of the twentieth century.

Two of his greatest "nature" poems, "Childe Roland to the Dark Tower Came" and "Caliban upon Setebos" offer first, a view of a materialistic natural world that would sit comfortably in T. S. Eliot's *The Waste Land* or Samuel Beckett's *Waiting for Godot*, and second, a Darwinian critique of the continuum of all life—from the lowliest self-replicating species to fully self-conscious human beings. In this regard, Browning is a forward-looking and eco-aware Victorian whose sensitivity to the natural world takes full advantage of an almost existential understanding that nature is not here for us; humans are only one part of a continuum of life that has not yet finished its process of evolution. This essay will reveal Browning's characteristic celebrations of the natural world, along with his surprisingly negative depiction of the natural world in at least one important poem, and his appreciation, later in his career, of the paradoxically complex multiplicity of Darwin's revelations about our nonhuman environment.

A number of Browning's most memorable poems contain important references to plants and animals, even if those references are not always the most memorable, or most often quoted, lines in these lyrics. Browning has a frequently commented upon ability to celebrate not just the beautiful and positive aspects of the natural world, but also the ugly, the grotesque, and the unseemly. He has a capacity, rare among poets in English, to embrace even those dimensions of human—and nonhuman—experience that have typically been rejected, despised, or completely ignored by most writers and commentators. Likewise, Browning has a level of sensitivity toward all living things that is found only in the most naturalistically inclined of poets: William Shakespeare, William Wordsworth, Percy Shelley, John Keats, Seamus Heaney and, in America, Walt Whitman, Emily Dickinson, Robert Frost, and Mary Oliver. Throughout his career, the natural world—in its material form—remains an important presence in Browning's poetry; it can never be all, or only, about the spiritual realm for this poet. He remains grounded in the physical, even in his most abstract and theoretical speculations. Again and again, Browning's poetry remains anchored, as he says in his "Parleying" with the Renaissance art theorist Gerard de Lairesse, in "Earth's common surface, rough, smooth, dry or damp" (V. 3). In this regard, the artist finds "abundant worth / In trivial commonplace" (ll. 32–3), and for Browning that commonplace always depends on the nonhuman world of natural beauty that surrounds us.

For Browning, nature is distinct from our human life but it has important links and lessons for humans. Indeed, he is one of the first major poets to fully recognize and incorporate the importance of Darwin's thinking into his verse. Alfred, Lord Tennyson also did so, of course, but most significantly before Darwin had even published, when the Poet Laureate's famous stanzas in *In Memoriam* (1850) anticipated—indeed, they almost quoted from—details of the biological genius nine years before the publication of his *On the Origin of Species* (1859). This anticipatory inclusion by Tennyson only confirmed Darwin's often repeated observation that he was not so much an original thinker as one who brought together the ideas of many early thinkers; he wove the currents of early nineteenth-century thought into the fabric of a unified theory. Tennyson made it his business to keep up on the work of Charles Lyell, Georges Cuvier, Alexander von Humboldt, and other earth and life scientists, and the result is an elegy for Arthur Henry Hallam that knew about fossils, about earlier species anticipating later species, and even about evolution as a system that favors the fit, not necessarily the strong. A tiny microbe or bloodstream weakness could bring low—could even kill—a living being like Hallam, a person who had many of the highest "powers" available to humans, especially intellectual powers. Yet Hallam was a member of the species *Homo sapiens* who was likewise subject to a tiny weakness in a thin blood vessel in his brain that resulted in an exploding aneurysm that killed him at the tender age of 22.

In addition, Tennyson and Browning both realized in their poetry the truth of Charles Kingsley's comment, in his own review of *In Memoriam* (1850), that the "dignity of Nature in all her manifestations" could be described as the "root idea of the whole poetry of this generation" (246). Indeed, many critics have noted the close link between literary descriptions of nature and the revolutions in both science and religious thinking—especially religious doubts—that were appearing in England during the reign of Queen Victoria (1837–1901). These revolutions brought science into ascendency in the minds of many thinkers, not only scientists, but also a wide range of social critics, politicians, and even artists. The concurrent doubts about orthodox religion became another defining characteristic of the era; as Bernard Richards says, these combined revolutions in thought in England "inevitably had a direct effect on attitudes to nature" (184). Henry James, as late as 1875, could link nature to science and then to the science of the mind, in ways I will explore later in this essay: "If the history of that movement toward a passionate scrutiny of Nature, which has culminated in our day, with Tennyson and Browning, could be scientifically written, we imagine it would be found to throw a great deal of light on the processes of the human mind" (41–2). This comment is especially significant because of the way it acknowledges the emerging power of the science that would come to be called "psychology."

Paul Johnson reminds us that Browning grew up in a Byronesque household menagerie full of pets, some tame, others more wild: "two dogs, a cat, a pony, monkeys, owls, hedgehogs, snakes, a magpie and at one time an eagle" (728). In addition, the young man "delighted" in his mother's "love of nature and wild life" (Ryals 3). As early as *Pauline* (1832), the poet's voice can identify completely—much as Keats can—with natural phenomena: "I can live all the life of plants ... I can mount with the bird / Leaping airily the pyramid of leaves ... Or like a fish breathe-in the morning air" (Kenmare 144). In *Paracelsus* (1835), Browning presents the natural world as a unified entity, an organic whole linked in spiritual, but just as completely, in material terms. Here, the Victorian poet (like a number of his

Romantic predecessors) anticipates the idea of "ecology" (the regional unity of groups of natural entities) three decades before its 1866 coinage by Ernst Haeckel, a German life-scientist.

Paracelsus presents its readers with a sixteenth-century alchemist, the dramatic monologue's speaker, who describes an earthly world organized along a hierarchical continuum of life. But this is also a Renaissance scientist who finds that same world filled with elaborate naturalistic beauty:

> Where the glossy kingfisher
> Flutters when noon-heats are near ...
> Where the shrew-mouse with pale throat
> Burrows, and the speckled stoat
>
> (V. 434–5, 437–8)

and "Where the quick sandpipers flit / In and out the marl [silt] and grit" (439–40). His vision culminates, appropriately for Browning, with the addition of mankind:

>   beetles run
> Along the furrows, ants make their ado;
> Above, birds fly in merry flocks, the lark
> Soars up and up, shivering for very joy;
> Afar the ocean sleeps; while fishing-gulls
> Flit where the strand is purple with its tribe
> Of nested limpets; savage creatures seek
> Their loves in wood and plain ...
> The inferior natures, and all lead up higher
> All shape out dimly the superior race,
> The heir of hopes too fair to turn out false,
> And man appears at last.
>
> (V. 673–80, 708–11)

In a letter written decades later, Browning noted the obvious connection between Paracelsus and Darwin: "all that seems *proved* in Darwin's scheme was a conception familiar to me from the beginning: see in *Paracelsus* the progressive development from senseless matter to organized, until man's appearance" (Hood, *Letters* 199). So Browning, like Tennyson, anticipated Darwin's thinking long before *Origin of Species* appeared, in Tennyson's case ten years earlier; in Browning's case, fifteen years earlier. In this regard, Darwin simply provided the name and the details of the mechanism—that is, "natural selection"—by which "lower" forms of life have evolved into "higher." Darwin makes it clear that any notion of hierarchy in evolution is imposed solely by human beings. Hierarchy is not a function of evolution itself, since any species, at any point, is just as likely to become extinct as any other. Just because one type of animal appears at a later stage in the process than another, it does not follow that the later arrival is superior to the earlier. All new species are just as subject to the forces of change that bring about extinction and the emergence of more new species as any other plant or animal.

Human understanding of nature and "the natural" changes dramatically during the nineteenth century, primarily because Darwin's research and understanding so completely transformed human beings' awareness of the nonhuman world around them and their place in it. Darwin not only laid out, he also established and supported, overwhelming evidence for a world in which all living things are connected, not only by their ancestry but also by some element of similarity that continues in and links the life—indeed, even the bodies of—all living creatures. Without any understanding of genetics, chromosomes, or inheritance whatsoever (that awareness would await the work of Gregor Mendel, published in 1866, but not appreciated until the early twentieth century), Darwin fully sees that an element in all living things passes down some traits, shuts off other traits, and modifies still others; the result is successful, or unsuccessful, adaptation. Browning's own understanding of Darwin is basic, but he appreciates the importance of heredity—traits inherited from one generation to the next or changed by individuals and generations over time—and even of primitive characteristics that more advanced creatures still to share with their ancestors. As Richards notes, "The relationship between Browning and evolutionary thought is more interesting than Tennyson's" (200). Thus, the creature Caliban, as we shall see, may be a primitive "monster," but he has ability to aspire upward, to seek an understanding of our shared world, and even to describe his own gods ("Setebos" and "The Quiet") beyond the realm of human (or certainly of "his" own) knowing. This, in turn, extends to an understanding of Caliban's own place in the natural world, a place that, while not fully human, is nevertheless self-conscious, analytical, and well able to understand numerous aspects of the life processes, and the living things, all around him.

One of Browning's most characteristic celebrations of the natural world appears in the 1845 lyric "Home Thoughts, from Abroad," the poem of a person who has lived long overseas and yet still misses his home country every spring:

I
O, to be in England
Now that April's there,
And whoever wakes in England
Sees, some morning, unaware,
That the lowest boughs and the brushwood sheaf
Round the elm-tree bole are in tiny leaf,
While the chaffinch sings on the orchard bough
In England—now!

II

And after April, when May follows,
And the whitethroat builds, and all the swallows!
Hark, where my blossomed pear-tree in the hedge
Leans to the field and scatters on the clover
Blossoms and dewdrops—at the bent spray's edge—
That's the wise thrush; he sings each song twice over—
Lest you should think he never could recapture
The first fine careless rapture!
And though the fields look rough with hoary dew,
All will be gay when noontide wakes anew
The buttercups, the little children's dower
—Far brighter than this gaudy melon-flower!

I quote this poem in its entirety because it so well reveals the way Browning's descriptions of nature indicate links between the precise parts, as well as the individual beauties, themselves. As Dallas Kenmare says: "the poet writes with a painter's awareness of colour, form, and grouping" (149). In this often-quoted lyric, all of the details fit together seamlessly, and the natural world reveals its ability to elevate the observer, even without any comment by him to that effect. The speaker lets nature speak for itself; he needs to make no comment beyond his simple, but beautifully careful, descriptions. Such objective observation gives us more than enough, as readers, to appreciate the world he describes in all of its richness and unity.

Even a poem like "Among the Rocks" has the ability to draw the reader into its obvious and accurate geological speculations:

> Oh, good gigantic smile o' the brown old earth,
>   This autumn morning! How he sets his bones
>   To bask i' the sun, and thrusts out knees and feet
>   For the ripple to run over in its mirth;
>   Listening the while, where on the heap of stones
>   The white breast of the sea-lark twitters sweet.
>
>   (1–6)

As Browning says in his play *A Soul's Tragedy*, "I trust in Nature for the stable laws / Of beauty and utility. Spring shall plant / And Autumn garner to the end of time" (*Luria*, Act I), by which he means that nature provides "laws," as either Isaac Newton or John Locke might have said, principles that humans choose to follow, or are often forced to follow. Human beings frequently have no choice in this matter, since they find themselves in a world of absolute, regular, and irreversible laws of matter and energy that they did not create. These are laws, like gravity and inertia, one of which pulls all things in the universe toward one another, into order, the other of which pulls all things apart, forever, into chaos. So spring creates life—it "plants"—while autumn destroys life—it "garners"; we might say more completely honestly, it kills.

So which principle dominates? The problem is, and has always been, that neither principle does dominate: out of life comes inevitable death, and out of every death always comes new life. We might say that these natural laws are the ones that organize existence into a never-ending cycle, a cycle in which each generation gives way systematically to the next, in which one season never lasts longer than its allotted time—it never "breaks" the law—but always turns into the next season, and the next, and the next, from now until infinity. Browning's emphasis almost always begins in the material aspect of nature—the flowers, the trees, the animals, the human body—but it is also always about the way this material element, one that is caught in time, and space, and matter, is linked to or leads toward a nonmaterial realm: an immaterial element, a supernatural world of spirits, and souls, and perhaps— who knows?—even God. From a physicist's perspective, this may turn out eventually to be the world of energy, the world of strange forces like light and heat—and of course gravity itself—that cannot be measured in terms of atoms or protons or neutrons, although we have now been given a world of quarks, and neutrinos, and even muons to describe the energetic entities. Browning's religion is—in this way—almost as cryptic as our current theoretical physics, always hard to pin down and always hard to understand fully, but it always begins in our own physical, and natural, world. At the same time, Browning's theology points toward, or gestures to, or may eventually lead us into another long-lasting, perhaps even an eternal, world. Brooke admits that Browning can at times represent "Nature as suddenly at one with us" (63), but he sees these moments as few and far between. He says that the usual way that nature connects to us in this poet is the way Ariel connects to Prospero and Miranda; Ariel was interested in their loves and welfare, but it was an "elemental," and "a wild, unhuman, unmoral, unspiritual interest" (63). Most of these moments of powerful and complete linkage between nature and humanity, as we might expect, occur for Browning during events connected to a loving relationship between two humans.

In "Two in the Campagna," for example, the speaker, who is also a lover, senses a "thought" that has "tantalized" him "many times" (6–7). But such a thought is always evanescent and fleeting. "Two in the Campagna" represents the desire for a form of communion, one of various forms of communion—and union—often sought in Browning's poems, but much less rarely achieved. Such communion can occur between individuals, as it does here between lovers walking in the rural outskirts of Rome. The "campagna" was a once rich and fertile farmland—during Roman times—that has deteriorated over the centuries into boggy swamps filled with malaria-infested mosquitoes and other disease-causing creatures. A vast region of not quite 1,000 square miles, it became one of the most often painted landscapes from the mid-eighteenth throughout the nineteenth centuries, when European artists scoured the countryside, seeking inspiring naturalistic landscapes. Here and now, in this nonhumanly beautiful Roman countryside, Browning's idea of this "thought" dashes ahead of the two lovers together; the "thought" is always expressed in terms of naturalistic metaphors "Like turns of thread the spiders throw / Mocking across our path" (8–9). In the next moment the speaker turns to his lover and makes an apparently simple request of her:

> *III*
> Help me to hold it! First it left
>   The yellowing fennel, run to seed
> There, branching from the brickwork's cleft,
>   Some old tomb's ruin: yonder weed
> Took up the floating weft,
>
> *IV*
> Where one small orange cup amassed
>   Five beetles,—blind and green they grope
> Among the honey-meal: and last,
>   Everywhere on the grassy slope
> I traced it. Hold it fast!

The thought dashes on ahead of them; it is a thought that is deeply connected to each of these precise organic details drawn from the natural world. The reason the speaker loves this place so much, in addition to loving his human lover, is that this Campagna is a place where nature rules and yet also a place where humans are welcome to perceive nature's power, almost to share in it:

> *VI*
> Such life here, through such lengths of hours,
>   Such miracles performed in play,
> Such primal naked forms of flowers,
>   Such letting nature have her way
> While heaven looks from its towers!

For humans, however, there is always a problem, the problem of unifying sensation and soul, body and spirit, even in as natural a setting as this one. Sometimes a human can almost get there, can almost arrive at fulfillment, can almost catch the "minute"; but then the minute is lost—then, it "goes":

> *X*
> No. I yearn upward, touch you close,
>   Then stand away. I kiss your cheek,
> Catch your soul's warmth,—I pluck the rose
>   And love it more than tongue can speak—
> Then the good minute goes.

This kiss and this rose both stand for this fleeting thought; they are not, however, *the same* as the thought. The fleeting mental sensation described by Browning comes and goes in an epiphanic natural moment of instant perception, a moment like the ones Browning is often drawn to and seeks to describe. But, here and now, even words fail this masterful poet, since words themselves are material, not spiritual. They must be spoken through blood-filled lungs and vocal cords or, they must be created with pens (or now computer keys) and ink. The poet-lover was just about to catch this good moment, just about to hold it (potentially forever?) but then it escaped again, leaving him with a lesson that is as painfully full of loss as it is stunningly beautiful:

XII
Just when I seemed about to learn!
    Where is the thread now? Off again!
The old trick! Only I discern—
    Infinite passion, and the pain
Of finite hearts that yearn.

So the speaker in this poem succeeds by failing. He loses the thread—one exactly like a spider's silk—as it races "off again," but he realizes at this moment that even a finite natural heart can embody infinite passion. In this poem, the natural world becomes the vehicle whereby humans realize that the world around them is finally a world beyond their knowing; there is more to the nonhuman world around us than we have the capacity to understand completely or to appreciate fully. Human beings, however, continue to seek such an understanding. As Morse Peckham notes of the Romantics and of the Romantic element in Browning, there was something redemptive in the nonhuman world, but it was only available as part of an "'aesthetic' response to nature, a tension-reducing feeling state elicited by nature and ultimately inexplicable"; this was the exact state that Wordsworth had, in his autobiographical *Prelude*, traced back to the "preconscious awareness of the infant in relation to its mother" (Armstrong 65).

Browning's sense of the beauties of nature, and his typically positive evocation of the nonhuman world, takes a surprising turn in "'Childe Roland to the Dark Tower Came,'" this poet's triumph of the naturalistic grotesque, which I have elsewhere called the "positive" grotesque (Nichols, "'Will Sprawl'" 157). This narrative poem presents readers with a cryptic, aphoristic fairy tale, drawn from the collective memory of cultural myth. The poem offers a vision of the modern self in a completely corrupted version of nature, presented among a set of Western symbols now turned sour within a legendary Victorian landscape of death and destruction. Roland's story is a tale full of terror mingled with existential triumph. All that this hero does is to arrive at a "place" that he has sought and struggled toward throughout the poem. He comes to his appointed location and yet, beyond that, nothing else happens. Childe Roland *came* to the dark tower, that is all he did; and yet, in doing so, he asserted his ability to act in a natural world that seems to offer little, if any, reason for action of any kind. There is not much hope here at all. Indeed, the landscape of this poem is directly influenced by Darwin (and perhaps Dante), at least insofar as Browning acknowledges that the "negative" elements of the natural world play just as central a role in this story as any positive dimension of nature. This landscape also anticipates T. S. Eliot's naturalistic vision of modernity; it is *the* "waste land" presented from within a Victorian sensibility: "I think I never saw / Such starved ignoble nature; nothing throve" (55–6), and thus nothing really lives here:

> As for the grass, it grew as scant as hair
>   In leprosy; thin dry blades pricked the mud
>   Which underneath looked kneaded up with blood.
> One stiff blind horse, his every bone a-stare,
> Stood stupefied, however he came there:
>   Thrust out past service from the devil's stud!
>
> Alive? he might be dead for aught I know ...
>
> (73–9)

This is not just a dying, deathly place; it is a self-killing place: "scrubby alders kneeled down over it [the "sudden little river"]; / Drenched willows flung them headlong in a fit / Of mute despair, a suicidal throng" (116–18), and yet Roland does not fully die; in fact, he joins his peers, all of the previous legendary heroes of song and story:

> ... all the lost adventurers my peers,—
> How such a one was strong, and such was bold,
> And such was fortunate, yet each of old
> Lost, lost! ...
>
> There they stood, ranged along the hill-sides ...
>
> (195–9)

Once gathered together here, in this "starved ignoble" place, Roland is the only one of this crowd of legendary Arthurian heroes who has apparently acted, at least recently.

Although this may be "the last of" Roland, with his "living frame" arriving here only "For one more picture!"; whatever the finality of this moment, the stagnant dead and dying landscape all around our hero still gives way to one more "dauntless" action. He sets the noble-sounding "slug-horn" (like Triton's "wreathed horn," I have argued) to his lips and blows the eponymous title of the very same poem we have just finished reading: "*Childe Roland to the Dark Tower Came"* (placed in quotation marks and italics by Browning to assure that we understand its role as a title [of the poem] *and* also as a description of a narrative [the actual story of the poem].) This is a remarkably postmodern recognition of the power of this lyric's title at once to *be* the story and also the power of the story to *be* its own title. Childe Roland *came* to this mysterious dark tower, nothing else; that is all that happens in this tale, and yet Browning manages to give us a modern version of the nonhuman natural world which, no matter how far drained of the Keatsian energy and Wordsworthian vitality of earlier Romantic nature, nevertheless provides us with a world in which Roland can still act, even if his action is just that of a human being moving through this nonhuman, yet still natural, world— recording its numerous discontents all the while.

Perhaps Browning's most significant poem from an ecocritical perspective is "Caliban upon Setebos," a powerful final example of what I have elsewhere called Browning's "positive grotesque," a poem in which the natural world becomes the index to Caliban's own unique genius and life. Caliban is the "missing link" sought by so many Victorians who had read *On the Origin of Species* and who understood that, though we were not descended from gorillas and apes, we shared a common ancestor with all of the great apes and primates that were part of our lineage. Although a grotesque monster, Caliban is given among the most beautifully written lines in Shakespeare's *Tempest*, one of the bard's most linguistically beautiful plays, perhaps his last drama ever written and performed (1611). Caliban embodies the way such an emerging evolutionary consciousness would be much more likely to see his creator in terms of the natural world around him; the subtitle is "Natural Theology in the Island." Browning's critique of Victorian natural theology (defining "God" through the natural world he supposedly created) delineates the way this self-aware creature wants to see his world as a reflection of the force that generated that world. Caliban's god Setebos is just such a reflection of the richly populated earth he created, while "The Quiet," on an even higher divine level, is a much more mysterious force, if "it" is an agent at all. This "Quiet" is much more like destiny or fate or "being" itself in the process of becoming. In Caliban, Browning finds the character he needs to paint one of his most complete and thoroughgoing visions of the numerous beauties (and the range of beauties) in the natural world:

> ['Will sprawl, now that the heat of day is best,
> Flat on his belly in the pit's much mire,
> With elbows wide, fists clenched to prop his chin.
> And, while he kicks both feet in the cool slush,
> And feels about his spine small eft-things course,
> Run in and out each arm, and make him laugh:
> And while above his head a pompion-plant,
> Coating the cave-top as a brow its eye,
> Creeps down to touch and tickle hair and beard,

> And now a flower drops with a bee inside,
> And now a fruit to snap at, catch and crunch,—
> He looks out o'er yon sea which sunbeams cross
> And recross till they weave a spider-web
> (Meshes of fire, some great fish breaks at times)
> And talks to his own self, howe'er he please,
> Touching that other, whom his dam called God ...]
>
> (1–16)

Here is a primitive-sounding creature who loves the "pit's much mire" as much as a human might love the cooling breeze on a sunny day. He feels the slithery salamanders running around his arms, and he joys in a fruit that drops right in front of his face, fresh for the eating: "snap at, catch, and crunch." Most of all, however, he relishes the opportunity he has to talk "to his own self," recognizing not only his self-awareness but also his ability to remember a conversation with his mother (now dead, we learn from Shakespeare) in which the subject must have turned to the topic of "that other," an identity his mother referred to only as "God":

> 'Thinketh, He made thereat the sun, this isle,
> Trees and the fowls here, beast and creeping thing.
> Yon otter, sleek-wet, black, lithe as a leech;
> Yon auk, one fire-eye in a ball of foam,
> That floats and feeds; a certain badger brown
> He hath watched hunt with that slant white-wedge eye
> By moonlight; and the pie with the long tongue
> That pricks deep into oakwarts for a worm,
> And says a plain word when she finds her prize,
> But will not eat the ants; the ants themselves
> That build a wall of seeds and settled stalks
> About their hole—He made all these and more ...
>
> (44–55)

Caliban is clearly a victim of Prospero's slave-holding servitude—as is Ariel—and yet this fishy reptilian, Darwinian-inspired creature is also a thoroughgoing lover of life (recall Fra Lippo Lippi?), a monster whose sense of his world is intimately tied to all of the living things around him, animal and vegetable, and even the inanimate natural objects with which he interacts on a regular basis:

> Look now, I melt a gourd-fruit into mash,
> Add honeycomb and pods, I have perceived,
> Which bite like finches when they bill and kiss,—
> Then, when froth rises bladdery, drink up all,
> Quick, quick, till maggots scamper through my brain;

> Last, throw me on my back i' the seeded thyme,
> And wanton, wishing I were born a bird.
> Put case, unable to be what I wish,
> I yet could make a live bird out of clay:
> Would not I take clay, pinch my Caliban
> Able to fly?—for, there, see, he hath wings,
> And great comb like the hoopoe's to admire,
> And there, a sting to do his foes offence …
>
> (68–80)

The sky darkens, and this "creature," the one that many modern readings say may not be a monster at all—"half reptile and half fish"—but rather may be seen as an indigenous Carib or Arrowack native Indian of this island place (near an island Shakespeare calls "the Bermoothes") finds himself terrified at the force outside of him, whatever it is, wherever it originates:

> [What, what? A curtain o'er the world at once!
> Crickets stop hissing: not a bird—or, yes,
> There scuds His raven that has told Him all!
> It was fool's play, this prattling! Ha! The wind
> Shoulders the pillared dust, death's house o' the move,
> And fast invading fires begin! White blaze—
> A tree's head snaps—and there, there, there, there, there,
> His thunder follows! Fool to gibe at Him!
> Lo! 'Lieth flat and loveth Setebos!
> 'Maketh his teeth meet through his upper lip,
> Will let those quails fly, will not eat this month
> One little mess of whelks, so he may 'scape!]
>
> (284–95)

The brackets here are Browning's, signifying that Caliban is thinking silently to himself, not yet speaking out loud, as he will do elsewhere, in halting ways, throughout the poem. Yet he does manage to invoke the complex theological concepts of penance, mortification, and sacrifice when he bites through his upper lip painfully until his teeth meet and then decides not to dine on those luscious-looking quail in front of him. Instead, he will let them escape and limit himself to eating a "little mess" of small shellfish as his main meal, perhaps for a long time.

 The Victorian poets, especially Tennyson and Browning, are clearly the first major English authors to appreciate the power of Darwin's emerging message about organic life, its origins, history, and even its possible futures. Numerous critics have noted the way Browning's characters go beyond the normal poetic level of observing nature toward a fusion of the human mind and the world around that mind. This fusion of the objective, external world of nature with the internal, subjective mind of the poet is precisely the one that Browning cites in his own powerful "Introduction" to the *Letters of Shelley* (1852), where he says that there is "no reason why these two modes of poetic faculty [the awareness of the inner, the perception of the outer] may not issue ... from the same poet" (Starzyk 35). Likewise, as Bryan E. Bannon has noted, artworks of a certain kind have the power to "provide alternative ways of envisioning the human relationship to nature and thereby present alternative modes of dwelling within it" (415). I want in this essay to emphasize this notion of "dwelling within," that is, the human ability to live within, in some sense fully to inhabit, the nonhuman world. Browning, as we have seen on numerous occasions, shows exactly what it means for a poetic human sensibility to lose its own self—in a version of what Keats calls "negative capability"—into a wider nonhuman world beyond the self. This is, of course, precisely the middle ground that is occupied by Caliban, perhaps to a greater extent than most humans, since he (in his earlier developmental stage) is that much "closer" to the external objects of his own consciousness. This is, after all, the same creature who feels as much at home in the "pit's much mire" as he does anywhere else and who has been described, on numerous occasions, as having received many of the most stylistically beautiful lines of pure lyrical poetry in Shakespeare's own imagining of this remarkable and redemptive drama.

As Park Honan has written, Browning possesses unalterable "sympathy for life," and for virtually all of life (13). Browning's power to express this sympathy is evident in many if his descriptions, for example, in his remarkable and startlingly beautiful description of a small cluster of mushrooms:

> By the rose-flesh mushrooms, undivulged
>   Last evening—nay, in to-day's first dew
> Yon sudden coral nipple bulged,
>   Where a freaked fawn-coloured flaky crew
> Of toadstools peep indulged.
>
> ("By the Fire-Side" 61–5)

There is no way to appreciate the nonhuman world without appreciating every aspect of that world. For Browning, there is no existential difference between rotting hemp and blooming hyacinths, warty toads and sparkling twilight, the mushrooms and the morning-dew. He wants, like his character Fra Lippo Lippi, to celebrate every aspect of the nonhuman world, from lowliest to most elevated, from most mundane to most exalted. In this respect, Browning is also an "anthropologist of experience" as defined and described by Frederick Turner. Browning produces lyrics in which the "intensity of perception is almost hypnotic" (Turner 90); when he describes human psychological activity in relation to the nonhuman world, he often records a "reflexive process in which we are only separated by our consciousness from nature in order to share in nature's own process of self-transcendence" (93).

Browning interrogates the activity of the human mind engaged with the natural world, partly in order to find the sources of that mind's ability to reach outside of itself, to identify with otherness in a way that leads toward a unity of this human self and this external world. Examples of this tendency occur throughout his poetry, especially in a number of the great dramatic monologues, but also in those personal love poems and lyrics that describe the most intense of personal experiences. More than either Tennyson or Matthew Arnold, Browning is able to let his readers share his personal emotions almost in the process of his own experience of them.

Browning's "natural world is not made by our thought, nor does it reflect our passions" (Brooke 59). Browning never conceives, "as Wordsworth conceived, of any pre-established harmony between us and the natural world"; rather, nature in Browning is always and forever "quite distinct from us" (59–60). The problem with this idea, of course, is the number of times that Browning identifies human activity with natural activity, or describes humans in terms of their connections to the nonhuman world: "Nature is alive in Browning, but she is not humanized at all, nor at all at one with us" (Brooke 66). But, as Browning's heroic Caponsacchi says in *The Ring and the Book*, "the true, / The good, the eternal" are to be found only in the "small experiences of every day"; thus, we are meant "To learn not only by a comet's rush / But by a rose's birth" (VI. 2090–5). As I have written elsewhere of this remarkable poem, "The ordinary rose's birth, perceived by a single consciousness, is as powerful as the comet's rush because of its potential to mean something to an individual" (*Poetics of Epiphany* 135). Of these ordinary natural phenomena—roses, comets, flowers, trees—Barbara Melchiori adds, no English poet "has mentioned so many birds by name as has Browning in *The Ring and the Book* ... The naturalist takes over at times from the poet in enriching the texture of the verse with a number of first-hand observations" (Armstrong 179). More modern descriptions of Browning's naturalism want to focus on his ability to appreciate and fully analyze the natural world, not just to observe and record its details in the mode of the natural historian.

To conclude a discussion of the ecocritical Browning is a complicated task, in part because the full range of Browning's poems often seems to favor spiritual possibilities over material realities. Yet, at the same time, in his poems the pure physical reality of the material nonhuman can overwhelm the spiritual realm. His spiritual world is admittedly a nonphysical place that remains abstract, detached, and necessarily distanced from the lived aspects of our human existence. Browning seems as though he often wants to elevate the spiritual over the material, but his own experience of the physical world does not always allow him to do so. Again and again, we find him drawn back to the quotidian, the sublunary, the mundane: that is, to the natural world. And time and time again, we see him celebrating the ordinary at the expense of the extraordinary, elevating the normal over the extra-normal or supernatural. We can conclude by saying that Browning anticipates a post-Darwinian, existentialist, or even a poststructuralist worldview, and yet at the same time he perfectly embodies Victorian uncertainties about Christianity, about organized religion in more general terms, and about the relationships between the human world and the world outside of humanity. Our world, however, is fully natural when it embodies bright green plants, warm lively animals, and clear water running over cool stones. Indeed, this world is especially natural when it reveals the complex, often beautiful, relationships between human beings and the wide evolving cosmos around us.

Works cited

Armstrong, Isobel. *Robert Browning. Writers and their Background*. Athens: Ohio UP, 1975.
Bannon, Bryan E. "Re-Envisioning Nature: The Role of Aesthetics in Environmental Ethics." *Environmental Ethics* 33 (2011): 415–36
Brooke, Stopford A. *The Poetry of Robert Browning*. New York: Crowell, 1902.
Browning, Robert. *Luria, and A Soul's Tragedy*. London: Moxon, 1846.
——. *Paracelsus*. Ed. G. Lowes Dickinson. London: Dent, 1898.
——. *Parleyings with Certain People of Importance in Their Day*. Boston & New York: Houghton Mifflin, 1887.
——. *Robert Browning's Poetry*. Ed. James F. Loucks and Andrew M. Stauffer. Norton Critical Edition, 2nd ed. New York: Norton, 2007.
Honan, Park. *Browning's Characters: a Study in Poetic Technique*. New Haven: Yale UP, 1961.
Hood, Thurman L. *Letters of Robert Browning*. Port Washington, NY: Kennikat Press, 1973.
James, Henry. "Review of Stopford Brooke's *Theology in the English Poets*." *The Nation* 21 January 1875: 41–2.
Johnson, Paul. *The Birth of the Modern: World Society 1815–1830*. New York: Harper Collins, 1991.
Kenmare, Dallas. *Browning and Modern Thought*. New York: Haskell House, 1970.
Kingsley, Charles. Unsigned rev. of *In Memoriam*, by Alfred Tennyson. *Fraser's Magazine* 42 (1850): 245–6.
Nichols, Ashton. *Beyond Romantic Ecocriticism: Toward Urbanatural Roosting*. New York: Palgrave Macmillan, 2011.
——. *The Poetics of Epiphany: Nineteenth-Century Origins of the Modern Literary Moment*. Tuscaloosa: U of Alabama P, 1987.
——. "'Will Sprawl' in the 'Ugly Actual': The Positive Grotesque in Browning." *Victorian Poetry* 21.2 (1983): 157–70.
Richards, Bernard. *English Poetry of the Victorian Period: 1830–1890*. London: Longman, 1988.
Ryals, Clyde de L. *The Life of Robert Browning*. Oxford: Blackwell, 1993.
Starzyk, Lawrence J. *The Dialogue of the Mind with Itself: Early Victorian Poetry and Poetics*. Calgary: U of Calgary P, 1992.
Turner, Frederick. "Reflexivity as Evolution in Thoreau's *Walden*." *The Anthropology of Experience*. Ed. Victor W. Turner and Edward M. Bruner. Urbana: U of Illinois P, 1986. 73–94.

4 "Truth to nature"

The pleasures and dangers of the environment in Christina Rossetti's poetry

Serena Trowbridge

> My first vivid experience of death (if so I may term it) occurred in early childhood in the grounds of a cottage … I lighted upon a dead mouse. The dead mouse moved my sympathy: I took him up, buried him comfortably in a mossy bed, and bore the spot in mind.
>
> It may have been a day or two afterwards that I returned, removed the moss coverlet, and looked … a black insect emerged. I fled in horror, and for long years ensuing I never mentioned this ghastly adventure to anyone.
>
> Now looking back at the incident I see that neither impulse was unreasonable, although the sympathy and the horror alike were childish.
>
> Only now contemplating death from a wider and wiser view-point, I would fain reverse the order of those feelings: dwelling less and less on the mere physical disgust, while more and more on the rest and safety; on the perfect peace of death, please God.
>
> Christina Rossetti, Time Flies 45

In her "Reading Diary" *Time Flies* (1885), Christina Rossetti describes the rotting corpse of a mouse, to which she links her early understanding of the nature of death and decay. Yet in the same book, she urges the reader to consider the beauty, and the moral message, of the forget-me-not flower. The natural environment thus provides a range of Christian parables for the Tractarian reader. One might argue that "Rossetti's flowers and plants are all a testimony to God's love" (Roe 23). It is difficult for a modern reader to overestimate the extent to which Christina Rossetti's poetry is shaped by her faith. As a Tractarian, Rossetti espoused a brand of High Anglicanism that juxtaposed a strong belief in the transformative powers of literature with respect for the world in which we live.[1] The Tractarian movement, itself a literary approach to faith, emphasized the importance of the natural world as a manifestation of God's work, and many of the texts produced by its adherents (and indeed works favored by them, notably the Romantic poets including Wordsworth)[2] offer something close to pantheism in their ability to "see" God's hand in the world around them, though their approach is distinct from this: the world is a reflection of God rather than a manifestation.

Isaac Williams, in *Tracts for the Times*, wrote of the typological symbolism which veils God's messages to his creation, seen in the world around us, a trope which Tractarian writers explore in their work. In Tract 80 (1837), Williams states: "There appears in God's manifestations of Himself to mankind, in conjunction with an exceeding desire to communicate that knowledge, a tendency to conceal, and throw a veil over it, as if it were injurious to us, unless we were of a certain disposition to receive it" (4: 3). Rossetti's approach is to extend biblical typology in her poetry, offering the natural world as symbolic of God's presence. This approach connects the corporeal to the sublime, and causes the environment and her faith to co-exist throughout her *oeuvre*.[3] Like her contemporary Tractarian Charlotte Yonge, Rossetti saw in the world around her an opportunity to learn more of the ways of God, offering lessons, as her comment about the dead mouse suggests, and also illustrative metaphors. Her work is suffused with her incarnational aesthetic, in which "the beauty of the physical world was shaped by [Christ's] continuing presence and incarnation" (Grass 361).

Yet Rossetti's poetic relationship with the world around her is a complex one. Early critics figured her as a poet of nature, flowers, and small animals, suggesting an uncomplicated "womanly" depiction of the natural world, but closer reading uncovers a more problematic approach.[4] Though strongly anti-vivisectionist and with an aesthetic appreciation of nature which appears in many of her poems, her sense of the beautiful and sublime is juxtaposed with a clearly delineated potential threat implicit in the beauties of nature: in the fruits and flowers, the birds and animals, and even in the landscape itself lie a seductive beauty which can lead one astray. The threats they offer are most clearly demonstrated in "Goblin Market," where the delicious fruits are tainted with evil, and the goblins become harbingers of death. This is perhaps the clearest manifestation of her concern that "reveling in nature could confuse moral judgment, thereby imperiling salvation" (Grass 361). I will thus explore how, for Rossetti, the experience of the natural world is filtered through the medium of faith, situating humankind in a landscape of delight and fear, a position which must be constantly and conscientiously negotiated. This positioning of the human subject is exemplified in her sonnet "The World," in which the duality of creation is personified:

> By day she wooes me, soft, exceeding fair;
>   But all night as the moon so changeth she;
>   Loathsome and foul with hideous leprosy
> And subtle serpents gliding in her hair.
> By day she wooes me to the outer air,
>   Ripe fruits, sweet flowers, and full satiety:
>   But thro' the night, a beast she grins at me,
> A very monster void of love and prayer.
>
> (1–8)[5]

This is Rossetti's representation of nature at its most abstract and metaphorical. What appears here is, as Antony Harrison suggests, a version of the Fall, where something which appears harmless may be an agent of evil:

> Rossetti uses a host of traditional images associated with both the Fall and English love sonnets. These include, on the one hand, serpent, fruit, and beast images; and, on the other, images of duplicitous beauty, the fickle moon, and "sweet flowers." These latter images are transposed from their originary Petrarchan contexts of admiration for a beloved. The moral dangers as well as the illusory quality of such images and their uses are exposed through juxtaposition with Satanic reality.
>
> (92)

The poem constructs an economy of good and evil, in which beauty and ugliness are balanced against each other, deceiving the senses in a complex web of allusions both literary and theological: this is not a "real" reflection of nature, but nature as symbol. The beauty that the day reveals is exposed by darkness as "a very monster." Though the beauty of nature might bring us closer to God, the poem implies, it may also seduce us from the path of righteousness, because beauty cannot be trusted, a concept she also relates to human beauty. For Rossetti, devout and contemplative, nothing can be taken for granted, and to make mistakes brings us to destruction, with "feet, cloven too" (14) which are animalistic as well as traditionally satanic, aligning the subhuman with evil. "The World" reminds us that though this beauty is God's creation, humanity is weak and may become ensnared in such beauty. The world is part of an implicit binary: good/evil, heaven/hell, God/Satan, but the boundaries are blurred, and Rossetti's poetry provides readers with the tools to use Christian judgment to distinguish them.

Rossetti's poems frequently construct a kind of Pre-Raphaelite "truth to nature" which, as Ruskin said, sees the world and reproduces it "rejecting nothing, selecting nothing and scorning nothing; believing all things to be right and good, and rejoicing always in the truth" (Ruskin 3: 624). The coexistence of the sublime and the wicked in the natural world, and the duty of the artist to render it, complements Rossetti's religious beliefs, yet her concept of "truth" is not entirely that of the Pre-Raphaelites, seeing the world with artists' eyes, but with "Eyes that have been supernaturalized," which can "recognize ... how darkness reveals more luminaries than does the day: to the eye pertains a single sun; to the night innumerable, incalculable, by man's perceptions inexhaustible stars" (*The Face of the Deep* 116).

How might Rossetti's poems be read in the light of modern ecocritical theory, then? Jonathan Bate writes of the "localness" of British nature writing (39), in the spirit of Wordsworth, suggesting that from love of a specific place of natural beauty grows love for all living things. This approach rarely applies to Rossetti, an urbanite whose love of nature, while genuine, was not rooted in specific places; for her, a love of living things grew from her love for God. Yet Bate also emphasizes Wordsworth's desire for the usefulness of poetry, for writing that made life endurable, if not enjoyable. Nature writing offers a refuge for all to learn from and appreciate the world around us, and this is a complex web of associations, as Victorians including Hazlitt, Ruskin, and Morris understood. Bate's discussion of how poetry might serve a specific purpose is one which Rossetti would well have understood; as a poet she was, like Charlotte Yonge, "writing as a Christian, with the glory of God in view" (228). Tractarian writing requires active reading, offering symbols, allusions, and glimpses of glory, providing an uplifting, spiritual, and deeply devotional reading experience. For Rossetti, the vehicle for her religious message is often nature, and to attempt to read one aspect without the other, as reviewers and critics have done occasionally, is to miss the point of her work entirely. This is not to suggest that "the biota has only a bit part," or serves as backdrop, a problem Lawrence Buell identifies (Hiltner 98); rather, it is part of Rossetti's poetics to focus on the tiny, accessible, and easily overlooked in order to point to the most serious matters, of life, death, and the soul. Her approach suggests a desire to create parity between all of God's creation, in which the earth looks to God as its creator and is thus egalitarian, not privileging humans as a superior species.

Sing-Song, Rossetti's book of nursery poems, demonstrates the range and depth of her connection with the world around her. In it, she constructs a textual world for children, complete with images by Arthur Hughes (based on her own drawings), and the book offers a carefully constructed Tractarian manual for children; this is truly "useful" poetry. *Sing-Song* provides an insight into the delicate ecosystem of the child's world. Informed by and situated within the framework of the Christian worldview, Rossetti presents the reader with an economy based on kindness, reciprocity, and duty that moves between humans and the natural world.

Frankel suggests that one purpose of an environmental approach to Victorian poetry "is to focus on the implications of such verse from the perspective of the reader's active experience and to argue ... that such writing itself constitutes a participatory environment, inviting us to enter the space it demarcates and so become an active participant in the world it sets out to remake" (630). In *Sing-Song*, Rossetti expects this participation from her child-reader, because involvement in both poetry and nature provides the child with a model for Christian adult life. The natural world offers relief from the man-made construction of manufactured threats and fears of the fallen world, *Sing-Song* suggests. Sharon Smulders writes that Rossetti's poems in *Sing-Song* "provide spiritual comfort by representing nature in accordance with the Tractarian principles of analogy and reserve. The ulterior or sacramental significance of 'Brown and furry,' for example, resides in the poet's use of nature to impart the mystery of the resurrection ... In 'Why did baby die?', on the other hand, nature supplies a tacit answer to the anguished question of infant mortality" (109). Moreover, the natural world in this theological view not only points to God, but also reminds the reader of the presumed innate innocence of the child, particularly in relation to the Romantic construction of the child.

Ulrich Knoepflmacher suggests that in Wordsworth's *Prelude* and more markedly still in "Tintern Abbey," the mother figure is conflated with nature, which becomes literally "Mother Nature" (13–14). The role traditionally expected of the mother, providing moral guidance, as well as a spiritual and emotional home, is here assigned to the environment. The sense of being nurtured by nature is a common trope in Wordsworth's poetry, present in poems such as "Influence of Natural Objects, in calling forth and strengthening the imagination in boyhood and early youth." This poem suggests that the "Wisdom and spirit of the universe" teach:

> The passions that build up our human soul;
> Not with the mean and vulgar works of man, –
> But with high objects, with enduring things,
> With life and nature; purifying thus
> The elements of feelings and of thought.
>
> (7–11)

These lines are particularly suggestive of the impact nature should have, rather than necessarily has, upon the child; the final line quoted combines the two crucial elements of the "purifying" effect of nature: feelings and thought. Moreover, in this idealized image of the child, it implies a creature of the most sensitive kind—that is, a Romantic child. Rossetti adopts, if not a Romanticist view of childhood, at least the idealization of nature that accompanies it. For example, she writes:

> When a mounting skylark sings
>   In the sunlit summer morn,
> I know that heaven is up on high,
>   And on earth are fields of corn.
>
> But when a nightingale sings
>   In the moonlit summer even,
> I know not if earth is merely earth,
>   Only that heaven is heaven.
>
> (1–8)

Rossetti here takes a Wordsworthian aesthetic approach in permitting the natural world to indicate the sublime. However, rather than describing scenery with lofty grandeur, she takes a homely approach which is more likely to appeal to children, rooting her spiritual meaning in familiar sights and sounds.

This approach is not only an extrapolation of Romantic ideals. It is also particularly embedded in Tractarian thought, with emphasis on the natural sublime as a motif emblematic of God's creation. Though Rossetti's approach to nature is by no means straightforward, she broadly follows the comments of Keble in Tract 89, "On the Mysticism Attributed to the Fathers of the Church," in which the relationship between the natural world and the spiritual is explained through "a particular set of symbols and associations, which we have reason to believe has, more or less, the authority of the Great Creator Himself" (6: 143). The path from earthly to spiritual is laid out here as a typological method for human understanding. It is precisely this form of extrapolation of the spiritual from the apparently mundane that Rossetti employs throughout her work. These "familiar Tractarian evidences of God in Nature" form the fundament of Rossetti's beliefs, and in particular provide her with ample material for Christian teaching (Tennyson 151).

For Rossetti, the natural world and the spiritual are connected specifically by mortality, since all on earth is temporal. *Time Flies* contains many incidents concerning spiders, birds and flowers, for example, in which it is not the sublime side of nature but its commonplaces, which Rossetti employs to teach her audience. In the passage quoted earlier, she concludes that we must learn not to reflect too much on the physical side of death but to consider with joy its spiritual element. This is reflected in her treatment of death in *Sing-Song*, using the natural world to accustom children to otherwise difficult or uncomfortable concepts. Distant from Wordsworth's approach to the natural world, the child can learn sometimes painful truths from Rossetti's depiction of nature. Perhaps inspired by the event detailed in *Time Flies*, a poem about a dead thrush in *Sing-Song* familiarizes the concept of death for a child:

> Dead in the cold, a song-singing thrush,
> Dead at the foot of a snowberry bush, –
> Weave him a coffin of rush,
> Dig him a grave where the soft mosses grow,
> Raise him a tombstone of snow.
>
> (1–5)

The dead bird might be read as a metaphor for the dead child which figures throughout the book, especially given the reverence with which the dead bird is treated. As a calm acceptance of the death of living creatures, it is a poem to accustom the child to the realities of the natural world.

However, it has been suggested that it is reference to infant mortality that has caused *Sing-Song* to fall out of favor as a nursery book. The fear of the death of a child is predominant, and features in several of the poems. Some poems feature the death of a bird or animal, but there are several which present the reader with a direct truth, of the possibility of the death of a child.

Death in *Sing-Song* does not only happen to children and animals; it can also deprive the child of its mother. Several poems offer a sense of security for the child with its present mother, but simultaneously raise awareness of the possibility of the mother's absence. Though there are more poems in the text that consider the death of a child, it becomes clear that, from the "motherless soft lambkin" to the "motherless baby," the poems are teaching that life is finite. The effect of this is mitigated through protective divinities: "Motherless children – / Cared for from their birth / By tender angels" (3–5), and also by social common sense: "Motherless baby and babyless mother / Bring them together to love one another" (1–2). The fact of death is considered more generally in other poems, so that the child would develop an awareness of the impermanence of life, often mitigated by being clothed in the child-friendly metaphor of the cycles of nature.

Other poems take a different yet still didactic stance. One of the most well-known poems in *Sing-Song* begs the child to:

> Hurt no living thing;
>   Ladybird, nor butterfly,
> Nor moth with dusty wing,
>   Nor cricket chirping cheerily,
> Nor grasshopper so light of leap,
>   Nor dancing gnat, nor beetle fat,
> Nor harmless worms that creep.
>
>   (1–7)

This simple poem appears little more than a list, but its range and descriptive powers are significant. Not only does Rossetti exercise a range of adjectives designed to appeal to children ("cheerily," "dancing," "fat"); she employs an alliterative mode that enables the apparently loosely structured poem to remain in the minds of her readers. The list begins with insects familiar from other nursery rhymes, brightly colored and appealing creatures, yet moves to those of which children (and indeed adults) are often afraid. By associating the gnat, beetle, and worm with the ladybird and cricket, Rossetti extends the range of insects of which, she implies, small children are the natural guardians. Jan Marsh comments that Rossetti was always uncommonly fond of insects such as spiders, beetles, and worms; here it becomes clear that rather than associating them with death and decay, she instead places them in the spectrum of God's creation, to be loved along with the rest of the natural world. As Gilbert White wrote, "The most insignificant insects and reptiles are of much more consequence and have much more influence in the economy of nature, than the incurious are aware of" (205). Another poem in *Sing-Song* suggests:

> Plodding toad, plod here and be looked at,
> You the finger of scorn is crooked at;
> But though you're lumpish, you're harmless too;
> You won't hurt me, and I won't hurt you.
>
>   (5–8)

The accompanying illustration to the poem shows two children looking at a toad, one holding out a hand towards it. The implication goes further than the need to treat animals kindly, carrying the implicit moral that the appearance may be deceptive, and kindness an imperative. Indeed, Rossetti's approach frequently places the child in kinship with small animals, particularly lambs, an idea replete with biblical connotations as well as familiar from Blake's poems.

Rossetti's poems include:

> A frisky lamb
> And a frisky child
> Playing their pranks
> In a cowslip meadow
>
> (1–4)

and "A motherless soft lambkin," in which the child cares for an orphaned lamb that seems akin to the "motherless baby" of another poem. Yet Blake's poems are darker; the "Chimney Sweeper" and the "flowers of London Town" ("Holy Thursday" 5) are in the shadows of Blake's poems, for which the reader has no agency to help, while for Rossetti's reader the darker troubles of the world are distant, though children are invited to alleviate suffering. The child is allowed to play an active role in a moral world in *Sing-Song*, visiting "The dear old woman in the lane" who "Is sick and sore with pains and aches," and offering solace: "We'll go to her this afternoon, / And take her tea and eggs and cakes" (1–4). The moral role of the child Rossetti introduces earlier in the book, of kindness to animals and respect for the natural world, is eventually transferred to the human world. As Christine Kenyon-Jones suggests, "[t]he association of children and animals is often taken for granted," and is used in Romantic writing onwards to develop both imagination and socialization (53).

The role of the child in the family is also represented by the animal world. While in many of the poems the mother is present only by presumption—that she is speaking the poems of love and play to the child—there are others in which she is either absent or irrelevant, the child's adventures taking place without her. Although Rossetti's depiction of the mother in *Sing-Song* is largely traditional and loving, paradoxically these poems explore the possibilities offered by freedom from the maternal influence. Poems such as "Minnie and Mattie" see three children exploring the countryside, discovering flowers and animals by themselves. The mother figure does feature in the poem, though only in the animal world:

> Cluck! Cluck! the mother hen
> Summons her chickens
> To peck the dainty bits
> Found in her pickings.
>
> (17–20)

This example of motherhood appears to serve more as a reminder of the absence of their own mother, perhaps with a note of guilt at the children's enjoyment of freedom from her presence. Indeed this could be read as a call to return home, which Minnie and Mattie ignore. The poem encourages this exploring, suggesting that they "Don't wait for roses / Losing today" (29–30), but rather free themselves from the nursery to enjoy the wider world instead.

For the more sophisticated child, who has learned the rules of nature, Rossetti's poems also include several nonsense rhymes, which provide a very different form of exploration: that of the imagination. Some poems are clearly intended to stimulate the imagination, exploring, for example, their own wishes and desires alongside the flowers in the garden:

> I am a King,
>   Or an Emperor rather,
> I wear crown-imperial
>   And prince's-feather;
>
> (1–4)

The poem goes on to assign roles of councilors and court to other plants, and the child's view of himself at the center of his universe is established, but within the safe domestic bounds of the garden.

The reader learns from *Sing-Song*, then, that nature is a model for society, from which we might learn a humane and sympathetic way to behave. However, Rossetti's other works by no means provide such an unproblematic approach. As the earlier discussion of "The World" implies, Rossetti's poems demonstrate an understanding of the natural world as ripe with implicit danger. "Goblin Market" has been read as a version of the Fall, and this is a subject she revisits in her poetry, from "Eve" and "A Daughter of Eve" to her "fallen women" poems; the effect of the Fall is her primary concern, but its cause, Satan working through God's creation, is also a concept to which her poems return. "Goblin Market" offers a warning fable of the dangers of succumbing to beauty, but it also explores the dialectics of desire, a trope that is manifest in her "Eve" poems. In "Shut Out," for example, the speaker can see Eden but no longer enter it, excluded by a man-made barrier:

> The door was shut. I looked between
>   Its iron bars; and saw it lie,
>   My garden, mine, beneath the sky,
> Pied all with flowers bedewed and green.
>
> (1–4)

The sense of oneness with the environment is all the stronger for being denied its pleasures; yet nature, in the form of the snake and the apple, caused Eve's exclusion from it. This conflict, between desire and danger, passion and reason, cause and effect, and ultimately good and evil, is one that is played out in many of Rossetti's poems. This construction is also indicative of a residual guilt, in which it is human behavior that resulted in punishment by separation from nature. A desire for excess, even for too much of nature's bounty, results in the ultimate destruction of its beauty: the girls in "Goblin Market," once wild creatures who explore their surroundings and listen out for the call of the goblin men, are tamed, kept inside by their domestic duties by the end of the poem—yet their memory of the strange fierce desire for the fruits remains to haunt them.

The possibilities offered by an ecocritical reading of "Goblin Market" are explored by Kelly Sultzbach, whose article suggests that the poem undermines traditional binaries, including those of gender, and the division between human and nature:

> non-human association is not just linked to the goblin men and does not function solely to aid in a bestial conspiracy of salacious temptation. Recalling the long outpouring of listed fruits, this passage provides a proliferation of beautiful natural similes for the two girls. They are animals, flowers, snow, and their flesh is rendered as objects of magical enchantment ... While not overtly challenging human agents' control over nature, "Goblin Market" does spin a revolving metaphorical mirror, thereby creating a dizzying array of human-like animals and animal-like humans and showing that humans and non-humans alike inhabit a single world in which all are dynamic players in life's tragedies and triumphs.
>
> (48–9)

This suggests a rather different reading from those which explore the poem as an allegory of salvation, both Eucharistic and of earthly redemption for fallen women, or as a marketplace economy in which women's bodies are currency. Instead, Sultzbach's reading conjures a world where nature and humanity are blended, and the signs must be read in order to escape damnation. It is also, of course, a framework of Christian morality, in which temptation must be identified and resisted, and forgiveness given and accepted; as Sean Grass writes, "Laura's failure in Tractarian terms to scrutinize nature for signs of a greater purpose than mere self-indulgence is redeemed by Lizzie's fundamentally Tractarian approach to the problem of redemption and salvation" (372). Rossetti's poems repeatedly insist on the dangers of attaching oneself too closely to the physical world, desiring only earthly things; her poems are suffused with a renunciatory attitude, particularly of temporal things, and "Goblin Market" illustrates the dangers that earthly desires can threaten. Similarly, "The Prince's Progress" demonstrates how the world might tempt one from the path by appearing seductive. Yet in both poems, the threat seems clear to the reader, signposted by Rossetti's language, and the temptations are thus revealed in advance. Her poem "Amor Mundi" makes explicit the dangers of the "love of the world": the poem moves from a walk on an easy, downhill path, through "honey-breathing heather" (6), until the peril that awaits the thoughtless walker is conjured: "'Oh what's that in the hollow, so pale I quake to follow?' / 'Oh that's a thin dead body which waits the eternal term'" (15–16). The body, which has become one with the landscape (illustrated in a painting by E. R. Hughes) offers a warning that the speaker is on "hell's own track" (18), because the beautiful world also contains within it death and decomposition.

Rossetti's approach to the environment can be explored most fully in *Time Flies*, a mature devotional work in which she invites the reader to see through Christian eyes which are trained to "read" the world around us as both emanations of the divine and harbingers of hell. *Time Flies* is a particularly appropriate text to examine Rossetti's approaches to nature; it is, as a daily devotional text, structured around the changing seasons and, of equal significance in the text, the liturgical calendar, seamlessly harmonizing faith and the environment. Many of her entries in this book suggest that, as with Wordsworth's poetry:

> Nature is not seen here as having values of itself, but as capturing the fleeting shadows of an invisible unchanging Platonic reality—even Heaven itself?—and it shares the values of that deeper reality precisely in so far as it is symbolic to the initiated eye of that hidden world. Without that invisible realm of absolutes its own changing phenomena would be meaningless.
>
> (Prickett 81)

Time Flies, with its anecdotes, poems and multiple approaches to Christian devotions, demonstrates Rossetti's belief that an understanding of the environment enables a true understanding both of the self and of God, as Todd O. Williams suggests. More than simply drawing attention to the beauty of creation, Rossetti uses analogy to construct every anecdote as a moral lesson, reminding the reader of God as well as providing moral instruction. For example, the entry for March 15 provides a clear moral lesson from nature, analogizing animals and flowers with humans:

> Thy lilies drink the dew,
> The lambs thy rill, and I will drink them too;
> For those in purity
> And innocence are types, dear Lord, of Thee.
>
> (1–4)

In this poem and many others, the "purity" of nature is provided as an example for humans, anthropomorphized to suggest the animals' sentience.

"Types" is a revealing word: Ruskin wrote that "what revelations have been made by humanity inspired, or caught up to heaven, of things to the heavenly region belonging, have been either by unspeakable words, or else by their very nature incommunicable, except in types and shadows" (4: 208). For Rossetti these "types and shadows" were a fundamental part of faith, in which Old Testament typology is expanded to provide all earthly objects and events with a heavenly counterpart. The innocence of nature is not related to lack of autonomy or conscious thought, in her schema, but to obedience to its creator. The poem expresses a wish to be "Not high, or great, or anxious overmuch, / But pure and temperate" (12–13), providing in the lamb and the lily—both obvious symbols of purity—a model of obedience and duty for human emulation.

Rossetti's choice of imagery makes it clear that her engagement with the environment comes primarily from the Bible. Her language is suffused with a biblical lexicon, but it is not only the words but also the sentiment behind them that her work both represents and transforms. In a poem for April 26, she writes, with reference to Psalm 121:

> When sick of life and all the world—
> How sick of all the earth but Thee!—
> I lift mine eyes up to the hills,
> Eyes of my heart that see
>
> (1–4)

The poem subsequently refers to the "Refreshing green for hearts and eyes" (6) of heaven. The speaker here is not refreshed by earth and its beauties, for she is "sick" of these also; it is the meaning behind them, which she can metaphorically see beyond the hills, which offers her hope. The concluding stanza refers to "the new Heaven and Earth" (33) where "There shall be no more blight" (35), and the restrictions and sadness of the current world will be dissolved. Her vision of a world perfected is one she returns to in *The Face of the Deep*, her study of the book of Revelation; her repeated insistence on a better world to come is one which reminds us that for Rossetti this world is fallen, doomed, and can only be a shadow of Heaven.

The poem for February 27 considers a mole and an earthworm: the mole ignores the earthworm, and they both tunnel blindly. A ploughshare, however, "Involved them in one common ruin" (16). The moral here is that death comes to all, however they behave. The use of such insignificant creatures to illustrate this *memento mori* suggests a complete equality not only between the analogous humans, but also between animals. This replication of an ecosystem is extended in a poem for July 5, which suggests that the environment exists *for* nature, not for humans. This is an important distinction, as Rossetti seems to imply that humans have not earned the right to exert power over the earth:

> Innocent eyes not ours,
> Are made to look on flowers,
> Eyes of small birds and insects small:
> ....
> Have just as clear a right
> To their appointed portion of delight,
> As Queens or Kings.
>
> (1–3, 10–12)

The poem appears to privilege the animal creatures of the earth over humans in their ability to enjoy nature with innocence. Their "right" to pleasure, and by implication to the green spaces of the earth, is asserted by the end. In fact this poem is extracted from a longer work, "To What Purpose is this Waste?," in which the speaker learns a lesson, moving from the superior view that nature is wasted when there is no one to see its beauty, to an understanding of nature as an independent ecosystem which does not require humankind. The title is taken from Matthew 26:8, in which Jesus is anointed with precious oil and his disciples question its use. The assertion that the oil is not wasted, but that the questioners do not understand its significance, provides a helpful context for the poem.

This consideration of who or what nature is *for* raises some important questions about the relationship between faith and environmental ethics in Rossetti's work. Lynn White's groundbreaking article suggested that "Christianity is the most anthropocentric religion the world has seen" and that "Christianity bears a huge burden of guilt" for the destruction of the natural environment (1205–6). This view has largely been overtaken by new readings of humanity's relationship to the natural environment in Genesis, but White's assertion seems to contain some historical truth. Yet Rossetti's approach is certainly not that of dominion as White suggests; his statement that "To a Christian a tree can be no more than a physical fact" (1206) is undermined by the body of her work. The solace of caring for nature, the responsibility for its creatures and plants, and its ability to point us towards God, suggest a more sympathetic ecological approach. Alastair McGrath writes of recent theological scholarship on the relationship between humans and the environment: "The creation is not ours; we hold it in trust for God … This insight is of major importance in relation to ecological and environmental concerns because it provides a theoretical foundation for the exercise of human responsibility towards the planet" (220). Re-readings of Genesis suggest that rather than mastery or dominion over creation, humans hold a position of guardianship or stewardship. This shift can be read as an issue of interpretation of biblical sources, yet its manifestation in Rossetti's work is apparent. When she writes in "Brother Bruin" of the dancing bear too weak to dance, who is beaten by his master, she is implicitly condemning the man whose lack of sympathy is evidence of his purely economic relationship with the creature. For him, it is true that "nature has no reason for existence save to serve man" (White 1207); the bear is his source of income and consequently the relationship is debased, rather than the sublime corollary her other poems depict. The man sells the bearskin after the bear's death, but the man's own death, alone and unloved, is seen as just punishment for his behavior. The natural world not only reflects God, it also reflects the state of the human soul: if we abuse it, we ourselves become soiled. As Sultzbach argues, "Her attitude isn't merely one of stewardship, but also one of respect for beings that have their own thoughts and emotions, which are undervalued and misunderstood by humans" (44). The poem for July 19 in *Time Flies* asks us to "Pity the sorrows of a poor old dog" (1) and concludes sagely, "Spare and be spared,—or who shall plead for thee?" (8). This is more than a reciprocal exchange in which displaying humanity might save one's soul: the poem makes clear the dependency of animals on humans, and suggests a two-way exchange. Moreover, Rossetti exhorts the reader to be selfless in relation to the natural world, replicating Christ-like compassion. Similarly, in a prose entry for July 6 there is an anecdote concerning frogs in which she parallels herself with a "scared frog" and, significantly, concludes: "it is quite certain that no day will ever come when even the smallest, weakest, most grotesque, *wronged* creature will not in some fashion rise up in the Judgement with us to condemn us" (129). Nature, then, as part of God's creation, may take on the role of judge against humanity that ill-treats it. This strongly worded warning makes clear the relationship Rossetti's work constructs between humankind and its environment. Humanity may be privileged, in terms of sentient thought and superior ability, but nature has its own eternal soul and must be treated with humility and kindness. Not only do we have a responsibility to care for the environment, but also we must resist the temptation to abuse it, for this will bring about our downfall.

It is possible now, in the context of modern critical developments, to see Rossetti's preoccupation with nature as an early form of ecotheology, in which humanity is the guardian of the world as well as standing in metaphorical relation to it as a manifestation of God's work. Modern ecotheological thought speaks to a tradition of the parson-naturalist, such as Gilbert White, who through the lens of faith constructed the ecology of the world in the light of their beliefs. Barri Gold says that we now need "different modes of ecological thinking" (221), and a theological approach to the environment in the nineteenth century is one such mode. As Sultzbach points out, "Rossetti's conflicted relationship with the worldly environment and the allegorical power of nature as a religious and cultural symbol becomes highly relevant to green scholarship" (39). Rossetti's approach to the environment fits into the framework of what Harold Bloom calls the "belatedness" of Victorian writers: an uncertainty about humanity's place in the world, particularly in light of developing industrial technologies, and the "long withdrawing roar" of past certainties in Matthew Arnold's "Dover Beach." For Rossetti, though, uncertainty about the world is underpinned with a desire to reach for the next world through this one, by replicating the behavior of God towards his creation. Her work invites the reader to view nature through Christian eyes, and to observe even the smallest details of creation: "Lichen and moss and sturdy weed, / Tell of His love who sends the dew" ("Consider the Lilies of the Field" 21–2). The Assisi Declarations of the Christian church, written nearly 100 years after Rossetti's death, seem in accordance with her doctrine: "At the risk of destroying himself, man may not reduce to chaos or disorder, or, worse still, destroy God's bountiful treasures" (Serrini). Laurence Osborn writes that the disobedience of humanity, from Adam and Eve onwards, has disrupted our relationship with God and thus with his creation. Now "barred from Eden," "violence corrupts the whole of creation" (89). There are threats in the world, then, of our own making, according to Rossetti's theology, and we must learn to read God's creation, which is temporal with death at its heart, in order to avoid damnation.

Notes

1 For discussion on specific beliefs of Tractarianism, and the background of the Oxford Movement, see Fairweather. Prickett and Tennyson provide thorough critical discussions of Tractarian poetry.
2 Stephen Prickett points out the "momentous effect" of Wordsworth on the Oxford Movement (92), particularly through Keble's *Lectures on Poetry*.
3 This is not to denigrate other influences on her work and her interaction with the natural world, however; her involvement with the Pre-Raphaelite Brotherhood must also be considered, given their interest in foregrounding nature rather than simply offering it as a setting, an idea manifested in *The Germ: Thoughts Towards Nature in Poetry, Literature, and Art* (1850).
4 An oversimplified approach was encouraged by W. M. Rossetti's edition of her poems, in which he reduces her work to "themes" including "A Love of Animals" and "The loveliness of the Rose."
5 All quotations from Rossetti's poetry are from *Christina Rossetti: The Complete Poems*, editor Rebecca Crump, and are cited by line number.

Works cited

Bate, Jonathan. *Romantic Ecology: Wordsworth and the Environmental Tradition*. London: Routledge, 1991.
Bloom, Harold. *The Anxiety of Influence: A Theory of Poetry*. New York: Oxford UP, 1973.
Fairweather, Eugene, ed. *The Oxford Movement*. Oxford: Oxford UP, 1961.
Frankel, Nicholas. "The Ecology of Victorian Poetry." *Victorian Poetry* 41.4 (2003): 629–35.
Gold, Barri J. "Energy, Ecology, and Victorian Fiction." *Literature Compass* 9 (2012): 213–24.
Grass, Sean C. "Nature's Perilous Variety in Christina Rossetti's 'Goblin Market.'" *Nineteenth-Century Literature* 51.3 (1996): 356–76.
Harrison, Antony H. *Christina Rossetti in Context*. Brighton: Harvester, 1988.
Hiltner, Ken, ed. *Ecocriticism: The Essential Reader*. London: Routledge, 2015.

Keble, John. "Tract 89: On the Mysticism Attributed to the Fathers of the Church." *Tracts for the Times.* Vol. 6. London: Rivington, 1840.
Kenyon-Jones, Christine. *Kindred Brutes: Animals in Romantic-Period Writing.* Aldershot: Ashgate, 2001.
Knoepflmacher, U. C. *Ventures into Childland: Victorians, Fairytales and Femininity.* Chicago: U of Chicago P, 1998.
Marsh, Jan. "The Spider's Shadow: Christina Rossetti and the Dark Double Within." *Beauty and the Beast: Christina Rossetti, Walter Pater, R. L. Stevenson and Their Contemporaries.* Ed. Peter Liebregts and Wim Tigges. Amsterdam: Rodopi, 1996. 21–30.
McGrath, Alastair E. *Christian Theology: An Introduction.* Chichester: Wiley-Blackwell, 2011.
Osborn, Laurence. *Guardians of Creation: Nature in Theology and the Christian Life.* Leicester: Apollos, 1993.
Prickett, Stephen. *Romanticism and Religion: The Tradition of Coleridge and Wordsworth in the Victorian Church.* Cambridge: Cambridge UP, 1976.
Roe, Dinah. *Christina Rossetti's Faithful Imagination: The Devotional Poetry and Prose.* Basingstoke: Palgrave Macmillan, 2006.
Rose, Andrea, ed. *The Germ: The Literary Magazine of the Pre-Raphaelites.* Oxford: Ashmolean Museum, 1992.
Rossetti, Christina. *Christina Rossetti: The Complete Poems.* Ed. Rebecca W. Crump. London: Penguin, 2005.
———. *The Face of the Deep: A Devotional Commentary on the Apocalypse.* London: SPCK, 1892; Bristol: Thoemmes, 2003.
——— *Sing-Song.* London: Macmillan, 1872.
———. *Time Flies: A Reading Diary.* London: SPCK, 1885.
Rossetti, W. M., ed. *The Poetical Works of Christina Georgina Rossetti, with Memoir and Notes.* London: Macmillan, 1904.
Ruskin, John. *Modern Painters. The Works of John Ruskin: Library Edition.* Ed. E. T. Cook and Alexander Wedderburn. 39 vols. London: Allen, 1903–1912.
Serrini, Lanfranco. "The Christian Declaration on Nature." *Assisi Declarations.* 1986. Web. 14 March 2015.
Smulders, Sharon. *Christina Rossetti Revisited.* New York: Twayne, 1996.
Sultzbach, Kelly. "The Contrary Natures of Christina Rossetti's Goblin Fruits." *Green Letters: Studies in Ecocriticism* 14.1 (2011): 39–56.
Tennyson, G. B. *Victorian Devotional Poetry: The Tractarian Mode.* Cambridge: Harvard UP, 1981.
White, Gilbert. *The Natural History of Selborne: with observations on various parts of nature and the naturalist's calendar.* London: Chidley, 1840.
White, Lynn. "The historical roots of our ecologic crisis." *Science* 155.3767 (1967): 1203–7.
Williams, Isaac. "Tract 80: On Reserve in Communicating Religious Knowledge." *Tracts for the Times.* Vol. 4. London: Rivington, 1840.
Williams, Todd O. "The Autobiographical Self and Embodied Knowledge of God in Christina Rossetti's *Time Flies.*" *Literature & Theology* 28.3 (2014): 321–33.
Wordsworth, William. *Selected Poems.* Ed. Stephen Gill. London: Penguin, 2004.
Yonge, Charlotte M. *Womankind.* London: Clay, 1876.

5 The zoocentric ecology of Hardy's poetic consciousness

Christine Roth

> What are my books but one plea against man's inhumanity to man—to woman—and to the lower animals?
>
> Thomas Hardy in an interview for the *Pall Mall Gazette*, 1901

The familiar historical division in the work of Thomas Hardy marks the striking shift the writer made from narrative, after the disappointing critical reception of *Jude the Obscure* (1895), to poetry, beginning with *Wessex Poems* (1898). But this division has the unfortunate effect of diminishing one of Hardy's most abiding ethical and aesthetic concerns. From 1860 to 1928, in both the form and content of his novels and poems, Hardy consistently challenged the prevailing anthropocentricism of Victorian culture, and his target across this entire period was the series of zoological links and institutional disjunctions that characterized "the animal." Moreover, Hardy's retirement from novels has been characterized as a retreat, the writer presumably spending his evenings "wooing the Muse of Poetry" (Hammerton 20), as if Hardy had shrunk from the openly political nature of fiction and shifted to the relative safety of poetry, with its neater, less confrontational, less expository compressions. Yet, precisely because he shifted his focus to poetry, Hardy got politically bolder; he took greater risks, not fewer. For he saw in this genre the opportunity to increase the *formal* pressure on the ethical concerns he had developed in his novels. In its tight, formal presentation, poetry could sharpen aesthetic realities that the novels had presented in looser, more expansive form.

Whether in novels or in poetry, however, Hardy's primary ethical interest, stemming from the new anthropology developed after Darwin's *On the Origin of Species* (1859), was the Victorian conception of the animal and, concomitantly, the kind of "human" that could be produced from this new consciousness of the nonhuman animal. To answer that question, readers needed to back up and ask what a "bird," or a "cow," or "dog" really was. What defined the "sentience" peculiar to each species? More reflexively, when does any *human* interest in a nonhuman species fall short or fail altogether? Such an ontological concern lies at the heart of what Lawrence Buell calls an "environmental text," one that encourages readers, in Randy

Malamud's deceptively simple terms, to "see animals without hurting them," respecting them "on their own terms," and thus leading readers to develop "a culturally and ecologically complex, problematized vision of what an animal means" (Buell 7; Malamud 44, 45). Keeping the value of "animals" *un*determined keeps them away from all the metaphors that would close them off as cultural commodities, safeguarding them, instead, as fully present beings in literal, biological, and bioregional terms: outside the cage of human language. A "cow" is not a "bird or a "dog" any more than it is also not a "human." Hardy does not "speak blithely of the Animal in the general singular"—a practice that Jacques Derrida marks as "perhaps one of the greatest, and most symptomatic idiocies of those who call themselves human" (Derrida 41). Challenging the minstrel use of animals as anthropocentric metaphors, for example, Hardy, in "Shelley's Skylark" (1887), presents the animal not as an incorporeal spirit or as a symbol for the "poet hidden / In the light of thought," but as "feather and bone"—a material bird—that has since turned to "dust" (101).[1] Nature bluntly impinges on symbol here. Even in his late elegiacal poems for animals, which might appear sentimental and anthropocentric, Hardy forces his readers out of the old symbols and into the difficult woods and streams of indigenous being (or into the shaming contexts of auctions, markets, and slaughterhouses), summoning from his copious notes about real animals the creatures' precise and alien behaviors. His poetry is continually divesting itself of Victorian fictions about those creatures, going so far as to anticipate modern discussions about speciesism and offering paradigmatic scenarios of Derrida's theorization of the "non-criminal putting to death" of animals.

Hardy begins, in both his poems and his novels, by assuming that any organism is a function of its environment, whether social or physical. This is classic nineteenth-century literary naturalism, in which a text reproduces the "ecology" of its characters. But the ethical heritage of naturalism is often hidden behind the severity of its philosophy (famously, though perhaps unfairly, characterized by Tennyson's comment about nature as "red in tooth and claw"). The word "ecology" had been coined in 1866 to denote a system of knowledge ("logos") that ensures the well-being of all living things residing together in a habitat ("oeco"), and this ethical dimension to "environmental" texts is where Hardy parts from the naturalists of the late nineteenth century. In narrativizing ecology, in which all forms of life—human and nonhuman—exist precisely because their environments have entitled them, Hardy not only treats "animals as though they are members of the variegated earth's family" (Sherman, "Hardy and Lower Animals," 308); he treats poetry as the system of knowledge (the "logos") by which this ecology might be understood.

As one who "was raised on the poetry of the Romantics" and was "heir in more than one sense" to them, Hardy had long seen poetry as a wellspring of natural compassion (Steinberg 184). Many Romantic writers had played a "polemically active" role in the cause of animal welfare, and, in their discourse, "animals could be said to have rights, much as humans have, to life, to justice, to their natural happiness": "God, it was often proved, loves *all* his creatures, and so accordingly must we" (Perkins 43, 3). Or, as Coleridge's Ancient Mariner attests, "the dear God who loveth us, / He made and loveth all" (*Rime* CXL). Throughout the Romantic period, poetry had been adopting religious poses in part because appeals to the divine—and thus to the Sublime—always entailed a rebuke of human industry: the presumption that the works of man could rival the works of God, or of nature. Indeed, some of the most robust arguments against animal cruelty came not only from writers like Wollstonecraft, Blake, Coleridge, Shelley, and Wordsworth but from religious writers as well. As David Perkins illustrates in *Romanticism and Animal Rights*, "The argument that God intends the happiness of *all* his creatures was, if you believed it, the most compelling one in the Romantic age for kindness to animals" (35). In this context, cruelty to an animal was ungodly, iniquitous. In the parallel context of ecology, fortified by the Darwinian notion of a "web of complex relations," cruelty raised not only scientific questions about human–animal connections and accountability but spiritual, ethical, and philosophical questions, as well. But, for all its vigor, religious rhetoric was ultimately impotent, Hardy thought. By 1913, he was still lamenting that, "after twenty centuries of what is supposed to be humane religion," people still failed to behave compassionately to their fellow creatures (Millgate, *Public Voice* 344). Perhaps poetry could do better.

Moving away from the melodrama and rhetorical excesses of Victorian fiction, Hardy opted for the verbal compression, exacting minimalism, and philosophical precision of modernist poetry. In doing so, he could, like a cubist, throw traditional anthropocentric falsehoods and cultural fantasies into stark relief against the circumstances and sensibilities of nonhuman animals, presenting readers with an efficient activist perspective that sprang from a new aesthetic ear and eye. In the first lines of poems like "The Puzzled Game-Birds," "Bags of Meat," and "The Bird-Catcher's Boy," Hardy focuses quickly and unrelentingly on the horror and cruelty of the scenes—asking pointed questions and making provocative and troubling observations without any cushion of exposition or introduction. He then closes the poems with the same briskness as he began them, offering no relief from the onslaught of sensory detail, multiple voices, exclamation points, question marks, and harsh realities. This pressure is especially strong in his eight-line triolets, in which the first and the last lines are identical. "The Puzzled Game-Birds," for example, opens and closes with "They are not those who used to feed us / When we were young—they cannot be!" The antecedent for "They" and "those" is momentarily suspended. The verbal "to feed," posed transitively, makes the subject, "who" (*not* "that"), into the actors, the givers of life, while "we" are made into their children. Hardy uses modernist concision to question, not to affirm, moral and ideological certitudes, and he answers the voice of "tradition" by overturning hierarchies and destabilizing divisions between animal and human, moral and immoral, humane and cruel.

Hardy also opted for poetry over fiction because of what it offered in Aristotelian terms: poetry presented its audience with a new form of experience, a way, emotionally and conceptually, to track motive from the smallest cause to the largest effect. Finding in Darwin's *On the Origin of Species* an "ethically intense attention to the whole range of nature" (Levine 37), Hardy argued in 1909 that "the discovery of the law of evolution, which revealed that all organic creatures are of one family, shifted the centre of altruism from humanity to the whole conscious world collectively" (Millgate, *Life and Work* 373). Poetry could create precisely this kind of experiential shift in perspective. That perspective was, a year later, elaborated in a letter to the Humanitarian League: "Few people seem to perceive fully as yet that the most far-reaching consequence of the establishment of the common origin of the species is ethical; that it logically involves a readjustment of altruistic morals by enlarging as a *necessity of rightness* the application of what has been called 'The Golden Rule' beyond the area of mere mankind to that of the whole animal kingdom" (Millgate, *Life and Work* 376–7). The relationship of humans to other animals was a continuum rather than a division. The post-Darwinian extension of ethical consideration to animals complicated the traditional animal–human binary: "reconceiving the binary as a single field of interrelations entails reconceiving the ethical aspects of relationship. When animals graduate from irrelevance to the status of beings in relation to which the human recognizes itself, animals come inside the circle of ethical consideration" (Crane 52). So a "cow" actually is partly a "dog" as much as it is partly a "human": no binary exists to separate each species fully. For Hardy, Darwin "introduce[d] a fundamental indeterminacy" about questions like "What differentiates one species from another? How do we tell where one species ends and another begins?" (Grosz 20–1). Hardy pasted excerpts from Conrad Guenther's *Darwinism and the Problems of Life* (1906) into his notebook: "In the eyes of science[,] man is not 'higher' than the other animals" (Hardy, *Literary Notebooks* 225). Man is an *other* (not a cow or a dog), but man is also *another* (part cow, part dog, all animal). The small cause of simple compassion had, therefore, the largest of effects, for it moved us from the natural impiety of cruelty to the godliness of global kinship.

One of the poetic devices through which Hardy untethers anthropocentric biases and breaks down the false distinction between human and nonhuman animals can be seen in his strict figuration of a "creature" as, in the words of the *Oxford English Dictionary*, both "a human being; a person, an individual" and "a living or animate being; an animal, often as distinct from a person." In *Jude the Obscure*, Hardy applies the word "creature" six times to a slaughtered pig; some examples include: a "long-legged creature" (58), a "poor creature" (58), an "artful creature" (59). Yet he uses "creature" sixteen times also to refer to humans. Jude considers a life of preaching and doing "good to his fellow-creatures" (123), for instance, and he is identified as a "purblind, simple creature" (332). Sue is a "creature of civilization" (141); an "ethereal creature" (179); a "poor miserable creature" (231); a "disembodied creature" (236); a "phantasmal, bodiless creature" (250); a "cold-natured, sexless creature" (256), a "pitiable creature" (328); a "refined creature" (332); a "vile creature" (338). The same crossover occurs in the poetry. In "Bags of Meat," a calf is "the creature sold" (808), and, in "Compassion: An Ode in Celebration of the Centenary of the Royal Society for the Prevention of Cruelty to Animals," animals are "Mild creatures, despot-doomed, bewildered" (822). Yet, in "The Cheval-Glass," the parson's daughter is a "creature of nameless charm" (360), and Hardy's deceased wife, Emma, is elegized in "He Prefers Her Earthly" as a "fond and fragile creature" (496).

Used in these richly imbued contexts, the word "creature" systematically undermines human exceptionalism and its varied teleologies that excuse us from the world and from our cruelty and instead enforces contingent human animality as an evolving project within nature, bound to its organic relationships. As Julia Lupton explains, the word "creature," derived from the future active participle of the Latin verb *creare* ("to create"), "indicates a made or fashioned thing, but with the sense of continued or potential process, action, or emergence built into the future thrust of its active verbal form"; it "is a thing always in the process of undergoing creation" (161). Elisha Cohn, who also builds on Lupton's definitions, argues that "creature" marks "a humanist domain concerned with the tragedy of failed agency" and that it links characters to both "images of damaged animality" and their own efforts at "alleviating animal suffering"; as a result, she understands the references to both the Durbeyfield children and the horse Prince as "creatures" in *Tess of the D'Urbervilles* to be a way of "simultaneously emphasiz[ing] their similarity and their difference, ultimately positing interspecies relationships as inherently ethical" (509–10). In this way, Hardy works "horizontally," in Cary Wolfe's term, to explore not only the condition of animals in his contemporary culture but also the "animality" of the humans in that culture (Wolfe xiii).

In Hardy, "creature" adumbrates the Heideggerian position of being "poor in the world," a pitiable, impoverished condition incapable of full access to the *Dasein* (the total being-ness) of humans (Heidegger 185). Like Frankenstein's "creature," Hardy's creatures often occupy a liminal position between conventional Victorian understandings of human animals and nonhuman ones. From a zoocentric perspective, the ability to regard cows, horses, birds, dogs, and cats as kindred beings is central to Hardy's appeal to extend ethical consideration and altruism to, in his words, "all organic creatures" (Levine 37). Indeed, some critics argue that "[w]hat made Hardy so upsetting to many of his contemporaries was precisely this sense that human life was merely the Darwinian extension of nonhuman life"—that "human beings are just another species in a long line of species" (Nichols

110–11). Increasingly, Hardy associated traits and feelings previously associated with humans only, such as compassion and charity, to animals, resulting in an ecology in which readers are called to transcend the human sphere by entering the collective biosphere. In fact, the emotions most often associated with animals in his poetry are those that commonly elevate humanity—the ones that constituted the antithesis of "animality," primitivism, predation—thus shifting the reader's response to Hardy's nonhuman characters from one of compassion to one of admiration, as readers are forced to see humans from the perspective of the animals, from the sporting gentleman ("The Puzzled Game Birds") and the fashionable dame ("Lady in Furs") to the grieving ("The Caged Goldfinch"), the frugal ("The Mongrel"), and the diligent ("A Sheep Fair") denizens of the human world, all now so seemingly inhuman.

Altruism and advocacy for animals became a formalized movement in the nineteenth century, and some of Hardy's passion for these issues can be traced to his own involvement in the Victorian humane movement, though he was attentive and responsive to the nonhuman world all his life.[2] Indeed, one of Hardy's earliest and most formative memories, from around 1844, focused on a time when he and his father "noticed a fieldfare, half-frozen, and the father took up a stone idly and threw it at the bird, possibly not meaning to hit it. The fieldfare fell dead" (Millgate, *Life and Work* 479). According to Hardy's own narrative, he never forgot how the starved bird felt in his hands. About thirty years later, Hardy's journals note his concern for a horse during a coach journey in September 1882, and he records a London trip during which he "was moved to compassion" in January 1889 by London horses who "struggled and struggled" on the greasy city streets (Millgate, *Life and Work* 225). Hardy's concern for horses extended to their use in warfare, and he argued in 1899 that they should not "be employed in battle except for transport" (Millgate, *Public Voice* 151)—an argument he repeated in "Horses Abroad," published twenty-five years later, in which the "unwitting" horses of war, doomed to be simply "war-waste," appear "wrenched awry / From the scheme Nature planned for them,—wondering why" (785–6). Then, in 1911, while serving as a Dorchester magistrate, Hardy instigated a case against a local drover and his employer for cruelly driving a tuberculous cow (Millgate, *Public Voice* 325–6). With an ardor that seemed to intensify as he grew older, Hardy championed the humane treatment of animals. His letters condemning blood sports, the inhumane treatment of zoo animals, vivisection, the cruel slaughtering of food animals, the caging of birds, forced animal performance, and the plumage trade appeared in *The Times*, *Animal's Friend*, *Humanity: The Journal of the Humanitarian League*, *Daily Mail*, *The Humanitarian*, *Glasgow Herald*, *Dorset County Chronicle*, and *Cruel Sports: The Official Journal of the League for the Prohibition of Cruel Sports*. By the time Hardy wrote "his final act of self-description" for the 1926 *Who's Who* entry, he wrote, "Holds Gold Medal of Royal Society of Literature; Member of the Council of Justice to Animals; is against blood-sport, dog-chaining, and the caging of birds" (Millgate, *Public Voice* 473).

This is not to say that Hardy opposed all human use of animals. As Ronald Morrison points out, "Hardy's intellectual and emotional responses to the specific goals and methods of the humane movement were extraordinarily complicated." Hardy "usually withheld unconditional support for humane causes"; he "was unable to embrace vegetarianism"; and he conceded "that experimentation on live animals might yield significant medical advances for humans" (Morrison, "Humanity" 67). To Hardy, though, such was the bigger picture of ecology: the prevention of suffering within the biosphere. For that reason, he could justify meat-eating and scientific experimentation as long as the animals were slaughtered humanely and not subjected to vivisection—in short, as long as suffering was minimal.[3] In his letters and in his poems, Hardy denounces power over animals that is wielded intemperately and asks that readers regard animals not only as providers of human sustenance, entertainment, and scientific advancement but as fellow creatures whose lives belong to themselves: each animal, like each human, is both *other* and *another*.

Toward this ethic, and contrary to the stance of most Romantic poets, Hardy did not stand apart from his animal subjects and argue on their behalf. Instead, he imagined them having a voice of their own. Sometimes he would communicate this voice through lyrical conventions; other times, he would imagine the creatures speaking in human language. For example, the musicality, the sibilant sounds, and the rhythm of bird song lend themselves especially well to poetry, and Hardy wrote approximately forty-five poems with significant reference to that peculiar voice.[4] Scholars have noted Hardy's ability to translate bird song into rhyme. George Witter Sherman writes that the greatness of "The Bullfinches" lies in Hardy's ability to mimic exactly the "right auditory tones, describing the finches' oscillating rhythm at times as one who has watched their soundless flight movement" (*Pessimism* 252). Referring to the same poem, Edmund Gosse calls Hardy "not only a very ingenious, but a very correct and admirable metricist" because readers "seem to hear the very voices of the birds warbling faintly in the sunset" (453). And Barbara Hardy claims that Hardy's choice of the "small-scale, repetitive, fixed and varied, and intricate metric" of the triolet allows him to "spea[k]—rather sin[g]—like a bird" in "Birds at Winter Nightfall" (199). Similarly, in "Winter Night in Woodland," Hardy recreates the fox's "sonorous and long" bark with an onomatopoetic "wong, wong, wong!" (734). The soft sounds of the deer's walk in "The Fallow Deer at the Lonely House" is recreated in the four-syllable line "Fourfooted, tiptoe" (598)—the fricative "f" sounds in "fourfooted" imitating the sound of the animal's hoof pushing through the snow, and the consonant, onomatopoetic "tiptoe" illustrating Hardy's familiarity with the breed's habit of walking on its third and fourth phalanges. Likewise, in "The Calf," the feet of the creature with "bewildered bleat" go "pit-pat" (945), the childlike staccato of the alliteration suggesting its distinctively raspy bovine cry and the light pattering of its hooves on the street.

If the sounds of individual species are specific and recognizable in Hardy's poems, individual animals themselves are not each a generic "it"; an animal is a "he" or a "she," often characterized by age, gender, breed, and species-specific behavior. In the words of contemporary H. C. Duffin (1884–1974), "Hardy never insults his animals by treating them as neuters" (qtd. in Sherman, "Hardy and Lower Animals" 305). In making these finer distinctions, Hardy resists reductive generalizations that deny agency to single animals, and so he emphasizes the plurality of animal life, suggesting what Derrida sought in the term "animot"—a homonym of "animaux"—to indicate not simply a nonhuman system of "words" ("mots") but "the plural *animals* in the singular" and thus to transcend "the single figure of an animality that is simply opposed to humanity" (Derrida 31, 47). The nonhuman characters in Hardy's poetry "look," "watch," "wonder," "get contemplative," and "humou[r] our queer ways." Like the agons of human tragedy, they even "strive in vain" against an "Immanent Will" before succumbing to their fate—perhaps the most significant mark of selfhood in Hardy's *oeuvre*.[5]

Many of Hardy's poems that advocate compassion and ethical treatment for animals are first-person monologues spoken by the creatures themselves. In the four-line poem "The Lizard," for instance, the reptile articulates the sort of "if ... then" proposition readers might encounter in formal logic or in a Renaissance sonnet:

> If on any warm day when you ramble around
> Among moss and dead leaves, you should happen to see
> A quick trembling thing dart and hide on the ground,
> And you search in the leaves, you would uncover me.
>
> (952)

The poem not only connects the shuffling of the reader to the scurrying of the lizard, both of whom are outside because of the warmth, both hardwired to detect peripheral movement; it calls attention to the "me"—the lizard as a person of sorts—hiding under the moss and dead leaves. The normal human–animal gaze is reversed so that the human "I"/eye (the otherwise dominant perspective from which the world is conceived) now becomes the observed "you": but only within the speaking voice. The form of the poem gives the altered perspective its being. The "trembling thing" that crawls on the ground suddenly can talk and can know itself through human eyes, and in that reversal of human perspective the directionless "rambling" acquires its tenor against the panicked "trembling" of a voice so small that it will shrink to mere "thing" if captured by human vision. In a similar reversal, the titular character in "The Calf" arrests her readers' attention with a declarative "That was I" as they are "passing by." She then individuates the "we" of the poem by breed—"Devon kind, / Shorthorns, or

Herefords"—but reduces her "masters" and "lords" to the generalized "human race" (945). Immersing readers in the sensory and emotional world of this one cow who hopes she is destined for a dairy farm—"if they let me live" (945) she adds—Hardy opens up animal "thingness" to consciousness and sympathy, and to the universal yoke of fear expressed through the individualized, autonomous voices of self-differentiating creatures.

From this first-person perspective, Hardy often rejects human-centered thinking altogether by moving into an animal-centered consciousness. In these cases, not only do animals display a voice and agency; they also have access to secrets and consolations that elude humans. In "An August Midnight," Hardy's speaker sits at a writing desk and attempts to find communion with four insects who have joined him—a "longlegs," a moth, a "dumbledore" (a bumblebee), and a fly (146). As they smear his ink and knock against his lamp, he refers to them all as "we five" and muses on their coming together, "At this point in time, at this point in space" (146). Intuitively, one might assume that the speaker could hardly identify with unthinking, insentient bugs, but the speaker ends by musing that these insects—"God's humblest"—"know Earth-secrets that know not I" (146). And they do: each animal's access to the earth is peculiar (though not, by definition, alien). Moreover, the speaker has, in disfigured grammar, expressed his own fear that the earth might not know him: that he might be an *it*, a *thing*. In "The Caged Thrush Freed and Home Again," the bird, relieved to be back among his "tribes in treen," declares,

> "Men know but little more than we,
> Who count us least of things terrene
> ....
> How happy days are made to be
> Eludes great Man's sagacity
> No less than ours."
>
> (147)

Again, creatures identified by their insignificance and minimality have access to enviable knowledge. These clear-sighted creatures, like the rural, intuitive children who populate the inner shrines of Romantic poetry, seem endowed with the secrets of eternity.

Animality has become a kind of heavenly, prelapsarian state. In "The Blinded Bird," the bird goes on cheerfully, unembittered, even though someone has tricked him into singing night and day by blinding him with a "red-hot needle" and "enjailed" him in "pitiless wire" (147). The speaker of the poem, observing the injustice, marvels, "So zestfully canst thou sing? / And all this indignity, / With God's consent, on thee!" (147). It is a typically Hardyesque "reproof to a supposedly loving God who has not provided an economy merciful to forms of life" (Kerridge 136). The speaker therefore acknowledges the bird's holiness:

> Who hath charity? This bird.
> Who suffereth long and is kind,
> Is not provoked, though blind
> And alive unsepulchred?
> Who hopeth, endureth all things?
> Who thinketh no evil, but sings?
> Who is divine? This bird.
>
> (446)

The bird's Blakean innocence and his personification of the lessons found in 1 Corinthians 13 make him a moral authority. The "this" in front of "bird" emphasizes the physicality and earthly presence of a specific, individual bird, discouraging any inclination a reader might have to understand it as simply a metaphor for human experience. Unfortunately, the bird's virtues cannot cure or eliminate the human brutality besetting the creature, but, ironically, the poem offers animality as a space for spiritual transcendence. The most recognizable example of this dynamic is found in "The Darkling Thrush." Though described in third-person voice, the thrush's "joy illimited" and "happy good-night air" seem inaccessible to the human speaker. Given that the bird is old, "frail, gaunt, and small, / In blast-beruffled plume," he "Had chosen thus to fling his soul / Upon the growing gloom." This mystifying act leads the speaker to conclude that the bird possesses some transcendent "blessed Hope, whereof he knew / And I was unaware" (150).

Whatever knowledge the birds have about spiritual matters, however, does not enable them to understand the reasons for human cruelty. Cruelty is incomprehensible to the animals in Hardy's poems. In "The Caged Goldfinch," the bird left on someone's grave shows "inquiry in its wistful eye" (491). The young animal in "The Calf" is a "creature with bewildered bleat" (945). A steer at auction, prodded by a drover's stick, enters with "a bewildered jump" in "Bags of Meat" (807). The cattle look on the humans:

> With a much-amazed reproachful stare,
>   As at unnatural kin,
> For bringing [them] to a sinister scene
> So strange, unhomelike, hungry, mean.
>
> (808)

The hissing sound of the sibilant words—"stare," "as," "sinister scene," "so strange"—expresses the animals' confused scorn, particularly toward fellow mammals who have become *other* through dumb cruelty. If, in a post-Darwinian world, "all organic creatures are of one family," as Hardy wrote, "shifting the centre of altruism from humanity to the whole conscious world" (Millgate, *Life and Work* 373), then the humans in this poem and others are indeed "unnatural kin." The cattle, which seem to understand this kinship intuitively, cannot make sense of this perversity in humans. A similar mystification haunts "The Puzzled Game Birds" when the very humans who have fed and nurtured the birds now "bereave and bleed" them. The birds cry out, "—If hearts can house such treachery / They are not those who used to feed us / When we were young—they cannot be!" (148). Because the poem is a triolet, the line "They are not those who used to feed us" is repeated three times (with the "When we were young—they cannot be" included in the first and third times). In the first case, the birds do indeed sound simply "puzzled." When they repeat the line, however, their puzzlement seems to turn to shock. By the third time, when it is followed by an exclamation point, the words suggest fear and grief. The lines formally recall the pig-killing scene in *Jude the Obscure*:

> they hoisted the victim on to the stool, legs upward ... The animal's note changed its quality. It was not now rage, but the cry of despair; long-drawn, slow and hopeless. "Upon my soul I would sooner have gone without the pig than have had this to do!" said Jude. "A creature I have fed with my own hands ... The dying animal's cry assumed its third and final tone, the shriek of agony; his glazing eyes riveting themselves on Arabella with the eloquently keen reproach of a creature recognizing at last the treachery of those who had seemed his only friends.
>
> (58–9)

The pig is not simply a squealing beast at slaughter; it is "the victim" of a crime, who gazes at his "only friends" with "eloquently keen reproach." This is a scene of "treachery," not butchery. In perhaps Hardy's most heart-wrenching poem about animal suffering, "The Mongrel," it is this same despicable act of betrayal that the animal finally discovers in its "unnatural kin." The dog's master tosses a stick into a harbor so the dog will chase after it and drown in the strong current, because "taxpaying day was coming," and the owner wants to avoid paying for the dog license. At first, the dog looks for help from "the man he held as a god enshrined, / With no suspicion in his mind / That this had all been meant," but then he experiences a "wakening to the treachery / He had loved with love so blind" and a "loathing of mankind" (877).

Hardy is able to shape affecting parallels between human and nonhuman emotions. The speaker watching the cattle at auction in "Bags of Meat," for example, imagines that "a tear runs down his [the young bull's] face / When the butcher wins, and he's driven from the place" (808). Yet, while this effort to establish nonhuman animals as akin to human ones relies on such an anthropomorphic architecture for acknowledging the personhood of nonhuman animals, Hardy is never anthropocentric. His poems explicitly resist the language of objectification and abstraction that would assimilate animals to human tropes for determining what an animal *means*. In "A Sheep Fair," for example, Hardy provides meticulous physical details about the "meek, mewed" auction sheep that are "consigned to doom" (732). They are "sodden" by the torrents of rain, their wool "is like a sponge," "Their horns are soft as finger-nails," and they "pant" in their "wet and woolly wear" (731–2). While the similes, alliteration, rhyme, and meter highlighting the artfulness of the scene might tempt a reader to see the animals as Blakean "meek" and "mild" lambs in "softest clothing wooly bright," the torrential rain, the panting, the heaviness of wet coats—these details keep the pedestrian suffering of 10,000 actual wet, dirty, sentient, individual sheep in focus, the poem resisting line by line the idealized literary symbols of human innocence, Christian sacrifice, or Romantic childhood.[6]

Even when he is writing poems to or about household pets, Hardy may use anthropocentric language, but he does not base the moral worth of the dogs and cats solely on their likeness to humans. In fact, he more often imagines the pets surpassing humans in profound ways. He attempts to describe them on their own terms. In the elegy "Last Words to a Dumb Friend," Hardy embraces what made his "friend" first and foremost a cat: the cat's morning mews, the way the cat arched his back when petted, his "bounding to the window-sill" (658). If sentimental, the poem consistently attempts to speak from an animal-centered position. When the speaker remembers how the cat "humoured our queer ways" or waited for humans "who loitered around" (657) (not understanding an apparent purpose for their activity), the poem clearly positions human behavior as the extrinsic, the mysterious, the "other." So, although the language of mourning anthropomorphizes the cat, it also compensates for the creature's otherwise diminutive role, for the death of this pet throws the poem's speaker into an ontological crisis that, as he points out, directly contradicts the animal's subaltern position in the household. The speaker first describes the cat as a "Timid pensioner of us Powers" and a

> speechless thing,
> Subject to our mastering,
> Subject for his life and food
> To our gift, and time, and mood.
>
> (657)

After death, though, when the cat "[takes] hence of its insignificance," it "[looms] as largened to the sense, / Shape as part, above man's will, / Of the Imperturbable" (657). The animal's transcendence into "the Imperturbable" and "the Dim" causes the earthbound, living speaker, "a prisoner, flight debarred, / Exercising in a yard," to feel "forsaken." The supra-human forces of time, nature, death, and love consolidate in the "small mound beneath the tree, / Showing in the autumn shade / That [he] moulder[s] where [he] played" (658). Here the poem refers to the pet cemetery in the front garden of Max Gate, where the household pets lie under square gravestones carved by Hardy himself. The elegy and the burial challenge any anthropocentric notions of how and for whom a person mourns for a being who means something that, in a zoocentric perspective, cannot be measured fully in human terms. Similarly, in "The Roman Gravemounds," Hardy sets up a deceased pet cat as insignificant—"A little white furred thing, stiff of limb, / Whose life never won from the world a thought," "a small furred life [who] was worth no one's pen"—only to then elevate it (albeit, in lines approaching bathos) to a memory that displaces the greatest of human legacies:

> "Here say you that Caesar's warriors lie?—
> But my little white cat was my only friend!
> Could she but live, might the record die
> Of Caesar, his legions, his aims, his end!"[7]
>
> (397)

In each case, the speaker celebrates the deceased animal's perspective as epistemologically relevant (because it is unassimilable to human forms of meaning) but also subtly calls attention to the power imbalances inherent in even the most intimate animal-human relationships.

Hardy continues to recognize the agency and personhood of his pets in "A Popular Personage at Home" and "Dead 'Wessex' the Dog to the Household." And he again uses anthropomorphic language and image to break down the species boundaries that would traditionally preclude people from acknowledging them. Both poems were written in remembrance of the family dog, Wessex, who died at 6:30 p.m. on 27 December, 1926—a dog who regularly trespassed conventional animal-human boundaries himself (and was apparently encouraged to do so). He walked on the dining table unchecked, challenging guests for each mouthful of food; slept on an eiderdown bed in Hardy's study; and ate goose and plum pudding at Christmas (Millgate, *Biography* 489). In the poem, Wessex comically regards his owners as "the folk I let live here with me" (800). It is therefore not surprising that Hardy would eulogize him not only as a person but also as an elevated "personage" of the household. Wessex's voice in "A Popular Personage at Home" is that of a Keatsian creature "not born for death." He guards the house, takes walks, sniffs to find the "rarest smells" (800), and generally lives unaware of his own mortality—a willfully ironic sensibility that Hardy attributes to him, given that Wessex was nearly put down for attacking postmen, guests, and servants. As he lives out his canine life, Wessex reflects:

> "No doubt I shall always cross this sill,
> And turn the corner, and stand steady
> ....
> And that this meadow with its brook,
> And bulrush, even as it appears
> As I plunge by with hasty look,
> Will stay the same a thousand years."

(800)

The first five stanzas of the poem immerse the reader in the dog's consciousness, oblivious to the very mortality that occasioned the poem. In the last stanza, however, Hardy, who himself would die just thirteen months later, merges death into the dog's narrative:

> Thus "Wessex." But a dubious ray
> At times informs his steadfast eye,
> Just for a trice, as though to say,
> "Yet, will this pass, and pass shall I?"

(800)

In "Dead 'Wessex' the Dog to the Household," Wessex speaks directly to the household that now longs for him. Addressing the humans as "Wistful ones" in each stanza—"Do you think of me at all, / Wistful ones?"; "Do you look for me at times, / Wistful ones?"; "You may hear a jump or trot, / Wistful ones"; "Should you call as when I knew you, / Wistful ones"—the self-aware spirit of the dead dog remembers his life as a vital co-presence whose daily activities intersected with the humans who "shared [his] home." In the end, though, he laments, "I shall not turn to view you, / I shall not listen to you, / Shall not come" (915–16). As with other poems, the gaze is pointed from the animal back to the human being, in this case as a final loving rebuke to the arrogance of human vision and voice.

Though the sheer volume of his literary work devoted to animal welfare would warrant his place in the history of the cause, Hardy struggled to envision his legacy in this regard. In "Afterwards" (1917), the autobiographical speaker imagines himself (like Dead Wessex) speaking from his grave and asking the living which activities remind them of him. In doing so, he focuses on the flapping of "glad green leaves like wings," the "dew-fall hawk" alighting the "wind-warped upland thorn," and "the full-starred heavens that winter see," hoping that people will remember him as "a man who used to notice such things" (553), someone who reached out to his larger environment. Yet he fears that his lifelong efforts to write the poetry of nonhuman life, like the efforts of religious authors exhorting readers to godliness, might have made only a passing difference:

> If I pass during some nocturnal blackness, moth and warm
>   When the hedgehog travels furtively over the lawn,
> One may say, 'He strove that such innocent creatures should come to
>   no harm
>   But he could do little for them; and now he is gone.'

(553)

By 1924, Hardy had a more hopeful but still mixed view of what he and other campaigners had accomplished on behalf of animals over the last hundred years. His polemical rallying cry, "Compassion: An Ode in Celebration of the Centenary of the Royal Society for the Prevention of Cruelty to Animals," celebrates the "larger clearer conscience" (compared to the "few fain pioneers / Before incredulous eyes" who began the society in 1824) that speaks on behalf of "mild creatures, despot-doomed," but he also recognizes that, despite the efforts of the RSPCA and groups like it, "still those innocents are thralls / To throbless hearts, near, far, that hear no calls / Of honour towards their too-dependent frail" (822). He closes by casting the killing of animals as a bloody, murderous, and shameful act committed in "secret nooks" and "hideous dens whereon none looks" (823), thinking perhaps of the dark and vulgar factories that feed human civilization. This is not the natural suffering of creatures who find themselves powerless. This is the avoidable, "tyrannical" cruelty of slaughter, but Hardy clings to hope:

> Cries still are heard in secret nooks,
> Till hushed with gag or slit or thud;
> And hideous dens whereon none looks
>   Are blotched with needless blood.
> But here, in battlings, patient, slow,
> Much has been won—more, maybe than we know—
> And on we labour stressful. "Ailinon!"
> A mighty voice calls: "But may the good prevail!"
> And "Blessed are the merciful!"
>   Calls yet a mightier one.
>
>   (823)

This call is a poem about voices—voices heard and voices unheard, the voices of the animals, the voices of the campaigners, even the voice of God. When the animals' voices are "hushed with gag or slit or thud," the voices of their advocates, both human and divine, rise up on their behalf. With the cry of "Ailinon!" (in Greek mythology, a ritual cry of lamentation), Hardy makes the struggle an epic one. With the line from the Sermon on the Mount ("Blessed are the merciful!"), he makes it a moral one. Behind all of the voices is Hardy's own, promoting a beneficent ideology through a poetry that earns a place among the century's great literature on behalf of a more humane, just, inclusive society.

Along with Hardy's twenty-five or so other poems explicitly calling for a more zoocentric perspective on the ways that humans and nonhumans relate to each other, "Compassion: An Ode" could be defined by its "spirit of commitment to environmental praxis" (Buell 430). In it, we find Hardy's trademark mix of realism and hope that threads through his various efforts to reconcile the human community with their fellow creatures. He extended the ethical, spiritual, even biological center of human consciousness to include those who had been shoved to its periphery. In fact, in an interview with William Archer in 1901, Hardy himself described his "practical philosophy" as "distinctly melioristic," adding, "What are my books but one plea against 'man's inhumanity to man'—to woman—and to the lower animals? ... Whatever may be the inherent good or evil of life, it is certain that men make it much worse than it need be" (Archer 535).[8] His poems foreground the interests and the well-being of the otherwise neglected, ignored, maimed, hunted, or slaughtered animals who share his habitat, and they dramatize the emotional and physical realities of all animals—both human and nonhuman—as members of an inter-species community.

Notes

1. As Barbara Hardy writes, "Hardy disagrees with the famous apostrophe, 'Bird thou never wert' insisting with brilliant commonsense that Shelley's skylark must indeed have been a physical individual. Hardy imagines, and makes us imagine, that bird as Shelley did not, as a real bird that lived and died, whose body was chemically recycled" (196). Quotations of Thomas Hardy's poetry are taken from *The Complete Poems of Thomas Hardy* and cited by page number.
2. Considerable work has been done on the nonhuman animal in Hardy's *oeuvre*. Ronald D. Morrison's two essays—"Humanity towards Man, Woman, and the Lower Animals: Thomas Hardy's *Jude the Obscure* and the Victorian Humane Movement," which provides a thorough assessment of how the "various rhetorical and ideological stances of the Victorian humane movement" influenced the novel, especially in relation to the movement's "ambiguous attitudes toward social class" (66), and "Thomas Hardy as Early Ecocritic: The Later Public Prose," which considers Hardy's public statements on behalf of animals to be "the foundation of what we might today regard as Hardy's developing ecocritical stance" (8)—were especially valuable to this project.
3. Hardy's will includes a clause of bequests to animal charities (specifically "to be applied as far as practicable to the investigation of the means by which animals are conveyed from their houses to the slaughter-houses with a view to the lessening of their sufferings in such transit").
4. This number is taken from Tim Armstrong "Sequence and Series" (391).
5. Quotations are from "The Fallow Deer at the Lonely House" (598), "The Calf" (945), "Dead Wessex" (916), and "A Sheep Fair" (732).
6. See William Blake's "The Lamb" from *Songs of Innocence*.
7. It is interesting to note that, in a 1901 interview with William Archer, Hardy confirmed that he lived on a Roman graveyard and added that he "decapitated a row of five Roman soldiers or colonists in moving the earth to make the drive," just next to where he located the household pet cemetery (Archer 531).
8. In working towards a more equal and just world for all living beings, Hardy also recognized that not all humans are equal, and he repeatedly anticipated the crossover between ecocritical, feminist, and postcolonial perspectives in his writing about cruelty towards those who were designated as "other" to the Western, white, male perspective. The alignment of female characters with animals in novels like *Tess of the D'Urbervilles* has been widely discussed. In 1906, he blurred the issues by writing to Millicent Fawcett that sport encouraged "so-called educated men" to "harass & kill for pleasure feeble creatures by mean stratagems," that slaughterhouses were "dark dens of cruelty," and that the

"father of a woman's child" was no one's "business but the woman's own, except in cases of disease or insanity" (*Collected Letters* 3: 238). In "The Wind Blew the Words," Hardy's speaker imagines the voice of Nature telling him that he is one and the same with the trees, the animals, and

> thy fellows who abound—
> Either of speech the same
> Or far and strange—black, dwarfed, and browned,
> They are stuff of thy own frame.
>
> (447)

Works cited

Archer, William. "Real Conversations: Conversation II.—With Mr. Thomas Hardy." *Pall Mall Gazette* 23 (1901): 527–37.
Armstrong, Tim. "Sequence and Series in Hardy's Poetry. "*A Companion to Thomas Hardy*. Ed. Keith Wilson. Oxford: Wiley-Blackwell, 2009: 378–94.
Buell, Lawrence. *The Environmental Imagination: Thoreau, Nature Writing, and the Formation of American Culture*. Cambridge: Harvard UP, 1995.
Cohn, Elisha. "'No insignificant creature': Thomas Hardy's Ethical Turn." *Nineteenth-Century Literature* 64.4 (2010): 494–520.
Crane, Susan. *Animal Encounters: Contacts and Concepts in Medieval Britain*. Philadelphia: U of Pennsylvania P, 2012.
"creature, n." *OED Online*. Oxford UP, June 2015. Web. 19 June 2015.
Derrida, Jacques. *The Animal That Therefore I Am*. Ed. Marie-Louise Mallet. Trans. David Wills. New York: Fordham UP, 2008.
Gosse, Edmund. *Some Diversions of a Man of Letters*. New York: Scribners, 1920.
Grosz, Elizabeth. *The Nick of Time: Politics, Evolution, and the Untimely*. Durham: Duke UP, 2004.
Hammerton, J. A. "A Look-In on Gilbert Parker: An Impression of the Author of 'The Seats of the Mighty.'" *Black and White: A Weekly Illustrated Record and Review*. 4 January 1902: 20.
Hardy, Barbara. *Thomas Hardy: Imagining Imagination in Hardy's Poetry and Fiction*. New York: Bloomsbury, 2001.
Hardy, Thomas. *The Complete Poems of Thomas Hardy*. Ed. James Gibson. New York: Macmillan, 1982.
——. *Jude the Obscure*. Revised edition. Ed. Patricia Ingham. Oxford: Oxford UP, 2002.
——. *Literary Notebooks of Thomas Hardy*. 2 vols. Ed. Lennart A. Björk. New York: New York UP, 1985.
Heidegger, Martin. *The Fundamental Concepts of Metaphysics: World, Finitude, Solitude*. Trans. William McNeill and Nicholas Walker. Bloomington: Indiana UP, 2001.
Kerridge, Richard. "Ecological Hardy." *Beyond Nature Writing: Expanding the Boundaries of Ecocriticism*. Ed. Karla Armbruster and Kathleen R. Wallace. Charlottesville: UP of Virginia, 2001. 126–42.
Levine, George. "Hardy and Darwin: An Enchanting Hardy." *A Companion to Thomas Hardy*. Ed. Keith Wilson. London: Wiley-Blackwell, 2009: 36–53.
Lupton, Julia. *Citizen-Saints: Shakespeare and Political Theology*. Chicago: U of Chicago P, 2005.

Malamud, Randy. *Poetic Animals and Animal Souls.* New York: Palgrave Macmillan, 2003.

Millgate, Michael, ed. *The Life and Work of Thomas Hardy.* London: Macmillan, 1984.

———. *Thomas Hardy: A Biography Revisited.* Oxford: Oxford UP, 2004.

———, ed. *Thomas Hardy's Public Voice: The Essays, Speeches, and Miscellaneous Prose.* New York: Oxford UP, 2001.

Morrison, Ronald D. "Humanity towards Man, Woman, and the Lower Animals: Thomas Hardy's *Jude the Obscure* and the Victorian Humane Movement." *Nineteenth-Century Studies* 12 (1998): 65–82.

———. "Thomas Hardy as Early Ecocritic: The Later Public Prose." *Kentucky Philological Review* 26 (2012): 8–14.

Nichols, Ashton. *Beyond Romantic Ecocriticism: Toward Urbanatural Roosting.* New York: Palgrave, 2012.

Perkins, David. *Romanticism and Animal Rights.* New York: Cambridge UP, 2006.

Purdy, Richard Little, and Michael Millgate, eds. *The Collected Letters of Thomas Hardy.* 7 vols. Oxford: Oxford UP, 1978–88.

Sherman, George Witter. *The Pessimism of Thomas Hardy.* Rutherford: Fairleigh Dickinson UP, 1976.

———. "Thomas Hardy and the Lower Animals." *The Prairie Schooner* 20 (1946): 304–9.

Steinberg, Gillian. *Thomas Hardy: The Poems.* New York: Palgrave, 2013.

Wolfe, Cary. "Introduction." *Zoontologies: The Question of the Animal.* Ed. Cary Wolfe. Minneapolis: U of Minnesota P, 2003. ix–xxiii.

6 Early Dickens and ecocriticism
The social novelist and the nonhuman

Troy Boone

This chapter examines nonhuman nature in the early novels of Charles Dickens. Although it has been over a century since Louis Cazamian linked Dickens to the idea of the "social novel," critics still treat Dickens as that novelist whose ethical concerns focus on interrelations between humans: in other words, the "social" realm, particularly the manifold human interactions associated with London as world metropolis and as represented in Dickens's large, and generally more highly regarded, later novels. This essay looks at Dickens's works before he became identified particularly as an urban novelist in order to investigate the relation between his works and the nonhuman world. Read ecocritically, Dickens's early fictions reveal a non-anthropocentric understanding of the human's place in the world and a critique of the centrality of the human in the social theories that are still profoundly with us.

How to make a social novelist

In his 1903 book *The Social Novel in England*, Louis Cazamian establishes Dickens as a chief practitioner of "the social novel": books that represented "a new emotional and intellectual response to the subject of social relations" in England, particularly the "rise of a compassionate interventionist spirit" responding to working-class urban poverty (3). Since, for Cazamian, the novel form itself[1] is "above all an emotional stimulant, with pathos frequently ... at its centre," the Victorian social novel can offer "an intuitive grasp of organic human relationships" (6) and aim at nothing less than "the total reform of human relations" (4).[2] Cazamian's focus is on Dickens's earlier works: from *The Pickwick Papers* (1836–1837) to *David Copperfield* (1849–1850), as he indicates in the now-outrageous statement that, if *Bleak House* and *Little Dorrit* "are still of some interest, the novels following them are negligible" (125).[3] According to Cazamian, in Dickens's early novels, nature exists only as an undeveloped, hackneyed pastoral setting that operates as a mere counterpoint to the novelist's real focus, the city: "Dickens, the literary pioneer of the great modern city, created it as a desert of bricks and mud, searing the mind in its horror" (142), and in early Dickens the "countryside is consistently described in idyllic terms: it is the oasis of refreshment lying between the muddy brick towns" (164). What Cazamian offers is Dickens as social and urban novelist, and what is excluded from his analysis, and seemingly from Dickens's works themselves, is nonhuman nature.

This way of reading his novels has been profoundly influential on twentieth- and twenty-first-century Dickens criticism, perhaps most obviously on the famous readings of the industrial novel by F. R. Leavis, Raymond Williams, and Sylvère Monod. For Leavis, as for Cazamian, Dickens "observes with gusto the humanness of humanity as exhibited in the urban (and suburban) scene" (267). Similarly, for Williams, Dickens offers "an imaginative judgement ... of social attitudes," and his positive values lie "in what he sees as the elements of human nature—personal kindness, sympathy, and forbearance" (93–4). Monod likewise argues that the "sincerity of Dickens' social feeling is not to be called in doubt. Few men have been so vividly struck as he was by the suffering of the poor, by the unfairness of fate, and by the frequent cruelty of privileged people" (444)— his impressions of which then form the ethical purpose of such works as *Hard Times* (1854). For more recent critics, Dickens continues to be the exemplary Victorian urban novelist, focused on human and social realms more than nonhuman natural realms. For a famous instance among many others, D. A. Miller treats Dickens's identity as a social novelist as self-evident: *Oliver Twist* (1837–1839) is "plainly written as a humane attack on the institutions that help produce the delinquent milieu" (4), and the discipline that the novel both attacks and exemplifies extends "down to the tiniest practices of everyday social life" (17). More recently and similarly, Elaine Freedgood states that the Victorian novel operated as if it would "eventually be taken for something very like social history" (34).

Even the relatively few critics who focus on Dickens's relation to the environment treat his works largely in these human and urban terms. Thus in an important 2009 essay, "Green Dickens," Karen Chase and Michael Levenson offer a reading of how Dickens links "modernization and social trauma" (133) and of how he emerges as a committed social activist. Like *The Social Novel in England*, Chase and Levenson's essay claims that, because "London will always be the privileged arena for Dickens," nature in his novels is relegated to "the memory of pastoral" (132) rather than being valued as an active ecosystem worthy of substantial representation. Indeed, one of the most telling features of Chase and Levenson's essay is the way in which it treats Dickens's social—that is, human and urban—concerns *as* ecology.[4] Descriptions of the commercial and social operations of "a metropolitan neighborhood" in one of the *Sketches by Boz* (1836) thus constitute for Chase and Levenson "economy as ecology, a self-contained system of human exchange (narrative as well as material) that exists in organic relation to the natural world" (132–3). But the "natural world" here is understood as thoroughly humanized and urbanized, as in the following summary by Chase and Levenson: "The river brings ships; the ships deliver coal, which the traders carry into the country; and when coal has been exchanged for cash, they return to convert it into food and drink and clothes" (133). Focusing on spurious uses of the natural—characters who flaunt "counterfeit pastoral" (135) like Mrs. Skewton in *Dombey and Son*, Harold Skimpole in *Bleak House* (1852–1853), and Mrs. Merdle in *Little Dorrit* (1855–1857)—Chase and Levenson can declare that in Dickens "'Nature' is left as a debased token of fashion, a privileged currency in polite conversation, but lacking any purchase as alternative to the failures of modernization" (136), namely the social, industrial, and human failures on which Cazamian, Leavis, Williams, and Monod also focus. Although Chase and Levenson make valuable arguments regarding mid-Victorian social concerns as a sort of early environmentalism—particularly commons preservation and the open spaces movement (139–44), as well as sanitation reform and opposition to the cruelty of animal slaughter at Smithfield Meat Market (138)—in their formulation, mid-Victorian ecological thought has everything to do with the human, and nature becomes "a debased token of fashion": aside from fried fish (135) purchased in the "ecology" of consumerism, practically the only "creatures" mentioned in their article are humans, such as the "caged urban creatures set free to exercise their limbs" (139).[5] Not to put too fine a point upon it, but, in this "organic" "ecology," what happened to the fauna and flora?

Part of the problem is that Dickens himself tells us to read him as a social novelist, for instance in the Preface to *The Pickwick Papers*, where he states that, if "any of his imperfect descriptions, while they afford amusement in the perusal, should induce only one reader to think better of his fellow men, and to look upon the brighter and more kindly side of human nature, he [the author] would indeed be proud and happy to have led to such a result" (*PP* c). And from the first readers have read him thus, as instanced by reviews of the early novels. Typically, John Forster, in a review of *Nicholas Nickleby* (1838–1839) in the 27 October, 1839 *Examiner*, remarks that the "knowledge of character, observable in the writings of Mr. Dickens, is never more apparent than are his kindness of heart and capacity for generous emotion" (qtd. in Collins 48). Similarly, in a review of Dickens's works up to *Nicholas Nickleby* published in the October 1838 *Edinburgh Review*, Thomas Henry Lister claims that Dickens is "the truest and most spirited delineator of English life, amongst the middle and lower classes, since the days of Smollett and Fielding," and Lister equally praises Dickens for his "comprehensive spirit of humanity" (qtd. in Collins 72–3). And Dickens's friend the poet Thomas Hood wrote to the novelist as if responding directly to the wish expressed in the Preface to *Pickwick*: "books which put us in better humour with the world in general must naturally incline us towards the Author in particular" (qtd. in Collins 95).

Part of the problem is also that, in contrast to Cazamian's statement that *Bleak House* is only of "some interest" and later novels "are negligible" (125), criticism in recent generations has focused so frequently on the urban novels of Dickens's later career—especially *Bleak House, Little Dorrit, Great Expectations* (1860–1861), and *Our Mutual Friend*—that advancing Dickens's status as a novelist who writes "about nature" is likely to seem at least a little strange. And so it seemed even to Dickens's earliest readers, such as Charles Buller, who stated categorically in a July 1837 article on "The Works of Dickens" in the *London and Westminster Review*: "It is easy to see that his observations have been mainly confined to London," and, "though he has sometimes described country life" it is not here "that his muse finds its favourite subjects" (qtd. in Collins 52). More caustically, John Ruskin declared in a 6 June, 1841 letter to W. H. Harrison that the author of *The Old Curiosity Shop* (1840–1841) should eschew natural description altogether: "It is evident the man is a thorough cockney, from his way of talking about hedgerows, and honeysuckles, and village spires; and in London, and to his present fields of knowledge, he ought strictly to keep for some time" (36: 26). Dominic Head would have it that these problems in the reading of Dickens are in fact problems in the form of the novel itself, given its interest in character, the human, and the social: "The tendency of the novel to focus on personal development, and on social rather than environmental matters (and on time rather than place) is sometimes said to create an impression of alienation from the natural" (236). However, instead of treating the novel as "peculiarly resistant to the operations of ecocritical inquiry" (237)—and instead of using such an ecocritical inquiry to offer an "exposure of what is left out" of the novel's "environmental bad faith" as a genre (237)—Head proposes that "a Green materialist reading ... cannot divorce the social from the natural" (236) and should offer an analysis of how "the represented landscape becomes a text in which human interaction with the environment is indelibly recorded" (236). What, in other words, if the fault lies not in the classic novel, Dickens's or otherwise, but rather with us as readers? What if we read other Dickens novels, and read all Dickens novels otherwise, to see what this supposed "social novelist" has to say about the nonhuman world with which we coexist?

If we move away from the late novels and their emphasis on London and move back to early Dickens,[6] and if we attend to the non-urban settings of those still largely urban novels without dismissing them as mere pastoral interludes, we can see Dickens offering ethically important depictions of the nonhuman world, depictions that can in turn inform more complex ecocritical re-readings of the urban spaces in these early novels, and in Dickens's later ones. Such a reading in turn can enable us to ask what Dickens has to tell us about the effects of human actions on the natural world, and the danger of living, reading, and writing as if human social matters are what should concern us most centrally, in a novel or in our lives. Lawrence Buell has famously proposed that we should read for setting, so as to get away from the anthropocentric nature of the novel (254–6), but Dickens's status as urban novelist and social novelist means that reading his city novels for the setting, as so many readers have done, returns us to the human social realm as what is important about his books. However, instead of reading for character (as criticism of the novel usually has done) or for setting (as much ecocriticism does), or even for character-in-setting, we might be better off reading for inhabitants-in-environment, where inhabitants can be plants and human or nonhuman animals existing in the ecosystemic place that we call the setting of a novel.

Reading like an idiot

Early in Dickens's novel *Barnaby Rudge* (1841), the narrator provides the sort of description of London that for many readers characterizes Dickens's later novels:

> And, now, he [the locksmith Gabriel Varden] approached the great city, which lay outstretched before him like a dark shadow on the ground, reddening the sluggish air with a deep dull light, that told of labyrinths of public ways and shops, and swarms of busy people. Approaching nearer and nearer yet, this halo began to fade, and the causes which produced it slowly to develop themselves. Long lines of poorly lighted streets might be faintly traced, with here and there a lighter spot, where lamps were clustered round a square or market, or round some great building; after a time these grew more distinct, and the lamps themselves were visible; slight yellow specks, that seemed to be rapidly snuffed out, one by one, as intervening obstacles hid them from the sight. Then sounds arose—the striking of church clocks, the distant bark of dogs, the hum of traffic in the streets; then outlines might be traced—tall steeples looming in the air, and piles of unequal roofs oppressed by chimneys; then, the noise swelled into a louder sound, and forms grew more distinct and numerous still, and London—visible in the darkness by its own faint light, and not by that of Heaven—was at hand.
>
> (26)

This way of seeing London is not that of Gabriel Varden, who at this point in the novel is sleeping on horseback as his horse walks along "a road with which he was well acquainted" (26). Rather, this is the language of the narrator as social novelist, and perhaps that of the implied reader of the social novel: what we receive in this passage is the accumulation of detail after detail, mostly visual but also auditory, so as luridly to render the massive and intricate human and built environment of the city, rounding finally to the judgment of the narrator who observes that the light of the infernal metropolis is not "that of Heaven." This passage implies a way of reading trapped within the realm of the human and its creations—all the labyrinths, ways, shops, streets, lamps, squares, markets, buildings, church clocks and steeples, traffic, roofs, and chimneys, nonhuman life being signified ever so briefly by the "distant bark" of companion animals.

Lest we assume that Dickens simply and earnestly desires for us to read from this anthropocentric perspective, *Barnaby Rudge* offers us a very different way of seeing the world in which we live: the perspective of Barnaby Rudge, the "idiot" who observes his surroundings consistently in terms of their nonhuman inhabitants. Barnaby's view of the world outside London is precisely attentive to what the narrator's view of London so humanly excludes:

> There were wild-flowers to pluck—the bright red poppy, the gentle harebell, the cowslip, and the rose. There were birds to watch; fish; ants; worms; hares or rabbits, as they darted across the distant pathway in the wood and so were gone; millions of living things to have an interest in, and lie in wait for, and clap hands and shout in memory of, when they had disappeared. In default of these, or when they wearied, there was the merry sunlight to hunt out, as it crept in aslant through leaves and boughs of trees, and hid far down—deep, deep, in hollow places—like a silver pool, where nodding branches seemed to bathe and sport; sweet scents of summer air breathing over fields of beans or clover; the perfume of wet leaves or moss; the life of waving trees, and shadows always changing.
>
> (340)

This view of the world is directly opposed to that of the social novelist, as we enter Barnaby's stream of consciousness and enumerate with him each of the different sorts of wildflowers one can pick and each of the different sorts of creatures one can watch: Barnaby even attends, with a naturalist's care, to the difference between hare and rabbit. Reading like an idiot, we can follow Barnaby in tracing the finest gradations of sunlight, the subtlest scents ("beans or clover ... wet leaves or moss"), and the lives of "millions of living" nonhuman beings "to have an interest in," as opposed to the millions of people and their crooked ways on which the narrator elsewhere focuses, writing as a social novelist. Human happiness, this novel insists, accrues to those who read the world (and perhaps the world in novels) for all its diverse inhabitants—or, those who read like an idiot: "The world to him [Barnaby] was full of happiness; in every tree, and plant, and flower, in every bird, and beast, and tiny insect whom a breath of summer wind laid low upon the ground, he had delight," and thus "where many a wise son would have made her [Barnaby's mother] sorrowful, this poor lighthearted idiot filled her breast with thankfulness and love" (355).

It is important to note that Barnaby does not simply inhabit this extraurban natural realm as a preferred alternative to the ugly London depicted by the narrator. Barnaby is, in addition to being a happy observer of the flora and fauna and sunlight, an urban subject, equally attentive to the relations of the people by whom he is surrounded. Barnaby only sees London as a "city which enclosed ... horrors" (526) when the metropolis is overtaken by the violence of the Gordon Riots (1780), at which point that violence also taints Barnaby's experience of the countryside to which he flees:

> Awakened early in the morning, by the sunshine and the songs of birds, and hum of insects, he ... walked into the sweet and pleasant air. But he felt that on his jaded senses, oppressed and burdened with the dreadful scenes of last night, and many nights before, all the beauties of opening day, which he had so often tasted, and in which he had had such deep delight, fell heavily.
>
> (528)

In other words, rather than posing a simple opposition between the human relations of the city (the proper subject of the social novelist) and the natural world of the countryside (a mere "green refuge," as Chase and Levenson have it [131]), in Dickens's early works characters who interpret the world as Barnaby does experience both urban and nonurban worlds fully and as interrelated spaces. In addition, such a character can perceive a fuller urban ecosystem, one that includes the nonhuman. Thus in *The Old Curiosity Shop*, Nell's grandfather (also a sort of "idiot") gains pleasure from urban nature:

> In a small dull yard below his [Nell's grandfather's] window, there was a tree—green and flourishing enough, for such a place—and as the air stirred among its leaves, it threw a rippling shadow on the white wall. The old man sat watching the shadows as they trembled in this patch of light, until the sun went down; and when it was night, and the moon was slowly rising, he still sat in the same spot.
> To one who had been tossing on a restless bed so long, even these few green leaves and this tranquil light, although it languished among chimneys and housetops, were pleasant things. They suggested quiet places afar off, and rest, and peace.
>
> (93)

Dickens's early novels encourage us to read them, and the world they seek to re-present, from the perspective of such non-normative or idiot subjects as Barnaby and Nell's grandfather. Reading these novels in such a way, and not from the perspective of the reader well trained by the social novel and its cultural expectations, is the path to comprehending Dickens's ethical engagement with the nonhuman world.

Reading for animals

Dickens's early novels are especially attentive to the role of animal inhabitants of the environments that we share with them. For example, as another striking counterpoint to the social novelistic depiction of London from

Barnaby Rudge quoted above (with its distant barking dogs seemingly the only animals in the city), *The Old Curiosity Shop* offers this very different panoramic depiction of London:

> The town was glad with morning light; places that had shown ugly and distrustful all night long, now wore a smile; and sparkling sunbeams dancing on chamber windows, and twinkling through blind and curtain before sleepers' eyes, shed light even into dreams, and chased away the shadows of the night. Birds in hot rooms, covered up close and dark, felt it was morning, and chafed and grew restless in their little cells; bright-eyed mice crept back to their tiny homes and nestled timidly together; the sleek house-cat, forgetful of her prey, sat winking at the rays of sun starting through keyhole and cranny in the door, and longed for her stealthy run and warm sleek bask outside. The nobler beasts confined in dens, stood motionless behind their bars, and gazed on fluttering boughs, and sunshine peeping through some little window, with eyes in which old forests gleamed—then trod impatiently the track their prisoned feet had worn—and stopped and gazed again. Men in their dungeons stretched their cramp cold limbs and cursed the stone that no bright sun could warm. The flowers that sleep by night, opened their gentle eyes and turned them to the day. The light, creation's mind, was everywhere, and all things owned its power.
>
> (113–14)

Just as the sunlit countryside delights Barnaby and just as the sunlit London yard gives pleasure to Nell's grandfather, here the rising sun unites a range of inhabitants of the metropolis: birds, mice, housecat, zoo animals, humans, and flowers. The passage carefully balances the sense of renewal that comes with morning sunshine and a less-positive sense of imprisonment, perhaps confirming Chase and Levenson's notions that Dickens's city novels are focused on the plight of "caged urban creatures" (139); yet the creatures here are not only the human inhabitants Chase and Levenson discuss but also caged birds who "chafed and grew restless in their little cells" and the zoo animals whose artificial confinement is poignantly contrasted with the memory of "old forests" which "gleamed" in their eyes. The closely drawn parallel between these "nobler beasts" who "trod impatiently the track their prisoned feet had worn" and the men "in their dungeons" who "stretched their cramp cold limbs and cursed the stone that no bright sun could warm" is profoundly opposed to the anthropocentric view of the difference between the human and the nonhuman that is implicit in characterizations of Dickens as a social novelist. Dickens here opposes the investment in individualism that characterizes the social novel (as described by Cazamian and those who follow him) and that characterizes humanism in Western writing as described by Neil Evernden: "Exterior objects and events were mere stimulants, never the source of meaning. This system of belief would be compatible with the later focus on the individual, and on the person as the sole source of value and purpose, for it makes the human the final authority" (44).

It is also not the case in Dickens's early works that, as John Berger once put it, "animals are always the observed," the "fact that they can observe us" having "lost all significance" (16).[7] Nonhuman inhabitants who receive detailed characterization are often positioned in Dickens's early novels in such a way that they reveal (usually comically) the presumptuous views that humans have about human superiority. As Dickens remarks in the 26 October, 1850 *Household Words* article "Lively Turtle," "man may learn wisdom from the lower animals."[8] The pony in *The Old Curiosity Shop* is a winning case in point. Although the unpleasant Mr. Chuckster "emerged from the office door, and cried 'Woa-a-a-a-a!'—dwelling upon the note a long time, for the purpose of striking terror into the pony's heart, and asserting the supremacy of man over the inferior animals" (283), the novel reveals the futility and fatuousness of such an assertion, and the long-standing superiority of the pony over the human inhabitants with whom he shares his environment: "The pony preserved his character for independence and principle down to the last moment of his life; which was an unusually long one ... He did no work for two or three years before he died, but lived in clover; and his last act (like a choleric old gentleman) was to kick his doctor" (551). As his anthropomorphism ("like a choleric old gentleman") might suggest, Dickens does not treat animals as instances of a radical alterity relative to humans.[9] Rather, Dickens renders human and nonhuman characters as equivalent inhabitants of an environment—and, crucially, equivalent not only physically but also intellectually, as in the case not only of the independent pony in *The Old Curiosity Shop* but also of the raven Grip in *Barnaby Rudge* and other sagacious ravens in Dickens's writings.[10] Commenting on the death of one of his two pet ravens (the models for Grip) in a 12 March, 1841 letter to Daniel Maclise, Dickens remarks that the bird "behaved throughout [his fatal illness] with a decent fortitude, equanimity, and self-possession, which cannot be too much admired" (*Letters* 2: 231). John Ruskin certainly saw the raven Grip as superior to the humans in the novel. Ruskin, commenting on *Barnaby Rudge* (which he disliked) in an 1876 lecture, claimed there were only a few "elements of good, or life, in the filthy mass of the story" and singled out Grip: "The raven, however, like all Dickens's animals, is perfect: and I am the more angry with the rest because I have every now and then to open the book to look for him" (22: 467). As Dickens points out in his 1849 Preface to the Cheap Edition of *Barnaby Rudge*, Grip was "a compound of two great originals, of whom I was, at different times, the proud possessor" (xxiii). Dickens's description of himself as the "possessor" of his pets seemingly reinforces hierarchies that place humans over animals (as does my county's designation of me as the "owner" of the cat and two dogs in my family). However, Dickens goes on to describe his first raven as possessing "good gifts," which "he improved by study and attention in a most exemplary manner" to arrive at "preternatural sagacity," "superiority of … genius," and "acquirements and virtues"; Dickens's second raven (obtained after the first died from eating lead paint) was "older and more gifted," a "Sage" capable of "immense labour and research, to which he devoted all the energies of his mind" (xxiii). Like his first raven, the second one dies after ingesting a perfidious man-made substance, leading Dickens to comment that perhaps each bird was "too bright a genius to live long" (xxiv).

Indeed, in a 11 May, 1850 *Household Words* article titled "From the Raven in the Happy Family," Dickens speaks *as* a raven, places the bird-writer as superior to the humans he addresses, and critiques the view of nature entertained by humans from the Comte de Buffon onwards. "I tell you what. I like the idea of you men, writing histories of *us*, and settling what we are, and what we are not, and calling us any names you like best," the raven correspondent declares: "Now, I am not going to stand this.… I shall put down my opinions about you [humans]. As leisure and opportunity serve, I shall collect a natural history of you … I am open to contributions from any animal except one of your set; bird, beast, or fish, may assist me in my mission, if he will" (156–7). The raven was judged to be a popular enough correspondent that he reappeared in two succeeding issues of *Household Words*, and in a 25 August, 1850 article (also titled "From the Raven in the Happy Family") he finally pits animals against humans by declaring this about the nonhuman collaborators in his natural history of humankind: "I have communicated with plenty of 'em [*sic*], and they are all down upon you" (507). The importance of Grip, Dickens's pets, and the critical raven of *Household Words* reinforces the fact that we should view Dickens as an ecologically minded novelist concerned with the nonhuman at least as much as we view him as a social novelist concerned with the human: not only does Dickens lead his Preface to the 1849 Cheap Edition of *Barnaby Rudge* with a lengthy discussion of Grip and his raven models in the real world, but also Dickens claims an explicitly environmentalist reason for focusing on the raven—his recent reading of Charles Waterton's *Essays on Natural History, Chiefly Ornithology* (1838), which argues, as Dickens notes in the first sentence of his preface, "that ravens are gradually becoming extinct in England" (xxiii).

Dickens and the class Insecta

There are certainly occasions in his early works where Dickens seems to assert the importance of the human over the animal and plant kingdoms, for instance when the narrator of *Oliver Twist* animalizes a villain such as Fagin: "As he glided stealthily along, creeping beneath the shelter of the walls and doorways, the hideous old man seemed like some loathsome reptile, engendered in the slime and darkness through which he moved: crawling forth, by night, in search of some rich offal for a meal" (*OT* 120–21). Yet in his early career Dickens routinely calls into question the supposed centrality of the human, for instance in the regular reminders of how human lives are part of an ecosystemic life cycle no less than the lives of plants, so often treated as a much lower life form. Thus in *The Old Curiosity Shop* Nell and her grandfather, traveling between industrial cities, note that "carts came rumbling by, filled with rude coffins (for contagious disease and death had been busy with the living crops)" (336). Similarly, in *Oliver Twist* the people in the crowd watching Sikes on the rooftop "all waved to and fro, in the darkness beneath, like a field of corn moved by an angry wind" (*OT* 345). At one point in *The Old Curiosity Shop* the narrator moralizes in a manner that subtly proffers a humanist reading of ethical behavior, and then undermines it; describing the "effigies of warriors" in "a baronial chapel," the narrator remarks the "[b]roken and dilapidated" statues that "retained their ancient form, and something of their ancient aspect" (397–8). The narrator's main point here is to critique the pride that erects such monuments to human acts of violence misunderstood as valor: "Thus violent deeds live after men upon the earth, and traces of war and bloodshed will survive in mournful shapes long after those who worked the desolation are but atoms of earth themselves" (398). In order to critique the human presumption weightily represented by the "stark figures on the tombs" (398), this sentence first turns to the humanist tradition, as one would expect in the case of a social novelist concerned with human relations—namely, the narrator invokes the famous eulogy for Julius Caesar delivered by Shakespeare's Marc Antony: "The evil that men do lives after them, / The good is oft interred with their bones" (*Julius Caesar* III, ii, 77–8). Dickens's narrator agrees that the "evil that men do" (specifically, their "violent deeds") lives "after them" (in the form of such "mournful shapes" as those in the chapel, as well as in the form of continuing warfare and other types of violence). Crucially, though, Dickens's narrator elides Marc Antony's second point— that the good men do "is oft interred with their bones" instead offering the profoundly nonhumanist reminder that humans ultimately become "atoms of earth."

The most powerful ecological critique of the humanism implicit in the social novel's focus on human relations, and thus from an ecocritical perspective arguably the most ethically important moment in Dickens's writings,[11] occurs late in *Nicholas Nickleby*. Having squandered his youth under the guidance of the older debauchee Sir Mulberry Hawk, Lord Frederick Verisopht finally shows some spine and objects to Sir Mulberry's lecherous insults to Kate Nickleby, at which point the young aristocrat and his wicked mentor come to blows, and fight a duel:

> Sir Mulberry turned his face towards his young adversary for the first time. He was very pale, his eyes were bloodshot, his dress disordered, and his hair dishevelled. For the face, it expressed nothing but violent and evil passions. He shaded his eyes with his hand; gazed at his opponent, steadfastly, for a few moments; and, then taking the weapon

which was tendered to him, bent his eyes upon that, and looked up no more until the word was given, when he instantly fired.

The two shots were fired, as nearly as possible, at the same instant. In that instant, the young lord turned his head sharply round, fixed upon his adversary a ghastly stare, and, without a groan or stagger, fell down dead.

...

So died Lord Frederick Verisopht, by the hand which he had loaded with gifts, and clasped a thousand times; by the act of him, but for whom, and others like him, he might have lived a happy man, and died with children's faces round his bed.

The sun came proudly up in all his majesty, the noble river ran its winding course, the leaves quivered and rustled in the air, the birds poured their cheerful songs from every tree, the short-lived butterfly fluttered its little wings; all the light and life of day came on; and, amidst it all, and pressing down the grass whose every blade bore twenty tiny lives, lay the dead man, with his stark and rigid face turned upward to the sky.

(*NN* 665–6)

Initially the passage appears to be exemplary of the Victorian realist novel's focus on human social relations: in the frozen moment of time (the words "instantly" and "instant" appear three times total in three consecutive sentences) we are meant to grasp Sir Mulberry's debauchery, evil passions, and expertise where lethal violence is concerned; Lord Frederick's misplaced generosity and friendship; and the life of human social relations he might have lived, "a happy man," up to the prized moment of the Victorian deathbed scene, surrounded by "children's faces." Indeed, the fact that the villain is named Mulberry Hawk—suggesting the wine to which he is addicted, and his predatory nature—might seem to indicate a novelist anthropocentrically inattentive to nature except as metaphor. Yet Dickens undermines all of this—undermines precisely what a social novel by Dickens is supposed to be about—on several levels. The supposedly human-centered alternate life Lord Frederick could have lived as a happy family man is undermined by the fact that the novel *Nicholas Nickleby* is nothing so much as a depiction of failed family relations—most obviously Ralph Nickleby's cruel neglect of his son Smike, enmity to his nephew Nicholas, and pandering of his niece Kate, but also Mrs. Nickleby's incompetence as a parent, Nicholas's inability to aid his sister with anything but violence approaching that of Sir Mulberry, and so forth. More subtly and more powerfully, Dickens undermines the anthropocentric moral with the astonishing concluding paragraph focusing on the majestic sun, noble river, quivering leaves, cheerful birds, and fluttering butterfly: "all the light and life of day came on," utterly oblivious to the "dead man" whose last act—falling down dead—is finally placed not in the context of any human relations, desires, or histories but in the radically nonhuman context of the very precisely enumerated "twenty tiny lives" inhabiting each of the blades of grass pressed down by the body.[12] Dickens's vision of nature here is far more radical than the one in this famous and seemingly similar passage in George Eliot's *Middlemarch: A Study of Provincial Life* (1871–1872): "If we had a keen vision and feeling of all ordinary human life, it would be like hearing the grass grow and the squirrel's heart beat, and we should die of that roar which lies on the other side of silence. As it is, the quickest of us walk about well wadded with stupidity" (189).[13] Although Eliot's amplification of the unheard rest of nature resembles the way Dickens forces us to observe the unseen communities living around us, Eliot's point is really that we fail to see and feel for "all ordinary human life": the squirrel's heartbeat and the growing grass are merely illustrative counterpoints, the minor vehicles to the important tenor of her metaphor, the sounds that, in fact, we are not supposed to hear. By contrast, Dickens's representation of Lord Frederick's death calls attention simultaneously to the natural world's unconcern for human activities, the human's ultimate existence as mere matter, and the failure of the human to attend to vital matters such as the lives being led on the blades of grass. Indeed, Dickens is here akin not so much to George Eliot as to Rachel Carson, who notes that "[m]ost of us walk unseeing through the world, unaware alike of its beauties, its wonders, and the strange and sometimes terrible intensity of the lives that are being lived about us. So it is that the activities of the insect predators and parasites are known to few" (249). Dickens's novel asserts, finally, that the life or death of Lord Frederick Verisopht, or Ralph Nickleby, or any other human inhabitant of the world featuring in the tragic or comic plots of a work such as *Nicholas Nickleby*, is no more or less important than the lives lived on a blade of grass, so small as to be ignored by all but the most ecologically minded novelist and reader.

Notes

1 Although his interest is in the Victorian novel, Cazamian implies that many of his remarks could apply to the novel itself as a generic form: "in one sense, every novel dealing with human customs is a 'social novel'" (7).
2 Although Cazamian frequently uses phrases like "environmental conditions" (5) and "organic ... relationships" (6), his focus is resolutely anthropocentric, "environment" meaning for him exclusively the built and social environment. The only exceptions, where what we would call environmentalist issues creep into Cazamian's analysis, are the brief mentions of the campaigns against animal cruelty (104) and the sanitation reforms that imply industrial pollution (68–70, 104, 253, 273–4), though even in these cases the emphasis is on the human: "statutory suppression of wilful cruelty to animals" reflected humans' "[c]hanging moral standards" (104), and public health reforms showed how "the new middle class" became "vaguely aware that it shared a common interest in hygiene with the proletariat" (68). In the most sustained examination to date of the environmental aspects of the nineteenth-century social novel (including Dickens's *Our Mutual Friend* [1864–1865]), Agnes Kneitz similarly limits herself to a discussion of the effects of environmental degradation on humans, aligning

3 Interestingly, F. S. Schwarzbach has stated that *Dombey and Son* (1846–1848) is "the first of Dickens' novels which can be said without qualification to be a social novel; that is, its primary goal is to depict directly society and social relations" (101). Schwarzbach like many critics thus emphasizes Dickens's later novels as in some way fully realized, the implication being that Dickens all along sought to be a social novelist but that his early works were only qualified successes on this score.
4 This tendency to read human interactions as the ecology of Victorian fictions is noteworthy in works other than Chase and Levenson's. See for instance Richard Kerridge's 2001 essay "Ecological Hardy," which, for all its valuable readings of Hardy, similarly treats human interactions as the ecosystemic order of Hardy's canon: his works are "responsive to ecological concerns, since ecology is the study of relationships and interdependencies within shared local environments," such as interdependencies between characters who "ceaselessly make and remake each other's identity" and between humans and human-made things—"the flow of goods, information, and travelers" (130–1).
5 A refreshingly unsocial analysis of Dickens is provided by Taylor, who argues that *Bleak House* represents anthropogenic climate change specifically as an abstraction that exceeds human understanding, including social understanding, even as it affects human and nonhuman alike. Similarly, in a fascinating study of fictions with dog narrators in the Victorian Period, Mangum (esp. 42–3) argues that their popularity upsets the presumed privilege of the social novel in the period, with its emphasis on the realistic depiction of the problems of class.
6 Fully aware that claims about periodization are risky, I believe one can nevertheless argue that "early Dickens" is more than a mere category of convenience and that his novels before *Martin Chuzzlewit* (1843–1844) share certain affinities of a rising star novelist, though I do not actually plan to make that argument here; the business of this chapter is to show that these early works share a manner of representing nature that has been lost in critical attention directed more generally to Dickens's later novels. An extensive treatment of "early Dickens" as a particular phase in the novelist's career is Bowen. I have decided to treat as "early Dickens" the novels *The Pickwick Papers*, *Oliver Twist*, *Nicholas Nickleby*, *The Old Curiosity Shop*, and *Barnaby Rudge* (dealing briefly with the first two and more substantially with the latter three). In choosing my cut-off novel I share Alexander Welsh's sense that *Martin Chuzzlewit* marks "the time in early middle life" when Dickens arrives at "his sense of identity as a writer of literature" (vii), as indicated for instance by his intensifying wrangles over copyright matters. Of course, it is worth mentioning that large portions of such late-career London novels as *David Copperfield*, *Bleak House*, and *Great Expectations* are set in, respectively, Yarmouth, Lincolnshire, and Kent villages.
7 Jacques Derrida goes so far as to say that what characterizes "*all* philosophers" from Descartes to Levinas is the circumstance that they "have taken no account of the fact that what they call 'animal' could *look at* them, and *address* them from down there, from a wholly other origin" (13).
8 For a cogent summary of the changing norms governing the representation of the human-nonhuman interrelation, see Buell 179–216. In an analysis of paintings of animals (especially pets), Murray Roster has convincingly argued that a new understanding of human–animal relations characterized the Victorian period, in contrast with the eighteenth century: the Victorians were "sensitive to the emotional reciprocity between man and animal, a bond of comradeship and mutual loyalty between owner and animal which lent the latter semi-human qualities" (86).

9 I do not mean to imply, as critics often have, that anthropomorphism is simplistic or ideologically suspect. For an incisive discussion of anthropomorphism as a specifically ethical practice in literature, see Cosslett 181–3 and Knickerbocker 5–6. Cosslett provides a useful corrective to the standard account of how Victorian relations with animals constitute the triumph of anthropocentrism. For a canonical instance of this account, see Ritvo, for whom in the period "animals became significant primarily as the objects of human manipulation" (2).

10 For a discussion of Grip, Dickens's pet ravens, and how they enable us to think about "the limits or ends of the human," see Bowen 164–6. Similarly, Jerome H. Buckley argues that "[w]hereas Grip can approach or simulate human responses, Barnaby seeks to realize the attributes of a bird" and is "essentially a child of nature" (37–8). By contrast, Ritvo offers the rather byzantine argument that, by attributing sagacity to animals, the Victorians "actually reinforced human dominion" (37–8).

11 Ethically important in the terms with which Karl Kroeber defines an "ecological vision": "one that assumes that all human beings bear profound responsibilities toward others, not just other humans, but other life forms—along with their and our habitat" (61).

12 Batra (163) analyzes how, in the poems of Anna Letitia Barbauld, the respect for the life of insects manages to eschew anthropocentric claims for human superiority.

13 Thanks to Alexandra Valint for pointing me towards this quote from Eliot, whose works could use more attention from ecocritics. For a good, brief discussion of how an environmental focus changes standard ways of reading her politics, see Malachuk 370–84.

Works cited

Batra, Nandita. "Dominion, Empathy, and Symbiosis: Gender and Anthropocentrism in Romanticism." *The ISLE Reader: Ecocriticism, 1993–2003.* Ed. Michael P. Branch and Scott Slovic. Athens: U of Georgia P, 2003. 155–72.

Berger, John. *About Looking.* New York: Pantheon, 1980.

Bowen, John. *Other Dickens: Pickwick to Chuzzlewit.* Oxford: Oxford UP, 2000.

Buckley, Jerome H. "'Quoth the Raven': The Role of Grip in *Barnaby Rudge.*" *Dickens Studies Annual* 21 (1992): 27–35.

Buell, Lawrence. *The Environmental Imagination: Thoreau, Nature Writing, and the Formation of American Culture.* Cambridge: Belknap P-Harvard UP, 1995.

Carson, Rachel. *Silent Spring.* 1962. Boston: Houghton, 2002.

Cazamian, Louis. *The Social Novel in England 1830–1850: Dickens, Disraeli, Mrs. Gaskell, Kingsley.* 1903. Trans. Martin Fido. London: Routledge, 1973.

Chase, Karen, and Michael Levenson. "Green Dickens." *Contemporary Dickens.* Ed. Eileen Gilooly and Deirdre David. Columbus: Ohio State UP, 2009. 131–51.

Collins, Philip, ed. *Dickens: The Critical Heritage.* New York: Barnes & Noble, 1971.

Cosslett, Tess. *Talking Animals in British Children's Fiction, 1786–1914.* Aldershot, Hampshire: Ashgate, 2006.

Derrida, Jacques. *The Animal That Therefore I Am.* Ed. Marie-Louise Mallet. Trans. David Wills. New York: Fordham UP, 2008.

Dickens, Charles. *Barnaby Rudge: A Tale of the Riots of 'Eighty.* 1841. Oxford: Oxford UP, 1954.

———. "From the Raven in the Happy Family." *Household Words* 11 May, 1850: 156–8.
———. "From the Raven in the Happy Family." *Household Words* 24 August, 1850: 505–7.
———. *The Letters of Charles Dickens*. Volume 2. Ed. Madeline House, Graham Storey, and Kathleen Tillotson. Oxford: Clarendon, 1969.
———. *The Life and Adventures of Nicholas Nickleby*. 1838–1839. Oxford: Oxford UP, 1950.
———. "Lively Turtle." *Household Words* 26 October, 1850: 97–9.
———. *The Old Curiosity Shop*. 1840–1841. Oxford: Oxford UP, 1951.
———. *Oliver Twist*. 1837–1839. Ed. Kathleen Tillotson. Oxford: Clarendon P, 1966.
———. *The Pickwick Papers*. 1836–1837. Ed. James Kinsley. Oxford: Clarendon P, 1986.
Eliot, George. *Middlemarch*. 1871–1872. Ed. David Carroll. Oxford: Clarendon P, 1986.
Evernden, Neil. *The Social Creation of Nature*. Baltimore: Johns Hopkins UP, 1992.
Freedgood, Elaine. "Realism, Fetishism, and Genocide: 'Negro Head' Tobacco in and Around *Great Expectations*." *Novel: A Forum on Fiction* 36.1 (2002): 26–41.
Head, Dominic. "Ecocriticism and the Novel." *The Green Studies Reader: From Romanticism to Ecocriticism*. Ed. Laurence Coupe. London: Routledge, 2000. 235–41.
Kerridge, Richard. "Ecological Hardy." *Beyond Nature Writing: Expanding the Boundaries of Ecocriticism*. Ed. Karla Armbruster and Kathleen R. Wallace. Charlottesville: UP of Virginia, 2001. 126–42.
Kneitz, Agnes. "'As If the River Was Not Meat and Drink to You!': Social Novels as a Means of Framing Nineteenth-Century Environmental Justice." *ISLE: Interdisciplinary Studies in Literature and Environment* 22.1 (2015): 47–62.
Knickerbocker, Scott. *Ecopoetics: The Language of Nature, the Nature of Language*. Amherst: U of Massachusetts P, 2012.
Kroeber, Karl. *Ecological Literary Criticism: Romantic Imagining and the Biology of Mind*. New York: Columbia UP, 1994.
Leavis, F. R. *The Great Tradition: George Eliot, Henry James, Joseph Conrad*. 1948. Harmondsworth, Middlesex: Penguin, 1962.
Malachuk, Daniel S. "George Eliot's Liberalism." *A Companion to George Eliot*. Ed. Amanda Anderson and Harry E. Shaw. Walden: Wiley-Blackwell, 2013. 370–84.
Mangum, Teresa. "Dog Years, Human Fears." *Representing Animals*. Ed. Nigel Rothfels. Bloomington: Indiana UP, 2002. 35–47.
Miller, D. A. *The Novel and the Police*. Berkeley: U of California P, 1988.
Monod, Sylvère. *Dickens the Novelist*. 1953. Norman: U of Oklahoma P, 1968.
Ritvo, Harriet. *The Animal Estate: The English and Other Creatures in the Victorian Age*. Cambridge: Harvard UP, 1987.
Roster, Murray. *Victorian Contexts: Literature and the Visual Arts*. New York: New York UP, 1996.
Ruskin, John. *The Works of John Ruskin*. Ed. E. T. Cook and Alexander Wedderburn. 39 vols. London: George Allen, 1903–1912.
Schwarzbach, F. S. *Dickens and the City*. London: Athlone P, 1979.

Shakespeare, William. *Julius Caesar*. Ed. T. S. Dorsch. London: Methuen; Cambridge: Harvard UP, 1955.
Taylor, Jesse Oak. "The Novel as Climate Model: Realism and the Greenhouse Effect in *Bleak House*." *Novel: A Forum on Fiction* 46.1 (2013): 1–25.
Welsh, Alexander. *From Copyright to Copperfield: The Identity of Dickens*. Cambridge: Harvard UP, 1987.
Williams, Raymond. *Culture and Society, 1780–1950*. 1958. New York: Columbia UP, 1983.

7 Bleak intra-actions
Dickens, turbulence, material ecology

John Parham

The mid-twentieth-century criticism of writers such as Jerome Hamilton Buckley, Walter Houghton, and Mario Praz established a long-standing narrative about Victorian literary culture: that the Victorians were troubled by the discrepancy between an inherited Romantic idealization of the natural world and rural life, and the "realism" both of new scientific paradigms (evolutionary theory, thermodynamics) and the social, cultural, and environmental impacts of industrialization; and so, consequently, they sought to withdraw. Yet, as has long been recognized, this misattributes both Romanticism and Victorianism. The Victorians shared an understanding of nature's mutability, vitality, and perpetual (re)emergence—in all its social ramifications—with what Eric Wilson, via Coleridge, has called "romantic turbulence." Therefore, one might posit "turbulent materialism" as the concept that unites some of the more recent developments in Victorian literary criticism: new historicism, literature and science, and ecocriticism. In this essay, I will suggest another, "new materialism" or material ecology, a live field of debate that encompasses science, philosophy, literary criticism, feminism, and (material) ecocriticism. This essay will examine what Victorian literature, Dickens, and *Bleak House* can tell us in terms of analyzing, representing, and living within a human material ecology.

Parameters of material ecology

The main dimensions to this new ecological materialism can be formulated as:

1. Jane Bennett's notion of "thing power";
2. The "materiality of the social" (see Tuana 210); and
3. "Trans-corporeality" (see Alaimo).

I will consider each in turn.

Matter is not passive; it has agency. That is a view captured both by Bruno Latour's notion of the "actant"—"something that acts [not necessarily human] or to which activity is granted by others"—and Bennett's "thing power." Bennett's underlying thesis in *Vibrant Matter* is that nonhuman things have an ability to "act as quasi agents or forces with trajectories, propensities, or tendencies of their own" (viii). Much of her emphasis falls on debris (dirt, rubbish, and waste products). She argues that such phenomena, which we have got used to ignoring, have increasingly become transformed into "stuff that commanded attention in its own right, as existents in excess of their association with human meanings, habits, or projects" (4). This affective power in "things" could of course be applied (as in the eco-phenomenology of David Abram) to the attention elicited by (say) mountains, forests, birds, or, for that matter, birds' nests. However, roughly paralleling the Victorians' shift from post-Romantic idealism to dark immersion in social critique, Bennett's focus encapsulates an ecologically apposite emphasis on material entanglements we would like to ignore, but ought to confront. This takes on perhaps its most sinister element when she describes the ongoing vitality of things that remain active long after their initial function has been fulfilled—waste products, by-products, garbage, residue, contaminants, run off, and the like.

Writers on material ecology have emphasized waste, dirt, and pollutants in order to alert us to how human and social networks, of whose pervasive presence we are all too aware—economic, political, cultural, and scientific (see Alaimo 20)—are themselves embedded in matter as well as to the urgency with which, in the face of apparent ecological crisis, we must now confront this. Consequently, the second key element determining this new ecological materialism is what Nancy Tuana has called the "materiality of the social" (210), a "viscous porosity" by which the agency of nonhuman things seeps into human society and human being. This she illustrates via Hurricane Katrina. The concept that most clearly articulates this has been Karen Barad's notion of the material "intra-actions" (128) that connect all entities. Given the pervasiveness of industrial and technological modes, the impacts of climate change, or the manacles of environmental justice, those intra-actions are, indeed, often bleak. Moreover, Barad's preference of *intra* over "*inter*action" develops the principle that human selves cannot be extricated from the networks of matter in which we are entangled—matter embodying, infecting, and inseminating us. This view carries over into the final, underlying principle of this new ecological materialism.

Stacy Alaimo gives literal body to new materialism through the concept of "trans-corporeality," the movement of matter across bodies and the understanding that we are constituted of the matter that passes through us. Here, again, environmental and ecological risk scenarios concocted by the contemporary world confront us with our own "trans-corporeality" just as the industrial and social risks of Victorian society had done. Not unconnected to Bennett's "thing power," "trans-corporeality" takes on its own sinister element in relation to the toxicity arising from contemporary life. This is captured in Alaimo's anecdote about participating in a Greenpeace campaign in which people were asked to send in a sample of their hair to be tested for mercury contamination. Having done this, she acquired disturbing data that measured "the toxicity of one's own body" and rendered "palpable one's own corporeal connection to global economic, industrial, and environmental systems" (19–20). This, then, is what the new materialism tells us: that matter, the power of "things" seeps into every juncture of ecological connection—from the Great Pacific Garbage Patch to the strands of our own hair—and that it does so with often toxic consequences.

Social and literary material ecologies

Indicating that the material (and often toxic) power of things partially arises from economic and industrial systems, Alaimo signifies a dialectical relationship between material and social ecologies. Arguably sometimes obscured in discussions about the new materialism, Lucy Bell reminds us that the "materiality of the social" is "inseparable from the sociality of the material." Therefore, while "thing power" and Barad's "intra-action" are essential insights in qualifying anthropocentric paradigms that have themselves created ecological risk, we ought nevertheless to remember that political ideologies, and economic and societal practices, also create these material entanglements that, at times, can rebound upon us. Bell, moreover, reminds us of at least two further dimensions to this dual material–social ecology.

First, and to the forefront of Alaimo's "trans-corporeality," are the environmental injustices by which contemporary societies' increasingly toxic and risky material ecologies rebound disproportionately on the poor. To illustrate, Bell draws on Zygmunt Bauman's book *Wasted Lives*, forging an all too real ecological connection. Bauman describes two interconnected problems: human lives cast aside as the "waste" products of modernity, and the "acute crisis of the human waste disposal industry" (6). Problems that "weigh ever more heavily on the liquid modern, consumerist culture of individualization," they are partially solved, he suggests, by delegating waste disposal to those people and places (whether the indigenous poor, displaced migrants, or backwaters of globalization) that are, themselves, the human "waste" of modernity. There is, then, literal, perilous, and toxic material intra-action for those humans subsisting as "slumdogs" in India, for villagers in places such as Giuyu, China, now junkyards for electronic goods (Bauman 59–60), or, in Bell's example, the rubbish pickers (*catadores*) in South America. Second, for all that, Bell argues, the material agency of waste might "productively be utilised by a corresponding *human* agency." Hence, her essay discusses Latin American *editoriales cartoneras*, small, independent publishing houses which, by making books out of recycled cardboard, enhance, alike, biophysical sustainability, the economic sustainability of the people who collect and sell the waste cardboard, and cultural sustainability (by increasing very low public reading levels).

Regarded, in part, as a reaction to critical theory, new historicism, the "linguistic turn," or poststructuralism, ecocriticism in general has been reminding us of our material being. Understood as a dialectic between matter and sociality, material ecology does not so much reverse the "linguistic turn," replacing discourse with matter, as connect them. Matter and discourse intra-act, they shape each other (Iovino and Oppermann 454); this has been the central insight of '"material ecocriticism." The turbulent play of matter and discourse offers a niche, in other words, for literature to underline our understanding of humans' materiality (see Iovino and Oppermann 469–70). Considered in relation to a contemporary stress on toxic or risky materiality we can see this, for example, in Susan Signe Morrison's suggestive notion of a "waste aesthetics" wherein "literature enables culture to acknowledge what it has to deny, such as ... bodily, cultural and societal waste—material and metaphorical aspects of our world" (464). The ubiquity of "waste," in all these dimensions, is central in several of Dickens's works, for instance *Our Mutual Friend*, a novel which I have examined elsewhere (see Parham "Dickens in the City"). *Bleak House*, though, confronts these matters directly, and in so doing, also addresses two caveats that might be raised about material ecocriticism in its still, admittedly, embryonic stage: first, that it has not really dealt with *affect*. Not much has been put forward, for example, in terms of literary models that might help shape a sense of our material ecology; second, that material ecocriticism has remained ahistorical and/or fixed in the (contemporary) moment.

Iovino and Opperman have suggested that "Material ecocriticism is not committed to a specific literary genre" and that an examination of literary texts in order to understand our material ecology should be "something more than a critical correlate of toxic narratives" (459). Certainly, a use of language, discourse, and literature to articulate a phenomenological sense of our material connection with the nonhuman can be found, as they attest, in the nature writing of David Abram (459) or, as Jonathan Bate has argued, in poetry (258). Indeed, poetry could be particularly effective in conveying the immediacy or shock of a toxic trans-corporeal moment. Nonetheless, extended narratives, such as the novel, do seem fitted for embodying and (as much as possible) disentangling the complex intra-actions between social, economic, and political forces, and matter.

"Thing power" and the transmissions that constitute our trans-corporeality are invisible or barely perceptible, intricate, and complex. As such, this might suit the fragmentations and unexpected connections that characterize postmodern fiction (see Iovino and Oppermann). Yet, as Dominic Head has pointed out, the classic realist novel also has "complex layerings" and "pointed textuality" (66). Hence, it is similarly equipped to capture the "viscous porosity" that only ever partially separates humans from their environment. Writing about Disraeli and Gaskell, I have argued that the Victorian "condition of England" novels of the 1840s and 1850s "allowed for subtle, complex representation of the ecological realities governing human existence ... the dialectical relation of political economy, society and physical environment" (Parham, "'For You'" 26). This arose, though, as Catherine Gallagher has pointed out, from these novelists being informed by a "bioeconomic" perspective that saw political economy in terms of the relation/interconnection of food supply, production, and exchange with matter and nonhuman life (see Gallagher 3). Gallagher goes on to suggest that bioeconomics was articulated via what she calls a "somaeconomics"—"emotional and sensual feelings that are both causes and consequences of economic exertions" (3). In literary terms, this gave rise, I would argue, to a principally affective mode of response—poetic inflections intra-acting with the narrative weave of the novel form. This is precisely the mode one might expect to be triggered by a perception of "thing power" heightened and haunted by a sharp (bioeconomic) awareness of human material ecology, perceptions that compel some kind of narrative untangling and clear-sighted response. Indeed, such a "waste aesthetic" seems particularly applicable to Dickens. For his melodramatic narratives dabble incessantly with the dark presence of an intangible, spectral, and menacing materiality in everyday life.

This parallel between Victorian literary culture and contemporary material ecology is not so much coincidental as evidential. The Victorians swam in intellectual currents that preceded contemporary ecologism. The immersion of novelists and poets in the new paradigms of evolutionary theory and energy physics, as extensively documented in research on Victorian literature and science, enabled them to anticipate the scientific ecological paradigm that slowly formed throughout the nineteenth century (Ernst Haeckel coined the word "ecology" in 1866). "So far," that is, "as Victorian writers were interested in science they were interested in precisely those components—evolutionary theory and thermodynamics—that would come to form ecological science" (Parham, *Green Man* 64). Yet, the interest was riven by anxiety. And while the more brutal dimensions of evolution and the discovery of the second law of thermodynamics (entropy) darkened an inherited theological and/or Romantic attention to nature, this was heightened by a perception of the risks being created by a new, toxic industrialism.

Christopher Hamlin notes, "Putrefying matter claimed a great deal of attention in mid-Victorian cities." "Enormous accumulations of rotting matter—in stagnant sewers and cesspools, in heaps of garbage and excrement, in churchyards so packed with bodies that corpse-parts continually surfaced" generated an anxiety that dwelled on trans-corporeal intra-actions and, ultimately, health (93–4). Indeed, as Bruce Haley puts it in *The Healthy Body and Victorian Culture*, no topic more occupied the Victorian mind because, for the Victorians, "the body was the summation of all the constituents and properties of the organism, including their individual relations to the total environment" (19). It does not take much, then, to figure out that Victorian writers understood and had the language to describe material entanglement. Hence, Hamlin's conclusion, that the

Victorians' fascination with decomposing matter indicates an "environmental sensitivity that has been insufficiently appreciated" leads us to conclude that this encompassed an anticipation of the central insights of the "new" ecological materialism.

Dickens's material ecology

Dickens's interest in science was, in many ways, patchy, passing, and often aesthetic or metaphorical in nature. Nevertheless, that interest has been underestimated. He was, as I have argued elsewhere, sufficiently grounded in evolutionary theory and energy physics for it to be suggested that a proto-ecological perspective flavored Dickens's observations and commentaries where these focused on the Victorian environment ("Dickens in the City" 4–9). Those observations took (as will be no surprise) a social turn. Aggravated by his scathing critique of and anxieties about Victorian industrial political economy, these were likewise impelled by an attentiveness to matter, invariably the pollution and putrefaction that Hamlin describes.

Dickens's perception of material ecology was captured by his interest in miasma theory. According to the UK Science Museum's online definition (accompanied by an image from a Glasgow street in 1868), miasma theory postulated disease caused by "the presence in the air of miasma, a poisonous vapour in which were suspended particles of decaying matter ... characterised by its foul smell" ("Miasma Theory"). Exemplifying both "thing power" and "intra-action," Dickens spoke about miasma in speeches and, here drawing on the authority of science, in *Dombey and Son*: "Those who study the physical sciences, and bring them to bear upon the health of Man, tell us that if the noxious particles that rise from vitiated air were palpable to the sight, we should see them lowering in a dense black cloud above such haunts" (738). The Science Museum web page notes that, ultimately, miasma theory was disproved and displaced by germ theory, but the theory had been valuable in instigating improvements to housing, sanitation, and health. Hamlin, likewise, suggests that the Victorians addressed the health ramifications of putrefying matter via a new "civic gospel" (94) of waste disposal, sanitation, and environmental improvement, that recognized "ecological problems in the most fundamental sense" (123). Ultimately, Dickens's engagement with material ecology was itself centered around sanitation. While he may have been wrong about the scientific particulars (of miasma), his instincts were right.

His engagement with material ecology took three interrelated forms. The first was practical campaigning. In 1850 and 1851, Dickens spoke to the Metropolitan Sanitary Association and worked alongside Sir Edwin Chadwick in campaigning to bring London into the provisions of the 1848 Public Health Act. The second was a commitment to raise awareness about the issue of poor sanitation, notably in his magazine *Household Words*, which ran from 1850 to 1859. Prior to its launch, Dickens wrote, "I hope to be able to do the Sanitary cause good service, in my new periodical" (*Letters* 6: 18–19). This, he did. For instance, as evidence of the editorial control that Dickens exerted over the journal, the editors of a collection of his contributions to it note two occasions on which Dickens intervened on behalf of the "sanitary cause." In 1854, as cholera raged through England and Wales, Dickens, on holiday in France, was so "ashamed" by what he took to be the "frivolous" content of two recent editions of *Household Words* that he hastily penned a piece for the next issue that entreated laborers to campaign for better sanitary conditions (*Letters* 7: 421). In the same year, he commissioned and then amended an article on sanitation, "A Home Question," actually written by Henry Morley, who had been recruited on the strength of his own writings about sanitation (Dickens, *Uncollected Writings* 1: viii–ix; 2: 656). And, in November 1854, *Household Words* published Morley's "People's Charter" which advocated properly constructed housing, the abolition of cesspools, and "a constant and unlimited supply of wholesome water" (see *Letters* 7: 436). The main phase of Dickens's interest in and activity around sanitation also broadly coincided with the composition and publication of *Bleak House*. And so, the literary novel was the final way in which Dickens engaged not just with sanitation but material ecology more generally.

Material ecology in *Bleak House*

For Dickens, sensible always to the turbulence of nature and society, the perception of "thing power" was second nature. What he perceived in the countryside and the city took different forms, though, up to a point. The environment around Lord and Lady Dedlock's country house, Chesney Wold in Lincolnshire, is verdant, mature, and abundant with a "wholesome growth" that "made the whole air [around] a great nosegay" (228); goodness permeated and shaped the house itself, signifiers of wealth, such as "old stone balustrades and parapets" and "wide flights of shallow steps," all "seamed by time and weather" (471). Yet, even here, the power of nonhuman things to permeate the human, of society to be reflected in matter, was not entirely "wholesome." Wet land, moist air, plentiful rain, begat "stagnant" ground water, seemingly stand as metaphor for the Dedlocks' fading aristocratic power. The nearby church is "mouldy," its "oaken pulpit breaks out into a cold sweat" (7–8), while "the cold and damp" stole in to the house itself (357).

Nevertheless, in the city, this power of things was more pronounced and literal. Indicative of a certain genteel squalor, the Jellybys' rooms have a "marshy smell" (36) while the solicitor, Vholes, lives in "an earthy cottage situated in a damp garden at Kennington" (509). His office, moreover, testifies to a civilization putrefying in the matter it consumes: "A smell as of unwholesome sheep, blending with the smell of must and dust, is referable to the nightly (and often daily), consumption of mutton fat in candles, and to the fretting of parchment forms and skins in greasy drawers" (502). Often, this power of things remained a mystery. The "street mud" collects in London but "is made of nobody knows what, and collects about us nobody knows whence or how" (124). In turn, specters haunt the Victorian mind. Shortly before discovering the store-keeper Krook's death by spontaneous combustion, the clerks, Guppy and Jobling (or Weevle), sense an environment "haunted by the ghosts of sound—strange cracks and tickings, the rustling of garments that have no substance in them, and the tread of dreadful feet that would leave no mark on the sea-sand or the winter snow" (414–15). Lurking beneath the material is the (barely perceptible) immaterial—the damp, smells, infections, and diseases whose consequences we cannot see. In *Bleak House*, Dickens is attempting to read and unravel the complex turbulence of these intra-actions.

What becomes immediately apparent, also, is the materiality of the social. Colored by Dickens's concern with miasma, the repository, in many ways, of this intra-action is the air, the atmosphere. Esther Summerson seeks out Lincolnshire, and the opportunity to be "in the fresh air all day long," as she convalesces from the fever (462). Conversely, before Guppy and Jobling's discovery of Krook's remains they routinely assume that the soot, greasiness, closeness, and foul taste of the air are pollution (408, 413). Such an identification of the air with the bleak intra-actions that characterize the novel is, of course, established at the very beginning of the book: "Smoke lowering down from chimney-pots, making a soft black drizzle, with flakes of soot in it as big as full-grown snow-flakes—gone into mourning, one might imagine, for the death of the sun" (1) gives way to an extended description of the fog (i.e., smog) as inescapably "everywhere" (1). It "rolls" across "the waterside pollutions of a great (and dirty) city"; it "flows among green aits and meadows"; it can be found "cruelly pinching the toes and fingers" of a boat's apprentice boy, "hovering in the rigging of great ships," "creeping" into "the cabooses of collier-brigs," and the tobacco of the boat's skipper. Dickens describes the smog as actant. Knowingly, he captures its agency in the continual use of active verbs: "rolls," "flows," "lowering," "making," "creeping," "hovering."

The pervasive and visceral way in which Dickens describes the movement and agency of things marks, as I have suggested elsewhere, not so much an environmental as an ecological mode of description ("Dickens in the City" 11). The agency of matter exerts itself not *on* or *around*, but *in/to* the ground or the air, and onto animals and humans. These intra-actions are trans-corporeal. The fog, for instance, ultimately makes its way into "the eyes and throats of ancient Greenwich pensioners, wheezing by the firesides of their wards" (1). Analyzing the ecological connotations of junk, Marland and Parham have argued that there are two dimensions to the inescapable materiality of human being: our embodiment in the materiality of the social and our existential condition, the fact that we humans are all mortal and "will all ... be reduced to junk" (1–8). As elements of the book's trans-corporeal perspective, Dickens highlights both these in *Bleak House*. The latter we find, for instance, in his description of Tulkinghorn's office. Here, the "lowering magazine of dust" (another actant) signifies an active force, "the universal article into which his papers and himself, and all his clients, and all things of the earth, animate and inanimate, are resolving" (280). This extended sense that human mortality resides in our trans-corporeal intra-actions with matter arrives with the observation that even the Dedlocks cannot escape. The cold and damp that steals into Chesney Wold can "eke into Sir Leicester's bones"—even with central heating, cushioned doors, screens, and curtains—but, more to the point, "the levelling process of dying" is "communicated" through the family bloodline via hereditary gout (200–1). Notwithstanding that, what ultimately is made clear in *Bleak House* is that the extent to which our trans-corporeal connection to the materiality of the social, our likelihood of being "junked," is closely connected to the extent of our exposure to socially determined waste matter.

Dickens's description of this takes many forms, from the Greenwich pensioners to Phil Squod, disfigured externally, in the face, and internally, in his throat, by a life working in factories. Yet, more than anything, our trans-corporeal connections are forged in the air, most notably in the "fever" infusing the streets. While not exclusively so, exposure to the "fever" is proportionate to social class. For instance, taken, in the course of a police enquiry, to the slum street of Tom-all-Alone's, Mr. Snagsby, the law stationer, has never seen anywhere like it. He "passes along the middle of a villainous street, undrained, unventilated, deep in black mud and corrupt water—though the roads are dry elsewhere—and reeking with such smells and sights that he, who has lived in London all his life, can scarce believe his senses" (285). Feeling as though he has descended to Hell, in "a dream of horrible faces," Snagsby encounters "the fever coming up the street," in the shape of a "shabby palanquin" borne towards them. His companion, Inspector Bucket, tells him: "the people 'have been down by dozens,' and have been carried out, dead and dying, 'like sheep with the rot'" (285). A central component to *Bleak House* is, then, environmental injustice, the extent to which this material ecology rebounds disproportionately on the poor.

Early in the novel, Esther encounters London for the first time and notices "extraordinary creatures in rags, secretly groping the swept-out rubbish for pins and other refuse" (44). Yet, this observation of the social *environment* of London is supplemented, increasingly thereafter, by a more *ecological* sense of matter permeating down through social life and into the dwellings, things, and bodies of the people themselves. Shortly after, moving in the philanthropic circles that Dickens derides, Esther encounters a brickmaker telling Mrs. Pardiggle that his daughter is, indeed, washing in dirty water. "Smell it! That's wot we drinks. How do you like it, and what do you think of gin, instead!" His place is "nat'rally" dirty and "onwholesome"; five of his children have died in infancy: "better for them, and for us besides" (98).

The epitome, however, of "wasted" life, around which the depiction of environmental injustice turns, is Jo, the crossing-sweeper. Jo is the victim of thing power and social power alike. He lives in the "black, dilapidated street" of "Tom-all-Alone's":

> Now, these tumbling tenements contain, by night, a swarm of misery. As, on the ruined human wretch, vermin parasites appear, so these ruined shelters have bred a crowd of foul existence that crawls in and out of gaps in walls and boards; and coils itself to sleep, in maggot numbers, where the rain drips in; and comes and goes, fetching and carrying fever, and sowing more evil in its every footprint …
> (237)

As "foul" things fetch and carry the fever that will afflict Jo he is, more broadly, caught in the forces of the city. Illiterate, Jo's "whole material and immaterial life is wonderfully strange" (203); he is estranged. Jo perceives that he is regarded as no better than an animal. As Dickens narrates and so deciphers, what he deciphers, in Bauman's sense, is Jo as "waste": "To be hustled, and jostled, and moved on; and really to feel that it would be perfectly true that I have no business, here, or there, or anywhere" (203). The materiality of the social—spanning from the largely benevolent nature that "seams" Chesney Wold to the malevolent infections and diseases running through the air, and masonry and bodies of the city—does not just illustrate "thing power" or even the consequences of carelessly flaunting thing power. What it illustrates is the force, also, of social power. The materiality of the social remains a social materiality; human actants shape the political economy and, so, the physical environment in which other human lives, other human bodies dwell.

Following the revelation that Lady Dedlock is her mother, Esther's apprehensiveness about her past and future seems to be experienced through the prism of "thing power." The "balustrades and parapets … seamed by time and weather" are replaced, as she proceeds along "long lines of dark windows," by "eccentric shapes, where old stone lions and grotesque monsters bristled outside dens of shadow, and snarled at the evening gloom over the escutcheons they held in their grip" (471–2). What she experiences are the hidden social forces—spectral but tangible, as real (ultimately) as thing power—that shape her social being. Revealing the source of these strange intra-actions is the stuff of Dickens's novel, as becomes clear in the question, pivotal to *Bleak House*, that he poses ahead of a description of Jo:

> What connexion can there be, between the place in Lincolnshire, the house in town, the Mercury in powder, and the whereabouts of Jo the outlaw with the broom, who had that distant ray of light upon him when he swept the churchyard-step? What connexion can there have been between many people in the innumerable histories of this world,

who, from opposite sides of great gulfs, have, nevertheless, been very curiously brought together!

(202)

The answer, implied in what follows, is that much of this connection is forged by the "fine gentlemen in office" personified as Lord Coodle, Sir Thomas Doodle, the Duke of Foodle—and others of their ilk (202). Likewise, at the start of the novel, the matter pervading London—smog and mud and gas—never lies as deep, Dickens writes, as the "High Court of Chancery, most pestilent of hoary sinners" (2). Thing power is often, if not always, generated and exacerbated by the power of people.

Dickens and beyond

The "material turn" in the humanities has sharpened our awareness of the fundamental, dialectical precepts of material ecology: that the social world is never rid of the materiality that underpins human life; but also that human material being, in particular times and places, is always (in part) socially wrought. While that awareness has been facilitated and forwarded by the perception of environmental crisis, and, in an intellectual sense, by neat formulae such as Barad's material "intra-action," Alaimo's trans-corporeality, or, what is perhaps material ecology's most arresting insight, Bennett's "thing power," in many ways Dickens's legacy has always encompassed a representation of the insights of material ecology.

Dickens's images and melodramatic narratives constitute a powerful lure for readers, now as then. Correspondingly, the Dickensian connection between the dirt, waste, pollutants of modern Victorian cities, and those cities' "wasted" human lives, signifies a flipside to modernization that has seeped into national and indeed global cultural traditions offering a touchstone for a strikingly visceral, materialist critique of environmental injustice. I am reminded constantly of Dickens, for instance, in watching what has been called "New Chinese Cinema" (see Lu and Mi). Films such as Jia Zhangke's *Still Life* (2006) or Ye Lou's *Suzhou River* (2000) parallel environmental or ecological corrosion (the filth, in the latter, of Shanghai's principal river) with the human waste of forcible removal, displacement, and homelessness that occurs (in *Still Life*) because of the Three Gorges Dam Project in Hubei Province. Likewise, Dickens shadows the British "punk poetry" of John Cooper Clarke that embodies the inner-city environment of Salford, Manchester where he grew up in the 1950s and 1960s. Having, in his own words, inherited a Victorian perspective (Parham "Flowers" 128), Cooper Clarke developed a spoken-word version of the punk aesthetic—notably a sharp, harsh, and aggressively regional accent— to articulate the duality of material conditions (dirt, disease, and decay) and social injustice that literally amounted, in Salford, to environmental health risk (134). A further, more uplifting example, analogous with Bell's essay, is the documentary *Waste Land* (2010).

Waste Land concerns a project by the Brazilian artist Vik Muniz with the *catadores* in Rio de Janeiro. Patricia Yeagar has described Muniz's work as a "queer ecology ... where the distinction between organism and environment disappears" (qtd. in Iovino and Oppermann 460–1). In the film, Muniz speaks about a previous project on the island of St. Kitts. Noting a discrepancy between the happy children of what, superficially, was an island paradise and their weary, careworn parents, and keen to isolate what had effected this sad transformation from childhood to adulthood, Muniz says that he found the cause in the sixteen-hour shifts the parents were working on the sugar plantations. Identifying this, then, as the work of sugar ("the sweetness is taken from the children") he formed the children from that substance in his art. "Transformation ... is the stuff of art," Muniz tells us, the "transforming [of] material into an idea." In *Waste Land,* he describes his motivation, similarly, as being "able to change the lives of a group of people with the same material that they deal with everyday." So, Muniz re-made canonical artworks, often religious paintings such as Jacques-Louis David's *Death of Marat*, out of the recyclable materials (glass, plastics, and metal) that the *catadores* gathered every day. The works drew attention, that is, to the material realities in which its human subjects are framed, while the project, at the same time, achieved social transformation, raising money to dignify, humanize, and transform the *catadores*' lives.

Muniz's example turns us towards the final consideration of this essay. If Dickens has assisted in bequeathing to global culture an awareness of our material ecology, how might a novel such as *Bleak House* likewise serve the associated, pragmatic intentions which, at the same time, were motivating Dickens's social campaigning? Dickens sometimes used *Household Words* to issue entreaties to others to do what they can, according to their means. The piece written in the wake of the cholera epidemic, "To Working Men," explicitly posits "wasted" lives, in referring to working families beset by "sickliness and pain," "imperfect development and premature decay," and being "set aside as food for pestilence." Dickens pressed laborers to campaign politically for better sanitary conditions but also exhorted journalists to "set themselves in earnest to improve the towns in which they live, and to amend the dwellings of the poor." If they failed in this duty they would be "guilty, before GOD, of wholesale murder." On that basis, it seems a fair assumption that Dickens regarded his novels in the same way and that, apparently, is corroborated when he writes, in the same article, of seeking "to turn Fiction to the good account of showing the preventible [sic] wretchedness and misery in which the mass of people dwell" (169). In that light, there are three ways in which *Bleak House* might have addressed the material problems—pollution, social injustice, and urban health—that it raises.

The first would be to posit governance and regulation as a solution. Graham Storey has written that while Dickens can be seen, in the 1840s and early 1850s, as "a politically progressive radical," he gradually "regressed" from this to become increasingly "authoritarian and exasperated" and cynical about government (67). While his period of radicalism would seem, just about, to encompass *Bleak House*, the stereotyping of establishment in the figures of Coodle, Doodle, Foodle, and others, coupled with broadsides at Parliament in "To Working Men," clearly suggests that by this stage exasperation had set in.

A second possibility returns us to the question of agency. Bell posits that the *catadores*-affiliated publishing houses of Latin America reverse both Bauman's conception of "wasted lives" and Bennett's "thing power" by harnessing material agency to a newfound human agency. Dickens, seemingly, flirts with a loosely related and more negative manifestation of this through Jo. Jo may be caught in the power of both things and the city, but his own "connection" to the rest of society is enacted as his disease passes up the rungs of society. Temporarily rescued via Esther's intervention, his disease passes first to Charley, Esther's maid, then to Esther herself. Disfigured by the illness, Esther prevents it from reaching her friend and confidante Ada, and, one might suggest, her guardian, John Jarndyce. The disease is stopped, that is, with the housekeeper (Esther) rather than with Jarndyce or his legal ward (Ada). These trans-corporeal networks seem also to have a social correspondence. Shortly before Jo's encounter with Lady Dedlock, Dickens compares him—in a trope of "wasted" human life—to a dog, but warns: "Turn that dog's descendants wild, like Jo, and in a very few years they will so degenerate that they will lose even their bark—but not their bite" (204). And yet, beyond Esther's disfigurement, the latent agency attributed to human "waste" remains largely unconsummated. Unable to escape the institutional forces (police and church) that persecute him, Jo succumbs to the fever and dies. The very limited agency which he has had, that which infects and scars Esther, he even recoils himself from, mortified at having damaged her.

In dwelling, nevertheless, upon the implications of the underlying threat, Dickens points the novel in a third direction. That direction had been signaled in *Dombey and Son*, where he ends the passage quoted earlier ("Those who study the physical sciences ...") by suggesting that the "noxious"' air of a social miasma would roll "slowly on to corrupt the better portions of a town." Furthermore, "if the moral pestilence that rises with them, and in the eternal laws of outraged Nature, is inseparable from them, could be made discernible too, how terrible the revelation. Then we should see depravity, impiety, drunkenness, theft, murder, and a long train of nameless sins ..." (738). Implied here is an "inseparable" material connection between an "outraged Nature" and a moral and social degeneration that will activate "terrible consequences" for the "better portions" of society. That danger, though, is even more explicitly spelled out in *Bleak House*:

> There is not a drop of Tom's corrupted blood but propagates infection and contagion somewhere. It shall pollute, this very night, the choice stream ... There is not an atom of Tom's slime, not a cubic inch of any pestilential gas in which he lives, not one obscenity or degradation about him, not an ignorance, not a wickedness, not a brutality of his committing, but shall work its retribution, through every order of society.
>
> (662)

Considered through Jo, "retribution" might mean, here, social revolution or trans-corporeal infection. Assuming either, one might interpret Dickens as indulging his readers' fears of the "lower" classes. That wasn't his intention, as we can gather from his social activism and the numerous speeches and articles that Dickens addressed to the "working man." Yet, because he did, ultimately, lack faith in the agency of the working class or dispossessed, Dickens largely deployed his narrative towards prompting us, his readers, to confront our own culpability and, thereafter, modify our practices. While aiming to alleviate the threats described above, this was also, genuinely, an attempt to repair society's material ecology.

Principally, this is enacted through Esther whose role, for much of the novel, is housekeeper. Writing about Marilynne Robinson's novel *Housekeeping*, Hannes Bergthaller contests the somewhat obvious ecological analogy often drawn from "housekeeping"—of extending "the traditional sphere of domesticity" towards tending the environment (84). Rejecting, explicitly, a non-turbulent Romanticism, he argues that because of its dynamism and fluidity nature can never be our home. However, "this does not excuse us from the task of keeping house—of defining and sustaining a meaningful relation to our natural environment" (96). Bergthaller goes on to suggest language as the most suitable tool for that task, precisely because, like nature, it is fluid in its discursiveness. In just this way, Dickens, in *Bleak House*, revolves, examines, revolves, and re-examines the complex intra-actions by which matter, society, and human lives are woven together. Yet, ultimately, "Esther's narrative" broadly stitches (keeps) the novel together. And what, in this context, her character represents is the necessity of acting, however hesitant and contingent those actions might be, towards developing material *and* social ties that nurture rather than wither human and nonhuman life.

Conclusion

This essay has argued for the provisional, double-edged but, nonetheless, profound and useful nature of the Victorians' anticipation of contemporary ecological paradigms. Focusing on "material ecology," *Bleak House* demonstrates that, however turbulent human ecology is, and however contingent analyses and remedies may be, the imbrication of our existence in both material and social intra-actions is all too real. Rather than withdrawing from the social, ecological, existential turbulence of new Victorian "realism," Dickens confronted it. In doing so, he forged a literature that, in novels such as *Bleak House*, cajoled "culture to acknowledge what it has to deny" and which, at least implicitly, conscripts us, his modern-day readers, to assume agency with regard to our own social and material ecologies. Only by doing so might we remove the modern day equivalents of Dickens's characters from the mire as well as the mercury from our bloodstream.

Works cited

Alaimo, Stacy. *Bodily Natures: Science, Environment, and the Material Self*. Bloomington: Indiana UP, 2008.

Barad, Karen. "Posthumanist Performativity: Towards an Understanding of How Matter Comes to Matter." *Material Feminisms*. Ed. Stacy Alaimo and Susan Hekman. Bloomington: Indiana UP, 2008. 120–57.

Bate, Jonathan. *The Song of the Earth*. London: Picador, 2000.

Bauman, Zygmunt. *Wasted Lives. Modernity and its Outcasts*. Cambridge: Polity Press, 2004.

Bell, Lucy. "Recycling Materials, Recycling Lives: Cardboard Publishers in Latin America." *Literature and Sustainability: Exploratory Essays*. Ed. Adeline Johns-Putra, John Parham, and Louise Squire. Manchester: Manchester UP, forthcoming 2016. [Quotes are from unpublished draft.]

Bennett, Jane. *Vibrant Matter: A Political Ecology of Things*. Durham: Duke UP, 2010.

Bergthaller, Hannes. "Like a Ship to be Tossed: Emersonian Environmentalism and Marilynne Robinson's *Housekeeping*." *Culture, Creativity and Environment: New Environmentalist Criticism*. Ed. Fiona Becket and Terry Gifford. Amsterdam: Rodopi, 2007. 75–97.

Dickens, Charles. *Bleak House*. London: Penguin Popular Classics, 1994.

——. *Dombey and Son*. Ed. Peter Fairclough. London: Penguin, 1985.

——. *The Letters of Charles Dickens*. Ed. Graham Storey et al. 12 vols. Oxford: Clarendon, 1965–2002.

——. "To Working Men." *Household Words*, 7 October, 1854: 169–70.

——. *Uncollected Writings of Charles Dickens: Household Words*. 2 vols. Ed. Harry Stone. London: Allen Lane/Penguin, 1969.

Gallagher, Catherine. *The Body Economic: Life, Death and Sensation in Political Economy and the Victorian Novel*. Princeton: Princeton UP, 2006.

Haley, Bruce. *The Healthy Body and Victorian Culture*. Cambridge: Harvard UP, 1978.

Hamlin, Christopher. "Providence and Putrefaction: Victorian Sanitarians and the Natural Theology of Health and Disease." *Energy and Entropy: Science and Culture in Victorian Britain*. Ed. Patrick Brantlinger. Bloomington: Indiana UP, 1989. 93–123.

Head, Dominic. "Problems in Ecocriticism and the Novel." *Key Words* 1 (1998): 60–73.

Iovino, Serenella, and Serpil Oppermann. "Theorizing Material Ecocriticism: A Diptych." *ISLE: Interdisciplinary Studies in Literature and Environment* 19.3 (2012): 448–75.

Lu, Sheldon, and Jiayan Mi, eds. *Chinese Ecocinema in an Age of Environmental Challenge*. Hong Kong: Hong Kong UP, 2009.

Marland, Pippa, and John Parham. "Remaindering: The Material Ecology of Junk and Composting." *Green Letters: Studies in Ecocriticism* 18.1 (2014): 1–8.

"Miasma Theory." *Science Museum* (UK). N.d. Web. 21 May 2015.

Morrison, Susan Signe. "Waste Aesthetics: Form as Restitution." *ISLE: Interdisciplinary Studies in Literature and Environment* 20.3 (2013): 460–78.

Muniz, Vik, perf. *Waste Land*. Dir. Lucy Walker. Prod. Angus Aynsley. Almega Projects/O2 Films, 2010.

Parham, John. "Dickens in the City: Science, Technology, Ecology in the Novels of Charles Dickens." *19: Interdisciplinary Studies in the Long Nineteenth Century*, 10 (2010). Web. 15 June 2015.

———. "'Flowers of Evil': Ecosystem Health and the Punk Poetry of John Cooper Clarke." *Fight Back: Punk, Politics and Resistance*. Ed. The Subcultures Network. Manchester: Manchester UP, 2015. 119–38.

———. "'For You, Pollution': The Victorian Novel And Human Ecology: Benjamin Disraeli's *Sibyl* And Elizabeth Gaskell's *Mary Barton*." *Green Letters: Studies In Ecocriticism* 14 (2011): 23–38.

———. *Green Man Hopkins: Poetry And The Victorian Ecological Imagination*. Amsterdam: Rodopi, 2010.

Storey, Graham. "Dickens in his Letters: The Regress of the Radical." *Dickens and Other Victorians: Essays in Honour of Philip Collins*. Ed. Joanne Shattock. Basingstoke: Macmillan, 1988. 65–74.

Tuana, Nancy. "Viscous Porosity: Witnessing Katrina." *Material Feminisms*. Ed. Stacy Alaimo and Susan Hekman. Bloomington: Indiana UP, 2008. 188–213.

Wilson, Eric. *Romantic Turbulence: Chaos, Ecology and American Space*. New York: Palgrave Macmillan, 2000.

8 Dark nature

A critical return to Brontë country

Deirdre d'Albertis

> This is certainly a beautiful country! In all England, I do not believe that I could have fixed on a situation so completely removed from the stir of society. A perfect misanthropist's heaven—and Mr. Heathcliff and I are such a suitable pair to divide the desolation between us![1]
>
> Emily Brontë, *Wuthering Heights*

So begins the tale of one of literature's most self-regarding, critically obtuse narrators: Emily Brontë's Lockwood invites readers of *Wuthering Heights* to share in his metropolitan traveler's gaze as he familiarizes himself with Yorkshire and its inhabitants, strange and wild as they turn out to be. An outsider's view of Brontë country as both "completely removed" and a "misanthropist's heaven" has been reflected in critical commentary ever since the novel's original publication in 1847. In her Editor's Preface to the 1850 edition, Charlotte Brontë characterizes *Wuthering Heights* as "moorish, and wild, and knotty as a root of heath."[2] The book, she suggests, shares aspects of the land that are hard to appreciate: what Lockwood refers to as "a beautiful country" would not have seemed so to many of his contemporaries.[3] As Lucasta Miller points out, the now iconic landscape of the Yorkshire moors came into view only as reception of Brontë's novel changed over time (154). Elizabeth Gaskell opens her *Life of Charlotte Brontë* (1857) on a similar note: it was this hostile, nonhuman terrain that shaped the imaginative resources shared by the three Brontë sisters. Haworth, writes Gaskell, is situated against the "wild, bleak moors—grand, from the ideas of solitude and loneliness which they suggest, or oppressive from the feeling which they give of being pent-up by some monotonous and illimitable barrier, according to the mood of mind in which the spectator may be" (55). The moors paradoxically "suggest" a "feeling" both of being lost in too much space and of being intolerably hemmed in by the earth itself. Isolation and oppressive confinement in relation to this "illimitable barrier" are subject to the spectator's "mood of the mind"; consciousness in (and of) the environment functions like a Möbius strip, contributing to the notorious unreliability of Brontë's multiple narrators.

This selfsame atmosphere of removal and desolation has the power to seduce. Lockwood insists on kinship with Heathcliff until events cause him to rethink easy identification with his landlord and his "bad nature" by the middle of chapter two (10). Just as quickly, readers of the novel begin to dissociate themselves from Lockwood and his shallow romanticism: narcissistic and condescending, he is "incapable of appreciating things that are so important here" (McCarthy 50). "His gracelessness makes readers feel infinitely more comfortable" in a strange text about a strange land, observes Laura Gruber Godfrey, not least because "Lockwood embodies the worst qualities of the Victorian tourist" (6, 9). Learning precious little from the narrative he transmits, he rhapsodizes, "there is nothing more divine than those glens shut in by hills, and those bluff, bold swells of heath" and wonders in the final sentence, "how any one could ever imagine unquiet slumbers for the sleepers in that quiet earth" (*WH* 233, 258). No reader could be as oblivious as the tenant of Thrushcross Grange—or so it would seem. Lockwood's self-congratulatory, "misanthropist" reading practices, I want to suggest, far from being exceptional, point to persistent problems in interpreting *Wuthering Heights* and to the limits of what Timothy Morton has theorized as our own "ecological imaginary" (1).

In this essay, I propose that we return to Brontë country and the harsh, unforgiving horizon of the moors as it appears in *Wuthering Heights*. Christopher Heywood has described the landscape in *Wuthering Heights* not as a detailed mapping of a "real" place but as a hybrid of locations in Yorkshire (Heywood 1998), coterminous with western, northern, and southern Pennine landscapes also found in *Jane Eyre* (Heywood 2001). It is this imaginary geography/topography that I refer to here as Brontë country.

Countless readings have explored the expressionistic role of landscape in *Wuthering Heights* and indeed in all the novels of the Brontës.[4] Yet this text is rarely if ever mentioned in literary ecocriticism or in cultural histories of the origins of environmentalism in nineteenth-century Britain.[5] I am interested in pushing hard on that omission. As Charlotte Brontë's Preface demonstrates, landscape or "setting" in the novel has been read in an explanatory or justificatory mode: harsh places create harsh people. Looking anew at Emily Brontë's representation of inhospitable moorland, I want to reverse that equation. Discerning the "wild" or "animal" nature of not just a few but *all* of her human characters radically changes our understanding of earth as it is bodied forth in the novel. Focusing on humanity's painful relationship to nature, I will draw on two recent, influential interventions in ecocriticism to limn Brontëan "dark nature": theorist Tim Morton's concept of dark ecology in *Ecology without Nature: Rethinking Environmental Aesthetics* (2007) and "Uncivilisation," a manifesto of the Dark Mountain Project begun by Paul Kingsnorth and Dougald Hine in 2009. Dark nature as a concept stands resolutely apart from Lockwood's anemic romanticism, refusing narrative shape and meaning in a novel structured to an obsessive degree around plotting and repetition.[6] In *Wuthering Heights* nineteenth-century readers were affronted by not only its alien vision of "wild, bleak moors" but also by the unremitting brutality between and among humans and animals "all wildered like"(223), a vision that retains the power to unnerve and challenge us today. Violence, abjection, grief, and mourning are integral to this vision of dark nature.

Bad nature

> The tone in which the words were said revealed a genuine bad nature. I no longer felt inclined to call Heathcliff a capital fellow.
>
> (10)

Having nurtured a fantasy of fellowship with his saturnine neighbor, Lockwood returns after an unsettling initial visit to find himself trapped among the denizens of Wuthering Heights, forced by a winter storm to shelter for the night. Ill at ease in a house where it is possible to mistake "a heap of dead rabbits" for "an obscure cushion full of something like cats" (8), he becomes increasingly discomfited by the inhabitants' speech (curses), behavior (clenched fists), and belligerent relations to one another (later referred to as "cat-and-dog combat" [25]). Heathcliff's unwillingness to provide a guide and indifference to his tenant's plight eventually drives the outsider to risk "being discovered dead in a bog, or in a pit full of snow" (13), striking out on his own in the blizzard, only to have the dogs set on him by a suspicious family retainer. Stranded at the Heights, Lockwood is *bewildered*, "lost in pathless places."[7]

When a disgruntled "Mrs. Heathcliff" murmurs that "a man's life is of more consequence than one evening's neglect of the horses," the narrator realizes that Heathcliff places more value on his draft animals than on his fellow man (14). Lockwood's at first outraged and then terrorized response to his landlord's obviously habitual brutality—the servant Zillah's tepid reproach, "are we going to murder folks on our very door-stones?"(15) says it all—provides a suitable frame for the reader's induction into the novel. Although no one wants actively to "murder" Lockwood, it is also true that no one will prevent him from perishing on the heath if it means defying the master of the house. Events unfold from this violation of Lockwood's claim to special regard as a gentleman, a neighbor, and a human being. Closeted finally for the night in an old-fashioned paneled bed, Lockwood withdraws to the secret heart of the house: Zillah cautions him to be quiet, for Heathcliff would "never let anyone lodge there willingly" (15). In this most enclosed of spaces he discovers traces of writing left long ago by Catherine Earnshaw and he dreams her back into the phenomenal world. "The branches of a fir tree" beating on the window that forms the fourth side of this curiously self-contained bed/room are transmuted into the "fingers of a little, ice-cold hand" that seize upon his own, a revenant with the power to summon in Lockwood all the violent ruthlessness of his host. "Terror made me cruel,"

Lockwood confesses, causing him to "pull its wrists onto the broken pane, and" rub "it to and fro till the blood ran down and soaked the bed clothes" in order to secure his release from the undead (20–1). Plaintive sobbing from a being that Lockwood refers to first as a child and then as "it," calls forth from the refined Londoner an answering (and distinctly human) cruelty.

The dreamer attempts to equate this weird apparition with his reading of Catherine's childhood scribblings before sleep ("an impression which personified itself" [22]). Soon he realizes, however, that for Heathcliff what wails beyond a now-broken windowpane is the ghost of Catherine Earnshaw Linton. Lockwood secretly watches as Heathcliff cries for her in the dark to no avail: "the spectre showed a spectre's ordinary caprice; it gave no sign of being; but the snow and wind whirled wildly through, even reaching my station, and blowing out the light" (23). Returning exhausted the next morning to Thrushcross Grange (guided by Heathcliff across "one billowy, white ocean, the swells and falls not indicating corresponding rises and depressions in the ground" [25]), Lockwood collapses "feeble as a kitten" to receive from Ellen Dean the family history of Wuthering Heights—explanation for the incomprehensible scenes he has just witnessed—in a form that he (and we) can better understand.

In these dense, hallucinatory opening chapters of Brontë's novel the reader too must stumble and wander—as Lockwood does—across a wilderness every bit as misleading and indecipherable as the snow-covered moors. The primal encounter with Cathy's ghost opens up questions that shape our understanding of the narrative as a whole: is her spirit "alive" and, if so, in what form? How does the wild whirling of snow and wind through the broken window-pane stand in for or actually give voice to her unquiet spirit? What does it mean to live as a human being along an apparent continuum between savagery or brute impulse on the one hand and incorporeal forces on the other?

From the start, Brontë erodes as meaningless any distinction between the wildness "out there" and "in here": nature is shown to be nothing more or less than wild. Heathcliff, whose very name represents a portmanteau of local topography, is described by Cathy as "an unreclaimed creature ... an arid wilderness of furze and whinstone" (80). He is not alone: every character in the novel demonstrates a capacity to "get wild" (91), granting full sway to emotions and instincts, whether intentionally or not. The first generation of dwellers at the Heights—Hindley, Catherine, and Heathcliff—are all described as violent, asocial, intemperate with one another as well as outsiders. Earnshaw, their father, frankly doesn't recognize himself in his children, disavowing Cathy ("I doubt thy mother and I must rue that we ever reared thee!" [34]) to embrace an adopted foundling over either of his progeny; soon too, his death opens up a chasm in a household without parents or legitimate authority. In childhood, Hindley violently hurls "an iron weight, used for weighing potatoes and hay" (31) at his foster brother and later, in his adult guise as "Devil Daddy," routinely victimizes his own boy. Although at pains to impress her suitor with fine manners and attire, the grown-up Cathy cannot resist pinching Nelly Dean and slapping her future husband.

Violence has a way of spreading and infecting others; wilderness can reclaim civilized places and people. Nelly, the most piously conventional character in the novel, maintains her affective ties with her childhood playmate Hindley, stoutly bantering with him as he vows to make her "swallow the carving knife" (57). Isabella and Edgar Linton, gracious and genteel though they may be, cannot look away from their Earnshaw peers, eroticizing the wildness they long to access and control in Heathcliff and Cathy. On the night of their elopement, Heathcliff hangs Isabella's springer Fanny from a tree limb in front of her mistress. He wishes to destroy "every being belonging to her," and his disgust at "that pitiful, slavish, mean-minded brach," drives him to violate his unhappy spouse throughout their marriage—"such a wilderness as this with you"—abusing her not as a woman but as an "abject thing" (118). Isabella, once one of the "petted things" at the Grange (38), begins to use her "tigress" nails once sexually aroused by Heathcliff. Mild-mannered Edgar Linton (dismissed as a "lamb" or "sucking leveret" [90, 91]) eventually closes with Heathcliff in physical combat, landing a sharp blow before retreating to safety. Introjecting something of his beloved's cruelty, Edgar possesses "the power to depart" from Catherine, observes Nelly Dean, "as much as a cat possesses the power to leave a mouse half killed, or a bird half eaten"(57). Desire in Brontë's novel is described as synonymous with predation; love means holding tight to the object of desire until both are dead (124).

The precarity of breeding shadows the second generation of *Wuthering Heights* even as it reminds Heathcliff and Nelly continually of their age mates who have predeceased them. "He has a bad nature," Nelly remarks of Heathcliff's neurasthenic heir, "he's your son" (219). Despised by others, sickly and sadistic, Linton is anathematized as "an abject reptile"(203), "a little perishing monkey"(208), a cowering "spaniel" (209), and a "cockatrice"(210) all within the space of a few pages. A sick animal, Heathcliff's son is clearly fated not to thrive or reproduce. Hareton, the "bear," and young Catherine, the "bird," the remaining offspring of pairings from the previous generation, adapt in different ways to the harsh environment of Wuthering Heights, each managing to survive and eventually escape the lair of this "fierce, pitiless, wolfish man" (81).

Regarded with both loathing and awe by others, Heathcliff is Brontë's paradigmatic instance of wild humanity. He doesn't talk, but rather "girns," or snarls, like a mastiff. With his lack of provenance—"where did he come, from the little dark thing?" muses Nelly not unsympathetically—Heathcliff is characterized by others as an "evil beast" (84), "goblin" (87), "ghoul" (251), "vampire" (252), and perhaps even the Devil himself (106). Isabella Linton Heathcliff, the woman with whom he is most physically intimate, flatly states on more than one occasion: "he's not a human being" (119,

134). "Inhuman" being, however, as we have seen, is hardly anomalous in the novel. Wildness is ubiquitous; moreover, it can be cultivated and taught. Heathcliff takes his own savage upbringing as the model of fosterage for Hindley's son Hareton (exulting "I've taught him to scorn everything extra-animal" [169]), the lad's presumably benign nature crowded out by ill-intended nurture. "Good things lost amid a wilderness of weeds, to be sure," Nelly remarks of her former nursling, "whose rankness far over-topped their neglected growth" (152). Hareton's cousin, Catherine, initially regards him as "like a dog" or "a cart horse": "what a blank, dreary mind he must have!" she exclaims as she watches him twitching in his sleep (237).

The animal/human divide plays into a long tradition of reading this novel in terms of binary structures: the contrast between Wuthering Heights and Thrushcross Grange has often been mapped onto a nature versus culture debate. The two places, in this account, are seen as fundamentally different. People in the novel resort to terms such as "heaven" and "hell" to describe their sense of Manichean forces at work in their lives. And both Lockwood and Nelly as narrators employ contrasting landscapes to "illustrate" this structuring conceit of polarity. Nelly Dean, for instance, hypothesizes:

> Doubtless Catherine marked the difference between her friends [Heathcliff and Edgar Linton] as one came in and the other went out. The contrast resembled what you see in exchanging a bleak, hilly, coal country, for a beautiful fertile valley; and his voice and greeting were as opposite as his aspect.
>
> (55)

How are we to think about nature as wilderness in *Wuthering Heights*, then, if not along these dualistic lines?

Wilderness, ecology without nature, and uncivilization

> I have a strong faith in ghosts. I have a conviction that they can, and do exist, among us!
>
> (220)

"The word 'wilderness,'" writes Greg Garrard, "derives from the Anglo-Saxon 'wilddeoren,' where 'deoren' or beasts existed beyond the boundaries of cultivation," gesturing towards "a place apart from, and opposed to, human culture" (60). Yet the boundary between nature and culture is nothing if not porous.[8] Animal as opposed to human status is frequently invoked in *Wuthering Heights* only to be confused through repeated variations upon the theme. The fierce dogs and cats populating the text across literal and figurative registers take on new significance if we consider seriously their presence as cohabitating members of both households. Indeed, animals assume pride of place in Brontë's imaginary world. Aloof

Grimalkin the cat, as well as Juno, Gnasher, Wolf, Throttler, and Skulker, who are provided with genealogies (Throttler being the son of Skulker), function less as familiars (young Catherine half-seriously threatens Joseph with her powers of witchcraft) than full-fledged companions in this most removed precinct of Brontë country.[9] Heathcliff's contempt for pets as opposed to working animals suffuses many of these interactions; all labor and live together. It is a distinct peculiarity of the narrative that we know more about the bulldog harrying twelve-year-old Catherine Earnshaw outside the walls of Thrushcross Grange, than we do about Isabella and Edgar Linton's mother and father firmly ensconced inside.

Such a system of antinomies—nature/culture, wilderness/cultivation—would be familiar and indeed "natural" to Lockwood and to Emily Brontë's Victorian readers. Yet the novel makes obscurely thinkable a third or alternative space along what Garrard identifies as "the boundaries of cultivation." Feral beings, animals belonging to domesticated species that have returned to the wild, belong wholly neither to one nor to the other domain. Cats and dogs, the animals most frequently represented and invoked in *Wuthering Heights*, are "in many parts of the world," Garrard points out, incompletely domesticated creatures, able to "move freely back and forward across the conceptual divide" between culture and nature, "suggesting that a detailed analysis of ferality as both theoretical construct and historical practice may be opportune in ecocriticism" (150). In his recent book, *Feral: Rewilding the Land, the Sea, and Human Life* (2014), environmental activist George Monbiot speaks passionately in favor of the "rewilding" movement. Allowing for ferality or "the desire for a fiercer, less predictable ecosystem," is an important step towards what he sees as the necessary "recognition that nature consists not just of a collection of species, but also of their ever-shifting relationships with each other and with the physical environment"(8–9, 11).

Perversely, it is not Juno or Skulker who turn out to be feral, but the humans who share home and hearth with these animals. As "feral" creatures, Cathy and Heathcliff, but also Isabella, Edgar, Hindley, Hareton, young Catherine, and Linton, can be seen as harbingers of a way of being in the world that imagines "nature" very differently. Construed as culture's other, nature "may be revered as wilderness or pristine animality," as Timothy Clark has written, "or feared as the bestial and cruelly inhuman" (75). Readings of *Wuthering Heights* have tended to mirror such a division. Discussions of pantheism, tellurism, and *Naturphilosophie* in Brontë's writing all replicate ecocriticism's signature move to "reverence" while nineteenth-century reviewers' objections to the text's "bestial and cruel" inhumanity participate in the flip side of this untenable dialectic.[10] Wilderness and the inhuman as intermingled and non-exclusive properly evoke both responses—reverence and fear—from readers, generating interpretive chaos but also insight and creativity.

"Putting something called Nature on a pedestal and admiring it from afar," contends *Ecology without Nature* theorist Timothy Morton, "does for the environment what patriarchy does for the figure of Woman. It is a paradoxical act of sadistic admiration" (5). Arguing on behalf of "ecology without a concept of the natural" (24), Morton agitates for a shift away from "ecologocentrism" to "the contingent and necessarily queer idea that we want to stay with a dying world: dark ecology" (185). What I call dark nature is a recognition of this dying world and Heathcliff as its avatar. Rather than see his destructive energies as alien or unnatural—the major work of the text being "to convey the rhythm of a larger natural life against which the inevitability of the individual evil represented by Heathcliff seems to dissolve" (Alexander and Smith 340)—I propose that we revalue what Dorothy Van Ghent long ago associated with Heathcliff's story: "the wilderness of inhuman reality" (157). Nature, approached from this perspective, as something beyond or apart from human meaning-making, ceases to exist. Dark nature is a name for one fragment, one vision of this broken dream.

Relinquishing the "myth of nature" allows us to access what Paul Kingsnorth and Dougald Hine have described as "an underlying darkness at the root of everything we have built." Disillusioned environmentalists, or "climate defeatists" as their critics have labeled them (e.g., Stephenson), Kingsnorth and Hine united in 2009 to create the Dark Mountain Project, an artists' collective dedicated to disavowing "humanity's delusions of difference, of its separation from and superiority to the living world which surrounds it." "Uncivilisation," a manifesto for "the age of ecocide," grapples with how to imagine and endure life during the twilight of the Anthropocene: "it is, it seems, our civilization's turn to experience the inrush of the savage and the unseen; our turn to be brought short by contact with untamed reality." Dark Mountain's focus is on mourning and grief not so much for the planet itself (which will endure) but for humanity's doomed relationship to a nature it both venerates and desecrates without respite.

Environmental justice and theory unmoored by essentializing constructions of nature work actively to unmake the nature/culture divide, yielding a new point of entry for readers to the "wildering" fantasia of *Wuthering Heights*. The second half of the novel charts an extended experiment by Heathcliff in the reverse engineering of humanity, a frank avowal of the work of "uncivilization" (at least until literacy apparently reclaims the narrative and allows for a marriage plot ending). Once Cathy slips from Heathcliff's grasp he longs to destroy life itself. "The more the worms writhe," he grimly avers, "the more I yearn to crush out their entrails" (119). He makes a wilderness of two estates, financially ruining his rivals, usurping their lands and holdings, and never relents in "exacting" what he sees as his "due from any one" (232). That is until he stops. Heathcliff's plots, once so strong and dark, fall away as he loses the will to punish his enemies for separating him from his love: "it is a poor conclusion, is it not" he asks Nelly, "an absurd termination to my violent exertions?" (247). He becomes absorbed instead by the environment itself and a violently receptive relation to the world around him: "in every cloud, in every tree—filling the air at night and caught by glimpses in every object by day. I am surrounded by her image ... [t]he entire world is a dreadful collection of memoranda that she did exist, and that I have lost her!"(247).

Abjuring human customs, keeping out of doors and clear of the domestic interiors over which narrators preside, Heathcliff neglects to nourish his body with food and even—at moments, Nelly tells us in the novel's final chapter—to breathe. As his physical vitality dwindles he begins to hear and to speak what Susan Pyke names "the language of the Moor," declaring: "my soul's bliss kills my body, but does not satisfy itself" (254). Heathcliff, like Cathy before him, no longer "sees" anything in the phenomenal world save for her genetic traces made manifest in the uncanny gazes of Hareton, her nephew, and Catherine, her daughter. These, he says, are "the only objects which retain a distinct material appearance to me; and that presence causes me pain, amounting to agony" (247). More than half-convinced that Heathcliff has committed suicide, Nelly refrains after his death from telling anyone "the fact of him having swallowed nothing for four days." Equivocating, she insists: "I am persuaded he did not abstain on purpose" (257).

In spite of Nelly's weak assurances and Lockwood's lack of comprehension, the reader can only conclude that self-destruction or self-murder is endemic to the indigenous population of *Wuthering Heights*. Hindley, Edgar, and Isabella all speak overtly of their wish to quit life. Cathy pines to depart for "my narrow home out yonder" (99) and both Edgar and Heathcliff dream eventually only of lying in the earth alongside her decaying body ("of dissolving with her, and being more happy still" [220]). Heathcliff strives in the end to erase all traces of his life's exertions along with his own existence: "how to leave my property, I cannot determine! I wish I could annihilate it from the face of the earth!"(254). Suicide, like ecocide, far from being "unnatural," may well be the most human reality we can imagine. "What ... if the exploitative and opportunistically destructive has always been characteristic of the species and its hominid predecessors," proposes Tim Clark of human life on earth, and "that there is no irenic natural human norm to be restored?" (79). Brontë's "dark nature" honors this drive toward dissolution in the grave as the most fearsome condition of "radical nonidentity" imaginable (Morton 13). Nature, Morton writes, "if it is anything at all, is what is immediately given, which at its simplest is pain" (182). *Wuthering Heights*, read in conversation with concepts of "ecology without nature" and "uncivilization," is nothing less than a paean to the suffering of all living, sentient beings and a reckoning not with evil or with nature, but with human dreams summoned forth by the empty horizon of the moors. "Like a ghost at the never-arriving end of an infinite series," nature is an idea that haunts humankind even as Catherine Earnshaw haunts Heathcliff (Morton 18).[11] Brontë's novel forces us to encounter the impossibility of knowing or possessing a "dark nature" "out there" that we can never accept "in here": teaching an ethics that looks like "perversion," with its never-ending grief and deep "acceptance of death" (Morton 183).

Conclusion

"There are scenes of savage wildness in nature which, though they inspire no pleasant sensation, we are well satisfied to have seen," writes one 1848 reviewer of *Wuthering Heights*.[12] No pleasant sensation: Lockwood and many readers have shared a certain distaste at the "scenes of savage wildness" that shape Emily Brontë's strange, dark book. Yet we cannot look away. Reading immerses us in the perverse satisfaction of witnessing a world fall apart. For all its preoccupation with genealogy (structured by two generations born to the ancient house of Earnshaw) and property (Heathcliff's diabolical manipulation of the law ultimately devours birthright and identity of all connected with Wuthering Heights), Brontë's work dwells ultimately in a place—beyond time and topography—of haunting and obsession.[13] Dark nature in this text is not a static entity but a way of being *in* and *of* the world, of realizing that "nature in itself always flickers between things—it is both/and or neither/nor" (Morton 18). Brontë shows us how to endure haunting, to live in awareness of what is and is not there. As Heathcliff insists, maddened to the point of his own extinction by her invisible presence, "so certainly I felt that Cathy was there, not under me, but on earth" (221). Brontë gives us a word for watching and feeling "both/and" and "neither/nor" in contrast to the flawed narrative certainties that bookend our experience of the pathless interiors we traverse in her fiction: *wuthering*.

"A significant provincial adjective," Lockwood informs the reader as any good tour guide should, *wuthering* as a place name is "descriptive of the atmospheric tumult to which its station is exposed in stormy weather" (4). Used as an adjective or adverb, "wuthering" here modifies the noun or place name of a house. Drawing on Old Norse and Old English associations with the verb "to whither," however, "wuthering" summons not an object but a range of human actions: "to move with force or impetus" and to "bluster or rage, as the wind", "to tremble, shake, quiver," and "to strike or beat forcibly; to throw wildly" (OED). Emily Brontë's novel pictures and performs all of these states of being. Nelly looks on helplessly as a fully feral Heathcliff labors *in extremis*, wuthering on the bourn between life and death: "his frame shivering, not as one shivers with chill or weakness, but as a tight-stretched cord vibrates—a strong thrilling, rather than trembling"(250).[14] *Wuthering Heights*, like the dark nature at its heart's core, also vibrates—it wuthers—sometimes showing itself, sometimes not, just beyond the limits of human meaning-making and awareness.

Notes

1. Emily Brontë, *Wuthering Heights* (ed. Dunn), 3. Further references will be cited parenthetically.
2. [Charlotte Brontë], "Editor's Preface to the New Edition of *Wuthering Heights*" (1850) qtd. in *Wuthering Heights,* ed. Dunn, 313.
3. See Susan Pyke's lyrical approach to the "eco-divine" in Brontë's writing of the moor as reimagined in latter-day interpretations by Anne Carson and Kathy Acker.
4. See for instance Jennifer Fuller's "Seeking Wild Eyre: Victorian Attitudes towards Landscape and the Environment in Charlotte Brontë's *Jane Eyre*," and "Natural History and the Brontës" in *The Oxford Companion to the Brontës* (Alexander and Smith).
5. No mention, for instance, is made of *Wuthering Heights* in canonical works of environmental criticism in English Studies such as Jonathan Bate's *The Song of the Earth* (it is Austen and Hardy who appear alongside Clare, Wordsworth, and Keats among others) or Harriet Ritvo's *The Dawn of Green: Manchester, Thirlmere, and Modern Environmentalism* (which focuses on the romantic roots of the movement in the Thirlmere Defence Association). Nature and the environment are typically viewed either as backdrop to the events at Wuthering Heights and Thrushcross Grange or as an opposing force to the cultural values exemplified by the Linton estate.
6. See J. Hillis Miller, "*Wuthering Heights*: Repetition and the Uncanny."
7. See "be wildered, adj." *OED Online.*
8. See Kate Soper's 1995 *What is Nature?* for a particularly cogent analysis of "textuality" in relation to ecological discourses around nature.
9. In her essay, "Animals and Violence in *Wuthering Heights*," Lisa Surridge demonstrates how Brontë's views on animal–human relationships were perceived to be radically outside her contemporary readership's frame of reference.
10. See Ngom and Guimarães for specific instances.
11. "Dark ecology is based on negative desire rather than positive fulfillment. It is saturated with unrequited longing" (Morton 186).
12. *Britannia* January 1848, qtd. in *Wuthering Heights* (ed. Dunn) 288.
13. J. Hillis Miller's classic reading of "Repetition and the 'Uncanny'" in *Wuthering Heights* argues that each new reading of the novel "performs a multiple act of resurrection, an opening of graves or a raising of ghosts" (71).
14. The adjective "feral" can mean both "wild" and "deathly or funereal."

Works cited

Alexander, Christine and Margaret Smith. *The Oxford Companion to the Brontës.* Oxford: Oxford UP, 2006.

Bate, Jonathan. *The Song of the Earth.* Cambridge: Harvard UP, 2000.

"be wildered, adj." *OED Online.* Oxford UP, June 2015. Web. 30 July 2015.

Brontë, Emily. *Wuthering Heights.* 1847. 4th ed. Ed. Richard J. Dunn. New York: Norton, 2003.

Clark, Timothy. "Nature, Post Nature." *The Cambridge Companion to Literature and the Environment.* Ed. Louise Westling. Cambridge: Cambridge UP, 2013. 75–89.

"feral, adj." *OED Online.* Oxford University Press, June 2015. Web. 1 August 2015.

Fuller, Jennifer D. "Seeking Wild Eyre: Victorian Attitudes towards Landscape and the Environment in Charlotte Brontë's *Jane Eyre*." *Ecozon@* 4.2 (2013): 150–65.
Garrard, Greg. *Ecocriticism*. New Critical Idiom Series. New York: Routledge, 2004.
Gaskell, Elizabeth. *The Life of Charlotte Bronte*. 1857. Ed. Alan Shelston. Harmondsworth, Middlesex: Penguin, 1985.
Godfrey, Laura Gruber. "'That Quiet Earth': Tourism, Cultural Geography, and the Misreading of Landscape in *Wuthering Heights*." *Interdisciplinary Literary Studies* 12.2 (2011): 1–15.
Guimarães, Paula Alexander. "'Over my boundless waste of soul': Echoes of the Natural World, or a Feminine Naturphilosophie, in the Poetry of Emily Brontë and Mathilde Blind." *Nineteenth-Century Gender Studies* 7.2 (2011). Web. 3 August 2015.
Heywood, Christopher. "Pennine Landscapes in *Jane Eyre* and *Wuthering Heights*." *Brontë Society Transactions* 26.2 (2001): 187–98.
——. "Yorkshire Landscapes in *Wuthering Heights*." *Essays in Criticism* 48.1 (1998): 13–34.
Kingsnorth, Paul, and Dougald Hine. "Uncivilisation: The Dark Mountain Manifesto." 2009. Web. 3 August 2015.
McCarthy, Terence. "The Incompetent Narrator of *Wuthering Heights*." *Modern Language Quarterly* 42.1 (1981): 48–64.
Miller, J. Hillis. "Fiction and the 'Uncanny.'" *Fiction and Repetition: Seven English Novels*. Cambridge: Harvard UP, 1982. 42–72.
Miller, Lucasta. *The Brontë Myth*. New York: Anchor, 2005.
Monbiot, George. *Feral: Rewilding the Land, the Sea and Human Life*. Chicago: U of Chicago P, 2014.
Morton, Timothy. *Ecology without Nature: Rethinking Environmental Aesthetics*. Cambridge: Harvard UP, 2007.
Ngom, Abdou. "Tellurism and the Apotheosis of Nature in Emily Brontë's *Wuthering Heights*." *Bridges: a Senegalese Journal of English Studies* 8.8 (1997): 144–62.
Pyke, Susan. "Healing Words and the Matter of Our Urban and Rural Moor." *TEXT* 20 (2013): 1–15.
Ritvo, Harriet. *The Dawn of Green: Manchester, Thirlmere, and Modern Environmentalism*. Chicago: U of Chicago P, 2009.
Soper, Kate. *What is Nature?* London: Blackwell, 1995.
Stephenson, Wen. "I Withdraw: A Talk with Climate Defeatist Paul Kingsnorth." *Grist Magazine*. April 2012. Web. 3 August 2015.
Surridge, Lisa. "Animals and Violence in *Wuthering Heights*." *Bronte Society Transactions* 24.2 (1999): 161–73.
Van Ghent, Dorothy. *The English Novel: Form and Function*. New York: Holt, Rinehart, & Winston, 1953.
"whither, v." *OED Online*. Oxford UP, June 2015. Web. 30 July 2015.

9 Anna Sewell's *Black Beauty*
Reframing the pastoral tradition

Erin Bistline

Anna Sewell's 1877 novel *Black Beauty: His Grooms and Companions. The Autobiography of a Horse* is frequently viewed simply as a children's novel and it has certainly influenced—and still influences—generations of youngsters. Narrated by Black Beauty, the novel begins and ends with the horse's positive feelings for the country: the idyllic farm and the Gordon estate where he lived before eventually being sold off to work in the city, and the "pretty, low house, with a lawn and shrubbery at the front and a drive up to the door" on the farm where he expects to end his days under the beneficent eyes of the women who have rescued him from the city and in the care of Joe Green, one of his first grooms with whom he has been reunited (210). Saved from the difficulties he experiences in the city, Black Beauty returns to the country toward the end of the novel, and he finds it an ideal situation equal to the one in which he lived early in his life. Feeling secure in his new, rural surroundings, Black Beauty explains, "Joe is the best and kindest of grooms. My work is easy and pleasant, and I feel my strength and spirits all coming back" (213). The new home reminds him of earlier, happier times: "often before I am quite awake, I fancy I am still in the orchard at Birtwick, standing with my old friends under the apple trees" (213). For Black Beauty, the country offers what some critics term an "idyllic"[1] retirement: an escape from the dangers of the city and a return to his childhood home. This view helps reinforce the childlike simplicity of the narrator and provides a romanticized happy ending.[2]

While Black Beauty, as a character, presents a simplistic and idealized understanding of the country and the city, the novel itself shows the country and the city to be equally dangerous for horses and people. The novel's often unnoticed complexities, manifest through its depiction of the treatment of horses and human workers, provides an opportunity to examine Victorian attitudes toward the environment,[3] especially their interaction with pastoral ideas based on the notion of a dichotomy between country and city in order to highlight the post-industrial understanding of the relationship between these environments. In this chapter, I will argue that, while the novel has characteristics of the traditional, literary pastoral, it actually exemplifies Raymond Williams's and William Cronon's more complex representations of the interaction between the country and the city, emphasizing the influence of humans within those settings, and shows the ultimate inadequacy of the simplistic dichotomy to represent that relationship adequately.

From a literary standpoint, pastoral literature, most simply, is fiction or poetry related to the country. Terry Gifford's introduction to the pastoral tradition offers two purposefully simplistic options for defining the term before further examining the tradition. First, he quotes Karl Marx's pithy and insightful quip, "no shepherd, no pastoral," noting that pastoral writing requires working inhabitants of the country, most explicitly people who care for sheep or other animals (Gifford 1). Gifford also defines pastoral as "any literature that describes the country with an implicit or explicit contrast to the urban" (2). Ultimately, Gifford offers a more nuanced explanation of the term later in the work by noting three different ways in which it may be employed: in its historical sense; as a representation of an idealized view of nature in contrast to urban settings; and as a negatively charged term that considers the problems associated with a simplistic view of nature and/or the country. Similarly, in "Pastoral," Greg Garrard divides the pastoral into multiple categories including the romantic pastoral, a category in which *Black Beauty* could easily be included. However, even Garrard's definition of romantic pastoral remains fairly simplistic.[4]

In ecocritical terms, the idea of pastoral literature is much more complex, as ecocritics seek to investigate and, in some cases, erase differences that create and separate traditional concepts of "country" and "city." While the idealization of the country certainly plays a part in pastoral literature, there are other ways to characterize the relationship between rural and urban environments. For example, Williams offers a more complex view of that relationship, tracing the changing representation of country and city in literature from classical times to the twentieth century. Williams says that often the country is presented positively and the city negatively—but not always. One way that Williams identifies more complex representations of the country and city is in the work of Thomas Hardy and Charles Dickens.[5] Hardy often writes of individuals isolated in the city and highlights the multifaceted nature of rural communities. Williams argues that for Hardy "[t]he originating pressures within rural society itself are accurately shown, and are given a human and social rather than a mechanical dimension" (208). There are dangers present in both the country and the city, and "[t]he pressures to which Hardy's characters are subjected are then pressures from within a system of living" (Williams 209). Just as Williams sees Hardy revealing a complex view of country life, he sees Dickens's relationship to the city as more complex than idealistic or overly negative. Part of Dickens's representation of the city hinges on his "characteristic way of seeing people and their actions," even in the city, as varied and individual despite the "uniform view" of the "new and industrial order" (Williams 153).[6] Dickens even "dramatize[s] those social institutions and consequences that are not accessible to ordinary physical observation" (Williams 156). Williams argues that "[the] physical world is never in Dickens unconnected with [humans]" (161). These ideas are reflected in later work in ecocriticism that highlights the close relationship between the country and the city for the humans that inhabit these regions—and who are responsible for "country" and "city" as ideological constructs.

For Cronon, the line between the country, the city, and the wilderness is even more complex and especially blurry due to the fact that the line itself comes from a "rural bias" (*Nature's Metropolis* xv).[7] He notes that "We carefully partition our national landscape into urban places, country places, and wilderness" but "we rarely reflect on how tightly bound together they really are" (*Nature's Metropolis* xvi). Despite the commonplace view of the city as being outside of nature, Cronon argues that the country and city "shared a common past and had fundamentally reshaped each other" (8). Both are shaped by human experiences and human needs and as a result cannot be separated completely. The country and the city are intricately linked to the point that, to put it bluntly, the simplistic dichotomy inherent in pastoral literature falls apart.

The idealization of the country and the cynical view of the city

In some ways, the character Black Beauty's descriptions of the environments in which he lives present the traditional literary view of the pastoral. Certainly, Black Beauty describes his original home in highly idealistic terms and uses it as a measure of comparison for his future homes. He is also consistent in presenting the city in more cynical terms. Black Beauty describes his birthplace as a peaceful and gentle country locale. He spends his days with his mother in "a large pleasant meadow with a pond of clear water in it" and "[w]hen it was hot, we used to stand by the pond in the shade of the trees, and when it was cold, we had a nice warm shed near the plantation" (3). Here, within the first chapter of the novel, the human impact on the country is highlighted as Cronon explains in his introduction to *Nature's Metropolis*. The horses' needs are taken care of and they are happy, but this is the result of human intervention and labor. The natural setting is not the sole cause of Black Beauty's happiness; instead, the people present in the country are responsible for his comfort and safety. His first home away from his birthplace, Squire Gordon's Birtwick Park, offers similar benefits. Squire Gordon, his family, and his workers respect and appreciate Black Beauty. Black Beauty describes the stable at Birtwick Park as "very roomy with four good stalls" and "a large swinging window [that] opened into the yard" (15). Again, the comforts of the country are dependent upon the presence of human work, for it must be humans who built the comforting stable. Also, Black Beauty loves and appreciates the people who bought him—ultimately viewing those humans as his family—and enjoys the company of the other horses at the Park. He explains that "The longer I lived at Birtwick, the more proud and happy I felt at having such a place," and he connects the family's behavior to that of his first owners (42). The Gordons are "respected and beloved by all ... good and kind to everybody and everything, not only men and women, but horses and donkeys, dogs and cats, cattle and birds" (42). This description, followed by Black Beauty's assertion that "If any of the village children were known to treat any creature cruelly, they soon heard about it from the Hall" (42), recalls an earlier scene in the novel when his previous owner punished the farm hand Dick for throwing rocks at the horses. Here, only miles from his original home, Black Beauty sees a reaffirmation of ideas of respect and protection for both the human and the nonhuman.

Black Beauty also presents his final home in idealistic terms, showing that he still believes the country to be superior to the city. After living in the city for years and being worked nearly to death, he is sold back to the country. Black Beauty describes his final home in ways that parallel his descriptions of his earlier country homes. The women who buy him (Miss Blomefield, Miss Ellen, and Miss Lavinia) and the men who help him recuperate from his injuries (Willie and Mr. Thoroughgood) understand horses and consider them in a more positive and caring light than some of the city people Black Beauty describes. They exhibit genuine kindness in discussing his knees, scarred from injuries caused by the drunken stable master at Earlshall, the last country place he lived before being sold to an owner in the city. Mr. Thoroughgood explains that "many first-rate horses have had their knees broken through the carelessness of their drivers, without any fault of their own, and from what I can see of this horse, I should say that is his case" (211). Certainly Black Beauty's experiences confirm Mr. Thoroughgood's explanation—the accident Black Beauty suffered was due to his drunken rider and not a failure on the horse's part—and he sees their understanding of him as another example of how the country is superior to the city. The earl's wife, a devotee of city fashion (a point I will discuss later) ignored the circumstances of the accident and had Black Beauty sold because it was unfashionable to drive in a carriage pulled by a horse with scarred knees. In a more explicit link to his early home that further heightens the superiority of the country, Black Beauty also reunites with a figure from Birtwick Park and the Gordon family that Black Beauty loved so much. The women who buy Black Beauty from Mr. Thoroughgood employ Joe Green, the groom who, earlier in the novel, nearly caused Black Beauty's death by putting him up incorrectly and inducing colic. Joe is delighted to have the horse back in his care now that he, too, is wiser from his experiences.[8] At the end of the novel, Black Beauty is in what he terms his "last home"—the title of the final chapter—and he calls it his "happy place" where his "ladies have promised that I shall never be sold, and so I have nothing to fear ... my troubles are all over" (213).

Despite the variety of experiences he has over his lifetime, Black Beauty's view of the country remains simplistic and idealized, adopting an attitude that reflects the traditional pastoral. For example, he views the accident in which he suffers injuries at the hands of the stable master at Earlshall in a more positive light than might be expected. As he moves closer to the city, his knowledge of the dangers to and abuse of horses is associated with the urban environment, further reinforcing his simplistic (pastoral) view. After being sold by the earl because he has scarred knees, Black Beauty moves outside of families and becomes a working horse, being rented out to men who need temporary transportation. Within this section of the novel Sewell, through her character Black Beauty, often attributes instances of cruelty to ignorance and not purposeful unkindness, because city people do not have the experience and knowledge that country people do when working with horses.[9] For instance, a driver almost lames Black Beauty because the man "never knew that horses picked up stones before," which is one of the most basic dangers to a horse's well-being (113). The driver's ignorance is similar to that of the young stable hand Joe Green, who was too young to know that putting Black Beauty up hot and giving him cold water would cause an almost fatal instance of colic. But because Black Beauty is working as a job horse in the city, no one checks on the driver's work and saves Black Beauty from harm, as Joe's superior did. Black Beauty has some sympathy for these ignorant people; but in remarking on the behavior of the driver he reveals a change in his belief that humans are kind by nature, a precept he had learned from his mother, who was born and raised in the country. He displays a hint of contempt in wondering, "Whether the man was partly blind, or only very careless" (112). Other people who rent his services in his early days in the city suffer from ignorance due to their city upbringing and consequently treat him as machinery. Black Beauty describes these people as having a "steam-engine style of driving"; the comparison equates horses to trains, with which city people were much more familiar.[10] In some ways, city people's behavior is similar to that of the boys who overworked Black Beauty's friend Merrylegs in the country (114).

While people's ignorance may stem from their unfamiliarity with job horses, Black Beauty does not escape ignorant masters when he is sold out of his job horse position. In fact, the damage caused by human ignorance is heightened when he moves on. Black Beauty is sold to Mr. Barry, a man who, like the customers who abused Black Beauty when he was a job horse, has little knowledge of horses. Barry buys him anyway and relies (too much, as it turns out) on stable hands to care for him. While stable hands in the country are perhaps the kindest people with whom Black Beauty interacts, the stable hands Barry hires are lazy or greedy. Black Beauty receives poor care and little food because Barry does not know enough to protect him. Once again, although Black Beauty may not recognize the linkage, the negative treatment he receives in the city is not simply the result of the urban environment but more appropriately the result of humans who are supposed to tend to him. The behavior of the city men that Black Beauty encounters highlights for him the ignorance and selfishness that separate the city from the country.

The most significant negative experience that Black Beauty and other horses undergo in the city is their subjection to the bearing rein—the focus of Anna Sewell's fight against animal cruelty. In the novel, Black Beauty links the use of the bearing rein to humans within the city. The simple device, used in a variety of applications for horses, was not inherently dangerous. When used correctly, the rein keeps the horse from lowering his or her head and takes the strain off a driver's arms; however, when used incorrectly, it causes severe pain and shortens the lives of the horses subjected to it The rein pulls horses' heads dangerously high and impedes their ability to breathe as well as taxing their neck muscles and esophagus. This was especially dangerous in cart horses whose neck muscles and esophagus were already severely limited because of the added weight that they pulled. People were not unaware of these consequences even in the 1870s, when *Black Beauty* was written and published.[11] However, in *Victorian England and the Cult of the Horse*, which includes her definitive discussion of the history of bearing reins, Gina Dorré notes that the debate surrounding the use of the bearing rein focused on "utility, precision, rationality, and scientific understanding," not the cruelty towards the horses. This stratagem for framing the argument acted "as a distancing device" for the proponents of its use (101). Furthermore, arguments about the appropriateness of using the bearing rein only offered support for its correct use; unfortunately, this did not always occur.

Despite the negative characteristics of the bearing reins (expressed forcefully and dramatically in *Black Beauty* by the anthropomorphic horses), to humans in the nineteenth century, the bearing rein indicated fashion, so it is hardly surprising that those classes of society wishing to look smart on their drives would be engaged in debates over the use of the device. With few exceptions the people participating in the discussion viewed the working class as the people most at fault for any cruelty caused by its use;[12] workers were directly responsible for the horses, not the wealthy and aristocratic people who viewed the bearing reins as fashionable and demanded that those reins be used (Dorré 101). In reality, working-class people more often used the reins correctly, effectively avoiding harm to the horses, but that was not always the case—especially when instructed by their superiors to do otherwise. Regardless of who was at fault for the use of the bearing reins, the key point is that this negative aspect of life in the city for horses like Black Beauty hinges on human behavior. As Cronon argues, humans are the ones who create conditions for life in both the country and the city—breaking down the perceived differences between the two.

In the context of this discussion, it is worth noting that before Black Beauty even reaches the city, he is introduced to the bearing rein. Ginger, one of the other horses at Birtwick Park, explains the effect of the bearing rein to him. Having lived in the city and having "been very ill-used before she came" to Squire Gordon's farm, Ginger knows first-hand the very real dangers of the city (17). She is the only horse at Birtwick Park who can tell Black Beauty about the negative experiences related to bearing reins; none of the other horses had ever been subjected to their use.¹³ At this point, however, Black Beauty cannot understand the significance of what Ginger is saying, because his idealized vision of the country, developed from his limited experience and the information provided by his mother, does not allow him to imagine that the country also harbors dangers for horses. Later Black Beauty experiences the damage that bearing reins inflict, but he connects that danger to the city itself and not to the people who use the rein.

However, horses are not the only beings in danger in the city. Humans are also at risk, and this is shown by noting similarities in the discourse about mistreatment inflicted as a result of the use of the bearing rein, and the discourse regarding machinery and workers of the time. As discussed earlier, the bearing rein was created for a positive reason; in the same way, in the nineteenth century machinery was perceived as a way to increase efficiency and profit. Jamie L. Bronstein explains that the nineteenth century offered "streamlined production ... the increasing demand for fuel to power industrialization, and the mechanized transport of goods" (2). However, machinery often caused more problems for the workers than it solved. Bronstein explains that new machine technologies increased injury just as much as—or more than—they increased productivity as they were intended (2). They were so dangerous that many workers were injured and killed using machinery. Hence new inventions—bearing reins and machines—may have been created for positive reasons, but the end results were often far from salutary.¹⁴

The link between the bearing rein and machinery is not the only way that workers and humans are connected. The exchange between the Governor and Seedy Sam, a cab driver in London, highlights a larger question of who is most in danger in the cab industry, aligning the industry to many others in the city. While Seedy Sam sees that the horses are "downright tired," the Governor observes that both the workers and the horses experience difficulties and need assistance to overcome abuses perpetrated against them. This connection is continued through the discussions Black Beauty overhears, during which several workers show empathy for the horses that moves beyond an understanding of the horse as a mere tool. While Black Beauty describes some of the individuals who view horses as tools as "steam-engine style" drivers "who never had a horse of their own and generally travel by rail," this is not the only way people view horses (114). There are men who see horses as individuals and not machines, and these are often the men¹⁵ with whom Black Beauty has the closest emotional relationship. As passages such as these indicate, the dangers horses face in the city stem largely from their treatment by humans—another point that recalls Cronon's argument that humans are the creators of the country and the city and that humans, not the city itself, possess the power to harm others.

The dangers of the city for the workers also hinge on the actions of other humans. Workers in the city during the nineteenth century experienced situations similar to those of the horses. With few laws to protect them, working-class adults and children were often worked to death. Some of these deaths were related to the use of machinery, as discussed earlier in this chapter. However, as with Black Beauty, the workers could be physically overworked to the point of death or serious illness not related to machinery. Jerry, a cabby and one of Black Beauty's owners in the city, must retire to the country in order to escape certain death from overwork and damage from the unhealthy environment. Jerry is more fortunate than Seedy Sam, one of the other cab drivers, who dies "at four o'clock [one] morning" after "raving about Skinner, and having no Sundays. 'I never had a Sunday's rest,' these were his last words" (168). Jerry actively avoids Sam's fate, saving both himself and the horses he worked with from death caused by overworking. Sam, like many of the cab horses Dorré discusses,[16] dies without notice, even though he is human and not an animal. He is simply replaced when he can no longer work, because workers possess little or no more power and worth than the animals that surround them. As Black Beauty comes to learn, the same fate awaits many of the horses in the city. Ginger dies from overwork there, and Black Beauty eventually hopes to die as Ginger does in order to escape mistreatment. Aligning the workers and the horses so closely, and showing that the dangers come from other humans and not from the city itself, undermines the simplistic dichotomy between the country and the city suggested by conventional definitions of pastoral.

Negative aspects of the country and positive aspects of the city

Sewell's novel challenges the simple dichotomy of pastoral by failing to describe the country and the city exclusively in positive and negative terms. Instead, Sewell shows that the two environments are alike in many ways. In forming his consistently positive view of the country, Black Beauty overlooks significant negative events. For instance, when he is a colt, the young farmhand Dick torments the horses in the pasture by throwing rocks at them. Although Black Beauty says the horses "did not much mind him" (4), this episode presents an attitude towards animals that undermines the notion of the country as purely idyllic. In the country however, humans react more strongly to the mistreatment. Dick is caught, lectured by his master, and ultimately fired. Ironically, in this scene the horses have some empathy or understanding for the way the humans behave, while at least some humans are intolerant of cruelty toward animals. But it is also true that it is not the country setting, but the quick response of humans, that protects horses from ill treatment.

Another situation that Black Beauty overlooks in his idealization of the country not only shows mistreatment toward horses but also reveals different reactions from humans and horses. Rob Roy, an adult horse on the farm and "a good bold horse" with "no vice in him," according to Black Beauty's mother, Duchess, dies in a hunting accident in which the son of a neighbor is also killed (8). While the young horses see Rob Roy's death and comment on it, they are physically separated from the incident by a fence and emotionally distanced from it because Rob Roy, as an older, trained horse, is not part of their group. At the same time, the younger horses show no sympathy for the human. One young horse responds to the news that the boy died from a broken neck with, "serves him right, too" (8). Although Duchess stands in for the voice of reason, her response to the colt's statement does little to temper their reaction. Duchess tries to frame the situation kindly, but she clearly does not believe that humans are without blame here. She tells the colts they "must not state that"; humans, in their zeal to pursue pastimes such as hunting, "often hurt themselves, often spoil good horses ... all for a hare or a stag ... but we are only horses, and don't know" (8). Her argument that horses cannot understand human behavior neither idealizes nor diminishes the country and its inhabitants. In this instance, the humans mourn the horse as well as the young man, blaming no one. The loss of Rob Roy is not overlooked, as Black Beauty notes; people "rid[e] off in all directions, to the doctor's, to the farrier's, and no doubt to Squire Gordon's to let him know about his son" (8). Seeking the farrier and the doctor simultaneously suggests that human and horse are equally important. Perhaps because the incident occurs so early in Black Beauty's life it has no significant effect upon him; hence, he is able to remember his life in the country as perfect. The experience does, however, highlight for readers the presence and power of the humans, further affirming the notion that the link between the country and the city is their presence and influence.

While I have explained how the use of the bearing rein in the city created extremely harsh conditions for horses forced to wear it, its use in the country also has negative consequences for Black Beauty, even though he chooses to overlook its effects there. After Squire Gordon's wife becomes ill and the family must leave Birtwick Park, Black Beauty and the rest of his friends are sold. Black Beauty and Ginger stay together, going to Earlshall fifteen miles away. The setting seems very similar to Birtwick Park, and to the reader fifteen miles does not seem a great distance. The horses live in a "light, airy stable," but within days of arriving at their new home, the earl's wife demands the use of the bearing rein on the horses drawing her carriage. She intends to be fashionable in a way more regularly seen in the city and, regardless of whether she understands the effects of the reins, ignores the protests of the groom and the horses. Even though Sewell does not attribute the earl's wife's decision to her conscious emulation of city fashion, ideas about fashion typically originate in the city. The fluidity of these ideas across the borders of country and city highlights Cronon's point about the human influence in both places.

When he is first made to wear the bearing rein, Black Beauty finds it only a "nuisance not to be able to get my head down now and then," and he is able to overlook it (88). He can bear a gradual tightening (something the coachman does to preserve both horses pulling the carriage), though he realizes that "every little [change] makes a difference, be it better or worse"

(88). But soon the earl's wife demands the rein be tightened significantly and at once. The bearing rein becomes "almost intolerable." Ginger, who is paired with Black Beauty in trace, "went on plunging, rearing, and kicking in a most desperate manner" until she injures Black Beauty and is freed (89). Ginger's reaction reflects factual accounts of horses being forced to submit to bearing reins. York, the groom, understands the reasoning behind Ginger's actions and exclaims afterwards "confound these bearing reins!" Yet he does not have the power to alter the earl's wife's desire to follow fashion (90). Ultimately Black Beauty "suffered with that rein for four long months" and is "quite sure that, had it lasted much longer, either my health or my temper would have given way" (91). Although Black Beauty is unable to comprehend the danger Ginger attributes to the bearing rein when she tells him about its effects while the two are at Birtwick Park, once he experiences it himself, he understands her warning and begins to appreciate her very different upbringing away from the idealized country setting in which he grew up. Even though the abuse occurred on the Gordons' estate, Black Beauty does not alter his idealized view of the country. Unlike Ginger, who mistrusts humans and sees them as the source of danger, Black Beauty still does not understand that the connection between the country and the city—and therefore the danger he attributes only to the city—is the presence and power of humans in both environments. He attributes the differences between his experiences exclusively to the setting, instead of to differences in human behavior.

The negativity associated with the city is further undermined by the positive experiences Black Beauty overlooks in his description of his life there and by the plight of the workers whose lot is as bad as that of their equine partners. Jerry Barker certainly views Black Beauty and his other horses as co-workers and partners, not tools. Black Beauty explains that he worked together with Jerry as an equal instead of being used by him. He describes their relationship as one of trust that made them unbeatable "at getting through when [they] were set upon" (148). Jerry also frequently considers Black Beauty's well-being in the day-to-day operations of his cab. When being asked to drive on Sundays, Jerry does not think only of his own rest. He tells his customer "that God made man, and He made horses and all the other beasts, and bade that all should rest one day in seven" (152).

For Jerry, his horses are more than simply tools, as they are for some of the other cabbies; they are his partners. John Manly, a worker in the country who appears earlier in the novel, exhibits similar care. These men's actions highlight Cronon's points about how closely entwined the country and the city are, especially given Black Beauty's own association of the two men through his description of Jerry as "as strong for the right as John Manly" (145). From their first introduction, John understands Black Beauty and appreciates him as an individual with consciousness. He tells Squire Brown that "many horses will not pass [travelling] carts quietly," but Black Beauty does, showing that John understands that not all horses will react the same way, as machines and tools will (19). Black Beauty also notes that John "seemed to know just how a horse feels," implying that John understands that horses have feelings beyond simple pain (20).[17] The alignment of these two men undermines the differences Black Beauty repeatedly sets up and shows just how similar the country and the city are, even if Black Beauty himself misses those similarities.

Sewell also shows that the city provides better opportunities for improving conditions for both workers and horses. In the country, workers have little to no control over the treatment of horses, but as workers in the city struggle to protect their own rights, they have the chance to protect animals as well. Jerry Barker clearly thinks about the rights of horses along with those of men, and, because he owns his own cab and horses, he can give the horses those rights. Through discussion and example, Jerry can influence others to provide horses with some rights. While Jerry does not have more power than the other cabbies, his Christian beliefs, his eloquence, and his leadership abilities allow him to shape others' opinions. He convinces the Governor to support these ideas, showing he truly can influence people in power, and he urges the other cabbies to follow his practices. As owners and operators, these men have control over their own horses; furthermore, they can benefit many more individuals and animals through their positive influence. If Jerry convinces one man who then convinces another and so on, he may create significant change in his community and ultimately change the city itself. However, men in the country such as York, the earl's wife's groom, do not have that ability. York cannot even offer ease for Black Beauty and Ginger, though he is directly responsible for their welfare. The owners of the horses have more influence here and the workers have little power. These differences undermine Black Beauty's belief in the superiority of the country, but again highlight that humans are still the most significant factor in his life in both locales.

The blurred line between country and city

Not only does *Black Beauty* offer clear evidence of positive and negative aspects of both the country and the city, the novel ends on an uncertain note regarding the future for Jerry and Black Beauty when they retire to the country. Unquestionably, both experience considerable danger in the city and ultimately find themselves near death from those dangers. Jerry's doctor tells him that he must leave the city and go to the country in order to recover from his illness. Jerry's daughter describes their proposed new home as one "that will just suit us, with a garden, and a henhouse, and apple trees" and a job for both her father and her brother (193–4). Certainly a future in the country looks positive for Jerry and his family, but the novel offers no real evidence of what occurs after they move there. Only the optimistic thoughts of Jerry's daughter suggest that they will be better off; the novel offers no real confirmation that the family is happy in their new surroundings. Very similarly, Black Beauty returns to the county after the city nearly kills him from overwork. Undoubtedly, returning to the country saves him from certain death. The farrier convinces Skinner, his owner at the time, to rest him and then sell him to a new owner rather than send him to the knacker (one who kills and renders animals) because he cannot work. As I have noted earlier, Black Beauty's describes his "final home" (as the chapter is titled) in idealistic language, but his belief about the permanence of that home is open to challenge. His only evidence for believing that he will live there for the rest of his life rests on the promise of the women who bought him that they will never sell him. These women have little power (although admittedly more power than Black Beauty does). There is no guarantee that his return to the country has not started the cycle again and that he will never return to the city.

Conclusion

Reading Sewell's novel in light of theories about the country and the city espoused by Raymond Williams and William Cronon provides a framework for highlighting the contradictions within Sewell's novel and reveals an important point about pastoral: Place alone does not guarantee bliss or agony; instead, a state of Edenic tranquility depends largely on human behavior regardless of the environment. Black Beauty's idealization of the country and vilification of the city overlooks dangers that affect horses and humans alike in both settings. Exposing the complicated view of the country and the city in *Black Beauty* calls into question the underlying assumptions about pastoral literature represented in many earlier descriptions of the genre. These contradictory elements should be examined in other texts of the time to expand our understanding of the country and the city in the Victorian era.

Notes

1. Both Moira Ferguson and Robert Dingley refer to the country settings of *Black Beauty* as idyllic.
2. Black Beauty is not only a character, he is the narrator of the novel. Copeland, Hansen, Colombat, Gavin ("Autobiography"), and Cosslett all discuss the novel as an animal autobiography. For an examination of the genre as a whole, see DeMello; this volume includes chapters by Hansen and Copeland.
3. Although it is a broad generalization, many writers in the Victorian era did in fact idealize nature in a variety of ways. Often this idealization can be attributed to a reaction against industrialization and urbanization. John Parham attributes this feeling to individuals who participated in what Peter Gould calls the "'Back to Nature and Back to the Land' movement influenced by figures such as Carlyle and Ruskin" (65).
4. Both Gifford and Garrard exclude women writers from most of their discussion of pastoral literature, although Gifford does bring women authors into his discussion of the anti-pastoral. They also both elaborate on their definitions of the pastoral later in their texts.

5 Williams returns to discussions of Hardy and Dickens throughout *The Country and the City*. I have simplified Williams's points here due to space constraints.
6 In fact, Williams argues that our modern understanding of the city of London was created by Dickens and his fiction (153).
7 Cronon examines Chicago in *Nature's Metropolis*, but his arguments can easily apply to England and other Western cultures as well. As Williams shows in *The Country and the City*, the examination and comparison of the urban and the rural occurs in a variety of ways through a long history of literature. In "The Trouble with Wilderness," Cronon argues that the wilderness is also constructed by humans; however, a consideration of wilderness is outside the focus of this chapter.
8 Black Beauty has forgiven or forgotten this, although Joe has not. He introduces himself to Black Beauty as "little Joe Green that almost killed you" (212).
9 Williams discusses this idea in his analysis of the country as good and the city as bad. Throughout *The Country and the City* Williams highlights the cyclical nature of the way the dichotomy works.
10 Gina Dorré examines the relationship between horses and trains in *Victorian Fiction and the Cult of the Horse*. In her chapter "Handling the 'Iron Horse': Dickens, Travel, and the Derailing of Victorian Masculinity" she argues that the trains are symbolic not just of progress, but of the conflict related to that so-called progress.
11 Several critics examine Sewell's novel as making other social statements. Peter Stoneley, Robert Dingley, and Moira Ferguson examine the novel in terms of its alignments to abolitionist thought. Peter Hollindale and Adrienne Gavin discuss the novel's commentary—or lack of commentary—about war. Gina Dorré connects the novel to the treatment of women by correlating the bearing rein and the corset. Sewell's more explicit argument about the treatment of animals features only minimally in most discussions of the novel.
12 Sewell's novel follows this belief to a point. However, there are notable variances. As I will discuss later in the chapter, the earl's wife overuses the bearing rein against the recommendations of her groom, but one of the kindest owners Black Beauty has is a cab driver.
13 Ginger and Black Beauty experience the use of the bearing rein together at the earl's estate, a point discussed later in this chapter. Ginger's tale is even more horrific than Black Beauty's. Like him she is sold by the earl to an owner in the city, and later dies from overwork.
14 Although Cronon describes humans as having the power to define both the city and the country, by showing the horses and the workers as similar, *Black Beauty* argues that many humans are powerless to affect their environment. In the novel, human workers lose that power largely due to their position in a class-based social system; many have control of very little because of their lower status. Unfortunately, an extensive discussion of class is outside of the focus of this chapter.
15 With only a few exceptions, the majority of humans that Black Beauty bonds with are men. See Ferguson for an analysis of some of the novel's gender implications, including their connections to social class.
16 As Diane L. Beers explains: "On one street, [citizens] might see a driver whipping a team of horses ... On another street, they might hop onto an omnibus meant to carry thirty or forty passengers but struggling instead with double that number" (63–4). She also notes that "approximately twenty-five thousand streetcar horses died from overwork annually" at the end of the nineteenth century and "Typically, a driver would simply unhitch the dead animal and deposit the body along the curb" (Beers 64).

17 Pain as a means of differentiating humans from nonhuman animals remains a topic of discussion within animal rights discourse even in the twenty-first century. Peter Singer discusses this in *Animal Liberation* and notes that "pain is a state of consciousness" which is the key to the ongoing debate. If dissenters do not believe animals have consciousness, they cannot believe that animals feel pain.

Works cited

Beers, Diane L. *For the Prevention of Cruelty: The History and Legacy of Animal Rights Activism in the United States*. Athens: Ohio UP, 2006.

Bronstein, Jamie L. *Caught in the Machinery: Workplace Accidents and Injured Workers in Nineteenth-Century Britain*. Stanford, CA: Stanford UP, 2008.

Colombat, Jacqueline. "Mission Impossible: Animal Autobiography." *Cahiers Victoriens et Édouardiens* 39 (1994): 37–49.

Copeland, Marion. "'Straight from the Horse's Mouth': Equine Memoirs and Autobiographies." In DeMello 2013, 179–92.

Cosslett, Tess. "Child's Place in Nature: Talking Animals in Victorian Children's Literature." *Nineteenth-Century Contexts* 23.4 (2002): 475–95.

Cronon, William. *Nature's Metropolis: Chicago and the Great West*. New York: Norton, 1991.

———. "The Trouble with Wilderness; or Getting Back to the Wrong Nature." *Uncommon Ground: Rethinking the Human Place in Nature*. Ed. William Cronon. New York: Norton, 1996. 69–90.

DeMello, Margo, ed. *Speaking for Animals: Animal Autobiographical Writing*. New York: Routledge, 2013.

Dingley, Robert. "A Horse of a Different Color: *Black Beauty* and the Pressures of Indebtedness." *Victorian Literature and Culture* 25.2 (1997): 241–51.

Dorré, Gina M. *Victorian Fiction and the Cult of the Horse*. Aldershot: Ashgate, 2006.

Ferguson, Moira. "Breaking in Englishness: *Black Beauty* and the Politics of Gender, Race and Class." *Women: A Cultural Review* 5.1 (1994): 34–52.

Garrard, Greg. "Pastoral." *Ecocriticism*. 2nd ed. New Critical Idiom Series. London: Routledge, 2012. 33–58.

Gavin, Adrienne. "The Autobiography of a Horse?: Reading Anna Sewell's *Black Beauty* as Autobiography." *Representing Victorian Lives*. Ed. Martin Hewitt. Leeds, England, UK: Leeds Centre for Victorian Studies, 1999. 51–62.

———. "Black Beauty: Pacifist Novel?" *The Journal of Children's Literature Studies* 1.2 (2004): 1–13.

Gifford, Terry. *Pastoral: The New Critical Idiom*. London: Routledge, 1999.

Hansen, Natalie Corinne. "Horse Talk: Horses and Human(e) Discourses." In DeMello 2013, 207–30.

Hollindale, Peter. "Plain Speaking: Black Beauty as a Quaker Text." *Children's Literature* 28 (2000): 95–111.

Parham, John. *Green Man Hopkins: Poetry and the Victorian Ecological Imagination*. New York: Rodopi, 2010.

Sewell, Anna. *Black Beauty*. New York: Signet Classics, 2011.

Singer, Peter. *Animal Liberation: The Definitive Classic of the Animal Movement*. Updated Edition. New York: Ecco, 2009.

Stoneley, Peter. "Sentimental Emasculations: *Uncle Tom's Cabin* and *Black Beauty*." *Nineteenth-Century Literature* 54.1 (1999): 53–72.

Williams, Raymond. *The Country and the City*. New York: Oxford UP, 1975.

10 The environmental politics and aesthetics of Rider Haggard's *King Solomon's Mines*
Capital, mourning, and desire

John Miller

Henry Rider Haggard's depiction of phenomenal riches concealed within a sexualized African landscape in his breakthrough novel *King Solomon's Mines* has been variously taken to support and contest vested economic interests at a time of expanding British imperial influence and developing commodity culture. Published in 1885, the same year that the Berlin Conference formalized European colonial intentions in Africa, Haggard's romance for "big and little boys" (38) for all its apparent otherworldliness is an unavoidably political text, as a significant body of criticism has established. The discovery of diamonds in South Africa in 1867 and gold in 1885 transformed the region, in Laura Chrisman's words, "from a service station en route to India to a global centre of industrial production" (23). *King Solomon's Mines*, for Chrisman, is both a response to and a rewriting of "the narrative of modern capitalism in South Africa" that "mythologize[s] imperial history and its extraction of mineral wealth" (24). As such, Haggard's novel operates, in Anne McClintock's words, as a "disavowal of the origins of money in labour" (257) through which historical processes are transfigured into a mythic imaginary that evades meaningful engagement with empire's material impacts.

But while in Chrisman's and McClintock's analysis Haggard's recourse to a mythological frame of reference operates as part of his legitimation of colonial capitalism, Gerald Monsman has taken a different approach that seizes on a 1905 speech of Haggard's in Toronto published as an appendix to his autobiography *The Days of My Life* (1926). Here Haggard insists on an alternative conception of value to the merely economic:

> of what use is wealth unless you have men and women—healthy men and women—these are the real wealth of the nation. You remember the old Greek fable of Antaeus, how, whenever he fell to earth he arose fresh and strong. So it is with us. Do not believe, gentlemen, that wealth is everything ... The strength of a people, gentlemen, is not to be found in their Wall Streets, it is to be found in the farms and fields and villages.
> (2: 271)

Haggard's polemic against what he saw as a widespread disregard for rural interests proceeds from a reflection on the denouement of *King Solomon's Mines* in which the novel's three heroes, Allan Quartermain, Captain Good, and Sir Henry Curtis, find themselves starving in a cave, "surrounded by all the diamonds and all the gold of a continent." Haggard pointedly asks his listeners, "of what use were those diamonds and that gold to them?" (271). Developing Haggard's interest in Victorian social anthropology, Monsman concludes that *King Solomon's Mines* revolves around the belief that "the commercial and technological wealth of urban life is valueless apart from an Antaeus-like contact with the land and its fertility" (281).[1] Consequently, for Monsman, the novel's central narrative dynamic is not straightforwardly acquisitive, but structured around an anti-materialist desire for a return to the land in which is contained the "power of rebirth, renewal" (281) in an era notable for its emphasis on the manifold perils of cultural and physical degeneration.

The tension between Chrisman's historical materialist approach and Monsman's anthropological focus hinges on a readily observable contradiction in Haggard's writing which is the focus of this essay. On the one hand, Haggard's work recurrently evinces an economic agenda; his novels abound with lost fortunes and fantastic financial possibilities. On the other, his writing repeatedly privileges a landscape aesthetics that often serves as the focal point for a stinging critique of industrial modernity. Describing the African landscape in his first published article, "The Transvaal" (1876), for example, Haggard reflects in explicitly utilitarian terms on the region's future:

> those wastes, now so dismal and desolate, are at no distant date destined to support and enrich a large population; for underneath their surface lie all minerals in abundance and when the coal of England and of Europe is exhausted, there is sufficient stored up here to stock the world.
> (qtd. in *A Farmer's Year* 399)

Set against this entrepreneurial prognosis, however, are the sharply opposing sentiments of the eponymous narrator of *Allan Quartermain* (1887), the sequel to *King Solomon's Mines*. At the novel's outset, Quartermain, living idly in England, finds himself hankering after Africa's "wild land" for reasons that have nothing to do with economics: the "thirst for wilderness was on me ... I began to long to see the moonlight gleaming silvery white over the wide veldt and mysterious sea of bush, and watch the lines of game travelling down the ridges to the water" (9). Utility, then, rubs shoulders with mystery in Haggard's imagining of Africa, the profit motive offset by the anticipation of an environmental profundity in which material, mineralogical value dissolves into the gleam of the moonlight.

The paradox of Haggard's concurrent support of and retreat from the culture of Victorian capitalism has not been lost in recent criticism. Francis

O'Gorman explains how Haggard's fiction occupies "a strikingly multiple position in accounts of the relationship between high capitalism and literature," so that his novels transform capitalism's "narratives into aesthetic delight even while, at the level of plot, loudly censoring its workings" (172). O'Gorman's assertion that contrary views are present in individual texts provides a salutary corrective to the assumption that the oscillation between capitalist and anti-capitalist positions corresponds to Haggard's public versus private opinions, expressed, one might suppose, alternatively in his nonfiction and fiction. Norman Etherington's suggestion, for instance, that "very little of the imperialism which Haggard preached from public platforms and in the press is written into his romances" (91) appears rather dubious now given Chrisman's and McClintock's conclusive accounts of the ways in which *King Solomon's Mines*, among other texts, engages with imperial politics. That Haggard was both a conspicuous public figure and a popular novelist does not itself account adequately for his consistent inconsistency when it comes to ideologies of capital in relation to African landscape. Both his fiction and his nonfiction contain numerous uncertainties and contradictions on the topic of imperial economics in relation to environment and nation that merit more detailed consideration.

Crucially, the key effect of Haggard's fluctuation between capitalism and anti-capitalism is to allow the divergent approaches of Chrisman and Monsman to sit alongside each other with a surprising degree of coherence. Not only might *King Solomon's Mines* be read as either a justification of imperial exploitation of African resources *or* a denunciation of the same in favor of an idealization of the natural, the unspoiled, and the primitive, but it might also legitimately be understood to be both of these at the same time. Haggard's novel, it seems, encourages precisely what it disapproves. Chrisman argues that this very duality is a central part of Haggard's complicity with imperial ideologies as the "attempt to deny, in the very site of capital accumulation, any association with the dynamics of capitalism itself" (57). Certainly, this argument has weight. The disavowal Chrisman identifies, however, operates through the subordination of capital to the antimaterialist priority Monsman summarizes as the quest for a "lost primordial identity" (292), which tells us not just about the dynamics of capitalism, but also about the dynamics of Haggard's early strain of environmentalism, a theme not directly addressed by Chrisman. Unpacking the ideological investments of *King Solomon's Mines* leads us toward what today we would call Haggard's environmental politics, that is to say the ways in which his vision of the South African landscape as the site of economic opportunity and mythic dwelling embodies particular kinds of ecological consciousness: the instrumentalist view of land as resource alongside a view that privileges the natural world as the primal home of humanity.

"Prosperity to the plough": Squire Haggard's environmental nation

Lindy Stiebel, whose study of Haggard's depictions of South African landscapes is the closest thing to date to an ecocritical approach, casts Haggard as something approaching an environmental prophet. "The efforts to preserve 'Nature' as wilderness," she writes, "enclosed and contained for future generations is one of the most positive spinoffs from Haggard's romanticisation of the African landscape he so loved" (134). These identifications of Haggard the environmentalist revolve around his imagining of two distinct ecological categories, the farm and the wilderness, and two distinct geographical arenas, the overdeveloped metropolitan center and the underdeveloped colonial outpost, most frequently Britain and Africa. Appreciation of the nuances of Haggard's environmental vision, then, pivots to a large extent on the interrelations between these modes, specifically the ways in which the management of agricultural land and the celebration of uncultivated land unfold and rely on a paradigm of colonial relations.

Turning first to the agricultural, as himself a professional farmer initially in South Africa and subsequently in his native Norfolk from 1889 until 1920, Haggard's interests in the land ran deep. Agricultural reform comprised a prominent part of his unsuccessful 1895 attempt to gain election as Conservative Member of Parliament under the slogan "prosperity to the plough" and his writings on rural life are voluminous. His daughter Lilias remembered that he wrote "more than fifty articles on the agricultural situation for the *Daily Express* and the *Yorkshire Post*" which he later assembled into his two-volume magnum opus *Rural England* (1902) (181). This work comprised, Haggard insisted, "the heaviest labour of all my laborious life" in which meticulous county by county adumbrations of the condition of the English countryside amount to a *cri de coeur* against "our national neglect of husbandry" (1: 2). Preceding *Rural England* had been a volume of reflections on his own farming experiences in *A Farmer's Year* (1899); following it were the similarly oriented *A Gardener's Year* (1905) and *Rural Denmark and its Lessons* (1911). *A Farmer's Year* and *Rural England* in particular drew a considerable amount of critical approval (a fate not always shared by Haggard's fiction). A review of *Rural England* in the *Contemporary Review* praised it as, "written with a professional charm and a whole-hearted love of the soil, of growing things, of country sights and sounds" (qtd. in Cohen 174). Despite his celebrity as a writer of romance, Haggard's fiction at times seemed an unfortunate distraction from his more momentous agricultural work. By the end of the century he confessed himself haunted by the desire "to do something in my day more practical than the invention of romance upon romance" (qtd. in Ellis 153). At one moment in his autobiography he regretted that "although I should have liked to place on record my views on Irish agriculture, in place thereof I have found myself obliged to edit certain of the reminiscences of Mr Allan Quatermain" (2: 85). Rather than a peripheral consideration at the margins of his more significant literary ventures, questions of agricultural policy are absolutely central to reaching a full appreciation of the environmental ideology at work in Haggard's writing.

Although some forms of farming, principally in its manifestation in large-scale monoculture, may now be far from immune from implication in our global ecological crisis, Haggard's rural ideal was a long way distant from this kind of corporate practice. The rural prosperity he campaigned for did not involve a crude maximization of the land's economic potential, but in fact aspired to a redistribution of agricultural wealth. His most prominent and controversial aim was the division of land into a series of smallholdings that would prevent "the race of yeoman [from] becoming extinct," and thereby restore the rural landscape, re-installing the "love of the soil" after many years of desperate agricultural decline, characterized perhaps most starkly by accelerating rural depopulation (*Rural England* 2: 569, 546). For all Haggard's reputation as the hidebound conservative squire, there is a radical edge to his agrarian politics that he was fully aware of. Haggard pondered, "what would be thought of one who, posing as a member of the Tory party, yet earnestly advocated the division of the land amongst about ten times as many as hold it at present, thereby spoiling a great many great estates?" (*Days* 2: 108). A further aim of this rural regeneration was to address that most prevalent of Victorian social anxieties, urban poverty, defined by Haggard as "the problem of every civilised country of the earth" (*Days* 2: 188). Often in his disquisitions on this favorite hobby horse of his, Haggard frames the problem in a wider geographical context, emphasizing the environmental contrast between urban Britain and the wide open spaces of Britain's colonies: "the glutted, foul, menacing cities, the gorgeous few, the countless miserables! And beyond the empty land which could feed them all and give them health and happiness from the cradle to the grave" (*Days* 2: 188). Haggard's work with the Dominions Royal Commission during and immediately after the First World War was devoted to precisely this problem; he travelled widely through the empire with a view to securing land for the resettlement of returning soldiers on agricultural plots in which they could sustain themselves and their families while alleviating Britain's urban congestion.

The overarching premise behind Haggard's agrarian vision, then, is an interconnection between land, nation, and subjectivity that coheres into an essentially, but problematically, ecological trope that Gail Low has designated "racial environmentalism." This view, Low explains, "details a paradigm in which external forces ... mould the racial character and physical attributes of the various human groups" (16–17). At its most basic level "racial environmentalism" expresses a widespread "correlation between environment and health" (18) that is strikingly apparent, as Low illustrates, in Haggard's report on Salvation Army colonies in Britain and the United States, *The Poor and the Land* (1905). While Haggard saw the towns breeding "puny pygmies," the country yeoman in stark contrast was eulogized as "the blood and sinew of the race" (qtd. in Low 18). Ideologically charged imaginings of Britain as the greatest of nations hinged, therefore, on an ideal of natural life exemplified by rural laborers (the central point of his Toronto speech). As Low puts it, the "principle of the healthy body was a national and racial imperative" (19). By extension, as Haggard continually exhorted, the sound environmental management that would facilitate this was the key to the nation's success. "Agriculture," he explains in the preface to *A Farmer's Year*, "that primaeval occupation and the cleanest of them all ... means more than the growing of grass and grain. It means, among other things, the engendering and achievement of patient, even minds in sound enduring bodies" (ix). Haggard's argument ultimately proceeds along the lines that restoring the yeoman class restores the land that restores the nation.

Haggard's environmental aesthetics

Framing these contentions in the language of later environmental movements, we might think of Haggard's ideas as a form of social ecology through which social and environmental problems are understood in intimate relation. In current environmentalist terminology, Haggard's emphasis is evidently broadly anthropocentric. As he writes in *Rural England*, "the land should support men, not men the land" (2: 543). But for all this stress on the land as livelihood, there is also a consistent attention to the nonhuman in Haggard's writing that exceeds mere use value. The ornate final words of *The Days of My Life* spell out Haggard's sense of his own deep affiliation to the natural world: "So ends the chronicle of Henry Rider Haggard — ... a lover of flowers, a lover of the land and of all the creatures that dwell thereon, but most of all perhaps, a lover of his country" (2: 232). As Haggard arrives at the climax of his florid list, we reach a connection of nature and nation that for all its ideologically charged patriotic fervor, relies on the incorporation of other organisms into his idealistic nexus of agrarian culture, labor, and national health. Consequently, Haggard's environmental ethos bears comparison to that of another farmer/writer, the influential American conservationist Aldo Leopold, whose formulation of a land ethic, in particular, elucidates the environmental implications of Haggard's rural vision. "The land ethic," Leopold writes, "enlarges the boundaries of the community to include soils, waters, plants, animals, or collectively: the land" (204). Haggard's inclusion of "all the creatures that dwell thereon" (what Leopold would have called the "biotic community") indicates that there is more to his ecological leanings than just pragmatics, however pressing those pragmatics may be.

Consequently, Haggard's attention to the good stewardship of the British countryside is invariably accompanied by an aesthetic discourse that includes the nonhuman in its depiction of a deeply valued rural life. Any number of passages from either his fiction or nonfiction could be chosen to illustrate Haggard's merging of the agricultural and the literary into prose that finds much to rejoice about in the flora and fauna of the English countryside. Indeed, even the driest of Haggard's agricultural treatises are interspersed with descriptive passages stimulated by landscapes of "exceptional loveliness" (1: 27). One notable extended evocation of Haggard's own rural Norfolk is the now little read novel *Colonel Quaritch V.C.* (1888),[2] which the publisher Charles Longman considered "the best description of English country life in the nineteenth century" (Haggard, *Private Diaries* 116). Setting the scene in the first chapter, Haggard has Quaritch reflect on the long history of his home, built by monks in the fifteenth century:

> And as they built it, so, with some slight additions, it had remained to this day, for in those ages men did not skimp their flint, and oak, and mortar. It was a beautiful little spot, situated upon the flat top of a swelling hill, which comprised the ten acres of grazing ground originally granted, and was, strange to say, still the most magnificently-timbered piece of ground in the country side. For on the ten acres of grass land there stood over fifty great oaks, some of them pollards of the most enormous antiquity, and others which had, no doubt, originally grown very close together, fine upstanding trees with a wonderful length and girth of bole.
>
> (6)

Although Haggard had not yet at this point attained his own farm, an agriculturalist's perspective is unmistakable in the assessment of the ten acres of grazing land, an amenity that, vitally, appears inseparable from the appreciation of this "beautiful little spot." Haggard's landscape aesthetics here are familiar as a paradigmatic depiction of the English countryside in which the key element is a depth of history, emphasized by the "enormous antiquity" of the oaks that surround Quaritch's venerable abode. As Haggard wrote in *A Farmer's Year*, "the crown and charm of rural England is its antiquity" (7). Politics and aesthetics converge in a traditional mode of country living in which the harmony of the scene is affirmed by a sense of ecological thriving. Haggard's Norfolk is a mixture of nostalgia and utopianism, in which the "primaeval occupation" of agriculture reveals the world as it was meant to be: man, landscape, livestock, trees and flowers joined in an ancient coexistence that precedes the vulgar aberrations of urban modernity.

This nostalgic investment in the country also, significantly, leads Haggard away from a materialist register towards language that is at times unabashedly spiritual. Introducing *A Farmer's Year* as the thoughts of one "who lives a good deal in the company of Nature, who loves it and tries to observe it as best he may," Haggard finds himself drawn to the "inner meaning and mystery of things," concluding grandiloquently that "Nature is a spirit who must be worshipped with the spirit as well as admired with the eyes" (1–2). Haggard immediately counters this flight of prose, bringing it straight back to earth as he advises, "Let the reader of utilitarian mind have patience, however, for there will be a practical side to this book. I am a farmer and engaged in a desperate struggle to make my farming pay" (2). The sudden turn in Haggard's mood from the mystic to the practical man, who devotes a good proportion of the ensuing pages to complaining about prices, provides an apt summary of the doubled stakes of Haggard's agrarian discourse. Rather than an irreconcilable opposition, the spiritual and the material appear as complements to one another; the soil, for Haggard, is both work and meditation, humdrum and transcendent, at the same time.

Haggard's interest in the land's history fuses with the poetic account of his birth that begins *Rural England*: "I was born in a farmhouse, among high-edged pastures near to the silence of a great wood, and I suppose the first sounds that my ears heard were the lowing of kine and the bleating of sheep" (1: 10). Such a reflection on his rural biotic community identifies Haggard as a countryman to the core, but also connects with a macrocosmic sense in his writing of the broader human past and a broader still obsession across his *oeuvre* that McClintock describes as "an unusually intense preoccupation with origins" (236). Vitally, Haggard's interest in anthropology hinges on a fascination for mythic beginnings and lost histories that coheres with his concern for agricultural heritage. The overarching question for Haggard is our "lost primordial identity," to return to Monsman. Just as Haggard establishes his own origins in the natural world by re-imagining the first sounds he heard of animal life, so he looks to human origins in a mystic union of man and land that is revisited in the day-to-day work of tilling the soil. Accordingly, what is left for Haggard in the money-driven, technologized urban age is a profound sense of mourning. In his diary Haggard wrote poignantly on the sale of the Bradenham farm on which he was born: "Now it has gone and doubtless soon the axe will bring down all its familiar woods and even the great copper beech on which every one of us cut his name, while probably the Hall itself will become a farmstead or a ruin" (133). The carved names on the condemned trees reveal the loss of this estate as something much more than the loss of a farm; the sale of Bradenham stands in for modernity's wiping away of a rural past that Haggard clings to as the expression of the primal identity of himself, his country, and of humanity. As such, Haggard's conception of environmental value must ultimately be understood to problematize the bottom line of capitalist modernity with an insistence on a traditional mode of rural living driven by subsistence and a deep sense of the aesthetic, rather than by the intention to maximize profit margins.

Romance, wilderness, nostalgia

The year 1885 was something of a high point for agrarian nostalgia. Richard Jefferies's novel *After London: Wild England*, for example, presents a reactionary depiction of the collapse of industrial civilization that takes significant pleasure in the simple rural culture that takes hold in post-apocalyptic England. "The Relapse into Barbarism" Jefferies depicts in the first section of his novel overwrites capitalist modernity with a back-to-the-land gesture that aims to consummate a widespread fantasy of the return of the rural in the years of England's agricultural crisis. Evidently, *King Solomon's Mines* as a novel about Africa does not comprise a direct commentary on the condition of rural England in the way that *Colonel Quaritch V.C.* would three years later, or Haggard's flood of nonfiction on either side of the turn of the century. Moreover, *King Solomon's Mines* does not offer any tangential commentary on English agricultural practice through an African example as *Allan Quartermain* does with its depiction of a system of smallholdings practiced by the lost white race, the Zu-Vendis. As Quartermain approvingly reports, "Agriculture is the great business of the country, and is really well understood and carried out" (160). Despite this brief but pointed allusion to agricultural reform, Africa generally functions for Haggard in direct environmental contrast to England. In *Allan Quartermain*, our hero's "thirst for wilderness" appears as a response to his dissatisfaction with the "prim English country, with its trim hedgerows and cultivated fields" (9). Even a well-ordered English countryside is no match for Africa in Quartermain's sensibility. But, importantly, if Haggard's agrarian politics comprise one aspect of his criticism of an urban culture of capital, his depiction of wilderness constitutes another.

The Africa of *King Solomon's Mines* is exactly the wilderness that Quartermain desires. As Quartermain and companions depart into the African interior in search of Curtis's lost brother (with the lure of diamonds an added, if initially uncertain incentive), Haggard lingers not just on the difficulty of the landscape they traverse, but on its extraordinary aesthetic appeal. Even as the adventurers face a slow death from thirst in a remote desert there is space for Quartermain's first-person narrative to marvel as the sun comes up at the "spear upon spear of glorious light flashing far away across the boundless wilderness, piercing and firing the veils of mist, till the desert was draped in a tremulous golden glow and it was day" (88). Having survived this first ordeal, they find themselves in a somewhat friendlier terrain that still allows Haggard to keep up his purple prose. A brook "babbled merrily away at our side, the soft air murmured through the leaves of the silver trees, doves cooed around, and bright-winged birds flashed like living gems from bough to bough. It was like Paradise" (108). "The magic of the place" then leaves Haggard's heroes charmed "into silence" (109). Haggard's evocation of wonderment as a principal mode of experience in this distant location evidently taps into a well-established romantic discourse of nature. There is perhaps a degree of incongruity in the rough and ready trader Quartermain's elevated poetic tone in such passages, but nonetheless this attitude forms a key part of Africa's function in Haggard's broader environmental imaginary. At the edges of empire, beyond the reach (or so we are meant to think) of even the most intrepid white traveler, there remains a primal world that has a deep influence over those few strangers that visit it.

Such writing illustrates the central environmental premise of the romance form that Haggard adopts in *King Solomon's Mines* for the first, resoundingly successful time. Romance hinges on quest, which operates through the journey away from familiar territory into the unknown, a movement that implies a kind of geographical epistemology, that is to say a belief that the world might still contain areas at the end of Britain's imperial century with its exhaustive mapping and classifying that have not yet been brought into the pale of colonial knowledge. Haggard's extensive writings on romance reveal something approaching an obsession about the relationship between the advance of industrial modernity and the wild, environmental resources left available to the romancer. In the *African Review* he lamented, "Soon the ancient mystery of Africa will have vanished … where will the romance writers of future generations find a safe and secret place unknown to the pestilent accuracy of the geographer, in which to lay their plots? ("Elephant Smashing and Lion Shooting" [66]). Across Haggard's commentary on romance, then, is a consistent emphasis on the environmentality of form.[3] Nor was this connection lost on early commentary on *King Solomon's Mines*. Chrisman cites an article in *The Spectator* in which a reviewer wonders in relation to Haggard's novel, "now that the whole earth is being searched as with a microscope, and that we are really approaching its secret places—the centre of Africa, the great unexplored islands like New Guinea … whether we shall ever find anything really marvellous" (qtd. in Chrisman 26). Haggard's fiction is precisely about preserving an imaginative (which is also an ecological) space for the marvelous. If romance relies on distance, secrecy, and wildness as a kind of geographical *sine qua non* of its narrative structure, then romance evidently carries with it a certain anti-modern energy, despite its implication in the "progressive" attitudes of colonial politics. Development, for Haggard, appears as an impoverishment that once again emphasizes the investment of his literary aesthetics in the nonhuman.

Haggard's writing, therefore, craves wilderness, an orientation that links him strongly to one of environmentalism's oldest but most problematic tropes. As William Cronon explains, "wilderness serves as the unexplained foundation on which so many of the quasi-religious values of modern environmentalism rest" (80). The cultural privileging of wilderness as, in Cronon's words, the "ultimate landscape of authenticity" (80) hinges on the apprehension of the land as empty of a human presence, "virgin" land that ostensibly recapitulates the primal experience of man alone with unforgiving nature. There are many problems with his position, perhaps most significantly the way in which the Western "discovery" of wilderness operates as an erasure and/or dehumanization of an indigenous presence. Despite the continuous habitation of many "wilderness" areas for several thousand years, native histories and cultures are routinely denied or reduced to the weary trope of savagery, noble or otherwise, that services the colonial fantasy of the wild landscape. The establishment of national parks at the start of the twentieth century in particular often came at a considerable cost to indigenous people who were relocated to make way for an "authentic" wilderness experience. Stiebel's identification of wilderness conservation as a "positive spinoff" of Haggard's romanticized Africa then depends very much on perspective. The idea of wilderness evokes knotty questions of race, social justice, and imperial polity.

This is starkly apparent in Haggard's narration of the grisly fate of the African servant Khiva in *King Solomon's Mines*. The novel's fourth chapter, "An Elephant Hunt," represents a paradigmatic account of the colonial adventurer in the wilderness that is subtly advertised by Haggard in his prelude to the action as something approaching a definitive model of this kind of experience. Beginning with the disclaimer, "Now I do not propose to narrate at full length all the incidents of our long journey up to Sitanda's kraal" (70), Haggard announces the following events as that kernel that has survived his swathing editorial reductions, very much the heart of the matter. The landscape is precisely what would be expected from a colonial archetype of wilderness adventuring: the "kloofs in the bush were covered with dense bush," as around Quartermain and his companions spreads "the great sea of pathless, silent bush" in a "spot of peculiar loveliness" (72). What follows, however, is strikingly grisly as the men come to grips with the teeming game of this remote corner of Africa. Good first takes a potshot at a giraffe, "shattering the spinal column" (72). Shortly afterwards, they observe the singular sight of a "sable antelope bull" with a "magnificent black-maned lion" "transfixed" by its horns. Quartermain concludes that the "lion, unable to free himself, had torn and bitten at the back and the neck of the bull, which maddened with fear and pain, had rushed on till it dropped dead" (72). Such gruesome attention to the minutiae of agony is characteristic of Haggard's writing, although, perhaps ironically, Haggard himself would eschew blood sports later in life after a mysterious dream of his dog Bob that convinced him of "the intimate ghostly connection between all members of the animal world" (*Days* 2: 162).

Nonetheless, Haggard's fiction remained deeply invested in violence against animals as a sign of the primal human or nature interaction, which in the chapter's denouement sees Khiva come to a macabre end when he heroically interposes his body between Good and a charging elephant. "With a scream of pain the brute seized the poor Zulu, hurled him to the earth, and placing his huge foot on his body about the middle, twined his trunk round his upper part and *tore him in two*" (original emphasis 79). Haggard's italics impart a chilling relish to the scene's gory conclusion that illustrates the necessity for any reclamation of *King Solomon's Mines* as an environmentalist text to face head-on such violence as a central aspect of its evocation of wilderness. Crucially, Khiva's body is sacrificed to an ideal of primitivism that for all Haggard's curmudgeonly disapproval of capitalist modernity also buttresses the novel's economic logic. It is only after the

168 *John Miller*

"wonderfully fine lot of ivory" garnered from the hunt is "carefully buried in the sand" that the adventurers turn to the apparently less urgent task of burying the Zulu's remains (79). The subordination of native labor to the imperatives of capital is here inseparable from the landscape aesthetics that structures Haggard's African romances. If the journey into the continent's heart constitutes a journey back to primal nature, it is a primal nature that immediately invites commodification for the benefit of the white intruder and at the expense of African life, both human and animal.

Africa's body

The relationship between the ecological and the economic in Haggard's depiction of Africa in *King Solomon's Mines* is perhaps best understood, then, as an intricate pattern of desire and disavowal, to return to McClintock's and Chrisman's term. In desiring Africa's primal mythic "Nature," Haggard disavows the materialist modern world, but only to reproduce capital's all-consuming drive in the site of its supposed absence. Such complex dynamics unfold perhaps most notably in the sexual topography that Haggard writes onto the African interior. In part, this trope represents a conventional feminization of the natural world that emphasizes fruitfulness and nurture. In this vein, the Scottish poet James Thomson wrote in "A Voice from the Nile" (1881), a text mediated through the river's perspective, of the "Earth, All-Mother, all-beneficent, / Who held her mountains forth like opulent breasts / To cradle me and feed me with their snows" (3). Given Haggard's obsession for all things Egyptian, it is hard to imagine that Thomson's poem would not have reached his notice. The idea of nature's breasts at any rate appears to be a favorite metaphor of Haggard's in the 1880s. At the opening to *Allan Quartermain*, the eponymous hero writes of the longing to "lay us like little children on the great breast of nature that she perchance may soothe us" (14). *King Solomon's Mines* is notorious for the way in which this trope forms part of a broader eroticization of Africa, which has been identified as central to the text's participation in discourse of imperial capital.

The first hint of the adventure's bodily metaphorics comes with Quartermain's narrative of the treasure map he acquires, drawn by the sixteenth-century Portuguese speculator Da Silvestra as he lay dying in a cave "on the north side of the nipple of the southernmost of the two mountains I have named Sheba's Breasts" (56). Since the map functions as the key to becoming "the richest king since Solomon" (56), and appears, as several critics have pointed out, as an inverted and crudely sexualized representation of female anatomy, Haggard's corporeal register clearly connects with the discourse of colonial profit. The adventurers' descent into the mines at the novel's climax represents, in a sense, their moment of triumph. Leaving with enough gemstones to make them "exceedingly wealthy men" (232), they consummate the fantasy of a fantastic prosperity that awaits the bold imperialist. As McClintock explains, "the diamond mines are simultaneously the place of female sexuality (gendered reproduction), the source of treasure (economic production) and the site of imperial contest (racial difference)" (5). The exploitation of Africa's mineral resources is legitimated as a masculine entitlement, connected, as McClintock continues, to a "long tradition of male travel as an erotics of ravishment" (22) through which the landscape is imagined as passively inviting colonial domination. For William J. Scheick, the fantasy of Africa as body operates as a "'dirty joke' with mythic overtones" (21) in which "imperialism, racism and sexism coalesce" (27). As an apparent blueprint for environmental violence, this pattern seems to move us a long way from the ecological Haggard that Stiebel lauds, yet it is precisely in the imagery of Africa's body that Monsman finds the strongest evidence for Haggard's anti-materialism. "Sheba's breasts," he argues "are not narrowly indicative of the rapist-imperialist's sexual oppression of women," but part of a rhetoric of "human identity and its relation to nature in terms of a mother/mistress analogue in which birth and death are expressed by a female landscape both generative and fatal" (285).

A good deal of evidence can be marshaled from *King Solomon's Mines* and elsewhere in Haggard's *oeuvre* in support of Monsman's much greener reading. Quartermain's first glimpse of the curious mountains, for example, offers more than a blunt eroticism:

> there, not more than forty or fifty miles from us, glittering like silver in the early rays of the morning sun, were Sheba's breasts; and stretching away for hundreds of miles on each side of them was the great Suliman Berg. Now that I, sitting here, attempt to describe the extraordinary grandeur and beauty of that sight language seems to fail me. I am impotent before its memory.
>
> (93)

Clearly, Quartermain's gaze displays many familiar patterns of colonial writing. His estimation of the distances and dimensions of the landscape before him establishes himself as the organizing center of the scene as he instinctively prepares a mental cartography. If the equalization of the topography adds a certain male excitement to the economically driven act of imperial incursion, this energy is crucially offset by Quartermain's impotence before the "grandeur and beauty" that elevates the landscape beyond his carnal aspiration and marks Africa off from the coarsely erotic. Monsman makes much of the novel's wider engagement with the theme of impotence. Each of the three adventurers suffers from some kind of injured leg which, he argues, responds to the nineteenth-century slang "leg-business" to assert an erotic failure rather than ravishment.[4] Africa, significantly, is unavailable to the apparently crude attentions of Quartermain and his companions. After the initial view of the "breasts of Sheba," the mountains disappear into a "curious, gauzy mist" that veils them in "cloud-clad privacy" (94) as Africa withholds itself from colonial desire, even freezing and starving the adventurers as they seek comfort "under the nipple of Sheba's left breast" (99).

Moreover, as Haggard's Toronto speech insists, the supposed image of economic triumph in Solomon's mines, with the adventurers surrounded by "boxes full of gold" and the "dim glimmer of diamonds" (229) functions as anything but a celebration of capital. Rather, as Quartermain and his companions finally escape through a trapdoor to reappear above ground from what Haggard insistently denotes as the "bowels" of the mountain, the atmosphere is one of humiliation. "Smeared all over with dust and mud" (229) they are "shat out like lumps of excrement" in Monsman's evocative terminology (289). Africa it seems derides their eroticized mission with a scatological rebuff that displays the text's wider discomfort with the imperial obsession with profit. Accordingly, as he bids farewell to the white men, the newly installed king Ignosi bitterly perceives that "it is the bright stones ye love more than me, your friend" and pointedly debars his land to "traders with their guns and rum" (234).

The trope of Africa's body, then, signals the alienation of the colonizer from the regenerative potential of the land and reveals the continuity of Haggard's wilderness aesthetics with his broader agrarian politics. For Monsman, Haggard condemns "the choice of wealth by trade rather than the adoption of the land's mystic plenitude" (291). "A Tale of Three Lions," a short story from 1889, strengthens the sense of Haggard's opposition between capital and spirit as Quartermain, prospecting for gold, throws down his "pick and shovel in disgust" to "look out over the glorious stretch of country—the smiling valleys, the great mountains touched with gold—real gold of the sunset, and clothed in sweeping robes of bush, and stare into the depths of the perfect sky above; yes and thank Heaven I had got away from the cursing and coarse jokes of the miners" (188). Materialism is sordid, much like *King Solomon's Mines*' crudely sexualized treasure map, while the landscape, by contrast, is spiritually uplifting. The "real gold" of the African sunset ironically uses a mineralogical frame of reference to criticize the banausic culture of resource extraction, a technique that also appears in the description of the morning sun above "Sheba's breasts" "glittering like silver." And yet, for all the ecological worthiness that these arguments might associate with *King Solomon's Mines*, the novel concludes with a tacit endorsement of imperial speculation. Although Quartermain, facing starvation in the mines, saw the fantastic wealth before him as "a valueless thing at the last" (222), a letter from Curtis in the novel's final chapter identifies the value of a small portion of the stones the men make away with as "a hundred and eighty thousand" (243). What remains for all Haggard's earnest environmental rhetoric is a sense, as Chrisman argues, of the "legitimacy of imperial capitalism" (46) despite the novel's emphasis on its deleterious effects.

Clearly then, Haggard is more than a little torn. In the diary of his return to South Africa in 1914, he laments the "huge and hideous blue-grey dumps of the refuse ground dug from the mines" at Kimberley, but the unrelenting imaginative plundering of Africa throughout the remainder of his remarkably productive career continued to revolve around the drama of various kinds of resource extraction.⁵ In confirmation of a growing amount of work under the aegis of postcolonial ecocriticism, this paradox reveals that rather than diametrically opposed, there is an intimate relationship between imperial capital and environmental consciousness. Elizabeth DeLoughrey and George B. Handley argue that the late twentieth century witnessed a "naturalization of capitalism" whereby corporations involved in environmental violence might also simultaneously identify themselves as ecologically "responsible" (19). Such uncomfortable formulations are inextricably involved with current debates about sustainability, but are also part of a longer history of thinking about empire and ecology. Haggard's writing constitutes a significant example of an early form of environmentalism that simultaneously resists and encourages the determinations of capital. This is not to say that Haggard did not remain, as we have seen, critical of many aspects of Britain's economic development, or that he was employed in a deliberate, even conspiratorial, attempt to obfuscate the environmental impacts of empire: far from it. Instead, Haggard's incorporation of an ecological sensibility into a discourse of global capital illustrates the intractable problem of the imbrication of mainstream environmental thought in precisely the world order it appears to contest.

Notes

1 The allusion to Antaeus that Monsman addresses resonates with what may be identified (at least in part) as the conceptual foundations of the modern green movement. The son of Gaia and Poseidon in Greek mythology, Antaeus was an invincible wrestler as long as he remained in contact with the land, and so with his earth-goddess mother, but became weakened once that contact was broken. Antaeus, therefore, symbolizes an ecologically oriented interdependence between human and planet all the more powerful now for the biologist James Lovelock's adoption of Gaia as the figurehead of his hypothesis of the earth as a single system of life.
2 A curious twist to the novel's afterlife is the role of one Colonel Quaritch in James Cameron's 2009 ecological blockbuster *Avatar*. As a mining company in pursuit of the valuable mineral *unobtainium* set about devastating a distant, idyllic moon, the villainous Quaritch takes a lead role in attacking the indigenous Na'vi people, who are determined to protect their unique environment. The name is surely too unusual to be coincidental and indicates, if nothing else, Haggard's significant and ongoing legacy in popular culture.
3 For a full discussion of the environmentality of later Victorian romance, see John Miller, *Empire and the Animal Body* (2012).
4 Monsman explains that "Allan Quartermain has been mauled by a lion and his leg continues to pain him. Good's leg has been badly wounded by a native tolla; and Sir Henry is accidentally shot in the leg by Quartermain's son" (289).

5 See, for example, the 1917 Allan Quartermain novel *The Holy Flower*, in which it is Africa's botanical riches that lure the adventurers into the interior.

Works cited

Chrisman, Laura. *Rereading the Imperial Romance: British Imperialism and South African Resistance in Haggard, Schreiner and Plaatje*. Oxford: Oxford UP, 2000.
Cohen, Morton. *Rider Haggard: His Life and Works*. London: Hutchinson, 1960.
Cronon, William. "The Trouble with Wilderness; or, Getting Back to the Wrong Nature." *Uncommon Ground: Rethinking the Human Place in Nature*. Ed. William Cronon. New York: Norton, 1997. 69–90.
DeLoughrey, Elizabeth, and George B. Handley. *Postcolonial Ecologies: Literatures of the Environment*. Oxford: Oxford UP, 2011.
Ellis, Peter Beresford. *Rider Haggard: A Voice from the Infinite*. London: Routledge and Kegan Paul, 1978.
Etherington, Norman. *Rider Haggard*. Boston: Twayne, 1984.
Haggard, H. Rider. *Allan Quartermain*. Oxford: World's Classics, 1995.
——. *Colonel Quaritch V.C.: A Tale of Country Life*. Gillette: Wildside Press, 2000.
——. *The Days of My Life: An Autobiography*. 2 vols. London: Longmans, 1926.
——. *Diary of An African Journey*. Ed. Stephen Coan. New York: New York UP, 2000.
——. "Elephant Smashing and Lion Shooting." *African Review*, 9 June 1894: 762–3.
——. *A Farmer's Year*. London: Longmans, 1899.
——. *A Gardener's Year*. London: Longmans, 1905.
——. *The Holy Flower*. London: Ward, Lock, 1917.
——. *King Solomon's Mines*. Peterborough: Broadview, 2002.
——. *The Private Diaries of Sir Henry Rider Haggard, 1914–1925*. London: Cassell, 1980.
——. *Rural Denmark and its Lessons*. London: Longmans, 1911.
——. *Rural England*. 2 vols. London: Longmans, 1902.
——. "A Tale of Three Lions." *Allan's Wife*. London: Macdonald, 1963.
Haggard, Lilias. *The Cloak That I Left*. London: Hodder and Stoughton, 1957.
Jefferies, Richard. *After London: Wild England*. Oxford: World's Classics, 1995.
Leopold, Aldo. *A Sand County Almanac and Sketches Here and There*. Oxford: Oxford UP, 1987.
Low, Gail Ching-Liang. *White Skins, Black Masks: Representation and Colonialism*. London: Routledge, 1996.
McClintock, Anne. *Imperial Leather: Race, Gender and Sexuality in the Colonial Conquest*. London: Routledge, 1995.
Miller, John. *Empire and the Animal Body: Violence, Ecology and Identity in Victorian Adventure Fiction*. London: Anthem, 2012.
Monsman, Gerald. "Of Diamonds and Deities: Social Anthropology in H. Rider Haggard's *King Solomon's Mines*." *English Literature in Transition (1880–1920)* 43.3 (2000): 280–97.
O'Gorman, Francis. "Speculative Fictions and the Fortunes of H. Rider Haggard." *Victorian Literature and Finance*. Ed. Francis O'Gorman. Oxford: Oxford UP, 2007: 157–72.

Scheick, William J. "Adolescent Pornography and Imperialism in Haggard's *King Solomon's Mines.*" *English Literature in Transition (1880–1920)* 34.1 (1991): 19–30.

Stiebel, Lindy. *Imagining Africa: Landscape in H. Rider Haggard's African Romances.* Westport: Greenwood Press, 2001.

Thomson, James. *A Voice from the Nile and Other Poems.* London: Reeves and Turner, 1884.

11 Jane Loudon's wildflowers, popular science, and the Victorian culture of knowledge

Mary Ellen Bellanca

"I have often heard," wrote Jane Webb Loudon in 1842, "that knowledge is power, and I am quite sure that it contributes greatly to enjoyment" (*Botany* vii–viii). For Loudon, "knowledge" meant factual knowledge—especially about the natural world—which had become a commodity in Victorian culture, deemed both valuable in itself and an avenue for personal growth and social mobility. In the nineteenth century's early decades, according to Alan Rauch, "popular, cheap, and readable texts," including periodicals, books, encyclopedias, almanacs, instruction manuals, and educational texts for children, served to make knowledge about science, history, geography, and a host of other subjects "a cornerstone of progress, improvement, and civilization … enthusiastically produced, received, and promulgated by the culture" (14, 24). Jane Loudon voiced a Victorian commonplace when she wrote that studying nature "has a tendency to elevate and ameliorate the mind; and there is perhaps no branch of Natural History which more fully illustrates the truth of this remark than Botany" (*Botany* viii). The study of plants had intrigued many Britons since the mid- to late-eighteenth century as a fashionable and wholesome "amusement" and a way to inspire awe for the wonders of creation. By the 1830s and 1840s, the passion for botany suffused the culture as people engaged in collecting, sketching, gardening, making fern cases and herbariums, and reading about botany (Allen; Barber; Merrill). Writers used many different genres and styles to interpret botanical science for readers in virtually every social class who were compelled by what Barbara T. Gates calls "the Victorian need to know" ("Those" 210).

Jane Loudon is both representative of this phenomenon and distinctive for her individual achievements. A self-supporting author of fiction and miscellaneous works since age seventeen, she embarked on writing nonfiction about gardens and plants after marrying the horticultural author-editor John Claudius Loudon ("Account" xl). When *British Wild Flowers* was first published in 1844, Jane Loudon had recently brought out *A First Book of Botany*, *Botany for Ladies*, and several garden books, including three volumes of her ambitious multi-volume series *The Ladies' Flower-Garden* (1840–1848). Prolific and successful, Loudon made her own way in a botanical print market that, in Ann B. Shteir's analysis, increasingly demarcated boundaries between "professionalizing" and "popularizing" agendas, between strictly scientific discourse about plants and the expressive, spiritual, and artistic writing that appealed to amateurs, especially women (153). *British Wild Flowers* offered a popular guide to wildflower identification with a measure of scientific heft for readers interested in further study: organized taxonomically, it lists plants with Latin nomenclature and technical terms for their parts. At the same time, it ranges freely among non-factual discourses—floral folklore, mythology, and poetry—that were being discarded from modern scientific texts. *British Wild Flowers* distinguishes itself from most of Loudon's other works with its full-page color illustrations, a feature captivating in its visual splendor, though regarded as problematic by some authors concerned about fostering scientific proficiency, as we will see. Drawing on a breadth of human and cultural reference, *British Wild Flowers* integrates scientific and aesthetic, fact-based and subjective ways of knowing the world of plants. In doing so, it exudes the confidence of an experienced woman writer operating skillfully in the contested field of Victorian popular science.[1]

Jane and John Loudon devoted their careers to disseminating scientific knowledge as the key to self-advancement and to more informed, therefore more rewarding, appreciation of plants, gardens, and landscapes. As Jane Loudon wrote, "We never can enjoy thoroughly anything that we do not understand" (*Botany* 2). According to Sarah Dewis, the Loudons' works reached out to expanding middle-class readerships with a "discourse of inclusion" (238): they offered practical, accessible information as "a cultural alternative to the predominantly literary and classical culture of the educated English elite" and "a means to augment the social status and power of the less wealthy, including women" (3, 4). While John Loudon maintained that one must "be a good botanist" to "be a good gardener" (Howe 54), Jane Loudon's early nonfiction books keep botany and gardening separate; her moderately priced garden books such as *Instructions in Gardening for Ladies* contain very little material on botany. But the *Ladies' Flower-Garden* series, a more expensive reference work for affluent women readers (Dewis 199), brings the two spheres of knowledge together. It presents exhaustive information on cultivated plants, including numerous beautiful color plates, through the framework of systematic botany, so as to "be very useful in giving young people general ideas of the [taxonomic] arrangement of plants, and thus facilitating their study" of plant science (*Ladies'* vii).

Similar to the *Ladies' Flower-Garden* in its large size (about eleven inches tall or twenty-seven centimeters), page format, color plates, and taxonomic orientation, *British Wild Flowers* is a kind of one-volume sister publication to, or offshoot of, the *Flower-Garden* series, on the subject of wildflowers rather than garden plants. Loudon defines the book's primary purpose as "to enable any amateur who may find a pretty flower growing wild to ascertain its name and some particulars respecting it." In addition, she has "ventured to add a few remarks on the botanical construction of most of the plants, in the hope of inducing such of my readers as may be unacquainted with botany to study a charming science" (*British* 1).[2] The subject should be part of everyone's education, she asserts: "Nothing would give me more pleasure than to see botany commonly taught in girls' schools," and she hopes that botany one day "will be considered indispensable to every well-educated person" (1–2).

The question of who should learn what, who should teach it, and in what manner was an issue of active debate, and gender was a significant factor in an era when different kinds of reading were prescribed for girls and boys, men and women. Since the later eighteenth century, women had published books popularizing natural history and botany for other women and for young people, often for mothers' use in teaching their children (Gates and Shteir 6–10; Shteir 81–3). In the early nineteenth century, as the market for popular science grew, some female authors began expanding their target audiences to include "adult males" along with women and children (Lightman, *Victorian* 124). While many of Jane Loudon's works were explicitly intended for "ladies," with *British Wild Flowers* she aimed for a more inclusive readership of "amateurs," and the second edition of her *Botany for Ladies* in 1851 was re-titled *Modern Botany*.[3]

In the 1830s, meanwhile, even as women popularizers sought to legitimize their authority to write books informing men, the sciences had begun consolidating disciplinary identities, and debate intensified about who was qualified to interpret botany and how popular texts should be written. Science was becoming professionalized, with male scientists and popularizers accruing cultural prestige and seeking to differentiate "real" science from the polite avocation of botany as practiced and written by women and amateurs. As Shteir explains, "Distinctions were emerging between those with a more aesthetic, moral, and spiritual orientation to nature study and those with a more utilitarian or scientific education" (152). Amid "tension about the gender identity of botany and botanists," some male authors sought to "defeminize botany by defining a scientific botany for gentlemen" (153, 157).

In this milieu, "Mrs. Loudon" maintained her "well-established brand," in Dewis's phrase (215), as a popularizer for amateurs who, after learning to "ascertain" the names of plants, might want a degree of rigor beyond that entry point. Loudon approached botany as "a difficult but worthy pursuit rather than an occasional diversion," to borrow from Judith Page and Elise Smith on Loudon's conception of gardening (165). Loudon assembled *British Wild Flowers* as a savvy author fulfilling a need identified in the marketplace: "The present work has been undertaken in consequence of its being suggested to me that a selection of British Wild Flowers, in one volume, on the same plan as my *Ladies' Flower-Garden*, would be useful for those who have neither time nor opportunity to consult the larger works" (1). If some readers wanted to learn about wildflowers, and if some favored the approach taken in the *Ladies' Flower-Garden*, then *British Wild Flowers* filled that niche. Loudon's report that someone "suggested" such a book shrewdly implies the usefulness and good reception of the *Ladies' Flower-Garden* as well as its author's competence to produce a guide to flowers *not* "common in gardens" (1). The references to the *Ladies' Flower-Garden* in *British Wild Flowers* suggest the existence of reading communities with overlapping interests and awareness of Loudon's previous works. Indeed, the claim that *British Wild Flowers* is intended for raw beginners is somewhat disingenuous, since the book uses technical terms for the parts of plants without defining them (perianth, calyx, corolla, sepals, panicles), so that readers who want to know what they mean must "consult the larger works on the subject" (such as Loudon's own *Botany for Ladies*, perhaps?), whether or not they have the "time or opportunity" (1).

Otherwise, *British Wild Flowers* follows through with its professed allegiance to the needs of "the student" (2). Well aware of the difficulties facing readers without access to a classical university education, Loudon seeks to dispel what we might call botany anxiety, taking issue with the unnecessary hurdles she sees erected by other books. Why, she asks, must botany texts begin with the diverse and populous order Ranunculaceae—which includes the common buttercup, crowfoot, clematis, delphinium or larkspur, anemone, marsh marigold, and columbine, among others—as if to baffle learners from the outset? She had similarly complained in *Botany for Ladies*, "Modern botanists seem to have placed this unfortunate order first, as though to terrify students on the very threshold of the science, and to prevent them from daring to advance any farther to penetrate into its mysteries" (10). *British Wild Flowers* elaborates further on this problem: other plant groups "may be recognized by the resemblance which their flowers bear to each other," but the flowers of Ranunculaceae are "so variable as to form no clue to their relationship .... Why then, the student may naturally ask, are all these plants classed together?" Loudon explains that the "resemblance lies principally in the construction of the flowers and the seed vessels, which it requires some knowledge of Botany to distinguish in the plants while in flower" (3). An empathetic teacher, she zeroes in on the source of confusion and untangles it. But she stops short of rearranging the botanical orders in her own book; her function is not to originate or revise systems, but to synthesize and mediate the knowledge constructed by the experts. Her major task as popularizer is the packaging of her subject, a task that necessitates a clear definition of her audience and the kind and quantity of information they will find useful and comprehensible, but not overwhelming.

If Loudon envisions her readers as novices, why does she assume they would need, or be interested in, scientific classification at all, much less a structure dictated by taxonomic orders? A wildflower guide could be organized in many ways, such as by locale and habitat; "alphabetically, as in the old herbals"; or by seasons of blooming, as in Catharine Parr Traill's 1868 *Canadian Wild Flowers* (Ainley 88). One present-day field guide to

British wildflowers groups them first by color, an expedient stunningly simple yet utterly logical, since "the colour of the bloom is also the most distinguishing identification feature of a flower for humans" (Eppinger 10). This guidebook includes scientific names only for precision, to prevent users from confusing species that closely resemble each other (8). To be sure, some nineteenth-century readers shrank from the technicalities of classification. Many women avoided taxonomy as raising the fearful shadow of excessive learnedness, having been inculcated with the notion that too much learning made women masculine and unmarriageable (Gates and Shteir 6–7; Shteir 117). Some authors pushed back against the tide of taxonomic fervor. In *Our Wild Flowers Familiarly Described and Illustrated* (1839), natural history author Louisa Anne Twamley tells her "dear young readers" that a *little* knowledge enhances the "charm" of enjoying flowers— "and yet, I have not learned much. I have very few of the 'hard names' by heart; and it is very seldom that I pull a flower to bits, to discover its class and order" (v). *Our Wild Flowers* tells the story of a girl learning botany from her aunt and fretting about the "strange, difficult, out-of-the-way words" that "are often enough to frighten one from opening books on botany or gardening" (2). The aunt reassures her niece that as "fond" as she is of flowers, she can "cultivate, admire, examine, and endeavor to imitate their beauty in drawings, without possessing either strictly scientific or classical knowledge" (3).

For more ambitious knowledge-seekers, the "hard names" of taxonomy came with the territory of intellectual engagement. With some knowledge of a classification system, a learner familiar with anatomical features of a certain plant group could identify a new species in that group by looking for similar features, a method that Loudon credited with smoothing her own entrance to botanical study, as discussed below. In *British Wild Flowers* she points out that scientific names are needed in part because, with the rapid discoveries of new plants worldwide and the importation of species from other continents, many simply do not have common names in English. Thus, "The prejudice against botanical names is every day declining, from the number of beautiful plants exhibited at Flower Shows which have no English appellations" (1). More people now had opportunities to encounter plants in such public venues: "The naming of the trees in Hyde Park and Kensington Gardens, and the establishment of so many new Botanic Gardens ... must also have great influence in familiarizing persons with botanic names" (1).

To help instill this familiarity, *British Wild Flowers* culls scientific information from John Lindley's *Synopsis of the British Flora*; in Loudon's view "a most excellent and useful book, which no botanical student should be without" (2). The technical descriptions for hundreds of plants come largely verbatim from this book, with due citations of "Lindley" and of his sources in turn. The "plan" or page format adopted from the *Ladies' Flower-Garden*, purportedly so useful as to create a demand for *British Wild Flowers*, involves the relatively easy-to-use layout of a reference work, with headings and white space for each plant's botanical specifications instead of continuous discursive paragraphs. Though still very text-heavy, this approach prepares the reader to expect information in a consistent template for making distinctions among, for example, the many species of vetch, vetchling, toadflax, or flowering pea. Each heading, centered to guide the reader's eye, contains the plant's common and scientific names and some identifying characteristics, such as leaf shapes, and climbing or spreading habits. Beneath the heading come paragraphs headed "Description, &c." with such matters as the plant's locations and habitats, uses, literary references or quotations, and recommendations whether to cultivate it in a garden or not, along with Loudon's own brisk, frequently pointed opinions on whether it is pretty (ivy-leaved toadflax), handsome (corn-mint, though it "has a very disagreeable smell, like that of decayed cheese" [264]), splendid (broad-leaved everlasting pea), elegant (wood vetch, wild snowdrop, narrow-leaved everlasting pea)—or not.

It is the color illustrations, however, that, like those in the *Ladies' Flower-Garden*, most visibly set *British Wild Flowers* apart from most of Loudon's other books. The volume contains sixty plates with engravings of 296 plants by H. Noel Humphreys, a much-published artist-writer who also illustrated other Loudon works (Leathlean). More akin to portraiture than technical illustrations, the plates create an effect strikingly different from Loudon's *Botany for Ladies*, which is a much smaller, lighter volume with many line drawings and diagrams but no color pictures. In contrast, a reader of the *Ladies' Flower-Garden* comes face to face, even before reaching the main title page, with a gorgeous rendition of one of the plates within. In the volume on annuals, for example, a riotous ten-figure group of convolvulus and related flowers appears in vibrant colors, dominated by an outsize violet-blue and white blossom shouldering into the foreground in bold, almost wanton self-display. In similar fashion, *British Wild Flowers* groups related species in graceful, pleasing designs and orients each individual plant to show all its relevant parts. A reader looking for the globeflower, for instance, immediately recognizes in the plate the eponymous spherical blossom in bright, cheerful yellow.

Here was another point of contention in botanical publishing: how, or even whether, to use illustrations. While large, sophisticated color renditions of plants had long been an essential element of botany, their rarity and expense made them inaccessible to all but a few. In the early nineteenth century, technological advances in printing led to more varied and affordable visuals in books, and Anne Secord points out that twenty-first-century readers should not underestimate the "novelty" of color plates and the "sense of revelation" felt by people seeing them for the first time (32). The dazzle of color pictures, Secord writes, led to spirited arguments among "expert practitioners" seeking new recruits to scientific botany. Recognizing the power of "allurement" to entice through visual pleasure, some botanists feared that lavish color representations would distract learners with "superficial" beauty and impede their development of precise observational skill. Others contended that the "allure of pictures" could be a helpful stimulus to learning at a deeper level, "an appetizer to a more substantial scientific feast" (Secord 40). According to Bernard Lightman, color images became a significant part of popularizing works by women, and "utilitarian" illustration for scientific instruction came to be pitted against the "ornamental" purpose associated with botany as polite avocation ("Depicting" 217, 220). Amid this debate, the color plates in Jane Loudon's books accomplish both purposes, the aesthetic and the pedagogical. *British Wild Flowers'* illustrations provide technical knowledge, but they also point to Loudon's recognition of beauty and pleasure as portals to botanical learning.

This recognition is evident in several of Loudon's works that ground the desire for knowledge in the contexts of readers' lived experience, their encounters with "pretty flowers" in garden, roadside, and field. She recalls her own first interest in botany—a subject she had found "excessively repugnant" as a child—arising as something to occupy her while she waited for John Loudon to tour large gardens (*Botany* iii). Using her own learning trajectory as a model, Loudon sets out two accounts of initiation from idleness into captivation. When she and John Loudon noticed attractive flowers, "I was continually asking the names, though alas! these names, when I heard them, conveyed no ideas to my mind, and I was not any wiser than before. Still the natural wish to know something of what we admire, impelled me to repeat my fruitless questions" (iii). After a period of frustration with systematic botany, she finds new inspiration at the Horticultural Society gardens, where "my attention was attracted by a mass of the beautiful crimson flowers of Malope grandiflora" (iv–v). Hearing from her preoccupied husband that this was "some Malvaceous plant," Loudon sees its resemblance to "the flowers of the crimson Mallow, the botanical name of which I recollected was Malva," and she is on her way to learning "every Malvaceous plant that was in flower in the garden" (v–vi).

More knowledge leads her to more investigative independence, according to another account whose descriptive imagery mirrors the lustrous provocation of unfamiliar flowers (while also relating the mini-adventure of a plucky explorer who transforms a parasol into a water-plant retrieval device):

> I shall never forget the pleasure I once had in finding out the name of a plant myself. I happened to be waiting for Mr. Loudon … just opposite a small pond, which was covered by some white flowers that I did not know. The flowers were small, but very beautiful, and as they shone with almost a metallic lustre in the sun, they looked like a silvery mantle thrown over the water. I was curious to know what they were, and having got one with some difficulty, and by the help of my parasol, I began to examine it botanically.
>
> (*Botany* 14–15)

Determined to identify the specimen on her own, without help, Jane Loudon took it home, consulted a flora, and determined that "it was *Ranunculus aquatilis*, the water crowfoot" (16). Her exemplary narrative of discovery becomes evangelistic didacticism, gently exhorting readers to go and do likewise: "In a similar manner, my readers may amuse themselves, by identifying the plants they meet with" (16). In the Victorian knowledge culture, "amusement" entails much more than a way to kill time:

> Whenever I go into any country I have formerly visited, I feel as though I were endowed with a new sense. Even the very banks by the sides of the roads, which I before thought dull and uninteresting, now appear fraught with beauty. A new charm seems thrown over the face of nature, and a degree of interest is given to even the commonest weeds.
>
> (vii)

Loudon's botanical conversion narrative resembles the rhetoric of discovery found in many other natural history works (Bellanca 30): with the transformative power of knowledge, the most mundane objects become new.

Thus Loudon treats the desire to know as arising from a broader set of stimuli than intellectual discipline or even curiosity alone. Writing for amateurs, she is unconstrained by the scientific professional's need to keep botany writing entirely "objective" and technical. Certainly her brisk, businesslike style contrasts sharply with the other end of the spectrum, highly sentimental discourses like the Victorian "language of flowers" with its semiotics of interpersonal messages and abstract meanings for various blossoms, or fashionable books celebrating flowers effusively for their beauty, "poetical" associations, and religious inspiration (see Seaton). Loudon could write of such attractions, as in the inaugural volume of the *Ladies' Flower-Garden*:

> The love of flowers is calculated to improve our best feelings, and subdue our bad ones; and we can hardly contemplate the beauty and richness of a flower-garden without feeling our hearts dilate with gratitude to that Almighty Being who has made all these lovely blossoms, and given them to us for our use.
>
> (i)

She thus echoes sentiments expressed by Louisa Twamley in *The Romance of Nature; or, The Flower Seasons Illustrated* on "the beautiful power [flowers] possess of awakening in our hearts feelings of wonder, admiration, gratitude, and devotion" (viii). But Loudon seldom continues at length in this vein, as Twamley does when writing that flowers themselves constitute "a universal language of love, beauty, poetry, and *wisdom*, if we read them aright," much less that "Wild Flowers seem the true philanthropists of their race" (ix). Loudon's floral discourse, whether on gardening or botany, centers on science and factual knowledge with other comment appended—in contrast, say, to Rebecca Hey's *The Moral of Flowers*, which centers on flower poems conveying "moral and religious hints" (v) with a smattering of modest botanical information, including flowers' scientific names in small print, but no taxonomy. Hey's purpose is to "draw such a moral from each flower that is introduced as its appearance, habits, or properties might be supposed to suggest" (5). Between the transience of flowers and the book's religious sensibility, in a dismaying number of cases—violets, rue, wild wall-flower, almond tree—the "moral" turns out to have something to do with death.

Jane Loudon concentrates much more on the living world, and on knowing rather than supposing. In *British Wild Flowers* she augments general knowledge on the snowdrop with personal observation: "The blossoms generally open in February, but this year (1846) I gathered snowdrops in our little garden at Bayswater the 16th of January" (293–4). The familiar British ivy may be "so common, that it scarcely needs description," but Loudon will not miss an opportunity to demolish error by noting "some things respecting it which are either only imperfectly known, or generally misunderstood. As for example, what are called its tendrils are, in fact, its roots." They do not "embrace" nearby objects, but "frequently attach themselves to a tree, by dilating themselves to fill up the interstices of the bark" (184).

For some plants *British Wild Flowers* includes what today we would call their ecological contexts, such as their habitats or the conditions in which readers may find them. The least toadflax is "found in the east and south-east of England in sandy fields"; the common celandine "is very abundant in church-yards and waste places in almost every part of England; but it flourishes most in calcareous soils" (254, 29). The adaptable traveler's joy "will grow in almost any soil where it is planted, and in all shows the same luxuriance. ... It is, indeed, well deserving of general cultivation, from the great rapidity with which it covers bowers and arbours, or spreads itself over dead walls" (5). The ivy-leaved toadflax, a "beautiful little trailing plant," is "common everywhere, particularly on old walls in London and other cities" (253).

Along with its mission of imparting botanical knowledge, *British Wild Flowers* incorporates kinds of information unlikely to appear in books for professional botanists, including cultural practices, myths, common-name origins, and the author's personal experiences and opinions. These multiple discourses, irrelevant or distracting for those seeking scientific fact only, explore the world of wildflowers with a broader frame of reference, integrating cultural meanings with the "pure" information on species' physical structure and taxonomic identity. Loudon evidently judged that the readers she envisioned would value other kinds of material as well, perhaps to link new information with readers' previous knowledge or to make connections that would help with wildflower identification, or simply to make the subject inviting.

For some flowers Loudon brings in linguistic and historical color through purported etymologies of their names. Often the bane of scientific botany, vernacular names can apply to more than one species, vary a great deal by region, and derive from fanciful or counter-factual beliefs. But Loudon considers bits of "floral lore," in Bea Howe's phrase (54), worthy of inclusion whether plausible or not. An alternative name for the celandine is swallow-wort, which "alludes to a superstition, which was formerly very generally believed, that young swallows could not see till the old birds had anointed their eyes with the juice of this plant" (29). Two plants have common names explained by their historical use by "beggars" to "excite pity": applied to the skin, the leaves of both celery-leaved crow-foot and traveler's joy, or "beggar's grass" as it is known in France, exacerbate wounds and ulcers. "These practices," Loudon assures her readers, "are gradually disappearing as the world becomes more enlightened, and the people well-informed" (5, 13). When skeptical she can be quite tart, as with the scientific family name of the enchanter's nightshade, Circaeaceae, which comes from that plant's "supposed magical properties. It is said to be the herb which Circe gave to the companions of Ulysses to turn them into swine; but if it was, it has greatly degenerated in modern times, for it has now no medicinal property whatever" (156).

Other medicinal uses, credible and less so, as well as culinary notes make up other non-scientific references. Transmitting traditional knowledge on such practical applications was a predominant function of the earliest printed works of plants, such as "herbals" or guides to useful species. These kinds of information were in the process of being shed from scientific texts, which took as their purpose to catalog what plants are like in themselves and in relation to each other, rather than what they can do for people. In one of his introductory books, John Lindley explains that when the first botany books were published in the sixteenth century, "Botany was nothing more than the art of distinguishing one plant from another, and of remembering the medical qualities, sometimes real but more frequently imaginary, which experience, or error, or superstition, had ascribed to them" (*Introduction* x). Lindley's own *Synopsis*, Loudon's major source for botanical facts, contains not a whisper about healing, much less cooking, or any other human-serving function of any plant.[4] But Loudon sees fit to mention that the new buds of the common marsh-marigold—whose alternative vernacular name is the "unpoetical" term "horse-blob"—are "pickled as a substitute for capers, and their acridity, when softened by the vinegar used in pickling them, gives them nearly the same flavour" (16). A claim about the common celandine comes with a decidedly unbotanical note from astrology: "if gathered when the sun is in the sign of the Lion, [it] is the best cure of all diseases of the eyes"; Loudon adds that it is an ingredient "of several quack medicines used for such complaints" (29). The hips of the dog rose, a ubiquitous shrub in English hedgerows, have a "pleasant flavour, and a kind of conserve of roses is sometimes made from them." More dubious is an old medicinal supposition: "The name of Dog Rose was formerly given to all the wild roses, because their roots were thought to cure the bite of a mad dog" (145). And readers learn that the lesser spear-wort is traditionally "used by the country people as an emetic. ... It acts instantaneously" (11).

Diverging most obviously from science are Loudon's breezy pronouncements on flowers' degrees of attractiveness, issued with the confidence gained from "having acquired some knowledge of plants and gardens during the eight years I had acted as [John Loudon's] amanuensis" ("Account" xl).[5] Such commentary leavens the book's technical material with expressions of pleasure, which Loudon identifies as the twin motivation, along with desire for knowledge, for wanting to determine the identities of "pretty flowers growing wild." The "brilliant little" dwarf gentian "only grows a few inches from the ground, but the intense brightness of its blue never fails to excite admiration" (236). The sweet briar or eglantine's "delightful fragrance makes it a general favourite"; the dog rose "decorate[s]" hedges "with its lovely blossoms" (144, 145). The yellow toadflax, while beautiful, "would be very greatly admired if it were not so common," but the reverse problem besets the least toadflax, "an inconspicuous little plant," whose flowers "have no beauty" (254). Unappealing flowers merit no further comment: the sum total of notice on the English catchfly, aside from its common and scientific names, is its dismissal as "an inconspicuous plant, with dingy white flowers" (76).

Then there is the poetry woven all throughout the book: many dozens of quotations from poems describing, celebrating, or assigning figurative meanings to flowers. *British Wild Flowers* draws on poetry to complement or embellish its botanical information; it does not hark back to the eighteenth-century practice of conveying science information in verse, as do Erasmus Darwin's epic-length *Botanic Garden* and poems by Charlotte Smith, and others that were just as concerned with plants' material facticity as with their figurative and cultural significations (Pascoe 193). Loudon's poetic choices seek to connect actual wildflowers with readers' literary familiarity. The lesser celandine, or pilewort, "appears to have always been a favourite of the poets, particularly of Wordsworth, who has celebrated it in some well known verses." Quoted stanzas of Wordsworth's "To the Small Celandine" then follow (11–12). The book designates quite a few flowers as poets' favorites, and Loudon excerpts lines and stanzas from twenty or more named authors, including Chaucer, Shakespeare, Milton, Robert Herrick, Thomas Cowper, Walter Scott, Robert Southey, John Clare, William and Mary Howitt, "Mrs. Hemans" (Felicia), and "Mrs. Robinson" (Mary), as well as names less enduring to literary posterity, such as "Miss Strickland" and "Mrs. Grant of Laggan."

For some flowers, such as St. John's wort and traveler's joy, the cultural and literary material rivals the scientific and factual for allotment space. Getting particularly carried away, the entry on two species of wild cherry in

England contains more non-botanical than botanical information, as Loudon discusses the beauty of the blossoms, the frequent use of cherry wood in the countryside, and the "Feast of the Cherries" held at Hamburg (133, 134). She is undaunted by the paucity of poems on cherries *qua* cherries: "Though I have not been able to find any poetry distinctly relating to the Cherry, nothing can be more common than allusions to it in poetical descriptions of beauty." As an example, "the beautiful lines Shakspeare [sic] has put into the mouth of *Helena* in her address to *Hermia*, will be familiar to every one." The lines she quotes compare the two characters in *A Midsummer Night's Dream* to "a double cherry, seeming parted; / But yet a union in partition" (133). Judging by Loudon's assumption of what "every one" will recognize, botanical literacy can work with cultural literacy in an environment where different kinds of knowledge interrelate, reciprocally informing and reflecting human experience.

In its canny identification with its audience and its fashioning of sought-after information, *British Wild Flowers* stands as but one instance of the expansive role of nonfiction print culture in mediating science knowledge in the mid-nineteenth century. It testifies as well to Jane Loudon's acumen in seizing or creating market opportunities and piquing readers' "natural wish to know something of what [they] admire" (*Botany* iii). That the book succeeded in indulging this wish is evident in at least two subsequent editions and numerous republications through at least 1859, according to WorldCat. Operating at a juncture of factual literacy about "flowers growing wild" and their multiplicity of cultural meanings, *British Wild Flowers* exemplifies the competing yet co-existing languages through which Victorians sought to articulate and understand the living world.

Acknowledgments

This essay was written with the support of a RISE grant from the Office of Research, University of South Carolina. I also thank Elizabeth Sudduth, director, and the staff of the university's Irvin Department of Rare Books and Special Collections.

Notes

1 Some scholars avoid the phrase "popular science" because of pejorative connotations it took on in the twentieth century, among other reasons (Lightman, *Victorian* 9–13; Topham 135–6). I use the term with the more neutral connotations summed up by Topham: "ease of understanding," affordable price, and commercial success (136).
2 The "botanical construction" of plants refers to the "natural system" of classification, which is based on a variety of physical characteristics, as opposed to the Linnaean system, which identifies plants according to features of their reproductive organs. The Linnaean system was beginning to fade from wide use, partly because its sexual focus carried a frisson of impropriety for respectable women. Jane Loudon, among many others, considered the Linnaean system

"unfit for females" and preferred the natural system, which has "nothing objectionable" (*British* 1). See Shteir 13–32 and 154–7 for more on this issue.

3 Shteir reads the title change as a move to make the book appear up-to-date and consistent with a gradual abandonment of sex-segregated texts (224–7). There is evidence that Loudon had thought the book "modern" from the first, though the appellation could be slippery. She originally proposed to call the book *Instructions in Modern Botany for Ladies* (Lightman, *Victorian* 122); the first edition came out as *Botany for Ladies*, though *Modern Botany for Ladies* appears on the introduction to Part I (1). And though the second edition was titled *Modern Botany*, the bindings of at least some copies, such as one that I examined via HathiTrust Digital Library, retained the title *Botany for Ladies* on the spine, possibly for consistency or familiarity since the second edition differs only minimally from the first.

4 Lindley takes up the contemporary science of medicinal plants in great detail in *Flora Medica*.

5 Loudon wrote out many of her husband's books and articles for him because he had lost his right arm to rheumatism, failed surgery, and amputation (Howe 49).

Works cited

Ainley, Marianne Gosztonyi. "Science in Canada's Back Woods: Catharine Parr Traill." In Gates and Shteir 79–97.

Allen, David E. *The Naturalist in Britain: A Social History*. London: Allen Lane, 1976.

Barber, Lynn. *The Heyday of Natural History 1820–1870*. London: Jonathan Cape, 1980.

Bellanca, Mary Ellen. *Daybooks of Discovery: Nature Diaries in Britain, 1770–1870*. Charlottesville: U of Virginia P, 2007.

Dewis, Sarah. *The Loudons and the Gardening Press: A Victorian Cultural Industry*. Farnham, England: Ashgate, 2014.

Eppinger, Michael. *Field Guide to Wild Flowers of Britain and Europe*. London: New Holland Publishers, 2006.

Gates, Barbara T. "Those Who Drew and Those Who Wrote: Women and Victorian Popular Science Illustration." In Shteir and Lightman 192–213.

Gates, Barbara T., and Ann B. Shteir, eds. *Natural Eloquence: Women Reinscribe Science*. Madison: U of Wisconsin P, 1997.

Hey, Rebecca. *The Moral of Flowers, Illustrated by Colour Engravings*. London: Longman, Rees, Orme, Brown, Green, & Longman, 1833.

Howe, Bea. *Lady with Green Fingers: The Life of Jane Loudon*. London: Country Life, 1961.

Leathlean, Howard. "Humphreys, (Henry) Noel." *Oxford Dictionary of National Biography*. Oxford UP 2004–2015. Web. 9 June 2015.

Lightman, Bernard. "Depicting Nature, Defining Roles: The Gender Politics of Victorian Illustration." In Shteir and Lightman 214–39.

———. *Victorian Popularizers of Science: Designing Science for New Audiences*. Chicago: U of Chicago P, 2006.

Lindley, John. *Flora Medica: A Botanical Account of All the More Important Plants Used in Medicine, in Different Parts of the World*. London: Longman, Rees, Orme, Brown, Green, & Longman, 1838.

———. *An Introduction to Botany*. London: Longman, Rees, Orme, Brown, Green, & Longman, 1832.

———. *A Synopsis of the British Flora*. 2nd ed. London: Longman, Rees, Orme, Brown, Green, & Longman, 1835.

Loudon, Jane Webb. "An Account of the Life and Writings of John Claudius Loudon." *Self-Instruction for Young Gardeners*. By John C. Loudon. London: Longman, 1845. ix–lviii.

———. *Botany for Ladies*. London: John Murray, 1842.

———. *British Wild Flowers*. 1844. London: William S. Orr, 1846.

———. *Ladies' Flower-Garden of Ornamental Annuals*. London: William Smith, 1840.

———. *Modern Botany*. 2nd edition [of *Botany for Ladies*]. London: John Murray, 1851.

Merrill, Lynn L. *The Romance of Victorian Natural History*. London: Oxford UP, 1989.

Page, Judith W., and Elise L. Smith. *Women, Literature, and the Domesticated Landscape: England's Disciples of Flora, 1780–1870*. Cambridge: Cambridge UP, 2011.

Pascoe, Judith. "Female Botanists and the Poetry of Charlotte Smith." *Re-Visioning Romanticism: British Women Writers, 1776–1837*. Ed. Carol Shiner Wilson and Joel Haefner. Philadelphia: U of Pennsylvania P, 1994. 193–209.

Rauch, Alan. *Useful Knowledge: The Victorians, Morality, and the March of Intellect*. Durham: Duke UP, 2001.

Seaton, Beverly. *The Language of Flowers: A History*. Charlottesville: U of Virginia P, 1995.

Secord, Anne. "Botany on a Plate: Pleasure and the Power of Pictures in Promoting Early Nineteenth-Century Scientific Knowledge." *Isis* 93.1 (2002): 28–57.

Shteir, Ann B. *Cultivating Women, Cultivating Science: Flora's Daughters and Botany in England, 1760–1860*. Baltimore: Johns Hopkins UP, 1996.

Shteir, Ann B., and Bernard Lightman, eds. *Figuring It Out: Science, Gender and Visual Culture*. Hanover, NH: Dartmouth College P, 2006.

Topham, Jonathan. "Publishing Popular Science in Early Nineteenth-Century Britain." *Science in the Marketplace: Nineteenth-Century Sites and Experiences*. Ed. Aileen Fyfe and Bernard Lightman. Chicago: U of Chicago P, 2007. 135–68.

Twamley, Louisa Anne. *The Romance of Nature; or, The Flower-Seasons Illustrated*. London: Charles Tilt, 1836.

———. *Our Wild Flowers Familiarly Described and Illustrated*. London: Charles Tilt, 1839.

12 Falling in love with seaweeds
The seaside environments of George Eliot and G. H. Lewes

Anna Feuerstein

George Eliot and George Henry Lewes fell in love on their 1856 trip to Ilfracombe and Tenby. While the two were already deeply attached before their seaside excursion, their rambles across seashores and tide pools opened their eyes and imagination to new forms of life with which they developed numerous intimacies. In her essay "Recollections of Ilfracombe," for example, Eliot recalls how "These tide-pools made me quite in love with sea-weeds ... so I took up Landsborough's book and tried to get a little more light on their structure and history" (267). Similarly, Lewes writes of his delight in uncovering his first *Anthea cereus*, *Clavelina*, and *Actinia* in ways one would write of their lover, as he says, "If these *first* thrills can never come back to us, there is ample compensation in the new vistas which open with increasing knowledge; the first kiss may be peculiar in its charm, but as the years roll on, we learn to love more and more the cheek on which we first found little besides that charm" (*Sea-Side Studies* 14). This love of seaweeds and anemones registers two competing relationships: an intimate connection that one would expect in discourses of pet keeping, and a sense of distance, one that can only be cleared by gathering new knowledge of radically different forms of life. The fact that Eliot and Lewes were writing about falling in love with small life forms far different from the Victorians' beloved dogs, cats, and horses, suggests a new valuation of plant and animal life that is intimately connected with a desire for increasing knowledge.

Eliot and Lewes were not the only Victorians obsessed with the seashore and the life inhabiting it. In the 1850s middle- and upper-class Victorians flocked to the sea in order to collect unfamiliar and striking life forms found in tide pools along the coasts of England. From polyps and seaweeds, to starfish and sea anemones, these creatures captivated the Victorian imagination while inspiring the production of domestic aquavivariums, enabling enthusiastic collectors to bring the sea inside their drawing rooms. Philip Henry Gosse's texts *A Naturalist's Rambles on the Devonshire Coast* (1853) and *The Aquarium: An Unveiling of the Wonders of the Deep Sea* (1854) popularized the seaside fascination, as did the new aquavivarium at the London Zoological Gardens in Regent's Park, which opened in May 1853. However, throughout all of this love, curiosity, and fascination lies another discourse of hierarchy, violence, and containment. Gosse's reverence for polyps and anemones is a reflection of his devotion to God, as he sees within sea creatures a reflection of divine intelligence rather than animal agency. Victorians collected sea animals out of fascination, yet frequently contained them at home in vivariums, and wreaked havoc to seashore environments and their multi-species inhabitants. And while Eliot and Lewes write about falling in love with sea life, they also enact violence upon these very same beings.

Thus discourses of natural history from the 1850s are often contradictory, and demonstrate varying ways of understanding animal life and the environment, what Victorians understood as the natural world. Although Eliot and Lewes have in common with Gosse and other Victorians a dual discourse of love and domination, they also stray from dominant understandings of the environment and the animals therein by embracing a secularized form of ecological thinking that emphasizes the interconnectedness of all life forms, and the alterity and agency of unfamiliar animal subjects. Their seaside writings, which include Lewes's *Sea-Side Studies* (1858) and *Studies in Animal Life* (1860), and Eliot's journal entries, letters, and essays from her time at the sea with Lewes, demonstrate a radical ecological thought that reveals a remarkable engagement with the environment, and an appreciation of nonhuman life forms, both plant and animal, that decenters the human and moves out of a hierarchical view of nature toward a more democratic ecological understanding. As such, Eliot and Lewes formulate an early ecological awareness quite different from other Victorian writers who engaged with seaside environments. For instead of seeing evidence of divine intelligence, I argue that they saw nonhuman agency, diversity, and connections between all life forms.

Ultimately Eliot and Lewes embrace what Timothy Morton has more recently articulated as the ecological thought: "the thinking of interconnectedness ... a practice and a process of becoming fully aware of how human beings are connected with other beings—animal, vegetable, or mineral" (*Ecological* 7). For Morton the ecological thought is an unromanticized view of nature that "has to do with love, loss, despair and compassion ... It has to do with amazement, open-mindedness, and wonder ... It has to do with delight, beauty, ugliness ... and pain ... It has to do with reading and writing ... It has to do with ideas of self and the weird paradoxes of subjectivity" (*Ecological* 2), and we can see these competing ideas within Eliot and Lewes's seaside writings. Thinking ecologically helps demonstrate how Eliot and Lewes challenge mid-Victorian discourses of natural history, as they reveal the implications of an enlarged perspective and a desire to know more intimately alternate life forms in themselves—not merely reduced to reflections of God's will—with which humans are connected. While Morton's ecological thought is a way to confront our own twenty-first-century ecological crisis, Eliot and Lewes's understandings of connections between life forms and radical ways of conceptualizing animal subjects, and the natural world more broadly, helps them make sense of their own cultural and political crisis: the increasing decentralization of the human subject, the destabilization of empirical epistemologies, and the burgeoning debates regarding evolutionary processes.

In this essay I examine the seaside writings of Eliot and Lewes from the 1850s to argue that both writers formulate an early ecological awareness that anticipates Morton's more radical twenty-first-century thought. Instead of seeing within their environment evidence of divine intelligence and a reverence for God, Eliot and Lewes describe nonhuman agency, diversity, and connections between all life forms. Below, I give a larger context for thinking through Eliot and Lewes's ecological thought by marking the mid-Victorian fascination with sea life, seen most prominently in the craze for tide pooling and drawing room aquariums, and describe how it spurred new ways of conceptualizing animal life and human relationships to the natural world. I then give a reading of Eliot and Lewes's seaside writings to demonstrate how their understanding of animal life veers from and challenges popular, natural-history discourses, even as they do not always operate outside of human power. As such, I hope to demonstrate the importance of Eliot and Lewes to Victorian ecological thought more broadly, for while they were not necessarily concerned with environmentalism as we conceptualize it today, their writings demonstrate how major literary and scientific figures were thinking ecologically even before the term "ecology" came into being.[1] Further, it helps to show how ecological thought in the Victorian period was not just concerned with confronting the problems of modernity, such as cities and industrialism, or trying to reconcile inherited romantic views of the environment with modernity, but how certain writers were critically engaged with completely reconceptualizing how one understood the multiplicity of life around them, and how it challenged the primacy of the human subject.[2]

Mid-Victorian natural history and the animals of the sea

The mid-Victorian seaside fascination has been well documented; accordingly I focus here on how sea creatures led to new understandings of animal life both within and beyond natural history writing, so as to better place Eliot and Lewes within this context.[3] By the 1850s, Victorians' most familiar animals were the pets—mostly dogs and cats—that were becoming increasingly valued and commodified within Victorian culture and society. Along with other domestic animals such as horses and cows, familiar animals were becoming subjects of sympathetic and political concern as an increasing wave of animal welfare discourses and anti-cruelty laws permeated Victorian society. Thinking ecologically, these more familiar discourses of human–animal relationships imagine a hierarchical connection, as they place humans in a dominant position of steward to the natural environment. Sympathy for animals was often founded on human–animal similarities, as early animal welfare advocates made their arguments by suggesting that animals could feel and think in ways similar to humans. This was also based on the certitude of human superiority, and the God-given responsibility of human care for the earth and its inhabitants. The seaside craze, however, brought new and radically different animals into the Victorian consciousness and imaginary, troubling current conceptualizations of animal subjectivity and sometimes, human superiority.

Certainly, people were interested in the sea and sea life before the mid-Victorian era, but writers such as Gosse popularized the expeditions to the English coast, giving Victorians an opportunity to see and engage with animals that according to one article, previously "have been only occasionally seen when cast up on our coasts or pinned down in our museums" ("Marine Vivarium"). David Allen has outlined important events that led up to this craze, such as the 1755 discovery by John Ellis that corallines (what Victorians broadly referred to as polyps) were animals, not plants; the fascination with seaweeds, particularly in the 1820s and 1830s; and the improvement and affordability of the microscope (126–8). In 1853, Gosse published *A Naturalist's Rambles on the Devonshire Coast*, which effectively produced a full-blown obsession with sea animals and tide pooling. Together with the discovery of plant oxygenation that proved necessary to the development of aquavivariums, and the production of tools useful for tide pooling, such as the dredge, Gosse's text and the ability to capture and keep sea animals brought Victorians closer than ever to new and fascinating animals that many had never before experienced.

Natural history is not without its connections to natural theology, and like animal welfare discourses, Gosse's famous text is rife with theological references, many which reinforce the human in a hierarchical position to the natural world. Although natural history was slowly moving away from its theological foundations into the more specialized disciplines of science and biology, Gillian Beer reminds us that these discourses "drew on a sense of natural beneficence, or prodigal creation" (120), which we can see in texts such as Gosse's *Rambles* and Charles Kingsley's *Glaucus*. Kingsley, who would later be an open supporter of Darwinian evolution, explains that a good naturalist should "estimat[e] each thing not carnally ... but spiritually, by the amount of Divine thought revealed to him therein" (233). Gosse similarly argues that one should study sea animals because they are God's creatures, suggesting that animals hold little reverential value in themselves. Indeed, in the opening of *Rambles* he asks if these "mean creatures" are "beneath our regard?" He answers,

> Surely no: God does not despise them ... the contrivances of their organization are the fruit of his infinite Wisdom, and elicit adoring wonder and praise from the hierarchies of angels; and the exquisite tints with which they are adorned are the pencillings of his almighty Hand. Yes, O Lord! the lowly tribes that tenant these dark pools are, like the

heavens themselves, "the work of thy fingers," and do as truly as those glowing orbs above us "declare thy glory," and "show thy work." If then they were worthy to be created and sustained by Thee, they are not unworthy to be examined by us with reverential regard.

(20)

Gosse's rationale for the study of "mean creatures" places them in a discourse of domination while limiting human appreciation of animal agency and autonomy; displays of animal agency are actually illustrations of divine intelligence. Animals are praised because they reflect the divine, and tide pools become a place of worship, where one studies animal life in order to contemplate a world made by God. As Amy King has suggested, Gosse's emphasis on the divine suggests a desire for order and fixity in a world that was questioning the stability of species ("Reorienting" 156), thus limiting the types of interconnections that will later be seen by Eliot, Lewes, and Darwin. Although King elsewhere correctly explains that both Gosse and Kingsley see within tide pools human concerns, the fact remains that animals are most often posited in theological terms that fit into more comfortable human epistemologies ("Tide Pools"). Ultimately, Gosse's popularization of the seaside was founded on a desire to contemplate the divine, rather than animals themselves, which reinforces humans in a hierarchical position.

The new aquavivarium at the Zoological Gardens, where Victorians could witness a radically different environment in miniature, and the availability of drawing room aquariums, further placed sea animals into the Victorian imaginary. Periodicals from the time of the vivarium's opening demonstrate a competing discourse of familiarity and alterity, as Victorians tried to understand how to place such radically different animals into their previous understandings of animal life. "The Aquatic Vivarium," for example, calls the tank's inhabitants "curious beyond conception," exclaiming that "their activity and rapacity present effects so curious that the most casual observer cannot help being struck with them." An article in *The Literary World* labels sea anemones "animal flowers," suggesting the liminality of certain sea creatures and the multiple epistemological borders they cross ("Marine Vivarium"). Similarly, in a letter to her friend Cara Bray, Eliot points out the necessity of viewing the "wondrous zoophytes and other marine queerities" in the new vivarium (*Letters* 2: 103), ultimately emphasizing the queerness of sea life. In this way, aquariums helped to push Victorian conceptions of animal alterity, as they showcased animals which Victorians could not always classify, sympathize with, or find points of similarity as they could with domestic animals. The vivarium and tide pools thus opened up a new perspective that showed the slight knowledge humans hold about the natural world.

One reaction to this abundance of queer life was to domesticate it, in order to place it more fully into human epistemologies. Articles such as "Sea Views" from *Household Words*, for example, focus on domestication rather than curiosity. The author suggests that with the rise of aquariums both in drawing rooms and at the Zoological Gardens,

> We can now bring the fishes, element and all, into our homes, watch them, and learn to know them as familiarly as dogs and cats ... we may look at the new world that has been lately spread before the eyes of men, and begin, as even naturalists have, only within this last year or two, began—to pick up an intimacy with the little people of the sea.
> (510)

As such, this author brings sea animals into what Ritvo has labeled the cult of the pet (86), suggesting the possibility of developing intimate relationships with non-domestic animals. In her detailed cultural analysis of the aquarium, Judith Hamera suggests that "The aquarium transforms the sea from untamed and inaccessible wilderness into manageable and restorative—because consumable—nature. It domesticates the sea" (60), and we can see how Victorians attempted to take control over animal alterity by domesticating it. Alterity becomes less radical and more manageable when placed alongside other pets in the drawing room and contained in a human environment. Indeed, as Hamera suggests, for many Victorians, Gosse especially, the aquarium is a miniature version of the sea: one made by God, the other by humankind (67). Thus the aquarium presents another space in which animals are placed in a position of subordination to a divine-like human subject, through the theological rhetoric underlying discourses of natural history and relationships with domestic animals.

Tide pools and aquariums became useful ecological metaphors, where one could witness the multiplicity of animals and relations between them. On a literal level, it was not until Joseph Priestley discovered that sea animals need oxygenation from plants that they could live in fabricated environments. This discovery that "the vegetable and animal worlds are made to play into each other's hands" ("Sea Views" 506) suggests an increasing awareness of ecological interconnectedness between varying life forms. The tank itself is a miniature world that allows the spectator to view a detailed environment and the ways in which animals interact with each other. "The Aquatic Vivarium" explains that you can see animals eat and be eaten, while one of its most striking aspects is the multiplicity of animal life: "The visitor may occupy the whole day in passing inside and outside the building from tank to tank, and yet every time see something new." For Gosse, the tide pool itself is a "natural vivarium" (*Rambles* 55), representing a space in which the human spectator can see nonhuman environments in a totality, while suggesting an inherent human authority over nature.

Although Eliot and Lewes never fully get away from human domination over animals—indeed, recognizing such control is part of thinking ecologically—they will transform these environments into a more radical ecological thought that challenges human superiority and embraces what

Morton calls the mesh: "a nontotalizable, open-ended concatenation of interrelations that blur and confound boundaries at practically any level: between species, between the living and the nonliving, between organism and environment" ("Queer" 275–6). Morton himself finds the mesh to be an important phenomenon of Victorian evolutionary science, as he claims that Darwin "sensed the mesh while pondering the implications of natural selection" (*Ecological* 28). Thus to conceptualize the environment more broadly as the mesh forces one to rethink hierarchy, reject the primacy of human epistemologies, and embrace alterity. Below I show how Eliot and Lewes also "sensed the mesh," and welcomed it even before the publication of *Origin*, where Darwin so astutely describes interconnectedness. If "Darwin brings ecological interconnectedness and thinking together" (*Ecological* 29), as Morton suggests, so do Eliot and Lewes as they embrace seaside environments in order to promote the scientific, literary, and political possibilities of rejecting human superiority and embedding themselves within the mesh of other life forms.

Eliot and Lewes at the sea

In 1856, Eliot wrote to her friend Bessie Rayner Parkes that she was heading off to the mesh. Gesturing toward her trip to Ilfracombe, she writes, "We mean to run away to mountains and mollusks and sea breezes, as soon as the weather gets warm" (*Letters* 2: 235). Eliot here conceptualizes both the living and the nonliving as a specific entity, a totality—a place to "run away to"—essentially noting the interconnectedness of all aspects of an environment while valuing each element equally. Indeed, Eliot's essay "Recollections of Ilfracombe" is one of the most representative mid-Victorian examples of the mesh, as she takes pains to minutely describe the entirety of the environment around her, from the buildings, which she viewed as an "ugl[y] cluster of human nests lying in the midst of beautiful hills" (264), the streams "fringed with Veronica and Stellaria" (265), the "lovely colours and forms of the Algae" (266), to caterpillars, and even the human friends they made on their visit. Lewes, however, thought of this trip as a way to "become more intimately acquainted with the organization of marine animals" (*Sea-Side* 4), demonstrating that his focus was on knowing more fully different kinds of animal life. Eliot too will prioritize animals, as her numerous journal entries from Ilfracombe detail her excitement in discovering new animals, calling their "hunts" "glorious," and those they find "treasures to us" and "splendid … beyond anything I had imagined of that kind" (*Journals* 60). Sea animals were thus highly prized and valued by Eliot and Lewes; at the same time they put pressure on human knowledge, and more fully allowed them to place themselves into an ecological totality in which humans were not always central.

Although one of Eliot and Lewes's larger goals on their trip was to capture animals—Eliot begins her essay "Recollections of Ilfracombe" by mentioning their "hamper of tall glass jars, which we meant for our sea-side Vivarium" (262) they do not always place the human in a dominant position to animals. While Hamera argues that vivariums "parlorize the sea" (59), pointing toward the domestication of seaside environments and their placement into more comfortable human epistemologies, sea life also dominates Eliot and Lewes. For example, Eliot writes to her friend Charles Bray that

> You would laugh to see our room decked with yellow pie-dishes, a *footpan*, glass jars and phials, all full of zoophytes or molluscs or annelids—and still more to see the eager interest with which we rush to our "preserves" in the morning to see if there has been any mortality among them in the night.
> (*Letters* 2: 252)

While generally the vivarium occupied a central position in the drawing room, here sea life and the objects to contain it spill over. Instead of placing the containment of animal life in a dominant position, Eliot and Lewes reject it to enclose themselves within it; indeed, here we get the sense that their entire room is a vivarium, with them as just one species among many.

Sea life also became embedded into their subjectivity, forcing them to confuse the human-animal divide, as Lewes writes,

> The typical forms [of sea animals] *took possession* of me. They were ever present in my waking thoughts; they filled my dreams with fantastic images; they came in troops as I lay awake during meditative morning hours; they teased me as I turned restless from side to side at night; they made all things converge toward them.
> (*Sea-Side* 34, emphasis in the original)

After leaving Ilfracombe and Tenby, Lewes notes, "Men began to appear like mollusks; and their ways of creatures in a larger rock-pool ... I caught myself speculating as to what sort of figure *he* [some 'friend of the family'] would make in the vivarium" (179). As such, Eliot and Lewes move out of a position of centrality into a totality wherein they are inundated with sea life, both physically and mentally. They experience and write about a merging of human, animal, and vegetable that erases boundaries and places them within a broader totality in which "there is no absolute center or edge" (Morton, *Ecological* 29). Human and animal environments and subjectivities merge together.

Indeed, one of the most famous passages from "Recollections of Ilfracombe" compares humans to mollusks in order to emphasize advantages of animals over humans, while showing how human centrality is challenged when placed in a larger ecological totality. First Eliot mentions that "In hilly districts, where houses and clusters of houses look so tiny against the huge limbs of Mother Earth one cannot help thinking of man as a parasitic animal—an epizoon making his abode on the skin of the planetary organism" (265), which as Mary Ellen Bellanca rightly mentions, challenges human superiority by lowering the human to a wildly different form of life (30). Eliot takes this even further, however, by then raising the mollusk's "architectural" capabilities above the human: "Whatever other advantages we may have over mollusks and insects in our habitations, it is clear that their architecture has the advantage of ours in beauty ... Look at man in the light of a shell-fish and it must be admitted that his shell is generally ugly" (265). Eliot's originality in how she destabilizes human superiority here is not only from the comparison of humans to more lowly creatures; rather, she places the human within a larger totality of both the living and the non-living—mountains, houses, animals, parasites—which emphasizes difference while forcing the human to be seen as any other form of life, rather than the dominant species.

Lewes also destabilizes human superiority by placing humankind in a larger totality of alternate life forms. In *Sea-Side Studies*, he anticipates Darwin's famous ending to *Origin*—the metaphor of an entangled bank to illustrate "ecological interdependence" (Beer 19)—by accentuating the multiplicity of life. Lewes writes, "In direct contact with Nature we not only learn reverence by having our own insignificance forced on us, but we learn more and more to appreciate the Infinity on all sides" (14). After discussing how polyps and mollusks will take salt and lime from ocean water, he asks, "Was I not justified in saying that the mollusk was deeply interesting in its relations to the great forces of the universe? Does not this one example show how the great Whole is indissolubly connected with its minutest parts?" (360). Thus Lewes highlights ecological relationships while stressing the infinity of life forms, demonstrating how discerning the multiplicity of life can remove the human from a central position in relation to others. Realizing how much life encircles the human forces Lewes to place humankind in a larger totality that posits him as "insignificant" in relation to the whole, rather than above all other animal life. Indeed, if Gosse suggests that we should study "mean creatures" to better worship God's creation, Lewes lessens human and divine superiority by suggesting we should study these creatures—"Frogs and parasites, worms and infusoria"—because "The life that stirs within us is also the life within them" (*Studies* 36).

Lewes further gives a Derridian critique of the category of "the animal" in order to put pressure on human categorizations that create arbitrary boundaries and erase profound differences. Derrida has famously critiqued the term "the animal" for its homogenization of difference. In *The Animal That Therefore I Am*, Derrida explains, "Beyond the edge of the *so-called* human, beyond it but by no means on a single opposing side, rather than 'The Animal' or 'Animal Life' there is already a heterogeneous multiplicity of the living ..." (31), and Lewes offers a similar critique. After discussing how we can tell whether or not the sea anemone is an animal or flower, Lewes suggests that we do not even know what makes an animal an animal;

indeed, as he suggests, nature itself does not even create "distinct confines" between animal and vegetable. He goes even further to suggest that

> *The Animal does not exist; nor does the vegetable*: both are abstractions, general terms ... used to designate certain groups of particulars, but having only a mental existence. Who has been fortunate enough to see the Animal? We have seen cows, cats, jackasses, and camelopards; but the 'rare monster' Animal is visible in no menagerie.
> (*Sea-Side Studies* 121, emphasis in the original)

Lewes demonstrates that to speak broadly of "the animal" as its own totality erases the profound differences that exist between animals. To call this category a "rare monster" suggests that to flatten all animal life into one category creates a monstrosity of the difference and multiplicity of life, and enacts a form of violence that for Derrida shows the "complicit, continued, and organized involvement in a veritable war of the species" (31). One can embrace a totality, but only if it remains a non-homogenous category. Lewes thus critiques human epistemological categories that seek to enact order within the natural world, demonstrating the failure of such order and the human ability to delineate and define the environment and its inhabitants.

While Lewes attempts to destabilize the superiority of scientific language in describing the environment, Eliot relishes it, using a specific vocabulary that distinguishes among animals of the same species. As such, her writings further function as a way to challenge the category of "the animal" by emphasizing particularities and differences among what seem to be similar kinds of life. In her journal, Eliot constantly notes the kinds of animals she and Lewes discover, at one point listing nearly fifteen different species of marine life, most often using their scientific names (*Journals* 60–1). In fact, it was this array of multi-species beings that spurred Eliot's desire for specificity, which later became a key element of her realism. She writes that

> I have never before longed so much to know the names of things as during this visit to Ilfracombe. The desire is part of the tendency that is now constantly growing in me to escape from all vagueness and inaccuracy into the daylight of distinct, vivid ideas. The mere fact of naming an object tends to give definiteness to our conception of it—we have then a sign which at once calls up in our minds the distinctive qualities which mark out for us that particular object from all others.
> ("Recollections" 272)

Here Eliot's "pleasure in acquiring a whole new vocabulary" (Harris and Johnston 260) functions as a way to mark distinct differences among various animals and develop the theory of realism she was formulating at the sea. Animal life proves to Eliot that one must entirely rethink how to describe a multiplicity of life in such a way that differences are emphasized, rather than flattened into a broad category of the nonhuman.

As such, these writings demonstrate how Eliot and Lewes's ecological thought puts pressure on human conceptions of animal life and the ability to faithfully record it. As we saw above, many Victorian commentators on sea life approached it with a mixture of strangeness and a desire to domesticate it. Eliot herself frequently articulates how such encounters challenge human thought and ways of seeing. She explains that "It is characteristic enough of the wide difference there is between having eyes and seeing, that in this region of Sea-anemones … we climbed for about two hours without seeing *one* Anemone" (265), questioning the authority of empirical dominance. As Peter Garratt has suggested, Victorians such as Eliot and Lewes "deny the clarity of the gaze, and describe the routine unreliability of the sensory foundations of sight" (104), and we can here see how the search for animal life demonstrates the limitations of human epistemologies. The mere trials of searching for animals in this context limits the classificatory and descriptive powers of human subjects, emphasized by Lewes's claims that "The truth is, one has to learn many little details about the animals—where to look for them, how to *see* them when there …" (*Sea-Side* 15).

Eliot and Lewes ultimately challenge human superiority and the theological overtones within natural history discourse, by demonstrating an ecological thought that embraces a totality and attempts to avoid hierarchical constructions of human–animal difference. They embrace all aspects of the environment in order to more fully place the human in a totality of life forms, which in turn lowers the dominance of humankind, connecting humans with radically unfamiliar, and at times undescribable, life forms. Morton's delineation of the effects of ecological thought helps emphasize how Eliot and Lewes will articulate an animal alterity that demonstrates how experiencing sea life forces them to reconceptualize animal subjectivity. Morton explains, "If we think the ecological thought, two things happen. Our perspective becomes very vast. More and more aspects of the Universe become included in the ecological thought. At the same time, our view becomes very profound. If everything is interconnected to everything, what exactly are the things that are connected?" (*Ecological* 38). We have already witnessed the expansion of Eliot and Lewes's perspective, but their ecological thought also invites them to more fully conceptualize the subjects of their vast outlook. In asking "what exactly are the things that are connected," Eliot and Lewes embrace a profound animal alterity that suggests humans cannot always adequately describe animal life, nor do they have unfiltered access to animal interiority; animal actions cannot necessarily be delineated in the theological and anthropomorphic categories dominating Victorian conceptions of animal subjects and the environment.

Lewes in particular emphasizes two important aspects of animal subjects in his work which enter into contemporaneous debates regarding conceptualizations of animal life: animal alterity and agency, and the non-fixity of species. As discussed above, many natural history writers placed most animal action in terms of divine intelligence. Gosse frequently mentions animal will and desires throughout *Rambles*, yet this often ties back to the divine. While many scholars have pointed toward the increasing desecularization of scientific thought, Lewes not only anticipates Darwin's arguments about the evolving nature of species, but challenges conceptions of animal agency by placing the ability to evolve within the animals themselves. By embracing an ecological thought, Lewes suggests animals are actors in their own evolutionary processes and registers a developing awareness of animal agency.

A specific example of how crabs change their dwellings by moving from shell to shell demonstrates the differing conceptualizations of animal agency—and its relationship to human superiority—between Gosse and Lewis. In describing the hermit crab's ability to appropriate abandoned shells, Gosse explains that

> it builds up a wall of sand-atoms, cemented by a glue of its own secreting, across the shell-aperture, leaving only a small central orifice, through which it may protrude its curious trunk. Thus we discern the infinite and inexhaustible resources of the Divine Wisdom in contrivances which have for their object the preservation, sustentation, and comfort of worms so obscure and humble as these. Discerning, let us adore!
>
> (*A Year at the Shore* 29)

While Gosse attributes crabs' actions to divine intelligence, placing species development in a theological framework that negates animal agency, Lewes will emphasize such agency. Writing of the same crab phenomenon, Lewes explains,

> Either we must suppose that the crab was originally so created,—designed with the express view of inhabiting shells, to which end his structure was arranged; or—and this I think the more reasonable supposition—that the hermit-crab originally was furnished with shell-plates for the hinder part of his body, but that these have become rudimentary in consequence of the animal's practice of inhabiting other shells,—a practice originally resorted to, perhaps, as a refuge from more powerful enemies, and now become an organized tendency in the species.
>
> (47)

Lewes's focus on the practices of hermit crabs and their desire to seek "refuge" suggests a level of agency in deciding to move from shell to shell, while demonstrating the non-fixity of species. Such animal agency, for Lewes, causes evolutionary development. Similarly, writing of sea hares, Lewes explains,

> One would fancy them slugs which had been troubled with absurd caprices of metamorphosis, and having first thought of passing from the form of slugs to that of hares, changed their weak minds, and resolved on being camels; but no sooner was the hump complete, than they bethought them that, after all, the highest thing in life was to be a slug—and so as slugs they finished their development.
>
> (*Sea-Side* 21–2)

In these examples, animals have enough agency and intelligence to enact their own evolutionary processes. Hence not only does Lewes suggest that species do in fact develop over time, but he places this ability to develop within the organisms themselves, suggesting that through their own actions and desires the bodies of hermit crabs have evolved to better suit their needs. Although Lewes is often in jest, relishing in the anthropomorphic techniques he later critiques, and admitting these anecdotes are mere "fancy," he does imagine the possibility of animal agency, taking their development out of the hands of God and into their own minds and bodies.

To conceptualize animals outside of a religious framework further exposes the limitations of human knowledge. Throughout *Sea-Side Studies*, Lewes castigates the frequency of anthropomorphism in scientific writing, even though he often relishes in this descriptive technique. Lewes solves the problem of anthropomorphism—which in his mind often leads to a misunderstanding of animal life—through an emphasis on alterity. In discussing the eyes and ears of mollusks, for example, Lewes attempts to defamiliarize the reader's understanding of human-animal difference:

> The mollusks, like heathen idols, have eyes for the most part, yet see not; organs of hearing, yet hear not; nevertheless, unlike the heathen idols, they are endowed with these organs for no "make-believe," but for specific purposes. A function there must be, and doubtless a good one; but we speak with large latitude of anthropomorphism when we speak of the "vision" of these animals. Molluscan vision is not human vision; nor in accurate language is it vision at all: it is not *seeing*, but *feeling*; it is not a perception of objects, but a sensation of light and darkness.
>
> (341)

By suggesting an animal has eyes and ears but does not see and hear Lewes evokes a profound animal alterity, even emphasizing foreignness through his reference to "heathen idols." Although mollusks are endowed with some of the same physical traits as humans, they use them in strikingly different ways. So while Gosse will posit the same molluscan vision in terms of a human–animal hierarchy, writing that "there exists ... every element needful for the due performance of vision, though, probably, the impressions thus conveyed may be neither so powerful, nor so distinct as those which are conveyed by the eyes of vertebrate animals. They are, however ... fresh proofs of the Divine wisdom and benevolence" (60), Lewes's understanding leads to completely divergent ways of understanding and interacting with the world. To have eyes with which one *feels* instead of *sees* forces one to imagine a radically unfamiliar mode of existence.[4] Thus, unlike those of Gosse, Lewes's descriptions of animal life succeed in decentering the human and positing animals outside of a hierarchical framework and into an ecological thought that forces humans to understand differently their relationships to and connections with other life forms.

Conclusion

Although Eliot and Lewes fall in love with sea life and develop intimate relationships, they do not always avoid the violence inherent in the ecological thought. While philosophically they establish an increasing awareness of interconnectedness, they still exert human domination over sea life, thus emphasizing how radical conceptions of human relationships with the environment do not always equate to a new kind of praxis. Throughout *Sea-Side Studies* and *Studies in Animal Life*, for example, Lewes carefully details the dissections he enacts upon animals he only sentences earlier labeled as his pets. While pet-keeping involves its own acts of violence, Lewes's ability to slide between pet and subject for dissection demonstrates the vast amount of interconnections between human and animal, and how, as Morton suggests, "Interconnectedness isn't snug and cozy. There is intimacy, as we shall see, but not predictable, warm, fuzziness" (*Ecological* 31). Lewes is fond of calling fish and mollusks his pets, explaining that often his only "consolation" after experiencing the death of a pet is to dissect him (52). While such dissection is not necessarily violent, as the animal is already dead, Lewes does admit that "Many a time I have had the unfeelingness to eye a pet with an undertaker's glance, almost wishing it would die, for the sake of its corpse" (52). In moments such as this, human dominance remains prominent, as it does when Eliot recognizes the unnaturalness of vivarium living for sea animals, but attempts to reinforce her dominance anyway: "When we put our anemones into our glass wells, they floated topsy-turvy in the water and looked utterly uncomfortable, and I was constantly called upon to turn up my sleeve and plunge in my arm up to the elbow to set things right" ("Recollections" 266). Eliot recognizes the discord between human and animal environments, and how it may affect animals, but attempts to "set things right" in an effort to force the animal into a space of human dominance.

Ultimately, Eliot and Lewes's seaside writings register a kind of thinking about human interconnections with the environment that veer from other natural history discourses, while still reasserting human dominance. At the same time, they anticipate Darwinian thinking about interconnections and the valuation of all life forms. Indeed, Darwin's famous ending to *Origin*

—the description of the entangled bank—seems like it could have come from Eliot or Lewes:

> It is interesting to contemplate an entangled bank, clothed with many plants of many kinds, with birds singing on the bushes, with various insects flitting about, and with worms crawling through the damp earth, and to reflect that these elaborately constructed forms, so different from each other, and dependent on each other in so complex a manner, have all been produced by laws acting around us.
>
> (*Origin* 397)

Eliot and Lewes carefully describe such entanglement in order to show the ecological connections between human, animal, vegetable, and mineral. Morton's privileging of Darwin, and thus Victorian thought more broadly, helps us draw Eliot and Lewes into a collection of writers who were trying to make sense of the environment and delineate the space of the human within it. Eliot and Lewes do not just stray from the theological discourse of natural history, although that is one of their key strategies in thinking ecologically, but they also defamiliarize themselves and their knowledge of other life forms in order to question human superiority and epistemologies, even as they remain a part of them. As such, Eliot and Lewes formulate divergent ways of describing animal interiority and subjectivity, as Darwin will attempt to do in later works such as *The Expressions of The Emotions in Man and Animals*. In order to comprehend how Victorians thought ecologically, then, we should include Eliot and Lewes's seaside writings into our understandings of environmental texts, particularly those that not only seek more secular and non-centrist ways of conceptualizing the environment, but that understand the environment's inhabitants—particularly animals—in ways that create a more inclusive and less hierarchical mode of thinking about, writing about, and interacting with alternate life forms.

Notes

1 German zoologist Ernst Haeckel first defined the term "ecology" in 1866. Jonathan Bate informs us that Haeckel was mostly inspired by Darwin's *Origin*, and his argument about the "'web of complex relations' by which all animals and plants are bound to each other, remote as they may be from one another in the scale of nature" (37).

2 John Parham's *Green Man Hopkins: Poetry and the Victorian Ecological Imagination* gives an excellent overview of Victorian ecological thought, where he more fully outlines these debates. See especially chapter 2, "The Trajectory of a Victorian Ecology."

3 The most representative of these works include those by David Allen, Lynn L. Merrill, and Lynn Barber.

4 Eliot makes a similar comment about animal vision in an 1856 letter to her friend Sara Hennell: "The conception of an all-wise Being does not compel us to suppose that he would endow all his creatures with the same duration of existence any more than with the same power of vision" (*Letters* 2: 265).

Works cited

Allen, David. *The Naturalist in Britain: A Social History*. London: Lane, 1976.
"The Aquatic Vivarium." *Literary Gazette* 28 May 1853: 529.
Barber, Lynn. *The Heyday of Natural History 1820–1870*. London: Jonathan Cape, 1980.
Bate, Jonathan. *Romantic Ecology: Wordsworth and the Environmental Tradition*. New York: Routledge, 1991.
Beer, Gillian. *Darwin's Plots: Evolutionary Narrative in Darwin, George Eliot, and Nineteenth-Century Fiction*. 1983. 2nd ed. Cambridge: Cambridge UP, 2000.
Bellanca, Mary Ellen. "Recollecting Nature: George Eliot's 'Ilfracombe Journal' and Victorian Women's Natural History Writing." *Modern Language Studies* 27.3/4 (1997): 19–36.
Darwin, Charles. *On the Origin of Species by Means of Natural Selection*. Ontario: Broadview, 2003.
Derrida, Jacques. *The Animal That Therefore I Am*. Trans. David Wills. New York: Fordham UP, 2008.
Eliot, George. *The George Eliot Letters*. Ed. Gordon S. Haight. 7 vols. New Haven: Yale UP, 1954–1978.
———. *The Journals of George Eliot*. Ed. Margaret Harris and Judith Johnston. Cambridge: Cambridge UP, 1998.
———. "Recollections of Ilfracombe." *The Journals of George Eliot*. Ed. Margaret Harris and Judith Johnston. Cambridge: Cambridge UP, 1998. 262–73.
Garratt, Peter. *Victorian Empiricism: Self, Knowledge, and Reality in Ruskin, Bain, Lewes, Spencer, and George Eliot*. Madison: Fairleigh Dickinson UP, 2010.
Gosse, Philip Henry. *The Aquarium: An Unveiling of the Wonders of the Deep Sea*. London: John Van Voorst, 1856.
———. *A Naturalist's Rambles on the Devonshire Coast*. London: John Van Voorst, 1853.
———. *A Year at the Shore*. London: A. Strahan, 1865.
Hamera, Judith. *Parlor Ponds: The Cultural Work of the American Home Aquarium, 1850–1970*. Ann Arbor: U of Michigan P, 2012.
Harris, Margaret and Judith Johnston, eds. *The Journals of George Eliot*. Cambridge: Cambridge UP, 1998.
King, Amy. "Reorienting the Scientific Frontier: Victorian Tide Pools and Literary Realism." *Victorian Studies* 47.3 (2005): 153–63.
———. "Tide Pools." *Victorian Review* 36.2 (2010): 40–45.
Kingsley, Charles. *Glaucus*. London: Dent, 1908.
Lewes, George Henry. *Sea-Side Studies at Ilfracombe, Tenby, The Scilly Isles and Jersey*. Edinburgh and London: Blackwood, 1858.
———. *Studies in Animal Life*. New York: Harper, 1860.
"The Marine Vivarium: At the Zoological Gardens, Regent's Park." *London Athenaeum* 28 May 1853: 511.
Merrill, Lynn. L. *The Romance of Victorian Natural History*. New York: Oxford UP, 1989.
Morton, Timothy. *The Ecological Thought*. Cambridge: Cambridge UP, 2010.
———. "Guest Column: Queer Ecology." *PMLA* 125.2 (2010): 273–82.
Parham, John. *Green Man Hopkins: Poetry and the Victorian Ecological Imagination*. New York: Rodopi, 2010.

Ritvo, Harriet. *The Animal Estate: The English and Other Creatures in the Victorian Age*. Cambridge: Harvard UP, 1987.
"Sea Views." *Household Words* 15 July, 1854: 506–10.

13 Agriculture and ecology in Richard Jefferies's *Hodge and His Masters*

Ronald D. Morrison

In comparing the ecological visions of Richard Jefferies and D. H. Lawrence, Rebecca Welshman recalls that the term "ecology" first appeared in print in an 1866 work by eminent German biologist Ernst Haeckel (51). Welshman reminds us that Haeckel created this new term by combining the Greek words *oikos* ("household" or "homestead") and *logos* ("study"); and, like other commentators before her, Welshman explicitly links the etymology of the word to Darwin's discussion of the "economy of nature" in *On the Origin of Species*. In emphasizing the literal dimension of the term—ecology as the study of the homestead—Welshman opens up a remarkably productive way of approaching much of Richard Jefferies's work. In this essay I examine a series of Jefferies's essays that first appeared in the Tory newspaper *The Standard* and that were later collected into his two-volume *Hodge and His Masters* in 1880. The individual pieces in this collection literally focus on the homestead, as Jefferies analyzes sweeping changes within the economic, social, political, and natural environments of agricultural communities in the southern county of Wiltshire in England during the late 1870s, in the midst of several years of severe agricultural depression. In this context, *Hodge and His Masters* offers a compelling account of the plight of middle-class farmers as well as agricultural laborers struggling to survive in a rapidly changing environment. In fact, *Hodge and His Masters* can be studied as an early example of what we today would call one variety of ecocriticism. As I shall argue, Jefferies's attitudes toward the environment are often (although not exclusively) based in conservative political and philosophical positions that are not always easily reconcilable with twenty-first century environmentalist thought. However, this ideological position links him to a modern-day version of the georgic and contemporary writers such as Wendell Berry in America.

Biographical and historical contexts for *Hodge and His Masters* offer a helpful place to begin, especially for readers familiar with only selections from Jefferies's large body of work. Jefferies was born in Wiltshire in 1848 the son of a small farmer, who, like several of the figures he describes in his collection, eventually abandoned farming out of economic necessity. Jefferies's imagination was deeply influenced by his rural boyhood, and he drew heavily upon his knowledge of country life throughout his brief but highly productive career as a writer. Discovering a talent for describing the natural world as well as local history, rural customs, and farming techniques, he found work as a journalist while still a teenager. By the late 1870s, Jefferies was becoming increasingly well known, especially after the 1878 publication of *The Gamekeeper at Home*, already in its fourth edition by 1880 (Keith, *Richard Jefferies* 19). Despite Jefferies's growing prominence as a "literary naturalist," it remains important to note that, over the course of many years, writing for the agricultural press provided Jefferies with a reliable if modest source of income, and he produced dozens of essays on agricultural subjects and rural culture; moreover, his early essays on hunting and game-keeping often include many references to agriculture as well, since these operations were interconnected on rural estates. During this same time frame, middle-class readers found it impossible to ignore the crucial importance of agriculture to the British economy. Several factors—including a succession of bad harvests, prolonged outbreaks of animal disease, and a glut of cheap imported grain, meat, and cheese from the Americas—resulted in an extended agricultural depression throughout Great Britain beginning in the 1870s.[1] Additionally, the efforts of Joseph Arch and other activists to unionize agricultural laborers resulted in increased attention paid to farming regions and to rural communities, and by 1880 there was considerable political pressure to extend the franchise to agricultural workers.

One of the initial problems in discussing Jefferies's works is the fact that critics from the Victorian Age to the present have struggled to situate his works into meaningful and consistent genre categories and ideological frames. To choose an obvious example, in *Hodge and His Masters* Jefferies often pushes beyond the usual boundaries of traditional journalism in employing techniques from fiction throughout the collection. Although in the Victorian Period and beyond many of Jefferies's works, most especially his early works on hunting, were considered to be part of the amorphous genre of "country books," it is disconcerting that Leslie Stephen's essay "Country Books," published in the *Cornhill* in 1880 and reprinted in later editions of *Hours in a Library*, never mentions Jefferies (despite the fact the two writers shared the same publisher at the time). As Stephen describes them, country books offer an idealized version of the country as a pleasant escape from the demands of industrialized, urban culture, and these works consistently avoid addressing politics or any of the harsh economic realities of rural life. Thus, as conceived by Stephen, Victorian country books generally exclude any meaningful discussion of agriculture at all. This context helps to explain W. E. Henley's complaint in his review of the book in the *Athenaeum* that Jefferies "would have done well to leave Hodge and Hodge's masters alone and keep to his beasts and birds and fishes" (180). Jefferies also frustrates Victorian expectations for country books in focusing on the actual concerns of middle-class farmers instead of idealized rustics. As Brian Morris describes the situation, Jefferies "writes out of sympathy with the class of small farmers to which he belonged by both birth and through marriage, and which had been particularly adversely affected by the depression years" (99). Despite Jefferies's expressions of concern regarding the growing political influence of agricultural laborers and what he feared was an increasing moral laxness among them, the full range of Jefferies's political views still remains more nuanced than Morris's pronouncement suggests. Unquestionably, many of his conservative views were squarely in line with those of the average readers of *The Standard*, such as his warnings about the effects of the unionization of agricultural workers. But Jefferies also emphasizes key ways in which agricultural laborers benefitted economically and socially from some of the recent developments in rural England. Moreover, the ever-practical Jefferies recognizes that British farmers do not have the luxury of going back in time before the advent of steam power, increased foreign competition, or demands for improved working conditions for laborers, and thus his essays generally focus on the state of agriculture as it is—rather than as it has been, or as it might be in an ideal state. Thus, while Jefferies does indeed hope to preserve certain productive features of the past, it is overly simplistic to label him as a reactionary conservative.

Critics from the twentieth century and beyond have also struggled to characterize Jefferies's stance toward the environment in consistent ways. Recent ecocritics have recognized Jefferies as part of an emerging environmental tradition in nineteenth-century Britain, concluding that his works are particularly rich because they can be approached both *from* an ecocritical perspective and because many of his writings might be considered *as varieties of* early ecocriticism. David Mazel, for example, includes an extract from Jefferies in his collection entitled *A Century of Early Ecocriticism*. In his Introduction to that work, Mazel claims that Jefferies "was one of the first authors to make a living by writing about nature" (12).[2] While this assertion has obvious validity, Jefferies nevertheless remains a problematic figure for critics hoping to discover a modern twenty-first-century environmentalist position in his work. Jefferies's focus in his early works on hunting and game-keeping is just one obvious sign of his difference from many of the writers in the tradition that Mazel identifies. And, as is true of their Victorian counterparts, modern critics have generally avoided Jefferies's work on agriculture altogether, simply accepting *Hodge and His Masters*, for example, as a "comprehensive survey of agriculture of the time" (Keith, *Richard Jefferies* 32). Other critics have reacted harshly to conservative elements in Jefferies's work. In the early part of the twentieth century, Edward Thomas dismissed *Hodge and His Masters* as a "partisan" work (90) written for a Tory audience unsympathetic to rural laborers and to reform, a claim that has been echoed by Raymond Williams and others.[3] It is understandable, then, that recent ecocritics have often focused on Jefferies's remarkable ecological disaster novel *After London, or Wild England* (1885), which describes the aftermath of an unnamed but horrific catastrophe that has wiped out most of the human inhabitants of Britain.[4] While such approaches have proven fruitful in exploring the ways in which Jefferies anticipates post-humanist ecological theory, this novel represents only one late stage of Jefferies's engagement with the environment and remains relatively atypical when compared to the rest of his large body of work.

Prior to the development of a full-fledged ecocriticism, critics often set up a false dilemma between considering Jefferies as a "nature writer" and as a chronicler of rural life and customs. But insisting upon a tidy division between the natural world and human interaction with nature was simply not possible for Jefferies, nor is it possible for contemporary ecocritics. W. J. Keith, anticipating key elements of ecocriticism, claims that, "For Jefferies a natural environment that excludes [humans] is inevitably incomplete ... while a human society that excludes nature is unthinkable" (*Rural Tradition* 128). Similarly, Kathleen Wallace and Karla Armbruster argue in their Introduction to *Beyond Nature Writing* that "Understanding how nature and culture constantly influence and construct each other is essential to an informed ecocriticism ... " (4). In much of his writing, Jefferies turns to agriculture as the liminal space where the traditional poles of nature and culture intersect and overlap. For Jefferies, the agricultural home place is bound up in a complicated tangle of connections not only with the natural environment but also with economic, legal, cultural, and natural forces that all have a tremendous impact on individuals, human communities, and the land itself. Thus *Hodge and His Masters* displays Jefferies's intense interest in what might be described as an ecological approach to analyzing agricultural communities. A focus on Jefferies's descriptions and analysis of Victorian agriculture as opposed to an abstract or idealized conception of nature untouched by human activity allows us, in the words of Barri J. Gold (writing about discourses of Victorian energy), to "avoid both an excessive literary anthropomorphism and a nostalgic vision of untrammeled nature" (214).[5]

There are additional reasons why it is crucial to explore Jefferies's treatment of agriculture. It is worth recalling that a great many of Jefferies's highly detailed observations of nature were originally gathered in the contexts of rural estates and farms in Jefferies's native Wiltshire. Even the famous complaint voiced by Jefferies's exasperated father about "our Dick poking about in them hedges" (quoted in Edward Thomas 47) underscores the fact that his son's most frequent engagement with nature occurred in the cultivated hedges that separated and protected plots of farm land, or in the carefully managed woods or parks surrounding large estates.[6] By 1880, Jefferies was tremendously invested in describing agricultural communities at a stage of tremendous change, and, in fact, *Hodge and His Masters* displays Jefferies's interest in exploring a path toward what today we would designate as a sustainable future for British agriculture.[7] While a handful of recent critics have come to regard *Hodge and His Masters* as an early variety of ethnographic or sociological analysis of rural occupations and agricultural communities,[8] Jefferies's focus remains broader, offering what can only be called an ecological approach to agriculture. Jefferies knew very well that agriculture serves as one of the primary means by which humans attempt to establish and maintain their relationships with the natural world in industrialized culture. The ongoing agricultural depression in the 1870s drew attention to the fact that all members of the society participated in the complex economic, political, and social networks created by agriculture. Furthermore, the entire culture had a vested interest in creating sustainable agricultural practices for the future. Jefferies witnessed spirited debates concerning various agricultural practices and their broader implications, including the sustainability of the land, the use of wild and domestic animals, and the dietary habits of the poor and working classes. Throughout his writings on agriculture, in one respect or another, Jefferies addresses each of these issues.

While Jefferies's works have often been described with the imprecise term "country books," it might be best to consider *Hodge and His Masters* as a nineteenth-century version of the georgic. Keith argues that the georgic tradition influenced rural writers such as Jefferies much more profoundly than did the more familiar—and more conventionally "literary"—pastoral tradition (*Rural Tradition* 5). In contrast to the pastoral, which idealizes rural life, the georgic allows for a broader and more realistic discussion of nature, agriculture, and rural culture. In his widely known introduction to ecocritical theory, Greg Garrard addresses the georgic only minimally, viewing it as one of several ideological positions that Western culture might take on the environment. For Garrard, the georgic tradition is part of a broader ideological stance on humans' relationship with the land that he describes through the trope "Dwelling," which he argues is "not a transient state; rather, it implies the long-term imbrication of humans in a landscape of memory, ancestry and death, of ritual, life and work" (117). Garrard laments that historically the georgic tradition has at times been co-opted by ideological forces that exploit the very people and land they ostensibly celebrate, but he nevertheless finds much to praise in contemporary georgic writers such as Wendell Berry. While the passage quoted immediately above is Garrard's characterization of more recent versions of the georgic, it also suggests many of the key features of Jefferies's agricultural writings as well.[9] Unfortunately, industrialized farming and the view of the land that it encourages threaten the ongoing imbrication of humans into their environment.

As is true with Berry, there are conservative elements in Jefferies's thought that may prove troublesome for ecocritics to accept, but these elements nevertheless fit his broader position on the environment. For example, in a section of the work entitled "The Juke's Country,"[10] Jefferies describes the manner in which a local fox hunt unites nobles, gentry, and, to a lesser extent, agricultural laborers (who, he claims, take pleasure and pride in witnessing such events) in a common purpose and celebration of community traditions and values. Jefferies expounds at length on the value of hunting in the rural community, claiming that hunting improves the breeding of the Duke's horses, and, more generally, asserting that hunting elevates the overall quality of life in the county. As Jefferies articulates it, hunting "gives a life, a go, a social movement to the country which nothing else imparts" (1: 193). Moreover, the chapter ends with a description of an agricultural show, sponsored by the local peer and attended by all members of the community regardless of social rank. Here Jefferies offers an extended account of an award ceremony honoring the service of various laborers, including an older worker who has remained on one farm for sixty years (1: 200)—for Jefferies, a clear indication of the prosperity and stability of the community and the careful stewardship of the land.

Both of these scenes exemplify the presence of what Katey Castellano terms "Romantic conservatism," a position which she convincingly demonstrates can be seen operating in the work of Romantic-era writers such as Burke and Wordsworth, but also evident in the work of more recent writers such as Berry.[11] Although twenty-first-century readers may presume that a "Green" view of nature is necessarily progressive politically, from Jefferies's perspective traditional class structures preserve crucial elements of nature in the cultivated parks and woodlands maintained by landowners and longstanding tenants. In contrast, "high farming," as we shall explore more fully below, too often encouraged unbridled agricultural production regardless of the economic, social, or environmental costs. For Jefferies, preserving the land also meant maintaining the deep-rooted social and economic structures that he believed promoted stability in both the human and natural environments. To illustrate the enduring benefits of a traditional rural community and natural environment, Jefferies offers the fictitious market town of "Fleeceborough" in Chapter XI as an example. One primary reason for the success of this community is the fact that the peer is willing to invest in new sheds, drains, and cottages for the laborers, along with a host of other material improvements. As a result of these actions, inhabitants of all social classes benefit—from the tenant farmers to the laborers. And thus, Jefferies concludes, "When the tenant is stationary, the labourer is also. He stays in the same cottage on the same farm all his life, his descendants remain and work for the same tenant family. He can trace his descent in the locality for a hundred years" (1: 264). And, just as important, the land—fields, pasture, and woods—benefits from such stability, just as do those who live upon it.[12]

From a twenty-first-century environmentalist perspective, we might expect Jefferies to oppose bitterly all aspects of the growing influence of science and technology upon agriculture—in other words, what was designated as "high farming." However, Jefferies's overall response remains considerably more nuanced. Based on his portrayal in these volumes, Jefferies remains relatively sympathetic to at least some of the farmers who determine they must enlist science and technology in order to survive. In a section entitled "Haymaking," Jefferies describes the host of difficulties encountered by Wiltshire dairy farmers—not the least of which is intense competition from cheesemakers in America and Canada, who can sell their products at considerably cheaper prices than can British dairy farmers (a factor that, significantly, forces these farmers to sell milk instead of cheese). Jefferies contends that more elements of the traditional dairy can be found in London than on Wiltshire farms, noting that "here in the heart of the meadows the romance has departed. Everything is mechanical or scientific. From the refrigerator that cools the milk, the thermometer that tests its temperature, the lactometer that proves its quality, all is mechanical precision" (1: 169–70). Jefferies further explains that the dairy farmer, Mr. George, remains ever mindful of "weather cablegrams from America," which influence him from the other side of the Atlantic (1: 174). Moreover, Jefferies continually emphasizes the fact that many of Mr. George's increased costs result from having to transport milk daily to the railroad station, where it is shipped to the metropolis. Inconsistent consumer demand and nagging concerns over the possibility of spoilage threaten his profits, as Mr. George works against the clock and the incessantly rainy weather to produce a high-quality hay crop necessary for his milk cows. Still, at least these technical innovations give him a chance to turn a profit and provide employment for the large number of laborers necessary to run a thriving dairy.

To choose another example of Jefferies's sympathetic stance toward ambitious farmers, in "A Man of Progress" Jefferies offers a portrait of Cecil, an educated young farmer who has purchased a small estate and who is resolutely determined to make "high farming" succeed. Cecil has spent several years of hard work incorporating such technical innovations as draining his farmland, installing a central irrigation system, and erecting modern cottages for his workers. Moreover, he has introduced the use of steam engines to power the farm's machinery and has launched an elaborate accounting system to keep track of expenditures. Based on the sympathetic tone of this chapter, Jefferies holds no special scorn for Cecil, since he concedes that the young farmer has been unduly influenced by a new farming model closely based on "commercial speculation":

> He began at the time when it was daily announced that old-fashioned farming was a thing of the past. Business maxims and business practices were to be the rule of the future. Farming was not to be farming; it was to be emphatically "business," the same as iron, coal, or cotton.
>
> (1: 46)

Despite his enthusiasm and his faithfulness to these guiding principles, the economic depression has caused Cecil to approach the limits of his capital, and he faces the gloomy prospect of mortgaging his property to pay for vaunted improvements that have yet to produce the promised monetary rewards. Jefferies suggests that Cecil possesses the right kind of temperament for farming, and he works diligently at improving his land, but the influence of the new agricultural business model threatens to ruin his prospects and may eventually cause him to lose his farm, with potentially disastrous results for laborers and the land.

Nevertheless, Jefferies holds special scorn for outsiders who would unthinkingly impose a quasi-scientific business model upon traditional farming without understanding or respecting the rhythms and values of rural life—let alone the challenging economic realities of trying to make a living from the soil. One example of these narrow-minded outsiders is the "professor," who in the opening chapter of the book delivers an address entitled "Science, the Remedy for Agricultural Depression" (1: 11) at a meeting for farmers in the fictional market town of Woolbury. In his paper, the professor blames the intractable farmers for the current state of agricultural depression and upbraids them for refusing to adopt up-to-date methods:

> Science could supply the remedy and science alone; if they would not call in the aid of science they must suffer, and their privations must be upon their own heads. Science said, Drain, use artificial manure, plough deeply, keep the best breed of stock, put capital into the soil. Call science to their aid, and they might defy the seasons.
>
> (1: 17)

The professor's speech is grounded in a long-standing belief among educated British citizens that "traditional husbandry ... [was] riddled with ignorance" (Keith Thomas 74), an assumption that Jefferies suggests may hold some validity, although new farming methods have as yet failed to offer sustainable alternatives. This passage serves as a representative example of Jefferies's tone and technique throughout the collection, in that he offers very few direct comments on the professor or his speech, allowing his readers to recognize for themselves that the professor's speech threatens to veer into self-parody, especially in the midst of a prolonged agricultural depression. Not surprisingly, the address ends disastrously when the professor cannot offer to the skeptical farmers even one concrete example of a farmer who has thriven using the advanced and expensive techniques the professor deems necessary for success.

Jefferies consistently reveals the potential harm of such doctrines preached by individuals who have neither money nor sweat invested in actual farming practices. To choose another example, in a section entitled "A Bicycle Farmer" Jefferies describes a young man named "Master Phillip," who, upon his wealthy father's recommendation, has come to the countryside while on vacation from his studies as an initial step toward becoming a gentleman farmer.[13] Rather than stay with a local farmer, Master Phillip resides with "a gentleman who had taken a country mansion and shooting for the season. His host had accumulated wealth in the 'City,' and naturally considered himself an authority on country matters" (1: 154). During this period, leasing hunting rights on estates became a common way of generating much-needed revenue for landowners, yet the practice, at least in irresponsible hands, represents an additional threat to the stability of rural estates, as becomes apparent when this new development is contrasted with the long-term care and respect for the land evident in "The Juke's Country." Young Master Phillip, as one might expect, has no practical experience whatsoever with farming (and he is unlikely to gain any from his affluent host), yet he spends his time and energies asserting that "The whole of rural England, in short, want[s] rearranging upon mathematical principles" (1: 165). In a section of the book more straightforwardly satirical than many others, Jefferies describes how Master Phillip plans to apply abstract principles gleaned from his classical education to farming, including geology, astronomy, botany, chemistry, and so on. But, tellingly for Jefferies, the chapter ends with a reference to Master Phillip's hand, which is "as white as a lady's" (1: 167), a small detail that confirms he has observed a great deal but has not worked at all. Despite the amused responses of local laborers, Master Phillip represents a new variety of farmer or landowner who may do great harm to the rural community, its land, and its inhabitants.

In a chapter entitled "The Borrower and the Gambler," Jefferies emphasizes that while many traditional farmers have been driven out of business, a new type of agricultural speculator has arisen, creating the two types of "façade farmer[s]" described in the chapter's title (1: 99). The first has borrowed so extensively throughout the county that his irresponsible practices threaten to pull down the entire economic structure, since the bank, most all of the merchants, and even the local squire have been entangled in his financial schemes, and all of them may be ruined if anyone calls in the promissory notes that keep the enterprise temporarily afloat. The second figure, "the Gambler," mechanically reinvests every penny he earns back into his farm, gambling on future successes while laying nothing aside for leaner times. While "the Gambler's" strategy is obviously not sustainable, Jefferies emphasizes that the most troubling consequences result from his view of the land itself, since the Gambler proclaims,

> the earth is like the Bank of England—you may draw upon it to any extent; there's always a reserve to meet you. You positively cannot overdraw the account. You see there's such a solid security behind you. The fact is, I bring commercial principles into agriculture; the result is, grand success.
>
> (1: 102–3)

Such unrealistic attitudes toward the land (as well as the basic economics of farming) were simply unsustainable, as any experienced farmer or landowner knew in the nineteenth century. Moreover, at the time of original publication, readers only needed to look at the deep depression in agriculture to see that any claim of "grand success" for these new methods was hardly credible. Although in various places in the work Jefferies admits that farmers may need to update some farming practices, he cannot endorse such shortsighted and destructive views of the land and such a blatant disregard for the laborers whose fortunes are so closely bound to it. Moreover, the actions of the Borrower and Gambler have far-reaching negative effects on the overall economic health of the community, since their principles have been adopted by virtually all members of the rural community. In a chapter entitled "County-Court Day," Jefferies explains that

> The labourer, like so many farmers in a different way, lives on credit and is perpetually in debt. He purchases his weekly goods on the securing of hoeing, harvest, or piece work, and his wages are continually absorbed in payment of instalments, just as the tenant-farmer's income is too often absorbed in the payment of interest on and instalments of his loans. No one seems ever to pay without at least a threat of the County Court … .
>
> (2: 39)

In contrast to descriptions of traditional and prosperous communities such as Fleeceborough, this community continually totters on the brink of economic and social collapse.

Prominent in Jefferies's descriptions of agricultural communities are the steam-powered traction engines that farmers found necessary to buy or lease with increasing frequency by the late 1870s, and Jefferies often describes the excessive noise, noxious smoke, and intense heat produced by such machines. At one point Jefferies offers an extended description of "the village factory," or the machine shop that rents and repairs these engines, and which has become something of a clamorous new center of village life, replacing, as we see in the quotation below, the village church:

> The ceaseless hum of wheels in motion comes from the rear, and the peculiar crackling sound of a band in rapid revolution round the drum of the engine and the shaft. Then the grinding scrape of sharp steel on iron as the edge of the tool cuts shavings from the solid metal rotating swiftly in the lathe. As blow follows blow the red-hot "scale," driven from the surface of the iron on the anvil by the heavy sledge, flies rattling against the window in a spray of fire. The ring of metal, the clatter, the roaring, and hissing of steam, fill the air, and through it rises now and then the shrill quick calls of men in command.
>
> Outside, and as it seems but a stone's throw distant, stands the old grey church, and about it the still, silent, green-grown mounds over those who once followed the quiet plough.
>
> (2: 72)

Twenty-first-century readers might assume that Jefferies's deep appreciation of the natural surroundings and his respect for quiet rural traditions would make him bitterly opposed to the introduction of such machinery. But other than a brief reference to the "original condition" (2: 78) of these formerly quiet villages before the arrival of steam power, his descriptions remain largely matter-of-fact, as though he is describing challenging weather conditions to which the inhabitants must respond in order to survive. According to Jefferies's account, especially in grain-producing regions, the use of steam-powered machinery has often helped to increase the wages of the workers, since these machines often increased the demand for additional labor, although the increased costs have been passed on to the farmers.[14]

Since a full, ecological analysis of rural communities must include all members of these communities, Jefferies spends a considerable number of pages focusing on women. Generally conservative and traditional in his attitudes toward gender roles, Jefferies nevertheless offers sympathetic and sensitive portraits of women from a range of social classes in these communities, as they negotiate dramatic changes occurring in their cultural and economic environments. Despite a general increase in wages for agricultural work—for men, women, and children alike—Jefferies reports that "the number of women working in the fields is much less than was formerly the case" (2: 133), since, as he puts it, "female labour has drifted to the towns" (2: 133). One reason for this change is that towns promise an easier life with regular work and with increased access to various consumer products, a factor which Jefferies considers as having an increasingly negative influence on rural communities in general. Even among the laborers, he notes that "With the exception of vegetables the cottager now buys almost everything and produces nothing for home use; no home-spun clothing—not even a home-baked loaf" (2: 168). While larger garden allotments represented one tangible benefit of agricultural reform, this new reliance upon consumer goods renders them far less self-sufficient than they have been in the past—and he believes that this factor alone has proven disruptive to the structure and stability of rural families.

The negative effects of this new consumerism, however, are not limited to the working classes by any means. In an early chapter entitled "The Fine Lady Farmer. Country Girls" Jefferies describes how tastes have changed dramatically in country homes as various cultural influences from the cities have filtered down to the countryside. For example, Jefferies notes that many of the local farmers subscribe to inexpensive illustrated newspapers (1: 249), a development that, despite offering obvious benefits, has tended to alienate young women, in particular, from traditional rural values and customs. Thus, in "Country Girls" he nostalgically remembers visiting a farmhouse some years earlier: "There was no disgrace in the touch of the plough—rather the contrary; now it is contamination itself" (1: 229). Still, Jefferies remains acutely aware that not even middle-class women have the luxury of keeping their hands clean, especially in the context of the ongoing depression. In a chapter titled "The Parson's Wife," Jefferies describes at length the efforts of a parson's wife to supplement her husband's income, which has diminished considerably since the prolonged depression has had a substantial impact on parish tithes, while at the same time the parson, like the farmers, must offer reduced rents and make additional improvements on the small amount of land from which he derives a significant part of his income. To compensate for these losses of income, the parson's wife has launched a whole series of money-making schemes, including raising goats, keeping poultry, and maintaining beehives, among others—but none of these attempts ultimately offers any reasonable return on her investments, despite her admirable ingenuity and persistent hard work. Under the present circumstances, subsistence farming simply does not pay in the new era of "high farming," which is a particularly troubling detail, given that large-scale farming is clearly not profitable either.[15]

But probably the most poignant description of changes in the role of women and its effects upon rural families appears in a chapter entitled "Mademoiselle, the Governess." In this chapter, the daughter of a successful farmer returns home for a brief visit (to borrow money from her father, we eventually learn). She has been provided with an advanced education for the time. First taught by her own London governess from an early age and then sent on to a finishing school, she has served as a governess and later as a paid companion to her former charge in a wealthy home in Belgravia. As a consequence, she has learned to detest all aspects of rural life in favor of urban life. Although "Georgie" earns nearly seventy pounds per year (a sum her father considers a wildly extravagant salary for a young woman), she spends the whole of her earnings on fashionable clothing, (since, as Jefferies puts it, "She found it necessary to dress equal to her place" [1: 252]), and she periodically must appeal to her parents for additional financial support. Georgie's situation, Jefferies concludes, is becoming all too frequent in farming families. With few opportunities to do anything else, and taught to regard rural life with scorn, many daughters of successful farmers take up "a scholastic life" (1: 255) as teachers or governesses in cities. But, as Jefferies observes, "The result is a continuous drain of women out of agriculture—of the very women best fitted in the beginning to be the helpmate of the farmer. In no other calling is the assistance of the wife so valuable … " (1: 255). Again, as Jefferies sees it, social and economic pressures from outside have a tremendously negative impact on rural families and threaten the long-term stability of the land and rural culture.

Space limitations prevent me from exploring additional examples, but there is much more that one might say about this extraordinary text. In many respects, *Hodge and His Masters* feels very familiar to twenty-first-century readers because the work—part novel, part sociological analysis, part treatise on farming, part study of the natural world—offers a complex and insightful analysis of the interrelations between humans and the environment through its focus on agriculture. In short, it has much in common with the modern georgic in the vein of such writers as Berry. Recasting this work as a forerunner of a modern version of the georgic helps to recapture Jefferies's aims and to understand the contexts of his conservatism as well as what should be described as his guardedly optimistic view of the future. "Conservation" and "conservatism" obviously share the same etymological roots and the same impulse. Although it may be entirely reasonable to characterize Jefferies as a conservative writer, that simple label does not contain the nuances of his views of the land and those who work upon it. Ultimately, writing in the depths of an extended agricultural depression, Jefferies seeks whatever measures might offer a sustainable future for British agriculture—and that broader view of sustainability is intimately connected to the land and the human families that live upon it.

Notes

1. The year 1879, in particular, produced heavy rains that ruined crops and caused outbreaks of disease in sheep and cattle (Keith, *Richard Jefferies* 28). P. J. Perry maintains that it is an oversimplification (perpetuated in part by the farmers, who were often reluctant to modernize their methods) to blame the depression solely on unfavorable weather conditions. Perry concludes that "Conservatism and prejudice were also responsible" (133). Also see Elizabeth Moss for an analysis of Jefferies's depiction of the depression.
2. Mazel includes Jefferies's essay "Nature and Books," which originally appeared in the *Fortnightly Review* in 1887 and which was included in the posthumously published *Field and Hedgerow* (1889).
3. Williams contends that Jefferies "was at times the class reporter or even the party hack" (194). More recently, John Rignall notes "an element of condescension and aestheticizing distance" (106) in Jefferies's treatment of agricultural laborers.
4. For two recent productive analyses of *After London*, see Heidi C. M. Scott (53–63) and Jed Mayer.
5. In this context, Gold is not writing about agriculture but about the discourses of Victorian energy. While Gold's focus and conclusions are quite different from mine, her article serves as an excellent general introduction to ecocritical approaches to Victorian literature. Also see John Parham's "Editorial" in the special edition of *Green Letters* devoted to Victorian ecocriticism.
6. In Jefferies's work, it often becomes impossible to separate descriptions of nature from accounts of human engagement with the natural world. Features that are produced and maintained by humans, such as the hedges that so intrigued the young Jefferies, eventually come to be regarded as "natural" parts of the landscape since they have been in place for many years, and since they often contain an astounding variety of plant and animal life.
7. Allen MacDuffie offers a helpful exploration of the Victorian use of the term "sustainability," which emphasizes the logical coherence and consistency of a process or policy rather than the ability of a process or policy to be continued indefinitely into the future (102).
8. For example, Sara L. Mauer refers to *Hodge and His Masters* as a "comic ethnography" (613), while Nick Freeman observes that Jefferies's early essays "typically adopt the techniques of informal interview pioneered by Henry Mayhew and other metropolitan sociologists" (171).
9. This observation deserves its own fully developed essay, but there are many parallels between *Hodge and His Masters* and Berry's *The Unsettling of America*, published nearly 100 years later.
10. The title comes from the laborers' characteristic pronunciation of the word "Duke."
11. See *Ecology* for her extended argument on British Romantic writers. In "Romantic Conservatism," she explicitly connects Burke and Wordsworth to Berry.

12 Over the course of several late chapters, Jefferies claims that traditional and prosperous regions contain few radicals among the agricultural workers: "The settled agricultural labourer, of all others, has the least inducement to strike or leave his work. The longer he can stay in one place the better for him in many ways" (2: 213). Significantly, the passage goes on to describe how long-term laborers improve the land on which they live, both for their own benefit and because of the affections they feel for it. See especially the chapter entitled "Landlords' Difficulties. The Labourer as a Power. Modern Clergy," which goes even further in detailing the increasing political and economic power of the laborers and the growing influence of what Jefferies sees as radical elements, often from outside of these rural communities.

13 The bicycle, upon which Master Phillip daily rides through the rural lanes, is also a new contraption and is viewed with wry amusement by the country folk.

14 In a statement that predicts life in the twenty-first century, Jefferies concludes that "The original idea was that the introduction of machinery would reduce all this labour. In point of fact, it has, if anything, increased it" (2: 263–4). See Roger Ebbatson for additional analysis of Jefferies's ambivalent treatment of steam power in various essays throughout his career.

15 Later in the work Jefferies argues that laborers attempting to make a living off of small plots of four or five acres inevitably fail. See "The Cottage Charter—Four-Acre Farmers" in Volume 2. Jefferies explicitly contrasts the failure of these small plots of land to the prosperity of traditional large estates.

Works cited

Berry, Wendell. *The Unsettling of America: Culture and Agriculture*. 1977. 3rd ed. Berkeley: Counterpoint, 1996.

Castellano, Katey. *The Ecology of British Romantic Conservatism, 1790–1837*. New York: Palgrave, 2013.

——. "Romantic Conservatism in Burke, Wordsworth, and Wendell Berry." *SubStance* 40.2 (2011): 73–91.

Ebbatson, Roger. "The Machine in the Wheatfield: Steam Power in the Victorian Countryside." *Green Letters: Studies in Ecocriticism* 14 (2011): 72–80.

Freeman, Nick. "Edward Thomas, Swinburne, and Richard Jefferies: 'The dead oak tree bough.'" *ELT* 51.2 (2008): 164–83.

Garrard, Greg. *Ecocriticism*. 2nd ed. New Critical Idiom Series. New York: Routledge, 2012.

Gold, Barri J. "Energy, Ecology, and Victorian Fiction." *Literature Compass* 92.2 (2012): 213–24.

Henley, William Ernest. *Views and Reviews: Essays in Appreciation*. 2nd ed. London: David Nutt, 1892.

Jefferies, Richard. *Hodge and His Masters*. 2 vols. 1880. New York: Cambridge UP, 2011. Cambridge Library Collection.

Keith, W. J. *Richard Jefferies: A Critical Study*. Toronto: U of Toronto P, 1965.

——. *The Rural Tradition: A Study of the Non-Fiction Prose Writers of the English Countryside*. Toronto: U of Toronto P, 1974.

MacDuffie, Allen. *Victorian Literature, Energy, and the Ecological Imagination*. Cambridge: Cambridge UP, 2014.

Mauer, Sara L. "National and Regional Literatures." *Cambridge History of Victorian Literature*. Ed. Kate Flynt. New York: Cambridge UP, 2012. 598–621.

Mayer, Jed. "A Darker Shade of Green: William Morris, Richard Jefferies, and Posthumanist Ecologies." *Journal of William Morris Studies* 19.3 (2011): 79–92.

Mazel, David. Introduction. *A Century of Early Ecocriticism*. Ed. Mazel. Athens: U of Georgia P, 2001. 1–19.

Morris, Brian. *Richard Jefferies and the Ecological Vision*. Victoria: Trafford, 2006.

Moss, Elizabeth. "'The wheat is beautiful, but human life is labour': Richard Jefferies and the Great Depression of British Agriculture." *EAPSU Online* 3 (2006): 24–36.

Parham, John. "Editorial." *Green Letters: Studies in Ecocriticism* 14 (2011): 5–9.

Perry, P. J. "An Agricultural Journalist on the 'Great Depression': Richard Jefferies." *Journal of British Studies* 9.2 (1970): 126–40.

Rignall, John. "Landscape, Labour and History in Later Nineteenth-Century Writing." *Ecology and the Literature of the British Left: The Red and the Green*. Ed. John Rignall, Gustav Klaus, and Valentine Cunningham. Burlington: Ashgate, 2012. 101–12.

Scott, Heidi C. M. *Chaos and Cosmos: Literary Roots of Modern Ecology in the British Nineteenth Century*. University Park: Penn State UP, 2014.

Stephen, Leslie. *Hours in a Library*. New Edition, with Additions. 4 vols. London: Smith, Elder, 1907.

Thomas, Edward. *Richard Jefferies: His Life and Work*. Boston: Little Brown, 1909.

Thomas, Keith. *Man and the Natural World: A History of the Modern Sensibility*. New York: Pantheon, 1983.

Wallace, Kathleen R. and Karla Armbruster. "Why Go Beyond Nature Writing, and Where To?" Introduction to *Beyond Nature Writing: Expanding the Boundaries of Ecocriticism*. Ed. Karla Armbruster and Kathleen R. Wallace. Charlottesville: U of Virginia P, 2001. 1–25.

Welshman, Rebecca. "Literature and the Ecological Imagination: Richard Jefferies and D. H. Lawrence." *Victorian Network* 3.1 (2011): 51–63.

Williams, Raymond. *The Country and the City*. Oxford: Oxford UP, 1973.

14 Edward Carpenter, Henry Salt, and the animal limits of Victorian environments

Jed Mayer

In one of Henry Salt's last publications, *The Creed of Kinship* (1935), published when the author was in his eighties, he reflects on a lifetime of efforts to bring about a "fusion of certain great causes," and recounts: "I felt flattered by the remark of a hostile journalist that I was a 'compendium of the Cranks,' by which he apparently meant that I advocated not this or that humane reform, but all of them. That is just what I desire to do" (qtd. in Preece 144). Despite criticism from "hostile journalists" and some of the more single-minded members of the emerging English socialist movement in which Salt participated, his inclusive approach to reform was in some respects typical of the activist climate of the 1880s and 1890s, when Salt formed the Humanitarian League with the aid of his friend Edward Carpenter. In his autobiography *My Days and Dreams*, Carpenter looks back fondly on the shared enthusiasm and sense of purpose among social activists in England during this period, which drew together a number of disparate groups:

> Hyndman's [Social] Democratic Federation, Edmund Gurney's Society for Psychical Research, Mme. Blavatsky's Theosophical Society, the Vegetarian Society, the Antivivisection movement, and many other associations of the same kind marked the coming of a great reaction from the smug commercialism and materialism of the mid-Victorian epoch, and a preparation for the new universe of the twentieth century.
> (240)

Despite Carpenter's optimism, the coming era was not to see the realization of such millennial hopes, but rather an intensification of the very ills he and his fellow activists labored against: economic inequality, deforestation, industrialized farming, and vivisection all flourished in "the new universe of the twentieth century," and are continuing to do so into the new millennium.

Given the urgency of present-day threats to the economically disenfranchised, to nonhuman animals, and to the biosphere, the unification of concerns addressed by Salt, Carpenter, and their circle—combining efforts for social justice with the liberation of animals and environmental activism—would seem all the more necessary. And yet these causes, which at the end of the nineteenth century could be regarded as unified, are now largely divided by what Paul Waldau describes as "the tyranny of small differences." "As one examines the relationship of the conservation movement to another vibrant, worldwide movement known by various names such as 'animal protection,' 'animal rights,' and 'animal liberation,'" Waldau argues,

> one finds *many* reasons these 'causes' ought to have an arm-in-arm relationship. Historically, however, the relationship between these two megamovements has often been described as tense—differences have at times prompted advocates of each of these social movements to remain silent about key insights of the other movement and, thereby, *ignore* fundamental features of nature.
>
> (27)

To cite just one example of the real-world impact this separation of perspectives has had, many of the most powerful and influential environmental organizations—including Sierra Club, Natural Resources Defense Council, Greenpeace, Amazon Watch, Surfrider, and Oceana—do not meaningfully address the problem of intensive animal agriculture, despite clear evidence that it is the single leading cause of global warming (significantly higher than the use of all fossil fuels combined).[1] The tyranny of small differences does not exist in the world of advocacy groups alone: a similar and puzzling split may be seen between the academic fields of ecocriticism and animal studies, despite their obvious commonalities. While the two fields emerged out of the principle that other-than-human lives matter, there remain fundamental differences in the ways they approach their subject. As Rebecca Raglon and Marian Scholtmeijer argue: "The most obvious difference emerges from the fact that environmental literature is frequently philosophically oriented toward a 'big picture' view, that is, concerned with nature's processes as a whole, or with ecosystems" (122). Erica Fudge similarly notes that "the ecological argument, in which the species rather than the individual is emphasized, sits at the heart of much literary ecocriticism, in which landscape and nature in general are the focus and animals perceived only as part of that landscape" (Cole et al. 93). While there have been notable attempts to think beyond these differences (Timothy Morton's unified theory of "hyperobjects," Bruno Latour's "actor-network" theory and notions of hybridity, and emerging discourses on biopolitics, to name just a few), ecocriticism and animal studies remain largely separate fields, despite their potential affinities.[2] Returning to the work of Henry Salt and Edward Carpenter, which emerged as first-wave environmentalism was underway, and animal rights was moving into a new phase with the antivivisection movement, might help to show us some of the ways in which these divided concerns might be unified as we try to think through the problems facing us in the new world of the twenty-first century.

Both writers sought to become closer to the natural world by leaving their bourgeois professional lives in town and living a simpler life in the country. Millthorpe, the seven-acre farm and cottage Carpenter established on the Yorkshire border near Sheffield in 1883, became the stuff of legend among figures like William Morris, Robert Blatchford, George Bernard Shaw, and other English socialists concerned about the environmental as well as the social impact of industrialization. Carpenter's dramatic change in lifestyle, from Anglican curate and tutor to rural farmer, inspired many in what would be called the "back to nature" movement (Gould 29–58; Goyder and Lowe 17–18). Among them was Henry Salt, who left an oppressive teaching post at Eton to set up a farm in rural Surrey with his wife Kate in 1884. Both writers were inspired by the model of Thoreau's *Walden*, and regarded their new lives as both radical social experiment and ethical awakening, though many of those who followed Carpenter's example would emphasize the former over the latter, retreating to a self-sufficient "simple life" of which Carpenter would later become critical (Rowbotham 245). Farm life awakened both writers to the ethical and physical values of vegetarianism, and a life lived closer to nature, as well as their growing awareness of the more-than-human, would come to inform their thinking on a wide range of social issues. They began to perceive fundamental connections between the plight of animals, the destruction of nature, the oppression of women and gays, and the flagrant use of corporal punishment in schools and prisons. In 1891, Salt would put these principles into practice by forming the Humanitarian League, which would work to promote "compassion, love, justice for every living creature; for in proportion as such gentleness is more and more inculcated and practised shall we be drawing nearer and nearer to a true civilization, a society in which all harmless and healthy life shall be free to develop itself unrestricted and uninjured" (*Humanitarianism* 26). Through lecture series, activism, and the League's journal *Humanity* (later *The Humanitarian*), Salt and Carpenter addressed a range of issues astonishing in its breadth and diversity, but all united under the common principle of an ethics that made no distinctions based on race, species, class, gender, or sexual orientation.

Yet while the League worked on the implicit principle of a "natural and necessary correlation between the various phases of humane sentiment, and that, if one be recognized, it is unreasonable to refuse acceptance to the rest" (*Humanitarianism* 26), there were many among their contemporaries who could not see beyond the tyranny of small differences. The eclecticism of activist causes in the *fin de siècle* was perhaps felt more in the aggregate of diverse groups working for social change than in individual groups or organizations. For every Anna Kingsford—vegetarian, antivivisectionist, medical reformer, feminist, and mystic—there was a more single-minded figure. Henry Hyndman, for example, the founder of the Social Democratic Federation, Britain's first socialist organization, took umbrage at the range of issues infiltrating the leftist platform. During a particularly contentious period in the Foundation's development, Hyndman said to Salt: "I don't want the movement to be a depository of odd cranks; humanitarians, vegetarians, anti-vivisectionists, arty-crafties and all the rest of them. We are scientific socialists and have no room for sentimentalists, they confuse the issue" (qtd. in Rowbotham 97). Both writers actively sought to win support for animal causes with the English left. In *To-day: The Monthly Magazine of Scientific Socialism*, Salt argued:

> When a Socialist sets aside the plea for humanity to the lower animals as a mere fad and crotchet, a Vegetarian might well retort that if the promptings of gentleness and mercy are deliberately disregarded in the case of the animals, it cannot surprise us if they are also excluded from consideration in those social questions where the welfare of human beings is concerned.
> ("Socialists and Vegetarians" 173)

Similarly, when writing for the socialist newspaper *The Clarion* in 1894, Carpenter stressed the affinities between antivivisection and the labor movement, arguing that the Labor Movement must "defend the dumb animals and creatures weaker than itself against the horrible exploitations of so-called Science" (qtd. in Rowbotham 177). Salt also addressed the split from the other direction, addressing the conservative middle-class members of the animal welfare movement on the topic of "The Animal Question and the Social Question," arguing that defenders of animals, "while in no way relaxing their efforts for the welfare of the animals, should also range themselves on the side of social progress. At any rate, to *oppose* such change, while pleading for justice to animals, is to undo with one hand the work that is being done with the other" (77). Such arguments suggest that, however broad the range of issues being addressed by activists in the period, their cooperation sometimes needed active encouragement. By doing so, figures like Carpenter and Salt honed their critique of all forms of exploitation, enabling them to look beyond the animal limits of some of their fellow socialists.

For Carpenter and Salt, leftist ideals of liberation could not be fully achieved without liberating animals, since humans and nonhumans suffer under similar ideologies of inequality. As Salt argues, "as long as the compassion which is claimed for men is denied to animals or extended only to certain classes of animals—so long will it be difficult to appeal successfully from the narrow selfishness of personal interests to the higher and nobler sentiment of universal brotherhood" (*Humanitarianism* 19). Peter Singer and Tom Regan have developed the term "speciesism" to describe the ideology that designates some species as intrinsically superior to others, and Cary Wolfe has shown the ways in which this ideology can be used to dehumanize marginalized human groups. He argues that "violence against human others … has often operated by means of a double movement that animalizes them for the purposes of domination, oppression, or even genocide—a maneuver that is effective because we take for granted the prior assumption that violence against the animal is ethically permissible" (Wolfe, "Human" 567). If "the discourse of speciesism ... can be used to mark any social other," then "[w]e all, human and nonhuman alike, have a stake in the discourse and institution of speciesism; it is by no means limited to its overwhelmingly direct and disproportionate effect on animals" (Wolfe *Animal* 7). For Salt, the only way of overcoming speciesism was to recognize a common kinship between humans and nonhuman animals: "Oppression and cruelty are invariably founded on a lack of imaginative sympathy; the tyrant or tormentor can have no true sense of kinship with the victim of his injustice. When once the sense of affinity is awakened, the knell of tyranny is sounded, and the ultimate concession of 'rights' is simply a matter of time" (*Animals' Rights* 21). In *Towards Democracy*, Carpenter implores his reader to "Behold the animals. There is not one but the human soul lurks within it, fulfilling its destiny as surely as within you" (5). This is not mere anthropomorphism, but a recognition of each animal's unique sense of itself, of its being "the subject of a life," in the words of Tom Regan (243). Carpenter's and Salt's imaginative sympathy resembles what Kari Weil calls "critical anthropomorphism," an "ethical relating to animals" in which "we open ourselves to touch and be touched by others as fellow subjects and may imagine their pain, pleasure, and need in anthropomorphic terms but must stop short of believing that we can know their experience" (16). Like Carpenter and Salt, Weil stresses that this mode of regard can also enable us to recognize that "the irreducible difference that animals may represent for us is one that is also within us and within the term *human*," thus working to counteract the animalizing of others described by Wolfe.

Imaginative sympathy may also inform encounters with the natural world in a more expansive sense, particularly in Carpenter's writings, where he stresses his sense of kinship to other-than-human life. In *Civilization: Its Cause and Cure*, he argues: "The life of the open air, familiarity with the winds and waves, clean and pure food, the companionship of the animals ... will tend to restore that relationship which man has so long disowned" (44–5). His study of Buddhism and Hinduism had shown Carpenter that other cultures developed alternative ways of relating to the nonhuman, finding a "kindred human life—in the animals, in the ibis, the bull, the lamb, the snake, the crocodile; in the trees and flowers, the oak, the ash, the laurel, the hyacinth; in the streams and water falls, on the mountain-sides or in the depths of the sea" (56). This perspective offers a corrective to the tendency to regard nature in the abstract, or as an ideal, in the manner of the Romantics. Salt speculated whether there is "some latent sympathy between plant and man," thus extending imaginative sympathy towards animacies not often considered sentient. Such perspectives work to counteract thinking of nature as something "over there," outside of us, a mode of thinking that ecocriticism often participates in when proffering the kind of "big picture" focus on ecosystems and species discussed earlier. The presence of animals, and the sense of animacy in the nonhuman world more generally, may subvert this conceptual framing, and help to shift the focus towards lifeforms as individuals. As Timothy Morton argues, "The question of animals—sometimes I wonder whether it is *the* question—radically disrupts any idea of a single, independent, solid environment," and

> the idea of "our" environment becomes especially tricky when it starts to slither, swim, and lurch towards us. The beings known as animals hover at the corner of the separation of inside and outside generated by the idea of a world as a self-contained system. Strangely enough, thinking in terms of 'world' often excludes animals—beings who actually live there.
> (*Ecology without Nature* 98–9)

Carpenter's and Salt's notion of environment is one that emphatically includes animals, who, like us, share their individual life-worlds with other organisms.

Just as the inequalities of human populations are in many ways fostered by the unequal treatment of other species, so the reduction of animals to nonsentient beings may facilitate the reduction of a living, diverse biosphere to the status of a resource. Eileen Crist argues:

> The objectification of animals has been primarily accomplished through the erasure of their mental lives. And the erasure of animal minds has produced an auspicious climate, and reinforced a deluded humanistic worldview, for the indiscriminate use of everything on Earth as a means to human ends.
> (57)

The view of animals proffered by the Enlightenment rendered animal behavior as merely reflexive, mechanical, and devoid of thought. Humans are regarded as exceptional beings, endowed with sentience, and this kind of human exceptionalism has enabled what Crist describes as exemptionalism: "Exemptionalism and exceptionalism are two sides of one coin: humanity has exempted itself from many of the biophysical limits that regulate and check animals, on the conviction that our ingenuity and technological savvy can (and should) successfully negotiate virtually any challenge" (48). Far from being merely a byproduct or collateral effect of environmental exploitation, "the long-standing denial or disparagement of animal minds is *causally* implicated in the devastation of the biosphere" (45). Voiding animals of agency makes them "construable as means for human ends," and consequently the "(apparently) nonsentient domains of forests, rivers, meadows, oceans, deserts, and mountains (in fact, of any landscape or seascape) were made accessible to the human race without accountability or restriction" (46). Carpenter and Salt noted similar parallels in the reduction of animals and other nonhuman life-forms to the status of resources. As Salt argues: "So long as pecuniary profit and self-interest are accepted as the guiding principles of trade, it will remain impossible to exempt the lower races from the results of an economic tyranny of which men are also the victims" ("Animal Question" 75). In *Towards Democracy* Carpenter envisions a future in which "The woods no more shall be merely a cover for wild animals, or so much value in timber—nor the fields for their crops alone" (338). Such statements make clear the abiding influence of their socialist critique of economic exploitation on their unique synthesis of the early green and animal welfare concerns of their contemporaries. This synthesis enabled them to see overlap and complicity between the ways in which human exceptionalism could render nonhuman animals and ecosystems as objects for appropriation and exploitation.

As a corrective to capitalist exploitation of animals and their environments, Salt and Carpenter portray animals as actors inhabiting vital life-worlds. Though they might be regarded primarily as polemicists, they effectively developed a new form of nature writing, one that draws from, but also corrects key tropes and motifs in, English and American natural history traditions. Their critique of environmental and animal exploitation is leavened by a sense of awe and reverence for nature, one that clearly draws from figures like Gilbert White of Selbourne, Charles Darwin, John Burroughs, and Henry David Thoreau, on whom Salt published a monograph shortly before forming the Humanitarian League. Though he takes the *Walden* author to task for his early love of hunting, he praises him for his later relinquishment of blood sport in favor of quiet contemplation, a transformation he would later contrast with naturalist Richard Jefferies. In *Richard Jefferies: A Study* (1894), Salt celebrates the amateur natural historian as a nature-poet who rose above his rural poverty to write some of the most vivid accounts of the natural world of the nineteenth century, but also notes that, while the "hunting instinct was strong in Jefferies; in Thoreau it was well-nigh extinct" (78). Salt published extensively on blood sport, and frequently emphasizes the complicity between masculinity and human dominance. Fox and pheasant hunting were frequently defended as encouraging manliness, but Salt derides them as merely desensitizing men to violence (see esp. *Killing*). This desensitization extends into the field of natural history. From the example of Jefferies, he observes more generally that "as things now are, a taste for sport is in many cases the precursor of a taste for natural history; it is the first and lowest rung of the ladder, up which a man may gradually climb from an insensate love of death-dealing to an exalted reverence for life," and regrets that it is "but one man in a thousand who at present emancipates himself in this way, and the ordinary sportsman-naturalist is a very dismal person indeed" (36). But Salt envisions "a really enlightened state of society" where "there would be other and better introductions to a familiarity with the open air" (36), an enlightened state he tried to bring about through his advocacy for humane educational reforms.

Strong as is his admiration for Jefferies in most respects, he finds in the naturalist a troubling tendency towards the kind of human exceptionalism he and Carpenter associated with exploitative attitudes towards animals and their environments. Praising the "essentially human aspect of his nature-creed," Salt notes that it is "in connection with the same subject that we note his most serious defects" (77). Discussing Jefferies's most philosophically rich work, his spiritual autobiography *The Story of My Heart* (1883), Salt argues: "Admirable as is the manner in which he exalts the human ideal as the crown of all culture, he not only goes too far, but weakens the efficiency of his own contention, when he isolates humankind from the rest of nature as something wholly unrelated and apart" (77). Contrary to Carpenter's recognition of a "human soul" in the animal gaze, Jefferies claims: "There is nothing human in any living animal" (14). Indeed, Jefferies goes so far as to state: "There is nothing human in the whole round of nature. All nature, all the universe that we can see is absolutely indifferent to us, and except to us human life is of no more value than grass" (14). Though this might be read as a skeptical avoidance of crude anthropomorphism, clearing a space for perceiving unique and distinctive qualities of other-than-human life forms without using man as their measure, later passages of *The Story of My Heart* suggest that Jefferies discursively voids the nonhuman world of a life apart from himself, preparatory to his consumption of it as a kind of imaginative resource. Describing a revelatory early encounter with nature, Jefferies describes how the "light coming across the grass and leaving itself on the dew-drops, the sound of the wind, and the sense of mounting to the lofty heaven, filled me with a deep sigh, a wish to draw something out of the beauty of it, some part of that which caused my admiration, the subtle inner essence" (70). Timothy Morton might describe this perspective as an example of Romantic consumerism, where images of nature are imaginatively imbibed as a way of purifying and beautifying the soul (*Ecology without Nature* 113). Reflecting on his ecstatic encounter with nature, Jefferies muses:

> After the sensuous enjoyment always came the thought, the desire: That I might be like this; that I might have the inner meaning of the sun, the light, the earth, the trees and grass, translated into some growth of excellence in myself, both of body and of mind; greater perfection of physique, greater perfection of mind and soul; that I might be higher in myself.
>
> (72–3)

Though for Jefferies the woods are not "merely a cover for wild animals" to hunt, "or so much value in timber," to repeat Carpenter's words from *Towards Democracy*, such passages clearly render nature as a resource for human consumption, even if it is only consumed through the eyes and spirit of the naturalist.

Romantic consumerism of the kind evoked by Jefferies may have consequences beyond the contemplative self. Noting how "Wordsworth's Lake District became the National Trust's Lake District," and "the American wilderness" has become a place to go "on holiday from an administered world," Morton argues that, beginning in the nineteenth century, "Environments were caught in the logic of Romantic consumerism" (*Ecology without Nature* 113). The very idea of "wilderness," he suggests, "can only exist as a reserve of unexploited capital, as constant tensions and struggle make evident" (113). In order for such a natural resource to work, it must be kept pure, pristine, lest it not satisfactorily beautify the souls of wayfaring consumers. "Exclusion and violence is the only way in which quietness and solitude can be guaranteed": witness the displacement of native populations from national parklands, or the extermination of "invasive" or feral species to maintain the purity of environments (113). Romantic constructions of natural purity may be seen as complicit in the categorization of undesirable life forms as alien or unnatural, laying the ground for their extermination or exclusion from ecosystems marked as wilderness. The alternative is to envision environments as always already under alteration, and this might include a different way of conceiving what we mean when we talk about pollution.

A distinctive element in the social criticism that came out of the early green movements of the 1880s and 1890s is its preoccupation with pollution, a signal difference from earlier traditions of writing about nature. While groups like the Selbourne Society for the Protection of Birds, Plants and Pleasant Places and the Coal Smoke Abatement Society existed primarily to maintain the kind of pristine nature valued by Romantic consumerism, the preoccupation of Victorian environmental criticism with the negative effects of modernity marks a dramatic shift of focus from the Romantic tradition. Urban environments figure prominently in Victorian green writing, shaped by trends in social criticism. From Carlyle's Irish widow dying of typhus in the open street and spreading it to seventeen other victims in *Past and Present*, to Dickens's sepia-toned prose portraits of Tom-all-Alone's in *Bleak House*, Victorian writers were uniquely attuned to the complex ecosystems spawned amidst urban sprawl. Such urban tableaus are deeply ecological, in the radical sense denoted by German evolutionary zoologist Ernst Haeckel in the first recorded usage of the word "ecology," which he defines as "the investigation of the total relations of the animal both to its organic and inorganic environment" (qtd. in McIntosh 7–8). Victorian critics of industrialization engaged in such investigations, describing in detail the effects of modernity on organisms, and the complex web of relations between living beings and their environments. Nature is not a refuge from culture, but a place always vulnerable to industrial intrusion. Over Thomas Hardy's pastoral Wessex landscape run the railway tracks where modernity "stretched out its steam feeler to this point three or four times a day, touched the native existences, and quickly withdrew its feeler again, as if what it touched had been uncongenial" (*Tess* 187). Walking through the Lune valley in Kirby, once "one of the loveliest scenes in England," John Ruskin visits a sacred spring to find it "choked up and defaced," surrounded by railings that had been crushed by felled trees, leaving it "in already rusty and unseemly rags, like the last use of a railroad accident, beaten down among the dead leaves" (28: 299–300). The fantasy of a nature pure and pristine rarely remains unsullied in Victorian green writing, and the attention to pollution offers an environmental vision that simultaneously holds industrialization responsible for spoliation, and makes nature unfit for Romantic consumerist consumption.

This focus on pollution is something Victorian environmental writing has in common with animal welfare and antivivisection literature, though the two are rarely discussed in the same context. Early RSPCA campaigns tended to focus on abuses of domesticated animals, such as horses, dogs, and cats, particularly in urban contexts, while early environmental organizations like the Kyrle Society and the Commons Preservation Society tended to focus on preserving green spaces; yet the use of pollution as a trope for modernity stretches across both discourses, suggesting strong, though rarely registered, affinities. Carpenter and Salt were attuned to these affinities, and used them to awaken their readers to the intimate relations between suffering humans and nonhumans, as well as to confront them with their complicity in consuming natural resources. In "Vivisection and the Labour Movement," Carpenter observes that "we all know it well enough— that our ways of life are about as unhealthy as they can be: the poor crammed down in narrow alleys without air or light, in dirt, and insufficiency of food" and that in such conditions it is "obvious that diseases *must* swarm; the only wonder is they do not swarm worse than is the case" (69). But rather than altering the conditions "which make health impossible for the poor," medical scientists "ignore these things, and turn instead upon the harmless animals, and maim and bake and crucify them, as if they were responsible for our sins" (69). This trope of pollution echoes the following passage from Carpenter's friend and fellow antivivisectionist Anna Kingsford: "when the vivisectors ask us angrily, 'What right have you to meddle with the researches of scientific men?' ... we turn upon them with greater anger and retort in our turn, 'What right have you to render earth uninhabitable and life insupportable for men with hearts in their bosoms?'" (qtd. in Freeman 99). For the Humanitarian League and their associates, the air was polluted by more than just factory smoke, but by the cries of suffering animals. Such rhetoric enables readers to consider animal and human environments simultaneously, and to see the ways in which animal exploitation diffuses a corrupting influence into everyday life.

Salt confronted his readers' tendency to compartmentalize animals from nature, and the nonhuman from the human. Addressing industries that profit from animal exploitation, he pushes supposedly humane consumers to consider the environments that supply their luxury goods. While "the confirmed sportsman, or amateur butcher, at least sees with his own eyes the circumstances attendant on his sport ... many of those who wear seal-skin mantles or feather-bedaubed bonnets," though they may be "humane enough ... are misled by pure ignorance or thoughtlessness" (*Animals' Rights* 70). By bringing readers out into the wild where such slaughter happens for their benefit, Salt at once obliterates their fantasy of pristine nature and shows the cost of that fantasy. Like green spaces, animals tended to be represented in idealized ways evoking a mythical past. Salt counters this by bringing his readers into the modern feedlot and slaughterhouse, where "the victims of the human carnivora are bred, and fed, and from the first predestined to untimely slaughter, so that their whole mode of living is warped from its natural standard, and they are scarcely more than animated beef or mutton or pork" (50). Animals are here denaturalized, thus displacing the sentimentality that frequently attended Victorian accounts of animals. The haunting vision of "animated beef or mutton or pork" challenges consumerist fantasies of happy cows, sheep, and pigs browsing in pastoral settings.

Salt and Carpenter recognized the ways in which ideologies of the natural could be used for exploitation, and Carpenter in particular had cause to be wary of arbitrary distinctions between what was considered natural or unnatural. As a gay man, Carpenter was acutely aware of the Victorian construction of homosexuality as unnatural, and of sodomy as a crime against nature, akin to bestiality. As Carpenter's monograph *Homogenic Love, And Its Place in a Free Society*, the first study of homosexuality published by a gay man, was going to the press, Oscar Wilde was under trial for committing "acts of indecency" under section of the Criminal Law Amendment Act of 1885. Max Nordau's *Degeneration* was being reviewed in the English press, and particular attention was paid to the sociologist's portrayal of homosexuality as unnatural and degenerate, while Wilde himself was called an "unclean beast" (Youngs 165–95). Not only the conservative press portrayed homosexuals in this way: the Independent Labour Party's *Labour Leader* described the trial as exposing the "uncleanness" behind the closed doors of the idle rich, living their lives of "filthy abomination" (qtd. in Rowbotham 194). Homophobic rhetoric could slide easily between constructing gays and lesbians as animals and as pollution, demonstrating the ways in which language associated with animal as well as environmental discourses could be used to dehumanize undesirable elements of the *polis*. Even sympathetic figures like Havelock Ellis, with whom Carpenter corresponded as they were both researching accounts of homosexuality, regarded it in terms of medical pathology as a deviancy from "healthy" heterosexuality (Rowbotham 189). Carpenter linked the emancipation of animals and gays, and noted complicity between the ways both groups suffered from misrepresentation, particularly by medical science. As with the connection made between the miserable lives of the poor and the victims of vivisection in the "Vivisection and the Labour Movement" essay discussed earlier, Carpenter also saw a connection between fears of pollution and contamination and the experiments on animals conducted by physiologists and medical pathologists. In *Civilization, Its Cause and Cure*, Carpenter argued:

> Medical science—and doubtless for very good reasons—makes a fetish of disease, and dances around it. It is (as a rule) only seen where disease is; it writes enormous tomes on disease; it induces disease in animals (and even men) for the purpose of studying it ... its eyes are perpetually fixed on disease, till disease (for it) becomes the main fact of the world and the main object of its worship. Even what is so gracefully called Hygiene does not get beyond this negative attitude.
> (23–4)

The scrutiny of homosexuals, in medical literature and the popular press, exhibited a similar fetishization of the supposedly diseased lifestyles of Wilde and others. Thus, while Carpenter campaigned against pollution from factory smokestacks, he was also attuned to the ways in which the trope of pollution could be used to degrade and dehumanize. As with romantic constructions of pristine nature, pollution discourses could serve as a pretext for singling out unwanted elements of the environment for expulsion.

Carpenter confronted the pathologizing rhetoric of medical science by co-opting it, representing the physiological laboratory as a polluted environment producing disease and degeneration. As with the antivivisectionist trope of animal experimentation creating a poisoned moral atmosphere, the laboratory itself becomes a polluted environment: "Is it not a strange kind of science, that which wakes the mind to pursue the shadows of things, but dulls the senses to the reality of them—which causes a man to try to bottle the pure atmosphere of heaven and then to shut himself in a gas-reeking, ill-ventilated laboratory while he analyses it" (*Civilization* 109–10). The scientist here resembles Carpenter's portrait of civilized man as a being who

> deliberately turns his back upon the light of the sun, and hides himself away in boxes with breathing holes (which he calls houses), living ever more and more in darkness and asphyxia, and only coming forth perhaps once a day to blink at the bright god, or to run back again at the first breath of the free wind for fear of catching cold!
> (32)

Illness, according to Carpenter, rather than being spawned through the phantasmatic influence of miasma or pestilence, comes from the experience of emotional and physical repression, division, and exclusion. True health could be achieved only through what he described as the "organic, vital, almost physiological morality of the Common Life—which means a quick response of each unit to the needs of the other units, and much the same in the body politic as health in the physical body" (237–8). Those excluded from the Common Life could become twisted out of their true nature, and Carpenter counters characterizations of homosexuals as degenerates by addressing "the great strain and tension of nerves under which those persons grow up from boyhood to manhood—or from girl to womanhood—who find their deepest and strongest instincts under the ban of the society around them" (*Homogenic* 58). It is hardly surprising that such conditions "should tend to cause nervous prostration or even mental disturbance ... and if such disturbances are really found to be commoner among homogenic lovers than among ordinary folk we have in these social causes probably a sufficient explanation of the fact" (58–9). Yet in this respect "homogenic lovers" (the term is Carpenter's own coinage) are no different from any being whose instincts have been repressed through alienation from the Common Life. Civilized man, generally, as well as the very scientists who contribute to the repressive narratives of deviancy, all suffer from unhealthy environments. Health is achieved, not through germophobic and homophobic tropes of purity and cleanliness, but through recognition of "organic unity, of the common welfare" of all beings, recognizing our affinities "through heredity and the fact that common ancestral blood flows in our veins" (*Civilization* 226–7). And this includes animals, "as beings, they too, who are climbing the great ladder of creation—beings with whom also we humans have a common spirit and interest" (232). By extension, Salt's "animated beef or mutton or pork" of the feedlot have similarly been made unnatural by their oppressive conditions, and are no less worthy of moral consideration or inclusion in the Common Life than any creature. Like those of a sexual orientation deemed unnatural, such creatures are so only in the sense of being forced to live under conditions contrary to their nature, and thus their liberation must follow from general recognition of unity and kinship.

Salt's and Carpenter's writings develop a radically inclusive model of being that challenges the compartmentalization of life-forms into human or animal, natural or unnatural. Such inclusivity enabled Carpenter to theorize his own homosexuality, and for Salt to theorize the complicity between masculinity and inhumane behavior. As with Carpenter, Salt's humane ideal was essentially an alternative model of being human, of performing humanness, which was in many ways connected to alternative models of performing masculinity. Cruelty, he argued, was largely a product of inhumane education in which boys in particular undergo an indoctrination in callousness. Linking hunting and collecting specimens for natural history study to other forms of cruelty, in "A Nature Study Exhibition and its Teaching" Salt argues: "To inculcate in children a wholesale disregard for the feelings and claims of the lower forms of life seems to us the surest way to encourage a similar disregard for the just claims of fellow citizens" (53). Consequently, the League called for reforms in education that would enable boys and girls to be raised along similar principles of compassion. In this respect, Salt's approach to gender anticipates the insights of ecofeminism, noting the complicity between patriarchy and dominance of the nonhuman, and theorizing alternative models of gendered behavior more conducive to peaceful coexistence. Greta Gaard stresses the importance of envisioning "eco-masculinities" that "would enact a diversity of ecological behaviors that celebrate and sustain biodiversity and ecological justice, interspecies community, eco-eroticisms, ecological economics, playfulness, and direct action resistance to corporate capitalist eco-devastations" (232). Such a project of redefining masculinity is especially crucial "because masculine gender identity has been constructed as so very anti-ecological, and thus its interrogation and transformation seem especially crucial" (232). For Salt and Carpenter, understanding the complicity of patriarchy in a wide range of oppressive behaviors was crucial to their mission of humane reform, and their work demonstrates the value of excluding no form of life from their sense of the common life presented in the sometimes separatist movements for change in the later-nineteenth century. By noting the animal limits of Victorian environmentalisms, their work offers solutions to the small differences that separate ecocritical and animal studies discourse in the twenty-first century.

Notes

1 According to the Food and Agricultural Organization of the United Nations' 2006 report, "Livestock's Long Shadow," animal agriculture is responsible for 18 percent of greenhouse gas emissions. According to Goodland and Anhang, however, more recent studies have demonstrated emission levels as high as 51 percent. For an account of environmental groups' silence on this issue, see *Cowspiracy: The Sustainability Secret*.
2 See Morton, *Hyperobjects: Philosophy and Ecology after the End of the World*; Latour, *Politics of Nature: How to Bring the Sciences into Democracy*, and *We Have Never Been Modern*; and Campbell and Sitze for an overview of biopolitics scholarship; and Wolfe, *Before the Law: Humans and Other Animals in a Biopolitical Frame* for a critique of biopolitics' animal limits.

Works cited

Campbell, Timothy and Adam Sitze, eds. *Biopolitics: A Reader*. Durham: Duke UP, 2013.
Carpenter, Edward. *Civilization: Its Cause and Cure*. 1889. New York: Scribner's, 1921.
——. *Homogenic Love: And Its Place in a Free Society*. Manchester: Labour Press Society Ltd., 1894.
——. *My Days and Dreams*. London: Allen, Unwin, 1916.
——. *Towards Democracy*. 3rd ed. Manchester: Labour Press Society Ltd., 1896.
——. "Vivisection and the Labour Movement." *Humanity: The Journal of the Humanitarian League* Nov. 1895: 68–9.

Cole, Lucinda, et al. "Speciesism, Identity Politics, And Ecocriticism: A Conversation With Humanists And Posthumanists." *Eighteenth Century: Theory and Interpretation* 52.1 (2011): 87–106.

Cowspiracy: The Sustainability Secret. Dir. Kip Anderson, Keegan Kuhn. AUM Films, 2014. DVD.

Crist, Eileen. "Ecocide and the Extinction of Animal Minds." *Ignoring Nature No More: The Case for Compassionate Conservation.* Ed. Marc Bekoff. Chicago: U of Chicago P, 2013. 45–61.

Food and Agriculture Organization of the United Nations. "Livestock's Long Shadow: Environmental Issues and Options." FAO Corporate Document Repository website 2006.

Freeman, Carol, Elizabeth Lean, and Yvette Watt, eds. *Considering Animals: Contemporary Studies in Human-Animal Relations.* Burlington, VT: Ashgate, 2011.

Gaard, Greta. "Toward New EcoMasculinities, EcoGenders, and Ecosexualities." *Ecofeminism: Feminist Intersections with Other Animals and the Earth.* Ed. Carol J. Adams and Lori Gruen. New York: Bloomsbury, 2014. 225–39.

Goodland, Robert and Jeff Anhang. "Livestock and Climate Change: What if the key actors in climate change were pigs, chickens and cows?" *WorldWatch* Nov./Dec. 2009: 10–19.

Gould, Peter C. *Early Green Politics: Back to Nature, Back to the Land, and Socialism in Britain, 1880–1900.* New York: St. Martin's, 1988.

Goyder, Jane and Philip Lowe. *Environmental Groups in Politics.* London: Allen & Unwin, 1983.

Hardy, Thomas. *Tess of the d'Urbervilles.* Ed. Tim Dolen. Harmondsworth: Penguin Classics, 2009.

Jefferies, Richard. *The Story of My Heart: My Autobiography.* London: Longmans, Green, 1883.

Latour, Bruno. *Politics of Nature: How to Bring the Sciences into Democracy.* Trans. Catherine Porter. Cambridge: Harvard UP, 2004.

———. *We Have Never Been Modern.* Trans. Catherine Porter. Cambridge: Harvard UP, 1993.

McIntosh, Robert P. *The Background of Ecology: Concept and Theory.* Cambridge: Cambridge UP, 1985.

Morton, Timothy. *Ecology Without Nature: Rethinking Environmental Aesthetics.* Cambridge: Harvard UP, 2007.

———. "Guest Column: Queer Ecology." *PMLA: Publications Of The Modern Language Association Of America* 125.2 (2010): 273–82.

———. *Hyperobjects: Philosophy and Ecology after the End of the World.* Minneapolis: U of Minnesota P, 2013.

Preece, Rod. *Animal Sensibility and Inclusive Justice in the Age of George Bernard Shaw.* Vancouver: UBC Press, 2011.

Raglon, Rebecca, and Marian Scholtmeijer. "'Animals Are Not Believers In Ecology': Mapping Critical Differences Between Environmental And Animal Advocacy Literatures." *ISLE: Interdisciplinary Studies In Literature And Environment* 14.2 (2007): 121–40.

Regan, Tom. *The Case for Animal Rights.* Berkeley: U of California P, 2004.

Rowbotham, Sheila. *Edward Carpenter: A Life of Liberty and Love.* London: Verso, 2008.

Ruskin, John. *The Works of John Ruskin*. Ed. E. T. Cook and Alexander Wedderburn. 39 vols. London: Allen, 1903–1912.

Salt, Henry Stephens. *Animals' Rights: Considered in Relation to Social Progress*. New York: Macmillan, 1894.

——. *Humanitarianism: Its General Principles and Progress*. London: Reeves, 1891.

——, ed. *Killing for Sport*. London: Bell, 1914.

——. "A Nature Study Exhibition and its Teaching." *The Humane Review* Sep. 1902: 50–3.

——. *Richard Jefferies: A Study*. New York: MacMillan, 1894.

——. "Socialists and Vegetarians." *To-Day: The Monthly Magazine of Scientific Socialism* 6.36 (1886): 172–4.

——. "The Animal Question and the Social Question." *Humanity: The Journal of the Humanitarian League* Oct. 1898: 75.

Singer, Peter. *Animal Liberation: The Definitive Classic of the Animal Movement*. New York: Harper Perennial, 2009.

Waldau, Paul. "Venturing Beyond the Tyranny of Small Differences: The Animal Protection Movement, Conservation, and Education." *Ignoring Nature No More: The Case for Compassionate Conservation*. Ed. Marc Bekoff. Chicago: U of Chicago P, 2013: 27–43.

Weil, Kari. "A Report On The Animal Turn." *Differences: A Journal Of Feminist Cultural Studies* 21.2 (2010): 1–23.

Wolfe, Cary. *Animal Rites: American Culture, the Discourse of Species, and Posthumanist Theory*. Chicago: U of Chicago P, 2003.

——. *Before the Law: Humans and Other Animals in a Biopolitical Frame*. Chicago: U of Chicago P, 2013.

——. "Human, All Too Human: 'Animal Studies' and the Humanities." *PMLA: Publications of the Modern Language Association of America* 124.2 (2009): 564–75.

Youngs, Tim. *Beastly Journeys: Travel and Transformation at the Fin de Siècle*. Liverpool: Liverpool UP, 2014.

Sources for further study

The *Works cited* lists that follow the essays in this volume provide scholars and students useful guides for further exploration into the burgeoning field of ecocritical studies, especially ones that may be of value to those interested in the Victorian writers' attitudes toward the environment. As a supplement to our contributors' work we are including this list of *Sources for further study* in our volume. Our bibliography is not comprehensive, but we have attempted to identify scholarship on a number of Victorian writers who have been the subject of scholarly study from an ecological perspective. A handful of selections are not targeted exclusively at Victorian literature and culture; we have included them because they contain discussions that researchers may find useful.

While we have included some entries that focus on the built environment, we have not included books and articles on animal studies or literature and science, except for ones that address environmental issues. These can be found in other publications (including our forthcoming collection of essays on Victorian animal studies). Most of the works cited below were published within the past thirty years; a few, however, are studies that provide a historical perspective on criticism aimed at understanding the Victorians and the natural world.

Adams, James Eli. "Woman Red in Tooth and Claw: Nature and the Feminine in Tennyson and Darwin." *Tennyson*. Ed. Rebecca Stott. Boston: Addison Wesley Longman, 1996. 87–111.
Agathocleous, Tanya. *Urban Realism and the Cosmopolitan Imagination in the Nineteenth Century: Visible City, Invisible World*. Cambridge: Cambridge UP, 2011.
Akilli, Sinan. "Henry Rider Haggard: An Early Ecocritic?" *The Future of Ecocriticism: New Horizons*. Ed. Serpil Oppermann, Ufuk Özdağ, and Scott Slovic. Cambridge: Cambridge Scholars, 2011. 300–9.
Allen, Michelle. "A More Expansive Reach: The Geography of the Thames in *Our Mutual Friend*." *Cleansing the City: Sanitary Geographies in Victorian London*. Athens: Ohio UP, 2008. 86–114.

Anderson, Kathleen, and Hannah Thulbery. "Ecofeminism in Christina Rossetti's 'Goblin Market.'" *Victorians: A Journal of Culture and Literature* 126 (2014): 63–87.
Archibald, Diane. "'Rogue's Paradise' or Honest Man's Arcady: Anthony Trollope's Australia and the Preservation of Home." *Domesticity, Imperialism, and Emigration in the Victorian Novel*. Columbia: U of Missouri P, 2002. 65–104.
Atwood Sara. "'The Earth-Veil': Ruskin and Environment." *Journal of Pre-Raphaelite Studies* 24.1 (2015): 5–24.
Azzarello, Robert. "Unnatural Predators: Queer Theory Meets Environmental Studies in Bram Stoker's *Dracula*." In *Queering the Non/Human*. Ed. Noreen Giffney and Myra Hird. Burlington, VT: Ashgate, 2008. 137–58.
Bate, Jonathan. "Culture and Environment: From Austen to Hardy." *New Literary History* 30.3 (1999): 541–60.
Beaumont, Matthew. "To Live in the Present: *News from Nowhere* and the Representation of the Present in Late Victorian Utopian Fiction." *Writing on the Image: Reading William Morris*. Ed. David Latham. Toronto: U of Toronto P, 2007. 119–36.
Beer, Gillian. "Charles Kingsley and the Literary Image of the Countryside." *Victorian Studies* 8.3 (1965): 243–54.
——. *Open Fields: Science in Cultural Encounter*. New York: Oxford UP, 1996.
Beinart, William, and Lotte Hughes. *Environment and Empire*. New York: Oxford UP, 2007.
Bellanca, Mary Ellen. "Gerard Manley Hopkins's Journal and the Poetics of Natural History." *Nineteenth-Century Prose* 25.2 (1998): 45–62.
Bennett, Michael, and David Teague, eds. *The Nature of Cities: Ecocriticism and Urban Environments*. Tucson: U of Arizona P, 1999.
Berard, Jane Helen. *Dickens and Landscape Discourse*. New York: Lang, 2007.
Bernstein, Susan. "Recycling Poetics: Amy Levy's London Plane Trees." *Nineteenth-Century Studies* 24 (2014): 101–22.
Bevin, Darren. "Mountain Thoroughfares: Charles Dickens and the Alps." *Dickens Quarterly* 29.2 (2012): 151–61.
Bevis, Richard. *The Road to Egdon Heath: The Aesthetics of the Great in Nature*. Quebec: McGill-Queens UP, 1999.
Bewell, Alan. "*Jane Eyre* and Victorian Medical Geography." *ELH* 63.3 (1996): 773–808.
——. "John Clare and the Ghosts of Natures Past." *Nineteenth-Century Literature* 65.4 (2011): 548–78.
Bilston, Sarah. "'They Congregate ... in Towns and Suburbs': The Shape of Middle-Class Life in John Claudius Loudon's *The Suburban Gardener*." *Victorian Review* 37.1 (2011): 144–59.
Boos, Florence. "An Aesthetic Ecocommunist: Morris the Red and Morris the Green." *William Morris: Centenary Essays*. Ed. Peter Faulkner and Peter Preston. Exeter: U of Exeter P, 1999. 21–46.
——. "*News from Nowhere* and 'Garden Cities': Morris's Utopia and 19th-Century Town Design." *Journal of Pre-Raphaelite Studies* 7.2 (1998): 5–27.
Bristow, Joseph. "'Dirty Pleasure': *Trilby*'s Filth." *Filth: Dirt, Disgust, and Modern Life*. Ed. William A. Cohen and Ryan Johnson. Minneapolis: U of Minnesota P, 2005. 155–81.

Brotton, Melissa. "Ecotheodicy and Animal Imagery in Two Poems by Robert Browning." *Victorians Institute Journal: VIJ Digital Annex* 40 (2012).

Buell, Lawrence. "Ecocriticism: Some Emerging Trends." *Qui Parle: Critical Humanities and Social Sciences* 19.2 (2011): 87–115.

———. *Writing for an Endangered World: Literature, Culture and Environment in the U.S. and Beyond*. Cambridge, MA: Harvard UP, 2001.

Bump, Jerome. "Hopkins, the Humanities, and the Environment." *Georgia Review* 28.2 (1974): 227–44.

Byerly, Alison. "Rivers, Journeys, and the Construction of Place in Nineteenth-Century English Literature." *The Greening of Literary Scholarship: Literature, Theory, and The Environment*. Ed. Steven Rosendale. Iowa City: U of Iowa P, 2002. 77–94.

Carroll, Alicia. "The Greening of Mary De Morgan: The Cultivating Woman and the Ecological Imaginary in 'The Seeds of Love.'" *Victorian Review* 36.2 (2010): 104–17.

Chen, Wenjuan. "Reading the Word Should be Connected to Reading the World: A Lesson from Wordsworth and Hardy." *Educational Studies* 31.1 (2005): 95–101.

Choi, Tina. "Forms of Closure: The First Law of Thermodynamics and Victorian Narrative." *ELH* 74.2 (2007): 301–22.

———. "Writing the Victorian City: Discourses of Risk, Connection, and Inevitability." *Victorian Studies* 43.4 (2001): 561–89.

Clayton, Jay. "Victorian Chimeras, or, What Literature Can Contribute to Genetics Policy Today." *New Literary History* 38.3 (2007): 569–91.

Cleere, Eileen. *The Sanitary Arts: Aesthetic Culture and the Victorian Cleanliness Campaigns*. Columbus: Ohio State UP, 2014.

Cohen, William. "Arborealities: The Tactile Ecology of Hardy's *Woodlanders*." *Interdisciplinary Studies* 19 (2014). Web. Accessed 1 March 2015.

Colley, Ann C. *Victorians in the Mountains: Sinking the Sublime*. Burlington, VT: Ashgate, 2010.

Coriale, Danielle. "Charlotte Bronte's *Shirley* and the Consolations of Natural History." *Victorian Review* 36.2 (2010): 118–32.

———. "Gaskell's Naturalist." *Nineteenth-Century Literature* 63.3 (2008): 346–75.

Costantini, Maria Concetta. "'The city tires to death': Images of Urbanization and Natural Corruption in Hopkins." *Hopkins Quarterly* 28.3–4 (2001): 114–29.

———. "'Strokes of Havoc': Tree-Felling and the Poetic Tradition of Ecocriticism in Manley Hopkins and Gerard Manley Hopkins." *Victorian Poetry* 46.4 (2008): 487–509.

Craig, David M. *John Ruskin and the Ethics of Consumption*. Charlottesville: U of Virginia P, 2006.

Cranfield, Jonathan. "Sherlock's Slums: The Periodical as an Environmental Form." *Textual Practice* 28.2 (2014): 215–41.

Critchley, Peter. *The Ecological Communism of William Morris*. Manchester, UK: Peter Critchley Books, 2006.

Csala-Gati, Katalin, and János Tóth. "The Socio-Biological and Human-Ecological Notions in *The Time Machine*." *Wellsian: The Journal of the H. G. Wells Society* 26 (2003): 12–23.

Cunningham, Gail. "Houses in Between: Navigating Suburbia in Late Victorian Writing." *Victorian Literature and Culture* 32.2 (2004): 421–34.

Cusick, Christine. *Out of the Earth: Ecocritical Readings of Irish Texts.* Cork: Cork UP, 2010.

Dahiya, Archana. "An Eco-Critical Reading of George Eliot's *The Mill on the Floss.*" *The Criterion: An International Journal in English* 4.3 (2013): 1–8.

Day, Brian J. "Hopkins' Spiritual Ecology in 'Binsey Poplars.'" *Victorian Poetry* 42.2 (2004): 181–93.

———. "The Moral Intuition of Ruskin's 'Storm-Cloud.'" *SEL: Studies in English Literature* 45.4 (2005): 917–33.

Denisoff, Dennis, ed. *Victorian Review*, 36.2 (2010). Special Issue: Victorian Environments.

Dennis, Richard. *Cities in Modernity: Representations and Productions of Metropolitan Space, 1840–1930.* Cambridge: Cambridge UP, 2008.

Desrochers, Pierre. "Victorian Pioneers of Corporate Sustainability." *Business History Review* 83.4 (2009): 703–29.

Dewan, Pauline. *The Art of Place in Literature for Children and Young Adults: How Locale Shapes a Story.* New York: Mellen, 2010.

Easterlin, Nancy. *A Biocultural Approach to Literary Theory and Interpretation.* Baltimore: Johns Hopkins UP, 2012.

Ebbatson, J. R. *An Imaginary England: Nation, Landscape and Literature, 1840–1920.* Burlington, VT: Ashgate, 2005.

———. *Landscape and Literature 1830–1914: Nature, Text, Aura.* New York: Palgrave Macmillan, 2013.

———. "Visions of Wild England: William Morris and Richard Jefferies." *Journal of the William Morris Society* 3.3 (1977): 12–29.

Egerton, Frank. *The Roots of Ecology: Antiquity to Haeckel.* Berkeley: U of California P, 2012.

Elder, John. "The Poetry of Experience." *New Literary History* 30.3 (1999): 649–59.

Elston, M. Melissa. "'A World Outside': George Eliot's Ekphrastic Third Sphere in 'The Mill on the Floss.'" *George Eliot-George Henry Lewes Studies* 62/63 (2012): 34–48.

Faldet, David. "The River at the Heart of Morris's Ecological Thought." *Writing on the Image: Reading William Morris.* Ed. David Latham. Toronto: U of Toronto P, 2007. 73–84.

Fletcher, Angus. "Another Literary Darwinism." *Critical Inquiry* 40.2 (2014): 450–69.

Flint, Kate, and Howard Morphy, eds. *Culture, Landscape, and the Environment: The Linacre Lectures, 1997.* Oxford: Oxford UP, 2000.

Foster, John Bellamy. *Marx's Ecology: Materialism and Nature.* New York: Monthly Review P, 2000.

Frankel, Nicholas. "The Ecology of Decoration: Environment in the Writings of William Morris." *Journal of Pre-Raphaelite Studies* 12 (2003): 58–85.

Freeland, Natalka. "The Dustbins of History: Waste Management in Late-Victorian Utopias." *Filth: Dirt, Disgust, and Modern Life.* Ed. William A. Cohen and Ryan Johnson. Minneapolis: U of Minnesota P, 2005. 225–49.

French, Elysia. "Designing Preservation: Waterways in the Works and Patterns of William Morris." *Brock Review* 11.2 (2011): 97–110.

Fromm, Harold. "Ecocriticism at Twenty-Five." *Hudson Review* 66.1 (2013): 196–208.

Frost, Mark. "The Organic Impulse: Ruskin, Trees, Architecture, and Society (1843–60)." *The Eighth Lamp: Ruskin Studies Today* 2.1 (2009): 1.

Fulton, Richard D., and Peter H. Hoffberg, eds. *Oceania and the Victorian Imagination: Where All Things are Possible*. Burlington, VT: Ashgate, 2013.

Fulweiler, Howard. "'A Dismal Swamp': Darwin, Design, and Evolution in *Our Mutual Friend*." *Nineteenth-Century Literature* 49.1 (1994): 50–74.

Gagnier, Regenia. "Twenty-First Century and Victorian Ecosystems: Nature and Culture in the Developmental Niche." *Victorian Review* 36.2 (2010): 15–20.

Gagnier, Regenia, and Martin Delveaux. "Towards a Global Ecology of the *Fin de Siècle*." *Literature Compass* 3.3 (2006): 572–87.

Gairn, Louisa. "Feelings for Nature in Victorian Scotland." *Ecology and Modern Scottish Literature*. Edinburgh: Edinburgh UP, 2008. 14–45.

Garson, Marjorie. "The Improvement of the Estate: J. C. Loudon and Some Spaces in Dickens." *Moral Taste: Aesthetics, Subjectivity, and Social Power in the Nineteenth-Century Novel*. Toronto: U of Toronto P, 2009. 173–238.

Gates, Barbara T. "Greening Victorian Studies." *Victorian Review* 36.2 (2010): 11–14.

———. *Kindred Nature: Victorian and Edwardian Women Embrace the Living World*. Chicago: U of Chicago P. 1998.

Gifford, James, and Gabrielle Zezulka-Mailloux, eds. *Culture and the State: Landscape and Ecology*. Edmonton, Alberta: CRC Humanities Studio, 2003.

Gilbert, Pamela K. "Medical Mapping: The Thames, the Body, and *Our Mutual Friend*." *Filth: Dirt, Disgust, and Modern Life*. Ed. William A. Cohen and Ryan Johnson. Minneapolis: U of Minnesota P, 2005. 78–102.

Glendenning, John. *The Evolutionary Imagination in Late-Victorian Novels: An Entangled Bank*. Burlington, VT: Ashgate, 2007.

———. "'Green Confusion': Evolution and Entanglement in H. G. Wells's *The Island of Doctor Moreau*." *Victorian Literature and Culture* 30.2 (2002): 51–97.

Gold, Barri. *Thermopoetics: Energy in Victorian Literature and Science*. Cambridge, MA: MIT P, 2010.

Gray, William. *Fantasy, Art and Life: Essays on George MacDonald, Robert Louis Stevenson and Other Fantasy Writers*. Newcastle Upon Tyne: Cambridge Scholars P, 2011.

Greenaway, Betty, ed. *Children's Literature Quarterly* 19.4 (1994–1995). Special Issue: "Ecology and the Child."

Grove, Richard H. *Green Imperialism: Colonial Expansion, Tropical Island Edens and the Origins of Environmentalism, 1600–1860*. Cambridge: Cambridge UP, 1995.

———. "Scotland in South Africa: John Croumbie Brown and the Roots of Settler Environmentalism." *Ecology and Empire: Environmental History of Settler Societies*. Ed. Tom Griffiths and Libby Robin. Edinburgh: Keele UP, 1997. 139–53.

Guelke, Jeanne Kay, and Karen Morin. "Gender, Nature, Empire: Women Naturalists in Nineteenth-Century British Travel Literature." *Frontiers of Femininity: A New Historical Geography of the American West*. Syracuse: Syracuse UP, 2008. 83–114.

Hamlin, Christopher. "Charles Kingsley: From Being Green to Green Being." *Victorian Studies* 54.2 (2012): 255–81.

Hanley, Keith. "In Wordsworth's Shadow: Ruskin and Neo-Romantic Ecologies." *Romantic/Victorian: Influence and Resistance in Nineteenth-Century English Poetry*. Ed. G. Kim Blank and Margot Louis. London: Macmillan, 1993. 203–33.

Hansson, Heidi. "Kinship: People and Nature in Emily Lawless's Poetry." *Nordic Journal of English Studies* 13.2 (2014): 6–22.

Henighan, Tom. *Natural Space in Literature: Imagination and Environment in Nineteenth and Twentieth Century Fiction and Poetry*. Ottawa: Golden Dog P, 1982.

Henson, Eithne. *Landscape and Gender in the Novels of Charlotte Brontë, George Eliot, and Thomas Hardy: The Body of Nature*. Burlington, VT: Ashgate, 2011.

Hess, Scott. *William Wordsworth and the Ecology of Authorship: The Roots of Environmentalism in Nineteenth-Century Culture*. Charlottesville: U of Virginia P, 2012.

Hill, Jen. *White Horizon: The Arctic in the Nineteenth-Century British Imagination*. Albany: SUNY P, 2008.

Hines, Maude. "'He Made *Us* Very Much Like the Flowers': Human/Nature in Nineteenth-Century Anglo-American Children's Literature." *Wild Things: Children's Culture and Ecocriticism*. Ed. Sidney Dobrin and Kenneth Kidd. Detroit: Wayne State UP, 2004. 16–30.

Holmes, John. *Darwin's Bards: British and American Poetry in the Age of Evolution*. Edinburgh: Edinburgh UP, 2009.

Hotchkiss, Jane. "'The Jungle of Eden': Kipling, Wolf Boys, and the Colonial Imagination." *Victorian Literature and Culture* 29.2 (2001): 435–49.

Hunt, Stephen E. "'Free, Bold, Joyous': The Love of Seaweed in Margaret Gatty and Other Mid-Victorian Writers." *Environment and History* 11.1 (2005): 5–34.

Hutchings, Kevin. *Romantic Ecologies and Colonial Cultures in the British Atlantic World, 1770–1850*. Montreal: McGill-Queens UP, 2009.

Hynd, Hazel. "A Sense of Place: Landscape and Location in the Poetry of John Davidson." *Victorian Poetry* 43.4 (2005): 497–512.

Jackson, Lee. *Dirty Old London: The Victorian Fight against Filth*. New Haven, CT: Yale UP, 2014.

Jessop, Ralph. "Coinage of the Term 'Environment': A Word Without Authority and Carlyle's Displacement of the Mechanical Metaphor." *Literature Compass* 9.11 (2012): 708–20.

Jones, Eric L. "The Land that Richard Jefferies Inherited." *Rural History* 16.1 (2005): 83–93.

Kehler, Grace. "Gertrude Jekyll and the Late Victorian Garden Book: Representing Nature-Culture Relations." *Victorian Literature and Culture* 35.2 (2007): 617–33.

Kennedy, Margaret. "Ectopian London: Morris's Geography of Conservation." *Environments in Science Fiction: Essays on Alternative Spaces*. Ed. Susan Bernardo. Jefferson, NC: McFarland. 101–17.

Kent, Eddy. "William Morris's Green Cosmopolitanism." *Journal of William Morris Studies* 19.3 (2011): 64–78.

Kerridge, Richard. "Maps for Tourists: Hardy, Narrative, Ecology." *Green Studies Reader: From Romanticism to Ecocriticism*. Ed. Lawrence Coupe and Jonathan Bate. New York: Routledge, 2000. 267–74.

Ketabgian, Tamara. *The Lives of Machines: The Industrial Imaginary in Victorian Literature and Culture*. Ann Arbor: U of Michigan P, 2011.

King, Amy Mae. *Bloom: The Botanical Vernacular in the English Novel*. New York: Oxford UP, 2003.

———. "Taxonomical Cures: The Politics of Natural History and Herbalist Medicine in Elizabeth Gaskell's *Mary Barton*." *Romantic Science: The Literary Forms of Natural History*. Ed. Noah Heringman. Albany: SUNY P, 2003. 255–70.

Knoepflmacher, U. C., and G. B. Tennyson, eds. *Nature and the Victorian Imagination*. Berkeley: U of California P, 1977.

Krasner, James. *The Entangled Eye: Visual Perception and the Representation of Nature in Post-Darwinian Narrative*. New York: Oxford UP, 1992.

Lampadius, Stefan. "Evolutionary Ideas in Arthur Conan Doyle's *The Lost World*." *Inklings: Jahrbuch für Literatur und Ästhetik 29: Der Andere Conan Doyle*. Ed. Dieter Petzold. Frankfurt: Peter Lang, 2012. 68–97.

Law, Jules. "A River Runs Through Him: *Our Mutual Friend* and the Embankment of the Thames." *The Social Life of Fluids*. Ithaca, NY: Cornell UP. 46–68.

Lawrence, Claire. "A Possible Site for Contested Manliness: Landscape and the Pastoral in the Victorian Era." *ISLE: Interdisciplinary Studies in Literature and the Environment* 4.2 (1997): 17–38.

Lear, Linda. *Beatrix Potter: A Life in Nature*. New York: St. Martin's Press, 2007.

LeMenager, Stephanie, Teresa Shewry, and Ken Hiltner, eds. *Environmental Criticism for the Twenty-First Century*. New York: Routledge, 2011.

Lightman, Bernard. *Evolutionary Naturalism in Victorian Britain: The 'Darwinians' and their Critics*. Burlington, VT: Ashgate, 2009.

Lipscomb, Susan Bruxvoort. "Introducing Gilbert White: An Exemplary Natural Historian and His Editors." *Victorian Literature and Culture* 35.2 (2007): 551–67.

Luke, Timothy W. "Karl Marx: Critique of Political Economy as Environmental Theory." *Engaging Nature: Environmentalism and the Political Theory Canon*. Ed. Peter F. Cannavo and Joseph H. Lane, Jr. Cambridge, MA: MIT P, 205–22.

Luow, Pat. "Identity, Place and 'The Gaze' in *The Woodlanders* by Thomas Hardy and *dream forest* by Dalene Matthee." *Alter*nation 14.2 (2007): 97–115.

MacDonald, Bradley. "William Morris and the Vision of Ecosocialism." *Contemporary Justice Review* 7.3 (2004): 287–304.

MacDonald, Graham A. "The Politics of the Golden River: Ruskin on Environment and the Stationary State." *Environment & History* 18.1 (2012): 125–50.

MacKenzie, Ann Haley. "An Analysis of Environmental Issues in 19th Century England Using the Writings of Charles Dickens." *American Biology Teacher* 70.4 (2008): 202–4.

MacKenzie, John. *The Empire of Nature: Hunting, Conservation, and British Imperialism*. Manchester: Manchester UP, 1988.

Manlove, Colin. "Charles Kingsley, H. G. Wells, and the Machine in Victorian Fiction." *Nineteenth-Century Literature* 48.2 (1993): 212–39.

Marsden, William E. "Ecology and Nineteenth-Century Urban Education." *History of Education Quarterly* 23.1 (1983): 29–53.

Martell, Jessica. "The Dorset Dairy, the Pastoral, and Thomas Hardy's *Tess of the D'Urbervilles*." *Nineteenth Century-Literature* 68.1 (2013): 64–89.

Mayer, Jed. "Germinating Memory: Hardy and Evolutionary Biology." *Victorian Review* 26.1 (2000): 82–97.

McCarthy, Jeffrey Mathes. "'A Choice of Nightmares': The Ecology of *Heart of Darkness*." *Modern Fiction Studies* 55.3 (2009): 620–48.

McElroy, James. "Ecocriticism and Irish Poetry: A Preliminary Outline." *Estudios Irlandeses* 6 (2011): 54–69.

Mee, Jon. "Dickens and the City: 'Animate London ... Inanimate London'." *The Cambridge Introduction to Charles Dickens*. New York: Cambridge UP, 2010. 43–63.

Metz, Nancy Aycock. "The Artistic Reclamation of Waste in *Our Mutual Friend*." *Nineteenth Century Fiction* 34.1 (1979): 59–72.

Miller, John. "Postcolonial Ecocriticism and Victorian Studies." *Literature Compass* 9.7 (2012): 476–88.

Morris, John. "The Emergent Stereotype of Man as Machine." *Exploring Stereotyped Images in Victorian and Twentieth-Century Literature and Society*. Ed. John Morris. Lewiston, NY: Mellen, 1993. 247–84.

Morrison, Ronald D. "Culture and Agriculture in 'The Dorsetshire Labourer' and *The Mayor of Casterbridge*: An Ecocritical Approach." *The Hardy Review* 15.2 (2013): 53–69.

———. "Tragedy and Ecology in the Later Novels of Thomas Hardy." In *Twenty-First Century Perspectives on Victorian Literature*. Ed. Laurence W. Mazzeno. Lanham, MD: Rowman and Littlefield, 2014. 185–202.

Mukherjee, Upmanyu Pablo. "Cholera, Kipling, and Tropical India." *The Oxford Handbook of Ecocriticism*. Ed. Greg Garrard. Oxford: Oxford UP. 80–97.

Murphy, Patricia. "Ecofeminist Whispers: The Interrogation of 'Feminine Nature' in Mathilde Blind's Short Poetry." *Nineteenth-Century Gender Studies* 11.1 (2015). Web. Accessed 15 May 2015.

Murphy, Patrick. *Ecocritical Explorations in Literary and Cultural Studies: Fences, Boundaries, and Fields*. Lanham, MD: Lexington Books, 2009.

Myers, Jeffrey. "The Anxiety of Confluence: Evolution, Ecology, and Imperialism in Conrad's *Heart of Darkness*." *ISLE: Interdisciplinary Studies in Literature and the Environment* 8.2 (2001): 97–108.

Nead, Lynda. *Victorian Babylon: People, Streets, and Images in Nineteenth-Century London*. New Haven, CT; Yale UP, 2005.

Nichols, Ashton. "Morris's Materialist Romanticism: Ecology, Gender, and Revolution in *News from Nowhere*." *William Morris: A Celebration of World Citizenship*. Instituto de Letras e Ciencas Humanas, Universidade do Minho, Braga, Portugal, *Actas do Coloquio*. Braga, 1996. 15–30.

Nixon, Jude. "'Death Blots Black Out': Thermodynamics and the Poetry of Gerard Manley Hopkins." *Victorian Poetry* 40.2 (2002): 131–56.

O'Connor, Martin. "John Stuart Mill's Utilitarianism and the Social Ethics of Sustainable Development." *European Journal of the History of Economic Thought* 4.3 (1997): 487–506.

O'Gorman, Francis. "Ruskin's Memorial Landscapes." *Worldviews: Global Religions, Culture & Ecology* 5.1 (2001): 20–34.

O'Sullivan, Paddy. "The Ending of the Journey: William Morris, *News from Nowhere* and Ecology." *William Morris and News from Nowhere: A Vision for Our Time*. Ed. Stephen Coleman and Paddy' O'Sullivan. Bideford: Devon: Green Books, 1990. 169–81.

———. "Struggle for the Vision Fair: Morris and Ecology." *Journal of the William Morris Society* 8.4 (1990): 5–9.

O'Toole, Sean. *Habit in the English Novel, 1850–1900: Lived Environments, Practices of the Self*. New York: Palgrave Macmillan, 2013.

Page, Michael R. *The Literary Imagination from Erasmus Darwin to H. G. Wells: Science, Evolution, and Ecology*. Burlington, VT: Ashgate, 2012.

Parham, John. *Green Letters: Studies in Ecocriticism* 14 (2011). Special Issue: Victorian Ecology.

——. "What is (ecological) 'nature'? John Stuart Mill and the Victorian Perspective." *Culture, Creativity and Environment: New Environmentalist Criticism*. Ed. Fiona Becket and Terry Gifford. Amsterdam: Rodopi, 2007. 37–54.

Peterson, Linda H. "Writing Nature at the *Fin de Siècle*: Grant Allen, Alice Meynell, and the Split Legacy of Gilbert White." *Victorian Review* 36.2 (2010): 80–91.

Pinkney, Tony. "Versions of Ecotopia in *News from Nowhere*." *William Morris in the Twenty-First Century*. Ed. Phillippa Bennett and Rosie Miles. Bern: Peter Lang, 2010: 93–106.

Plotz, John. "Going Local: Characters and Environments in Thomas Hardy's Wessex." *Portable Property: Victorian Culture on the Move*. Princeton, NJ: Princeton UP, 2008. 122–43.

——. "Speculative Naturalism and the Problem of Scale: Richard Jefferies's *After London* After Darwin." *Modern Language Quarterly* 76.1 (2015): 31–56.

——. "The Victorian Anthropocene: George Marsh and the Tangled Bank of Darwinian Environmentalism." *AJE: Australasian Journal of Ecocriticism and Cultural Ecology* 4.1 (2014): 52–64.

Post, Joseph. "A Voice for Nature: The Ecocritical Paradox and Gerard Manley Hopkins's Proxy Poetry." *Criterion* 7.1 (2014): 5–17.

Ranlett, John. "'Checking Nature's Desecration': Late-Victorian Environmental Organization." *Victorian Studies* 26.2 (1983): 197–222.

Rem, Tore. "Pip's Marshes and Wemmick's Castle: Nature in Dickens." *Q/W/E/R/T/Y: Arts, Litteratures & Civilisations du Monde Anglophone* 9 (1999): 61–8.

Ribner, Jonathan. "The Thames and Sin in the Age of Stink: Some Artistic and Literary Responses to a Victorian Environmental Crisis." *British Art Journal* 1.2 (2000): 38–46.

Rignall, John, Gustav Klaus, and Valentine Cunningham, eds. *Ecology and the Literature of the British Left: The Red and the Green*. Burlington, VT: Ashgate, 2012.

Ritvo, Harriet. "The View from the Hills: Environment and Technology in Victorian Periodicals." *Culture and Science in the Nineteenth-Century Media*. Ed. Louise Henson et al. Burlington, VT: Ashgate, 2004. 165–72.

Roth, Christine. "Green Victorianism." *Nineteenth-Century Studies* 24 (2010): 95–100.

Rowland, Susan. *The Ecocritical Psyche: Literature, Evolutionary Complexity, and Jung*. New York: Routledge, 2012.

Sagar, Keith. "Emily Brontë—The Crime Against Heathcliff." *Literature and the Crime Against Nature: From Homer to Hughes*. London: Chaucer P, 2005. 183–94.

Scott, Heidi C. M. "Subversive Ecology in Rossetti's *Goblin Market*." *Explicator* 65.4 (2007): 219–22.

Short, Brian. *The English Rural Community: Image and Analysis*. Cambridge: Cambridge UP, 1992.

Simo, Melanie Louise. *Loudon and the Landscape: From Country Seat to Metropolis, 1783–1843*. New Haven, CT: Yale UP, 1988.

Sipley, Tristan. "The Revenge of 'Swamp Thing': Wetlands, Industrial Capitalism, and the Ecological Contradiction of *Great Expectations*." *Journal of Ecocriticism* 3.1 (2011): 17–28.
Smith, Jonathan. "Heat and Modern Thought: The Forces of Nature in *Our Mutual Friend*." *Victorian Literature and Culture* 23 (1995): 37–69.
Sorensen, David R. "'Doom-Trumpet' in Elysium: The Death-Birth of the Pastoral Tradition in Carlyle's *The French Revolution*." *New Versions of Pastoral: Post-Romantic, Modern, and Contemporary Responses to the Tradition*. Ed. David James and Philip Tew. Cranbury, NJ: Associated UP, 2009. 31–44.
Steinlight, Emily. "Dickens's 'Supernumeraries' and the Biopolitical Imagination of Victorian Fiction." *Novel: A Forum on Fiction* 43.2 (2010): 227–50.
Stephens, Piers H. G. "John Stuart Mill: The Greening of the Liberal Heritage." *Engaging Nature: Environmentalism and the Political Theory Canon*. Ed. Peter F. Cannavò and Joseph H. Lane, Jr. Cambridge, MA: MIT P. 189–204.
Sumpter, Caroline. "Machiavelli Writes the Future: History and Progress in Richard Jefferies's *After London*." *Nineteenth-Century Contexts* 33.4 (2011): 315–31.
Tagnani, David. "Identity, Anthropocentrism, and Ecocentrism in John Clare's 'To an Insignificant Flower'." *Explicator* 72.1 (2014): 34–7.
Tague, Gregory. *Character and Consciousness: George Eliot, Thomas Hardy, E. M. Forster, D. H. Lawrence (Phenomenological, Ecological, and Ethical Readings)*. Palo Alto, CA: Academica P, 2005.
Talairach-Vielmas, Laurence. *Fairy Tales, Natural History and Victorian Culture*. Houndsmill, Basingstoke, England: Palgrave Macmillan, 2014.
Taylor, Angus. "Inhaling All the Forces of Nature: William Morris's Socialist Biophilia." *The Trumpeter* 14.4 (1997): 207–9.
Taylor, William M. *The Vital Landscape: Nature and the Built Environment in Nineteenth-Century Britain*. Aldershot: Ashgate, 2004.
Thompson, Paul. *Why William Morris Matters Today: Human Creativity and the Future World Environment*. London: William Morris Society, 1991.
Thornton, Kelsey. "Sentimental Ecology, John Clare, Gerard Manley Hopkins and Trees: A Note." *John Clare Society Journal* No. 31 (2012): 43–50.
Tiffin, Helen, ed. *Five Emus to the King of Siam: Environment and Empire*. New York: Rodopi, 2007.
Tondre, Michael. "George Eliot's 'Fine Excess': *Middlemarch*, Energy and the Afterlife of Feeling." *Nineteenth-Century Literature* 67.2 (2012): 204–33.
Waters, Michael. *The Garden in Victorian Literature*. Aldershot, England: Scholars P, 1988.
Weiss, Kenneth M. "'Nature Red in Tooth and Claw,' So What?" *Evolutionary Anthropology* 19 (2010): 41–5.
Wenzell, Tim. *Emerald Green: An Ecocritical Study of Irish Literature*. Cambridge: Cambridge Scholars P, 2009.

Editors and Contributors

Editors

Laurence W. Mazzeno is President Emeritus of Alvernia University in Reading, Pennsylvania. He is the author of books in Camden House's Literary Criticism in Perspective series on Matthew Arnold (1999) Alfred Tennyson (2004), Charles Dickens (2008), Jane Austen (2011), John Updike (2013), and Ernest Hemingway (2016). He is also the author of *Herman Wouk* (1994) in the Twayne U.S. Authors series and *James Lee Burke: A Literary Companion* (McFarland, forthcoming 2017), bibliographical studies of the Victorian novel (1989), Victorian poetry (1995), and the British novel 1660–1832 (1997), and more than 300 reference essays and book reviews. He edited *Critical Insights: Jane Austen's Pride and Prejudice* (2011), *Twenty-First Century Perspectives on Victorian Literature* (2014), and two editions of Salem Press's fourteen-volume *Masterplots* series. Since 1982 he has been affiliated with *Nineteenth Century Prose* and its predecessor, *The Arnoldian*.

Ronald D. Morrison is Professor of English at Morehead State University, where he teaches courses in Romantic and Victorian literature and literary theory. With colleagues from a variety of disciplines, he is currently leading an effort to establish an interdisciplinary Animal Studies program at Morehead State University. He is co-editor, with Laurence W. Mazzeno, of *Animals in Victorian Literature and Culture* (Palgrave, forthcoming in 2017). In that volume, he also has an essay on Charles Dickens and the Smithfield Market controversy. Recently he has published essays on Dickens and Smithfield Market in *Victorians: A Journal of Culture and Literature*, on Hardy and agriculture in *The Hardy Review*, and on connections between ecology and the conception of tragedy in Hardy's later novels in *Twenty-first Century Perspectives on Victorian Literature* (ed. Mazzeno). He has published on a variety of nineteenth- and twentieth-century authors in such journals as *CEA Critic, Critique: Studies in Contemporary Fiction, Nineteenth-Century Studies*, and the *CLA Journal*. He is also a long-time reviewer for *Choice*.

Contributors

Mary Ellen Bellanca is a professor of English at the University of South Carolina Sumter. The author of *Daybooks of Discovery: Nature Diaries in Britain, 1770–1870* (Virginia, 2007), she has published articles on George Eliot, Gerard Manley Hopkins, and Anna Barbauld, among others. Her most recent ecocritical publication is "The Monstrosity of Predation in Daphne du Maurier's 'The Birds'" in *ISLE: Interdisciplinary Studies in Literature and Environment*. Bellanca's article "After-Life-Writing: Dorothy Wordsworth's Journals in the *Memoirs of William Wordsworth*," a segment of her book project on Dorothy Wordsworth's reception history, received the prize from *European Romantic Review* for best essay in the journal in 2014.

Erin Bistline is completing a Ph.D. at Texas Tech University, where she is focusing on literature, social justice, and the environment in the nineteenth century. Her paper on Anna Sewell's *Black Beauty* delivered at the College English Association annual conference in March 2014 is the basis for the chapter in this volume.

Troy Boone is currently completing a book titled *Victorian Ecology, the Brontës, and the North of England*, and he has begun a study of Joseph Conrad, the South Seas, and the history of oceanic environments. His first book, *Youth of Darkest England: Working-Class Children at the Heart of Victorian Empire*, was published by Routledge in 2005. He is an Associate Professor of English at the University of Pittsburgh.

Deirdre d'Albertis is Professor of English at Bard College, where she coordinates programs in Victorian Studies and Irish & Celtic Studies. She is the author of *Dissembling Fictions: Elizabeth Gaskell and the Victorian Social Text* (1997) and editor of Elizabeth Gaskell's *Ruth* (2006). She has published articles and reviews in *Victorians Institute Journal*, the *Journal of the History of Sexuality*, and *Studies in English Literature, 1500–1900*.

Anna Feuerstein earned her PhD from Michigan State University and is currently an assistant professor in the Department of English at the University of Hawai'i at Manoa. Her research interests include Victorian politics and human–animal relationships, animal studies, and cultural studies. She is currently working on a book-length manuscript titled *The Political Lives of Victorian Animals*, which examines how Victorian liberalism influenced representations of animals and animal subjectivity, and how new understandings of animal subjects put pressure on existing political categories in Victorian Britain. She has published in *Society and Animals*, *Virginia Woolf Miscellany*, and *Journal of Victorian Culture*.

Mark Frost is Senior Lecturer in English Literature at the University of Portsmouth. A recognized authority on John Ruskin, he is the author of *The Lost Companions and John Ruskin's Guild of St. George: A Revisionary History* (2014) and articles on Ruskin in *Victorian Literature and Culture* (2011), *Nineteenth-Century Prose* (2011), *Green Letters: Studies in Ecocriticism* (2011), *Journal of Commonwealth Literature* (2010), and *The Eighth Lamp: Ruskin Studies Today* (2009).

Jed Mayer is Associate Professor of Victorian Literature at SUNY New Paltz. His current research focuses on the changing role of the nonhuman animal in scientific and popular discourses. He is currently at work on a book manuscript entitled *Scientific Dominion: Experimenting with the Victorian Animal*, which explores scientific, ecological, and political debates surrounding the nonhuman animal in nineteenth-century culture. His work has been published in *Victorian Studies, Nineteenth-Century Prose, Victorian Review, The Journal of Pre-Raphaelite Studies*, and *Victorian Poetry*, and in several recent anthologies in the field of animal studies.

John Miller is Lecturer in Nineteenth-Century Literature at the University of Sheffield. His professional interest focuses on the links between environmental aesthetics, conceptions of environmental and species value, and public policy. He is the author of *Empire and the Animal Body: Violence, Ecology and Identity in Victorian Adventure Fiction* (2012), and *Walrus* (2014). He is co-editor of *Romantic Ireland from Tone to Gonne: Fresh Perspectives on Nineteenth-Century Ireland* (2013) and *The Globalization of Space: Foucault and Heterotopia* (2015). He co-edited special issues of the *Journal of Victorian Culture* (2012) and *Green Letters* (2008). He has published chapters in *Popular Exhibitions, Science and Showmanship 1840–1910* (2012) and *The Apothecary's Chest: Magic, Art and Medication* (2009), and articles in *Gothic Studies, Symplokē, Journal for Critical Animal Studies, Journal of Victorian Culture*, and *Victorian Review*.

Ashton Nichols holds the Walter E. Beach '56 Distinguished Chair in Sustainability Studies and is Professor of English Language and Literature at Dickinson College. He is the author of *Beyond Romantic Ecocriticism: Toward Urbanatural Roosting* (2011), *Romantic Natural Histories: William Wordsworth, Charles Darwin and Others* (2004), *The Revolutionary "I": Wordsworth and the Politics of Self-Presentation* (1998), and *The Poetics of Epiphany: Nineteenth-Century Origins of Modern Literary Moment* (1987), and essays on British and American writers in several collections and journals focused on ecocriticism and postcolonialism.

John Parham is Lecturer in Media and Cultural Studies in the Institute of Humanities & Creative Arts at the University of Worcester. He is the editor of *The Environmental Tradition in English Literature* (2002), which included his seminal essay "Was There a Victorian Ecology?" and the author of *Green Man Hopkins: Poetry and the Victorian Ecological Imagination*. He has contributed essays to several important collections of ecocriticism, including *Culture, Creativity and Environment: New Environmentalist Criticism*, and *Ecodidactic Perspectives in English Language, Literatures and Cultures*. He has published articles on Victorian writers in *Ecozon@: European Journal of Literature, Culture and Environment*, *ISLE: Interdisciplinary Studies in Literature and the Environment*, *Nineteenth-Century Contexts*, *International Journal of Cultural Studies*, and *Key Words: Journal of Cultural Materialism*.

Valerie Purton is Professor of English at Anglia Ruskin University, having taught in Canada, Ghana, and at several universities in the United Kingdom. A recognized expert in the works of Dickens and Tennyson, she is a member of the Executive Committee and the Publications Board of the International Tennyson Society and Editor of the *Tennyson Research Bulletin*. She is editor of *Darwin, Tennyson and Their Readers* (2013), author of *Dickens and the Sentimental Tradition: Fielding, Richardson, Sterne, Goldsmith, Sheridan, Lamb* (2012), co-author of the *Palgrave Literary Dictionary of Tennyson* (2010), and author of *Two-Way Traffic: New Directions in Victorian Literature and Science* (forthcoming). She has also published on Iris Murdoch, Kazuo Ishiguro, and Tony Harrison.

Christine Roth is Associate Professor and Director of the Graduate English Program at the University of Wisconsin Oshkosh. She is the editor of John Ruskin's *The Two Paths* and author of articles on J. M. Barrie, Ernest Dowson, Victorian childhood, domestic workers in nineteenth-century England, and Oxford University. Her work has appeared in *Literature Quarterly*, *JASNA Newsletter*, *Nineteenth Century Studies*, *ELT: English Literature in Transition*, and *Victorian Studies*. She has also published the article "Green Victorianism" in a special issue of *Nineteenth Century Studies* for which she was a guest editor.

Serena Trowbridge is Lecturer in English Literature at Birmingham City University, UK. Her previous publications include *Insanity and the Lunatic Asylum* (Pickering & Chatto, 2014, ed. with Thomas Knowles); *Pre-Raphaelite Masculinities* (Ashgate, 2014, ed. with Amelia Yeates); and *Christina Rossetti's Gothic* (Bloomsbury, 2013). Her research interests include poetry; women's history and writing; Gothic literature; lunatic asylums and other nineteenth-century institutions; Ruskin; children's literature in the eighteenth and nineteenth centuries; and Pre-Raphaelitism in art and literature. She is editor of the *Review of the Pre-Raphaelite Society*.

Index

Abram, David 115, 117
Acker, Kathy 140n3
aesthetics 117, 124, 176; in Haggard 8, 157–71; in Hardy 79, 81; in Loudon 175, 180; in Rossetti 64, 67; in Ruskin 15, 16, 21–2
Africa 8, 157–73
agrarianism 8, 11n3, 161–2, 164–5, 170; *see also* agriculture
agriculture 3, 8, 9, 160–5, 220, 221; in Jefferies 205–18
Alaimo, Stacy 114–6, 124
Alexander, Christine 137, 140n4
Allen, David E. 174, 191, 202n3
Amazon Watch 221
Anglicanism 63
Anhang, Jeff 233n1
animal agency 83, 86, 87, 91, 113, 115, 189, 190, 192, 198–200, 225
animal autobiography 92, 142–53
animal cruelty (cruelty toward animals) 10, 81–3, 88, 94n8, 99, 109n2, 146–9, 190, 224, 232
animal rights 221; in Carpenter 10; in Salt 10, 81, 152, 155n17, 221–4
animal studies 7, 10, 221, 233
animals 20, 62, 99, 162, 206, 209, 217n6; in Brontë 8, 132, 134, 135–6, 140n9; in Browning 6, 47–53; in Carpenter 220–33; in Dickens 101, 103–9, 111n9, 111n10, 121, 123; in George Eliot 188–202; in Haggard 162, 164, 167–8; in Hardy 7, 79–94; in Lewes 188–202; in Rossetti 64–76; in Ruskin 17, 20–2, 25; in Salt 220–33; in Sewell 8, 142–53
animals, domestic 136, 190, 192–3, 209, 229
Antaeus 157–8, 171n1
Anthropocene 137
anthropocentrism 13–4, 18, 75, 111n9, 116, 162; in Dickens 97, 100, 102, 104, 108, 109n2; in Hardy 79, 80–2, 89–91
anthropology 79, 158, 164
anthropomorphism 73, 89, 90–1, 104, 111n9, 140, 198, 200, 208, 224, 227
anti-vivisection movement 64, 72, 85, 220–3, 229, 231
aquarium 190, 192, 193
aquavivarium 188, 191, 192
Arch, Joseph 206
Archer, William 94, 94n7
Aristotle 82
Armbruster, Karla 2, 208
Armstrong, Isobel 55, 61
Armstrong, Tim 94n4
Arnold, Matthew 29, 61, 76
Assisi Declarations 77
Atwood, Sara 27n5
Austen, Jane 140n5
Avatar (James Cameron film) 171n2
Avner, Jane 45, 45n2

Bakhtin, Mikhail 45
Bannon, Bryan E. 60
Barad, Karen 115–6, 124
Barbauld, Anna Letitia 111n12
Barber, Lynn 174, 202n3

Basso, Keith 33–4
Bate, Jonathan *Romantic Ecology: Wordsworth and the Environmental Tradition* 3, 30, 31, 65–6, 202n1; *The Song of the Earth* 117, 140n5
Batra, Nandita 111n12
Bauman, Zygmunt 116, 123, 126
bearing rein 147–8, 150–1, 154
Beckett, Samuel 48
Beer, Gillian 191, 196
Beers, Diane L. 154n16
Bell, Lucy 116, 126
Bellanca, Mary Ellen 9, 174–87, 196
Bennett, Jane 114–5, 124, 126
Berger, John 105
Bergson, Henri 17
Bergthaller, Hannes 127
Berry, Wendell 9, 205, 209, 210, 216, 217n11; *The Unsettling of America* 217n9
biotic community 162–4
Bistline, Erin 8, 142–56
Blake, William 70, 81, 88, 90, 94n6
Blatchford, Robert 222
blood sports *see* hunting
Bloom, Harold 76
Bonnefoy, Yves 44
Boone, Troy 97–113
botanical publishing 10, 36, 174–85
botany 10, 172n5, 174–86, 213
Bowen, John 110n6, 111n10
Bray, Cara 192
Bray, Charles 195
Bronstein, Jamie L. 148
Brontë, Charlotte 130–1; *Jane Eyre* 131, 140n4
Brontë, Emily 140n3, 140n9; *Wuthering Heights* 8, 130–41
Brooke, Stopford A. 47, 53, 61
Browning, Robert 6, 7, 47–62; "Among the Rocks" 52; "Caliban Upon Setebos" 48, 51, 57–9, 60; "'Childe Roland to the Dark Tower Came'" 48, 55–7; "Fra Lippo Lippi" 58, 60; "Home Thoughts, From Abroad" 51–2; *Paracelsus* 49–50; "Parleying with Gerard de Larisse" 48; *Pauline* 49; *The Ring and the Book* 61; *A Soul's Tragedy* 52; "Two in the Campagna" 53
Buckley, Jerome H. 111n10, 114
Buell, Lawrence 1, 3, 34, 66, 79–80, 93, 100, 110n8
Buller, Charles 100
Burke, Edmund 210, 217n11
Burroughs, John 226

Cambridge 30, 35
Campbell, Timothy 233
canon (literary) 3, 8, 10, 110n4, 111n9
capitalism 3, 11n3, 30–1, 226, 233; and colonial imperialism 157–71
Carlyle, Thomas 4, 153n3, 228
Carpenter, Edward 10, 220–35; *Civilization: Its Cause and Cure* 224, 231–2; *Homogenic Love, and Its Place in a Free Society* 230, 232; *My Days and Dreams* 220; *Towards Democracy* 224, 226, 227–8; "Vivisection and the Labour Movement" 229–31
Carroll, David 25–6
Carroll, Joseph 11n4
Carshalton, pool of 24–6
Carson, Anne 140
Carson, Rachel 109
Castellano, Katey 9, 210
catadores 116, 124–6
Cazamian, Louis 97–9, 104, 109n1, 109n2
Chadwick, Edwin 119
Chase, Karen 98–9, 103, 104, 110n4
Chaucer, Geoffrey 184
child, Romantic conception of 66–77
children's literature 8, 66, 142
Chrisman, Laura 157–9, 166, 168, 170
Christ, Carol 31, 32
Christianity 62, 90, 152; influence on Rossetti 63–77; influence on Ruskin 16
city *see* urban life
Clare, John 140n5, 184
Clark, Timothy 2, 30–1, 136, 138
Clarke, John Cooper 124–5
Coal Smoke Abatement Society 228
Cohn, Elisha 83
Coleridge, Samuel Taylor 81, 114

Colombat, Jacqueline 153n1
colonialism 41, 157, 160, 166–70
Commons Preservation Society 229
Comte de Buffon (George-Louis LeClerc) 106
Condition of England novels 117
conservation 162, 167, 221
conservatism (in environmental writing) 9, 205, 207, 209, 216–17
Copeland, Marion 153n2
Cosslett, Tess 111n9, 153n2
country (rural areas and life) 3, 4, 53–4, 222; in Dickens 97–8, 100, 103–4, 120; in Haggard 160, 161–4, 165, 170; in Jefferies 205–17; in Sewell 8, 142–53; Raymond Williams's concept of 8, 11n3
country books 206, 209
Cowper, Thomas 184
Crane, Susan 82
creature (living being) in Brontë 133, 136; in Browning 6, 47, 51–2, 53, 57–60; in Dickens 99, 102, 104, 122; in Haggard 162; in Hardy 80–83; 86–93; in Rossetti 67–76, 80; in Ruskin 16, 20–1; in Sewell 145 *also see* sea creature
Crist, Eileen 225
Cronon, William 8, 142–4, 147–8, 150, 151, 153, 154n7, 154n14, 166
Cuvier, Georges (Baron Cuvier) 20, 49

D'Albertis, Deirdre 8, 130–41
Danby, John F. 31–2, 34
Dante (Dante Alighieri) 56
dark ecology 8, 131, 137, 140n11
Dark Mountain Project 8, 131, 137
dark nature 8, 131–2, 137–9
Darwin, Charles 6, 7, 11n4, 13, 14, 20, 27n1, 33, 47–51, 56, 58–9, 61–2, 79, 81–3, 88, 191–2, 194, 196, 199, 201–2, 202n1, 205, 226
Darwin, Erasmus 184
Darwinism 13, 20, 33, 58, 82, 83, 88, 191, 201
David, Jacques-Louis 125
Decker, Christopher 38
deforestation 220
DeLoughrey, Elizabeth 171

DeMello, Margo 153n2
Derrida, Jacques 80, 86, 110n7, 196–7
Descartes, René 110n7
Dewis, Sarah 175–6
Dickens, Charles 4, 7–8, 41, 97–113, 114–29, 143–4, 154n5, 154n6, 154n10; *Barnaby Rudge* 101–3, 104–6, 110n6; *Bleak House* 7–8, 41, 97, 99–100, 110n5, 110n6, 114, 117, 120–8, 228; *David Copperfield* 97, 110n6; *Dombey and Son* 99, 110n3, 119, 126; *Great Expectations* 45, 100, 110n6; *Hard Times* 98; *Little Dorrit* 97, 99, 100; *Martin Chuzzlewit* 110n6; *Nicholas Nickleby* 99, 107–9, 110n6; *The Old Curiosity Shop* 100, 103, 104–5, 107, 110n6; *Oliver Twist* 98, 106–7, 110n6; *Our Mutual Friend* 100, 109–10n2, 117; *Pickwick Papers* 97, 99, 110n6; *Sketches by Boz* 98
Dickinson, Emily 48
Dingley, Robert 153n1, 154n11
Disraeli, Benjamin 117–18
domestic animals *see* animals, domestic
Dominions Royal Commission 161
Donne, W. B. 41
Dorré, Gina M. 147, 149, 154n10, 154n11
Duffin, H. C. 86

Eagles, Stuart 27n5
Ebbatson, Roger 218n14
ecocriticism (ecological criticism) 1–2, 4, 33, 221; Jefferies as early practitioner 205–17
ecodivine 140n3
ecofeminism 10, 233
ecological systems 2, 3, 6, 194–5, 202
ecological thought 4, 6, 13, 99, 111n11, 159; in George Eliot and Lewes 189–90, 197–9, 201
ecology 2, 5; as a scientific discipline 4, 13, 14–15, 27n1, 50, 202n1, 205; addressed in literature 10, 30, 75, 98, 110n4, 193; in Dickens 106, 107; in Haggard 160–71; in Hardy

80–94; in Loudon 182; in Ruskin 14–17, 21, 23, 27
ecology, dark *see* dark ecology
ecology, material 7, 114–19, 124–8; in Dickens 119–24
ecology, queer 10, 124–5, 137
ecomasculinity 233
ecotheology 7, 76
editoriales cartoneras 116
education (in Victorian Britain) 174–7, 232
Eliot, George (Marian Evans) 9, 188–204; *Middlemarch* 109; "Recollections of Ilfracombe" 188, 194–7
Eliot, T.S. 48, 56
Ellis, Havelock 230
Ellis, John 191
empathy 17, 148–9
energy 18, 25, 52, 53, 57, 118, 119, 208
entropy 118
environmental activism 1–2, 4, 13, 99, 106, 109n2, 136, 166, 171, 190, 220–1, 225, 228–9; in Carpenter 10, 226–7, 230–1; in Haggard 159, 160–2, 167; in Jefferies 205, 210; in Ruskin 14, 22–6; in Salt 10, 226–7, 232–3
environmental aesthetics 8; in Haggard 162–4
environmental criticism *see* ecocriticism
environmental ethics 75, 222
environmental justice 109–10, 115, 122–4, 137
environmentalism *see* environmental activism
Eppinger, Michael 178
Etherington, Norman 159
Evangelicalism 13–4, 16, 18, 20, 26, 27n4
Evernden, Neil 104
evolution 7, 50–1, 114, 118, 191, 194; in Browning 51, 57; in Dickens 119; in George Eliot 190; Hardy's view of 82; in G. H. Lewes 190, 199–200; in Ruskin 6, 13; in Tennyson 33, 49
exceptionalism 83, 225–7
exemptionalism 225–6

exotic, in Tennyson 39–44

Fairweather, Eugene 77n1
farming *see* agriculture
fashion (custom) 145–7, 150–1, 174, 181, 216
Fawcett, Millicent 94
ferality (feral creatures) 8, 136, 139, 140n14, 228
Ferguson, Moira 153n1, 154n11, 154n15
Feuerstein, Anna 9, 188–204
Fielding, Henry 99
Finley, C. Stephen 16
Forster, John 99
Fox, W. J. [space needed] 31
Frankel, Nicholas 11, 66
Freedgood, Elaine 98
Freeman, Nick 217n8
Fromm, Harold 1–2
Frost, Mark 6, 8, 13–28
Frost, Robert 48
Fudge, Erica 221
Fuller, Jennifer D. 140n4

Gaard, Greta 233
Gaia 171n1
Gallagher, Catherine 118
gardens 71, 90, 120, 215; in Loudon 174–85; in Tennyson 35–8, 43, 44, 54
Garibaldi, Giuseppe 44
Garrard, Greg 8, 135–6, 143, 153n4, 209
Garratt, Peter 198
Gaskell, Elizabeth 117; *Cranford* 31; *Life of Charlotte Brontë* 130
Gates, Barbara T. 174, 176
Gavin, Adrienne 153n1, 154n11
gender 9, 72, 86, 155n15, 169, 176, 215, 222, 233 *also see* sexuality
Genesis (Bible book) 20, 75
genre 5, 10, 30, 79, 100, 117, 153, 153n2, 174, 206
georgic 9, 205, 209, 216
Germ, The 77n3
Gifford, Terry 143, 153n4
Glotfelty, Cheryll 1–2, 30, 32
Godfrey, Laura Gruber 131

254 Index

Gold, Barri J. 5, 11n4, 11n5, 76, 208, 217n5
Goodland, Robert 233n1
Gordon Riots 103
Gosse, Edmund 85
Gosse, Philip Henry 188–9, 191–3, 196, 199–201
gothic 18
Gould, Peter C. 153, 222
Goyder, Jane 222
Grant, Anne 184
Grass, Sean C. 64, 72
Greenpeace 115, 221
griffin (in Ruskin's work) 18–21
Grosz, Elizabeth 82
Guenther, Conrad 82
Guild of St. George 26
Guimarães, Paula Alexander 140n10

habitat 3, 111n11, 166–7; in George Eliot 196; in Hardy 80, 94; in Loudon, 177, 179, 182; in Tennyson 31, 44
Haeckel, Ernst 14, 27n1, 50, 118, 202n1, 205, 228
Haggard, H. Rider 8, 157–73; *Allan Quartermain* 158, 165, 168; *Colonel Quaritch, V.C.* 163, 165; *The Days of My Life* 157, 160, 162; *Diary of an African Journey* 171; "Elephant Smashing and Lion Shooting" 166; *A Farmer's Year* 158, 160, 162, 163; *A Gardener's Year* 160; *The Holy Flower* 172n5; *King Solomon's Mines* 8, 157–73; *The Private Diaries of Sir Henry Rider Haggard* 164; *Rural Denmark and its Lessons* 160; *Rural England* 160–2, 164; "A Tale of Three Lions" 170; "The Transvaal" 158
Haggard, Lilias 160
Haley, Bruce 118
Hallam, Arthur Henry 31–1, 38–41, 49
Hamera, Judith 193, 195
Hamlin, Christopher 118–19
Hammerton, J. A. 79
Handley, George B. 171
Hansen, Natalie Corinne 153n2
Hardy, Barbara 85, 94n1

Hardy, Thomas 2, 3–4, 6, 7, 47, 79–96, 110n4, 140n5, 143, 154n5; "Afterwards" 92; "An August Midnight" 87; "Bags of Meat" 81, 83, 88, 89; "The Bird-Catcher's Boy" 81; "Birds at Winter Nightfall" 85; "The Blinded Bird" 87–8; "The Bullfinches" 85; "The Caged Goldfinch" 84, 88; "The Caged Thrush Freed and Home Again" 87; "The Calf" 85–6, 88, 94n5; "The Cheval-Glass" 83; "Compassion: An Ode" 83, 93; "The Darkling Thrush" 88; "Dead 'Wessex' the Dog of the Household" 91–2, 94n5; "The Fallow Deer at the Lonely House" 85, 94n5; "He Prefers Her Earthly" 83; "Horses Abroad" 84; *Jude the Obscure* 79, 82–3, 89, 94n2; "Lady in Furs" 84; "Last Words to a Dumb Friend" 90; *Life and Work of Thomas Hardy* 82, 84, 88; "The Lizard" 86; "The Mongrel" 84, 89; "A Popular Personage at Home" 91–2; "The Puzzled Game-Birds" 81, 84, 89; "The Roman Gravemounds" 91; "A Sheep Fair" 84, 89, 94n5; "Shelley's Skylark" 80; *Tess of the D'Urbervilles* 83, 94n8, 228–9; *Wessex Poems*; "The Wind Blew the Words" 95; "Winter Night in Woodland" 85
Harris, Margaret 197
Harrison, Antony H. 65
Harrison, W. H. 100
Hazlitt, William 66
Head, Dominic 100, 117
Heaney, Seamus 48
Heidegger, Martin 83
Heise, Ursula 11
Hemans, Felicia 184
Henley, William Ernest 206
hermeneutics 6, 14, 16
Herrick, Robert 184
Hey, Rebecca 182
Heywood, Christopher 131
Hiltner, Ken 98
Hine, Dougald 131, 137

Hollindale, Peter 154n11
homosexuality 230–2
Honan, Park 60
Hood, Thomas 99
Hood, Thurman L. 50
Hopkins, Gerard Manley 4
Houghton, Walter 114
Howe, Bea 175, 183, 186n5
Howitt, Mary 184
Howitt, William 184
Hughes, Arthur 66
Hughes, E. R. 73
human relationships 61; in Brontë 130–40; in Dickens 97, 102, 107, 108–9
human–animal relationships 4, 111n9, 190, 193, 194, 229; in Carpenter 224; in Hardy 7, 82, 83, 91; in Lewes 199, 201; in Ruskin 17; in Sewell 142–53, 154n10
Humanitarian League 10, 82, 84, 220, 223–4, 226, 229
humans' relationship with nature 4, 27, 31, 45, 60, 62, 103, 110n4, 118, 131, 137, 150, 201n1, 232; in Rossetti 62, 64, 75, 76, 77; in Brontë 132; in Loudon 190; in Lewes 196, 201; in Jefferies 209, 216; in Carpenter 236, 237
Humboldt, Alexander von 49
Humphreys, H. Noel 179
hunting 84, 94, 150–1, 167–8, 206–7, 209–10, 212–13, 226–7, 232–3
Huxley, T. H. 34
Hyndman, Edward 220, 222–3

Ilfracome 9, 188, 194–5, 197
India 116, 157
industrial novel 98–9
industrialization 3, 5, 76, 98–9, 114, 116, 118, 148, 153n3, 190, 206, 222, 228–9; in Dickens 119, 143; in Haggard 158, 166; in Jefferies 164–5, 209; in Tennyson 30–1
Iovino, Serenella 117

James, Henry 49
Jefferies, Richard 4, 226–7; *After London: Wild England* 164–5, 207–8, 217n4; *Hodge and His Masters* 9, 205–19; *The Story of My Heart* 227–8
Johnson, Paul 49
Johnson, Samuel 31
Johnston, Judith 197
Jordan, John O. 31, 32

Keats, John 32, 48, 49, 57, 60, 140n5; "Ode to a Nightingale" 42, 91
Keble, John 68, 77n2
Keith, W. J. 206–9, 217n1
Kenmare, Dallas 49, 52
Kenyon-Jones, Christine 70
Kerridge, Richard 1–2, 3–4, 87, 110n4
King, Amy 192
Kingsford, Anna 222, 229
Kingsley, Charles 49, 191–2
Kingsnorth, Paul 8, 131, 137
Kneitz, Agnes 109–10n2
Knickerbocker, Scott 111
Knoepflmacher, U. C. 67
Kroeber, Karl 3, 111n11
Kyrle Society 229

Labor Movement 220, 223, 231
land aesthetics *see* aesthetics
land ethic 162
landscape 45, 53–4, 221, 225, 228–9; in Brontë 130–1, 135; in Browning 56; in Dickens 100; in Haggard 157–9, 160–9; in Jefferies 217n6; in Rossetti 64, 73; in Ruskin 15, 23–4, 26, 27n8; in Tennyson 31, 34, 41, 42–3
language of flowers 181
Latour, Bruno 114, 221, 233n1
Lawrence, D. H. 205
Leavis, F. R. 98–9
Leopold, Aldo 162
Levenson, Michael 98–9, 103, 104, 110n4
Levinas, Emmanuel 110n7
Levine, George 82, 83
Lewes, G. H. (George Henry) 9, 188–204; *Sea-Side Studies* 188–9, 194–8, 200–1; *Studies in Animal Life* 189, 201

256 Index

Lightman, Bernard 176, 180, 185n1, 186n3
Lindley, John 178, 183, 186n4
Linnaean system of classification 185–6n2
Lister, Thomas Henry 99
Locke, John 52
London 4, 70, 84, 133 148, 154n6; Dickens's association with 97, 98, 100, 101–2; 103–4, 110n6, 119, 121–2, 124
London Zoological Gardens 188–9, 192, 193
Longman, Charles 163
Lou, Ye 124
Loudon, Jane Webb 4, 9, 174–87; *Botany for Ladies* (*Modern Botany*) 174, 176, 177, 179, 186n3; *British Wild Flowers*; *First Book of Botany* 174; *Instruction in Gardening for Ladies* 175; *The Ladies' Flower Garden* 174, 175, 176–7, 178–9, 181
Loudon, John Claudius 174–5, 180, 184, 186n5
Love, Glen 10
Lovelock, James 171n1
Low, Gail Ching-Liang 161–2
Lowe, Philip 222
Lupton, Julia 83
Lyell, Charles 49

MacDuffie, Allen 217n7
Maclise, Daniel 105
Malachuk, Daniel S. 111n13
Malamud, Randy 79–80
Manchester Corporation 24
Mangum, Teresa 110n5
Marland, Pippa 121
Marsh, George Perkins 14
Marsh, Jan 69
Martin, R.B. 32, 40
Marx, Karl *see* Marxist criticism
Marx, Leo 3
Marxist criticism 143
masculinity 169, 226, 232, 233
material ecology *see* ecology, material
material turn (in academic study) 124

materiality 7, 9, 18, 117–18, 121–3, 124
Mauer, Sara L. 217n8
Mayer, Jed 10, 217n4, 220–45
Mayhew, Henry 217n8
Mazel, David 207, 217n2
Mazzeno, Laurence W. 1–12, 31
McCarthy, Terence 131
McClintock, Anne 157, 159, 164, 168–9
McGrath, Alastair E. 75
McLuhan, H. Marshall 31
medicine 26, 85, 183–4, 229, 230–31
Meeker, Joseph 2
Melchiori, Barbara 61
Mendel, Gregor 51
Merrill, Lynn. L. 174, 202
Metropolitan Sanitary Association 119–20
Mi, Jiayan 124
miasma theory 7, 119, 121, 126, 231
Miller, D. A. 98
Miller, J. Hillis 140n6, 140n13
Miller, John 8, 11n5, 157–73
Miller, Lucasta 130
Millgate, Michael 81, 84, 91
Milton, John 184
modernism (literary movement) 32, 47, 56, 81
Monbiot, George 8, 136
Monod, Sylvère 98–9
Monsman, Gerald 157–8, 159, 164, 169–70, 171n1, 171n4
Moore, Bryan 2
Morley, Henry 120
Morris, Brian 206–7
Morris, William 4, 66, 222
Morrison, Ronald D. 1–12, 85, 94n2, 205–19
Morrison, Susan Signe 117
Morton, Timothy 8, 131, 136–7, 138–9, 140n11, 189–90, 194, 195, 198, 201–2, 221, 225, 227–8, 233n2
Moss, Elizabeth 217n1
Muniz, Vik 125

national parks *see* parks
natural history 47, 189–94, 199, 226, 232; and ecology 14; in George Eliot

and Lewes 190–4, 199, 202; in Loudon 174, 176, 178, 181
Natural Resources Defense Council 221
natural system of classification *see* taxonomy
naturalism, literary 80
naturalist 55–6, 76, 80, 102, 191, 206; Browning as 61; Jefferies as 226–7, 228
nature 6, 9, 13, 114, 118, 127, 140n8, 144, 166, 189, 221, 228–9; and culture 8, 135–6; ecologists' engagement with 13; idealized visions of 143, 153n3; in Brontë 132–5, 136–9, 140n5; in Browning 47–9; in Dickens 97–9; in George Eliot 189; in Haggard 160, 162, 163, 168; in Lewes 189, 197–9; in Loudon 174, 176; in Ruskin 14–16, 17–19, 23–7; nature tourism 17; realistic visions of 209; Romantic concepts of 3, 8, 11n2, 32, 33, 57, 63, 114, 165, 190, 228, 231; *also see* humans' relationship with nature
nature writers: Browning 51–7, 59–61; Dickens 100, 103, 106, 108, 109, 110n6, 128; George Eliot 109; Jefferies 9, 207–8, 210, 217n3, 226; Rossetti 64–9, 71–7; Ruskin 13, 14–27; Tennyson 29–32, 34, 44, 49, 80; Salt 229–30
nature writing 2, 3, 7, 11n1, 66, 117, 226, 228
New Critics 5
New Historicism 114, 117
Newton, Isaac 52
Ngom, Abdou 140n10
Nichols, Ashton 4, 6, 7, 47–62, 83
nonhuman environment 110n8, 120, 130, 220–1; Darwin's influence on perceptions of 51; Edmund Gosse's view of 193; in Browning 6, 47–8, 55, 57, 60–1
nonhuman subjects 115–16, 155n17; in Carpenter 10, 224, 226, 229; in Dickens 7, 97, 100–4, 106–7, 109, 110n5; in George Eliot 89–90, 189, 197–8; in Haggard 162, 167; in Hardy 7, 79–84, 86, 89, 92, 93–4, 94n2; in Jefferies 227; in Lewes 9, 189–90; in Salt 10, 224–5, 226, 229–30, 233
Nordau, Max 230
North, Christopher (John Wilson) 31

O'Gorman, Francis 159
Oceana Foundation 221
Old Testament 16, 74
Oliver, Mary 48
Oppermann, Serpil 117
Osborn, Laurence 77
Oxford Movement 77n1

Page, Judith W. 176
Palgrave, F.T. 43
Palgrave, W. G. (William Gifford) 43–4
Parham, John 4, 7–8, 11n4, 114–29, 153n3, 202n2, 217n5
Parkes, Bessie Rayner 194
parks 35–8; 167; 208; 210; 228
Parliament 126; 160
Pascoe, Judith 184
pastoral (literary genre) 3, 8, 209; in Dickens 98–9, 100; in Ruskin 25–6; in Sewell 142–53, 154n4
Peckham, Morse 55
Perkins, David 81
Perry, P.J. 217n1
pets (in Victorian life and fiction) 110n8, 190, 193; Brontë 135–6; in Browning 49; in Dickens 105–6, 111n10; in Hardy 90–2; in Lewes 201
place (location) 11n4, 135, 144, 153, 228; in Brontë 131–2, 134; in Browning 51, 54, 55–6; in Dickens 100–1, 124; in George Eliot 194; in Haggard 165–6; in Jefferies 208; in Rossetti 65–6; in Sewell 144–5, 150, 153; in Tennyson 6, 29–30, 32–8, 39–40, 41–4, 45
plant life 47, 174, 185n2, 186n4, 191; in Browning 6, 47–9, 51; in Dickens 106; in Loudon 174, 175–84; in Rossetti 63, 71, 75; in Ruskin 21; in Salt 224; in Tennyson 44
pollution 115, 228–9; as literary trope 229, 230; in Carpenter 231; in Louis

Cazamian's criticism 109n2; in Dickens 7–8, 119, 121, 124, 125–6; in Ruskin 25
popular science 9, 176, 185n1; influence on Loudon's work 175–85
Poseidon 171n1
practical criticism 5
Praz, Mario 114
Pre-Raphaelites 32, 65, 77n3
Preece, Rod 220
Prickett, Stephen 73, 77n1, 77n2
Priestley, Joseph 193
primitivism 8, 51, 58, 84, 159, 167
Public Health Act of 1848 119
Purton, Valerie 6, 29–46
Pyke, Susan 138, 140n3

queer ecology *see* ecology, queer

racial environmentalism 161
Rackham, Oliver 27n8
Raglon, Rebecca 221
Rauch, Alan 174
Regan, Tom 223
religion 6, 81, 166; in Browning 49, 53, 62; in Hardy 81, 92; in Lewes 199–200; in Loudon 181, 182; in Rossetti 65–6, 75–6; in Ruskin 13, 14, 18, 23; in Tennyson 44
Reuckert, William 2
Richards, Bernard 49, 51
Richards, I.A. 5
Rignall, John 217n3
Ritvo, Harriet 27n7, 111n9, 111n10, 140n5, 193
Robertson, Ben P. 11n2
Robinson, Marilynne 127
Robinson, Mary 184
Roe, Dinah 63
romance (literary genre) 35, 171; Haggard's use of 157, 159, 160, 164–8
Romantic conservatism 9, 210
Romantic consumerism 227–8, 229
Romanticism (Romantic writers) 3, 4, 6, 11n1, 17, 31, 70, 114, 118, 190, 228; relationship to ecology 13, 14; and animal rights 80–1

Romanticism, influence on Brontë 131; Browning 47, 49–50, 55, 57; Haggard 165, 167; Hardy 80, 85, 87, 90; Rossetti 67; Ruskin 15, 26; Salt 224; Tennyson 33, 36, 42–3; Tractarian Movement 63
Rossetti, Christina 6–7, 63–78; "Amor Mundi" 73; "Brother Bruin" 75–6; "Consider the Lilies of the Field" 77; "A Daughter of Eve" 71; "Eve" 71; *The Face of the Deep* 65, 74; "Goblin Market" 71–2; "Minnie and Mattie" 70–1; "The Prince's Progress" 72; "Shut Out" 71; *Sing-Song* 7, 66–71; *Time Flies* 63, 68, 73–5, 76; "To What Purpose is this Waste" 75; "The World" 64–5, 71
Rossetti, W. M. (William Michael) 77n4
Roster, Murray 110n8
Roth, Christine 7, 79–96
Royal Society for the Prevention of Cruelty to Animals (RSPCA) 83, 93, 229
rural landscape *see* landscape
Ruskin, John 3, 4, 6, 8, 13–28, 32, 65–6, 74, 100, 105, 153n3, 229; *The Crown of Wild Olive* 24; *Elements of Drawing* 18, 22; "The Law of Help" 6, 21–3, 25–6, 27n5; *Modern Painters* 6, 15–6, 18, 21, 27; *The Poetry of Architecture* 15; "The Work of Iron" 22–3, 27n6
Ryals, Clyde de L. 49

Salt, Catherine (Kate) 222
Salt, H. S. (Henry Stephens) 10, 220–35; *The Creed of Kinship* 220; "A Nature Study Exhibition and its Teaching" 232; *Richard Jefferies: A Study* 226–8
Salvation Army 161
Sammells, Neil 1–2
sanitation 99, 109n2, 119–20
Scheick, William J. 169
Scholtmeijer, Marian 221
Schwarzbach, F. S. 110n3

science, Victorians' knowledge of 9; instruction in 174, 176, 184, 185; materialist science 14, 17 *see also* ecology, evolution
Scott, Heidi C. M. 2, 30, 217n4
Scott, Walter 184
sea creatures 188–202
seashore 188–9
Secord, Anne 179–80
Selbourne Society for the Protection of Birds 228
Serrini, Lanfranco 77
Sewell, Anna 8, 142–56
sexuality in Haggard 8, 157, 168–9, 170; *see also* homosexuality
Shakespeare, William 48, 184; *Julius Caesar* 107; *A Midsummer Night's Dream* 185; *The Tempest* 57–60
Shaw, George Bernard 222
Shelley, Percy Bysshe 32, 47, 48, 80, 81, 94n1
Sherman, George Witter 80, 85, 86
Shteir, Ann B. 175, 176, 178, 185–6n2, 186n3
Sierra Club 221
Singer, Peter 155n17, 223
Sitze, Adam 233
Smith, Charlotte 184
Smith, Elise 176
Smith, Margaret 137, 140n4
Smollett, Tobias 99
Smulders, Sharon 66
social activism in Carpenter 10, 220; in Dickens 125–7; in Salt 10
social anthropology 158
social class 94n2, 154n15, 174, 175; in Dickens 122; in Jefferies 210, 215
social criticism 228
Social Democratic Federation 220, 222
social ecology 162
social novel 109n1; Dickens's fiction as 7, 97–101, 102, 103, 104, 106–8, 110n3; *Black Beauty* as 8
social, materiality of *see* materiality
socialism 220, 222–3, 226
Somervell, Robert 24
sonnet (literary form) 38–9, 45, 64, 86
Soper, Kate 140n8
South Africa 157, 159, 160, 171

Southey, Robert 184
space 99, 193, 229; in Brontë 130, 132, 136; in Dickens 100; in Haggard 162, 165, 166; in Jefferies 208; in Rossetti 75; in Tennyson 6, 30, 32–45
speciesism 80, 223–4
Spuybroek, Lars 17
Standard, The 9, 205, 207
Starzyk, Lawrence J. 60
Steinberg, Gillian 80
Stephen, Leslie 206
Stephenson, Wen 137
Stiebel, Lindy 160, 167, 169
Stoneley, Peter 154n11
Storey, Graham 125
Strickland, Agnes 184
Sturman, Christopher 35
sublime 7, 81; in Rossetti's poetry 64, 65, 67–8, 76
suicide 138
Sultzbach, Kelly 72, 76
Surfrider Foundation 221
Surridge, Lisa 140n9

taxonomy 175, 177–8, 182
Taylor, Jesse Oak 110n5
Tenby 188, 195
Tennyson, Alfred 4, 6, 29–46, 47, 48–51, 59, 61, 80; "Amphion" 35–6; "Audley Court" 38; "The Charge of the Light Brigade" 38; "Edwin Morris" 30; "Enoch Arden" 37; "The Gardener's Daughter" 37; "The Golden Year" 30; "Home" 35, 39; *Idylls of the King* 38; *In Memoriam* 29, 32, 33, 34, 37, 38, 40, 43, 44, 45, 48–9; "I weeded my garden" 36; "Lady of Shalott" 34, 38, 42; "Lines" 41–2; "Locksley Hall Sixty Years After" 30; "The Lotos-Eaters" 44; "Love of Home" 39; "Mariana" 38; "Mariana in the South" 40–1; *Maud* 30, 33, 37, 45; "Me My Own Fate" 39; "Ode to Memory" 36; "Pelleas and Ettarre" 38; *The Princess* 33, 34, 35, 37; "Tithonus" 38; "To Fitz" 37; "To Ulysses" 43–4; "The

Two Voices" 33; "Ulysses" 35, 38, 39–40, 41, 43, 45; "The Vision of Sin" 38
Tennyson, G. B. 68, 77n1
Tennyson, George Clayton 35–6, 41
thermodynamics 114, 118
thing power 114–5, 116–9, 120, 123–4, 126
Thirlmere reservoir 24, 27n7, 140n5
Thomas, Edward 207, 208
Thomas, Keith 212
Thomson, James 168
Thoreau, Henry David 3, 222, 226
Topham, Jonathan 185n1
Topography
tourism 17, 24, 131
Tractarianism 7, 63–4, 66, 67, 68, 72, 77n1
Tracts for the Times 64
Traill, Catharine Parr 177
transcendentalism 13, 14
transcorporeality 114, 115–16, 117, 118, 121–2, 124, 126, 127
Trowbridge, Serena 6–7, 63–78
Tuan, Yi-Fu 33–4
Tuana, Nancy 114–15
Turner, Frederick 60
Turner, J. M. W. 15
Twamley, Louisa Anne 178, 181
typology 64, 68, 74

uncivilization (concept) 131, 135–9
urban life 3, 4, 153n3, 158, 161, 163, 165, 206, 228, 229; contrasted with rural life 3, 8, 143, 144, 146, 154n7, 216
urban novel, Dickens's work as 7, 97–100

Valint, Alexandra 111
Van Ghent, Dorothy 137
vegetarianism 85, 220, 222–3
vivisection 84, 85, 220, 231 *see also* anti-vivisection

Waldau, Paul 221
Wallace, Kathleen 2, 208
Wandel River 25–6
waste aesthetics 115–19
Waterton, Charles 106
Weil, Kari 224
Welsh, Alexander 110n6
Welshman, Rebecca 205
Wheeler, Michael 3
White, Gilbert 69, 76, 226
White, Lynn 75–6
Whitman, Walt 48
Wilde, Oscar 230–1
wilderness 43, 144, 154n7, 193, 228; in Brontë 133–34, 135–8; in Haggard 158, 160, 164–8, 170
Williams, Isaac 64
Williams, Raymond 3, 8, 11n3, 98–9, 142–4, 153, 154n5, 154n6, 154n7, 154n9, 207, 217n3
Williams, Todd O. 73
Wilson, Eric 114
Wiltshire 9, 205, 208, 210, 211
Wolfe, Cary 83, 223–4, 233n2
Wollstonecraft, Mary 81
Wordsworth, William 15, 29–31, 38, 48, 57, 61, 63, 65–6, 73, 77n2, 81, 140, 210, 217n11, 228; "Influence of Natural Objects" 67; "Ode: Intimations of Immortality" 42; "Peter Bell" 32; *Prelude* 55, 67; "Tintern Abbey" 67; "To the Small Celandine" 184

Yeager, Patricia 125
Yonge, Charlotte M. 64, 66
Youngs, Tim 230
Zhangke, Jia 124

zoocentrism 7, 79–93
Zoological Gardens, London *see* London Zoological Gardens